Modern Scholarship
in the
Study of Torah

Modern Scholarship
in the
Study of Torah

Contributions and Limitations

edited by Shalom Carmy

Robert S. Hirt, Series Editor

The Orthodox Forum Series
A Project of the Rabbi Isaac Elchanan Theological Seminary
An Affiliate of Yeshiva University

JASON ARONSON INC.
Northvale, New Jersey
Jerusalem

"On the Morality of the Patriarchs in Jewish Polemic and Exegesis" by David Berger, which appeared in *Understanding Scripture: Explorations of Jewish and Christian Traditions of Interpretation*, edited by Clemens Thoma and Michael Wyschogrod, copyright ©1987, published by Paulist Press, is reprinted by permission of Paulist Press.

Reproduction of the diagram by Prof. Shama Friedman that appears in Yaakov Elman's essay is from "Perek ha-Ishah Rabbah ba-Bavli, be-Tzeruf Mavo Kelali al Derekh Heker ha-Sugya'," in H. Z. Dimitrovski, *Mehkarim u-Mekorot* I, reprinted by permission of the Jewish Theological Seminary of America.

Reproductions of parts of the *Valmadonna Pesahim* manuscript that appear in Yaakov Elman's essay are reprinted by permission of the Trustees of the Valmadonna Trust.

This book was set in 11 pt. Goudy Oldstyle by Alpha Graphics of Pittsfield, N.H.

Library of Congress Cataloging-in-Publication Data

Modern scholarship in the study of Torah : contributions and
   limitations / edited by Shalom Carmy
      p. cm.
   "The Orthodox Forum series, a project of the Rabbi Isaac Elchanan
Theological Seminary, an affiliate of Yeshiva University."
   Includes bibliographical references and index.
   ISBN 1-56821-450-2
   1. Bible. O. T.—Criticism, interpretation, etc., Jewish.
2. Talmud—Study and teaching. 3. Orthodox Judaism. I. Carmy,
Shalom.
BS1186.M63   1996
221.6'01—dc20   95-9837

Manufactured in the United States of America. Jason Aronson Inc. offers books and cassettes. For information and catalog write to Jason Aronson Inc., 230 Livingston Street, Northvale, New Jersey 07647.

THE ORTHODOX FORUM

The Orthodox Forum, convened by Dr. Norman Lamm, President of Yeshiva University, meets each year to consider major issues of concern to the Jewish community. Forum participants from throughout the world, including academicians in both Jewish and secular fields, rabbis, *rashei yeshiva*, Jewish educators, and Jewish communal professionals, gather in conference as a think tank to discuss and critique each other's original papers, examining different aspects of a central theme. The purpose of the Forum is to create and disseminate a new and vibrant Torah literature addressing the critical issues facing Jewry today.

The Orthodox Forum
gratefully acknowledges the support
of the Joseph J. Green Memorial Fund
at the Rabbi Isaac Elchanan Theological Seminary.

THE ORTHODOX FORUM
Fourth Conference

November 17–18, 1991, 11–12 *Kislev* 5752
The Jewish Center, New York City

PARTICIPANTS

Dr. Norman Lamm, Yeshiva University
Rabbi Marc Angel, Spanish-Portuguese Synagogue, New York
Dr. David Berger, Brooklyn College and Yeshiva University
*Rabbi Louis Bernstein, Yeshiva University
Dr. Moshe Bernstein, Yeshiva University
Dr. Rivkah Blau, Shevach High School for Women
Rabbi Yosef Blau, RIETS/Yeshiva University
Dr. Judith Bleich, Touro College
Rabbi Mordechai Breuer, Herzog Institute, Har Etzion
Dr. Elisheva Carlebach, Queens College
Rabbi Shalom Carmy, Yeshiva University
Rabbi Zevulum Charlop, RIETS/Yeshiva University
Rabbi Mordechai Cohen, Yeshiva Universtiy
Mr. Daniel Ehrlich, RIETS/Yeshiva University
Dr. Barry J. Eichler, University of Pennsylvania
Dr. Yaakov Elman, Yeshiva University
Rabbi Meir Goldwicht, Yeshiva University
Rabbi Irwin Haut, Morris, Duffy, Alonso and Farley
Rabbi Nathaniel Helfgot, Frisch Yeshiva High School

*Deceased

Dr. Basil Herring, Yeshiva University and Atlantic Beach Jewish Center
Rabbi Robert S. Hirt, RIETS/Yeshiva University
Dr. Ephraim Kanarfogel, Yeshiva University
Dr. Lawrence Kaplan, McGill University
Dr. Sid Z. Leiman, Brooklyn College and Yeshiva University
Dr. B. Barry Levy, McGill University
*Dr. David Maier, Hebrew University
Rabbi Israel Miller, Yeshiva University
Rabbi Yaakov Neuburger, Yeshiva University
Mrs. Dina Pack, Yeshiva University
Rabbi Michael Rosensweig, Yeshiva University
Rabbi Sol Roth, Yeshiva University and Fifth Avenue Synagogue
Rabbi Yonason Sacks, Yeshiva University
Rabbi Jacob J. Schacter, The Jewish Center, New York
Dr. Lawrence Schiffman, New York University
Rabbi Allen Schwartz, New York University
Dr. David Shatz, Yeshiva University
Dr. Michael Shmidman, Yeshiva University
Rabbi David Silber, Drisha Institute
Dr. Moshe Z. Sokol, Touro College
Dr. Moshe Sokolow, Yeshiva University
Dr. Haym Soloveitchik, Yeshiva University
Dr. Daniel Sperber, Bar-Ilan University
Dr. David Sykes, Yeshiva University
Rabbi Moshe Taragin, Yeshiva University
Rabbi Moshe D. Tendler, RIETS/Yeshiva University
Dr. Chaim I. Waxman, Rutgers University and Yeshiva University
Rabbi Mordechai Willig, RIETS/Yeshiva University
Dr. Joel Wolowelsky, Yeshivah of Flatbush High School
Rabbi Walter S. Wurzburger, Yeshiva University and Congregation
   Shaarey Tefilah

---

*Deceased

This volume is dedicated to the memory of David M. Maeir. Born in New York City in 1926, he was struck by an automobile outside his home in Jerusalem and left this world on December 14, 1992 (19 *Kislev* 5752).

Those who were fortunate to know him will never forget what a dynamic and commanding presence he was. His charm and charisma were both innate and the result of his many talents and diverse interests.

He was, in the truest sense, a modern Orthodox Jew. David Maeir was equally at home in a Beit Medrash as in a hospital, boardroom, and classroom.

He graduated from Yeshiva College and attended medical school in Ottawa. Following training in pathology, he joined the faculty of the newly formed Albert Einstein College of Medicine of Yeshiva University and was director of pathology at the college hospital, publishing on both experimental and human pathology.

In 1968, he was appointed the director general of the Shaare Zedek Hospital in Jerusalem and made *aliyah* together with his wife, Sheila (née Stillman), and three children, Alisa, Aren, and Joshua. The planning, development, and construction of the medical center was to become the major project of his professional life. David's ability to be equally at home with physicians and *talmidei hakhamim* allowed him to be the creative force behind the construction of a state-of-the-art hospital that would operate according to *halakhah*. This synthesis was his legacy.

David had both a strong allegiance to Jewish tradition and a sensitive appreciation of Jewish history. The tensions between "modern scholarship" and "Talmud Torah" were thus well-known to him and, indeed, were a part of his life. He faced the issues of modernity, whether in the sciences, the humanities, or public life and addressed them, as a thinking, religious Zionist Jew. David, while on a visit to New York, participated in The Orthodox Forum. Following the session, he presented challenging ideas for the use of modern scholarship in advancing Torah study. It is thus particularly appropriate that this collection of essays be dedicated to his memory. יהי זכרו ברוך

Contents

Preface

Shalom Carmy

"Modern scholarship" is what research universities claim to do; "Talmud Torah" is, first and foremost, the fulfillment of a Divine commandment, an act of religious devotion, the forging of a relationship with God. If the university were truly a place for the propagation of knowledge about all matters, as Newman regarded it, then "all branches of knowledge are connected together, because the subject-matter of knowledge is intimately united in itself, as being the acts and the work of the Creator."[1] If that were the case, then university scholarship in Jewish studies would be identical, in subject matter, procedure, and results, with Talmud Torah, and this book would lack a title.

But that is not the case. The universities pride themselves on rejecting, ignoring, or adopting methodological agnosticism about the truths taught by revelation. The corresponding attitude on the part of the *yeshivot* and the advanced schools for women that constitute the institutional home of Talmud Torah ranges from indifference to contempt. Two hallmarks of modern scholarship, the willingness to use all sources in the quest for truth, including those outside the canon of Torah proper, and a favorable attitude to new procedures and inquiries, are often viewed with suspicion in the *yeshivah* world.

There are reasons for this suspicion. Because modern scholarship prescinds from the knowledge provided by revelation, its conclusions often contradict Torah. Furthermore, the divorce between the modern

---

[1] John Henry Newman, *The Idea of a University*, Discourse V.

university and the religious dimension of Talmud Torah undermines the sanctity of traditional learning. Lastly, even when scholarship does not contradict Torah, it seems preoccupied with subject matter that is preparatory or trivial from the viewpoint of traditional Talmud Torah: prolonging secondary concerns with textual variants and background information while deferring, when not patronizing, the rigorous appropriation of the substance of Torah.

Some Orthodox thinkers and scholars have sought to overcome the alienation between the two sides. They have argued that the contradictions between Torah and scholarship can be eliminated, in some areas at least, either by improving scholarly method or by reexamining what propositions the Torah really teaches. They have demonstrated that many of the greatest religious authorities in earlier generations incorporated external sources in their analysis, and anticipated methods and results that have become prevalent in modern scholarship. They have countered the charge of irrelevance both by adducing instances where scholarship contributes to traditional Torah study and by appealing to precedents for interest in such matters by authoritative figures in earlier times.

Despite these efforts, the two terms in our title remain estranged. Many academic scholars come out of, and still participate in, traditional Talmud Torah; some *roshei yeshivah* cultivate a sympathetic or critical interest in academic work. Although these individuals presumably reflect on the connection between the two, their vocations and avocations generally remain in separate compartments, or else their achievement is perceived as an idiosyncratic combination of talents not to be extrapolated into a general approach.

This book is based primarily on the proceedings of the Fourth Orthodox Forum, held November 17–18, 1991 at Congregation Shearith Israel, New York. It is devoted to the two areas where the cognitive and experiential gap between modern scholarship and Talmud Torah is most dramatic: Bible and Talmud. Readers of this book should gain a great deal of knowledge about the problems, precedents, and solutions affecting these fields. But the principal thrust of this book is to challenge the compartmentalization to which we seem all too easily resigned, to discover whether, and to what extent, the methods of modern scholarship can become part and parcel of the study of Torah, conceived as a religious-intellectual way of life. Not "Modern scholarship *and* the Study of Torah," but "Modern Scholarship *in* the Study of Torah." My own essays are explicitly devoted to creating this frame of reference.

Barry Levy's thorough survey of Orthodox work in Bible and, even more importantly, his agenda of issues to be pursued by future study, set the tone for the Bible section. Barry Eichler offers an example of the way knowledge of ancient Mesopotamian law sheds light on the laws of the Torah; his concluding remarks point to some rarely confronted implications of his discipline for Jewish theology. Questions relating to the biblical text were not discussed at the conference, but Yeshayahu Maori kindly helped us to adapt his work in progress on that aspect of the problem arising from rabbinic literature.

The question of modern scholarship and the Bible cannot be limited to the issues discussed by university scholars of Bible. For this reason we have included the study by David Berger on the theological and psychological assumptions made in evaluating the personalities of biblical heroes.

For thirty years Rabbi Mordechai Breuer, arguably the most creative Orthodox student of the Bible born in this century, has courageously advanced his original approach to the data underlying what is commonly called the Documentary Hypothesis. We are privileged to present Rabbi Breuer's work, for the first time, in English, flanked by introduction and critique.

In Talmud the professors and the *talmidei hakhamim* share more by way of background and beliefs than do Orthodox students of the Bible and the university establishment. The papers by Daniel Sperber and Yaakov Elman illustrate the wealth of pertinent precedent in the field. In addition, Sperber examines the interaction of scholarship and *halakhah*, and Elman explores an original approach to history, based on hasidic sources, and seeks to comprehend the theological implications of changes in the nature of Talmud study over the ages.

My one remaining task as editor is one I have long looked forward to—the opportunity to thank those who have been instrumental in the production of this work. Dr. Norman Lamm, president of Yeshiva University, convener of the Orthodox Forum, has been a source of support throughout; his own example as a creative Jewish thinker, always ready to discover the interconnections among different areas in Torah and to apply our wisdom to the challenges of culture, has been an inspiration to me. As always, I enjoyed working with Rabbi Robert Hirt, Vice

President of RIETS. His commitment was fully reflected in that of his staff, whose assistance made my work easier. I cannot forgo thanking the entire staff of the Mendel Gottesman Library and Mrs. Ceil Levinson of the Yeshiva College Dean's Office, without whose supererogatory commitment, throughout my years at Yeshiva, it would have been impossible to combine writing and editing for publication with my primary responsibilities as a *mehannekh*. The Steering Committee of the Orthodox Forum has been, for me, the very model of collegial academic work. Other Forum participants have been helpful beyond the call of duty: Dr. Shneur Leiman at the inception of the project, Dr. Yaakov Elman at several stages along the way, and Rabbi Zevulun Charlop.

This book is dedicated to my friends and students, who have sustained and inspired me, both spiritually and intellectually, throughout my career. It is a special joy for me to mention those who provided assistance and encouragement in the course of this project. Hayyim Angel and Dov Fogel translated and helped edit the Maori and Breuer essays respectively; Seth Berkowitz and Kevin Taragin volunteered many hours to help with editorial chores. Rabbi Mordechai Cohen, Rabbi Nathaniel Helfgot, and Rabbi Moshe Taragin took part in the Forum and in subsequent discussions. Simeon Chavel and Avi Shmidman eagerly commented on various parts of the manuscript, as did Mark Kirschbaum, Yaakov Blau, and others. Special thanks are due my teacher and loyal friend Rabbi Moshe Wohlgelernter and my dear friends Bernard Stahl, Rabbi Yamin Levy, and Rabbi Yitzchak Blau.

If the volume in your hands succeeds in its task, it will speak much more to the future of our Torah study than about its past. It is the thinking religious individuals I have just mentioned, and many others like them, whose own lives and professional careers will determine our fate. They are the objects of my pride and the occasion of our hopes.

*****

However, neither rationalistic complacency nor agnostic despair nor mystical rapture will yield a solution to the religious problem of modern man. The homo religiosus calmly but persistently seeks his own path to full cognition of the world. He claims freedom of methodology; he has faith in his ability to perform the miracle of comprehending the world; and notwithstanding the asymmetrical appearance of the mysterium tremendum, *he eschews non-rational methods as a means to the realization of his goals.*

Rabbi Joseph B. Soloveitchik,
The Halakhic Mind

God willed man to be free. Man is required, from time to time, to defy the world, to replace the old and obsolete with the new and relevant. Only lonely man is capable of casting off the harness of bondage to society.

Rabbi Joseph B. Soloveitchik,
"The Community"

****

In the spirit of my revered teacher

Maran haRav

Yosef Dov ha-Levi Soloveitchik *zt"l*

I dedicate this volume

to my friends and students

the *Mishpaha ha-Lomedet*

with abiding affection

Shalom Carmy
Erev Rosh HaShana 5755

1

A Room with a View, but a Room of Our Own

Shalom Carmy

The unblemished saints do not complain about evil, but increase righteousness; do not complain about heresy, but increase faith; do not complain about ignorance, but increase wisdom.

—*Rabbi Abraham I. Kook*[1]

I think that trying to restrain an entire contemporary age is like a passenger in a carriage holding on to the seat in front of him in order to stop the carriage: he determines himself in continuity with the age, and yet he wishes to hold it in check. No, the only thing to do is to get out of the carriage, and so hold oneself in check.

—*Søren Kierkegaard*[2]

It is today possible that an Orthodox Jew who wishes to devote his professional life to the study of *Torah she-bi-Ktav* (the Written Torah) will seek to develop an orientation to the world of academic Bible scholarship. The Orthodox intellectual world is divided between those who

---

[1]*Arpelei Tohar* (Jerusalem: Rabbi Zvi Yehuda Kook Institute, 5743), p. 39.

[2]*Concluding Unscientific Postscript*, trans. David F. Swenson and Walter Lowrie (Princeton, NJ: Princeton University, 1941), p. 147.

1

welcome this situation and those who deplore it. The stakes in the struggle are greater than the small number of men and women involved in
academic activities would lead one to believe.

This is, first of all, because the study of Bible occupies a more delicate
position in the Orthodox curriculum than the study of Talmud. When
it comes to Talmud the *yeshivot* are already in possession of a *derekh
ha-limmud*, a set of well-established approaches to analyze and organize
systematically our learning. The academic Talmud scholar cannot hope
to supplant the regnant approaches; realistically he can only aspire to
augment the accepted canons with his own particular knowledge and
methodology.[3] Bible, however, has not received the same attention in
our schools. Any new trend is therefore likely to have far-reaching effects
on the study of Bible by nonspecialists.

Torah she-bi-Ktav and *Torah she-be'al peh* (Oral Torah) also differ with
respect to the characteristic interaction between piety and intellect. The
fervor with which the traditional student of Talmud applies himself to
the text is relatively independent of the content of the passage being
studied: an outsider, observing *benei Torah* in action, cannot determine
whether the topic under discussion carries immediate practical or existential implications or not. But with respect to other branches of Torah,
perhaps due to their secondary status, one expects the connection
between the subject matter and the religious experience of the student
to be more direct and explicit. Consequently, a shift in the mode of biblical study that detaches the reader from the exigency of the text, that
cools the ardor of confrontation, undermines the very raison d'être of
learning.

Because so much is at stake, the dispute is often carried on in terms
that are more heated than enlightened, more defensive than constructive, clouded by arbitrary assumptions, marred by bad logic and inhabited by straw men. The position I take in this introductory essay does
not conform to that of either side in the debate. Long-standing opponents of my position will no doubt find points to quarrel with. By stating
my general position at the outset, however, I hope to forestall the more
blatant misunderstandings, so that those who disagree with my approach
will at least know what it is that they object to.

---

[3] For more on this, see Chapter 9, "*Camino Real* and Modern Talmud Study."

1. Knowledge is a good thing. Specifically, reliable information about the historical, geographic, and linguistic background of the Bible can enhance our understanding of *Tanakh*. Authoritative control of such information requires a good deal of specialized training; even the preparation necessary to form an intelligent judgment about the work of experts in these fields presupposes an investment of time beyond that expected of most literate Jews. Nonetheless it is good that certain individuals master these disciplines and interpret them for the benefit of nonexperts. The potential value of such knowledge seems so evident as to need no argument: the example of preeminent *Rishonim* and *Aharonim* who availed themselves of Semitic philology, books on ancient religious practice, and historical-geographic data speaks for itself.

2. Most academic scholarship in Bible is conducted as if the fundamental tenets of Orthodox Judaism were false. At best, one affects methodological neutrality about the truth of these propositions. Sharp, irreconcilable conflict over fundamental presuppositions with wide-ranging implications—the authorship of the Torah, the reliability of the biblical canon, the authenticity and authority of the Oral Law—must, of necessity, preclude the development of consensus between Orthodox Jews and the academic establishment. Methodological agnosticism renders the Orthodox Jew an intellectual Marrano: compelled to feign neutrality in discussing matters on which he or she holds firm, unshakable convictions. To acquiesce outwardly, out of hunger for professional toleration, in a scholarly consensus the presuppositions and conclusions of which one judges false and pernicious, is an offense against intellectual honesty and a betrayal of human dignity.[4]

3. Jewish biblical study cannot be separated from the framework of Torah study and Jewish theological reflection as a whole. Even when the Orthodox student finds himself in agreement with secularist, Christian, or non-Orthodox writers about some particular issue, the context of interpretation differs considerably. Situating our own analysis within the continuum of Jewish biblical exegesis is more than a nostalgic exercise in historical piety: it defines an essential dimension of our study.[5] Style

---

[4]See below and my "The Nature of Inquiry: A Common Sense Perspective," *The Torah U-Madda Journal* 3 (1992): 37–51.

[5]Christian readers will detect similarities to the approach championed by Brevard Childs. See his *Introduction to the Old Testament as Scripture* (London

of presentation and choice of terms are not merely conventional, but trail clouds of theological significance.[6] This barrier to collaboration between Orthodox Jews and the academic establishment seems less absolute than the flat-out conflict mentioned in the previous paragraph: the Orthodox Jew is not asked to deny or suppress her beliefs, but merely to isolate one aspect of academic activity from the larger context of religious-intellectual existence and to desist from "parochial" vocabulary. Yet the threat is just as great, albeit more subtle: we lose contact with connections that we are constrained from expressing; when we are deterred from forming our insights in our own authentic words, their roots tend to wither away.

The principles I have spelled out invite further elaboration. I call my own *derekh ha-limmud* a *literary-theological approach*. Both terms carry a double meaning. By *theological*, we assert the conviction that Bible is to be encountered as the word of God, rather than primarily as the object of academic investigation; we also refer to the authoritative presence of the interpretive tradition. The adjective *literary* comes to stress that understanding the word of God is not only a matter of apprehending propositions, but also of hearing them in their literary and historical context; secondarily, we are reminded that the language we use to articulate our insight is also an integral aspect of our study.

In this essay we will first comment on the necessity to make our Bible study a true *derekh ha-limmud*, integrated within an overall program of *Mahashevet Yisrael*, Torah study and theological reflection, faithful to the Rav's conception of the *homo religiosus* who "calmly but persistently seeks his own path to full cognition of the world."[7] Next we will address the contentions of those who seek intellectual salvation in the greater integration of Orthodox Bible study within the academic world. Finally, I

---

and Philadelphia: Fortress Press, 1979) and *The Book of Exodus* (London and Philadelphia: Fortress Press, 1974). For analysis, see Mark Brett, *Biblical Criticism in Crisis?* (Cambridge: Cambridge University Press, 1991).

[6]See below and my "To Get the Better of Words: An Apology for *Yirat Shamayim* in Academic Jewish Studies," *The Torah U-Madda Journal* 2 (1991): 7–24.

[7]Rabbi Joseph B. Soloveitchik, *The Halakhic Mind* (New York: Seth Press, 1986), p. 4.

suggest that some tasks facing contemporary Orthodox Bible study, despite my general insistence on autonomy, can most honestly and most effectively be done, at present, within the walls of the secular university.

I

The Specter of Apologetic

How we are to study *Tanakh* is equivalent to the task of finding a way of learning (*derekh limmud*). To have a *derekh* of learning means that we have created a unified, integrated way of studying and teaching. When we are preoccupied with the novelty or strangeness of a certain methodology, when the novelty or strangeness interferes with the primary vocation of elucidating *devar ha-Shem* (the word of God) and hearing its message for our lives, we have not yet successfully incorporated that methodology as an integral part of our *derekh*. In particular, we cannot pursue the goals of Torah study when the truth of fundamental principles is rejected or doubted. If this is the case, then we surely cannot cultivate a *derekh* of Bible study in the hostile shadow of the academic establishment, an environment in which the bulk of our energy must be expended on defense rather than construction.

At this point an example may be useful. It is not a crucial or an especially exciting one, but it will serve our purpose precisely by illustrating the atmosphere in which we do our everyday work. In the speech that includes the opening of *Parashat Nitzavim* (Deuteronomy, chapter 29), Moses consistently addresses Israel in the second person plural. He shifts to the second person singular in only one passage (Deuteronomy 29: 11–12), which speaks of initiating the individual into the covenant to be instituted that day. Why the switch?[8] The Rabbis, commenting on verse 28, define a transition between two periods, marked by an expanded notion of responsibility on the part of Jews for the sins of their fellows; this idea is derived from the fact that several letters in the text are dotted, implying, according to midrashic principles, that the acceptance of

---

[8]For an alternative approach to this question, see *Keli Yakar*. See also *Haamek Davar* to Deuteronomy 31:26.

responsibility is somehow suspended during the intermediate stage.[9] Whether this comment can be adopted as a satisfactory explication of verse 28 (at the level of *peshat*) is, of course, highly debatable.[10] It occurred to me, however, that the idea underlying the midrashic interpretation of verse 28 might supply a key to the variation of persons in verses 11–12. I thought that the second person singular might refer to the undertaking of expanded responsibility connected to the covenant.

Having offered this modest suggestion in public,[11] I had nobody to blame when I got a scholarly rap on the knuckles. Naturally my critic was mildly annoyed by the infiltration of rabbinic tradition into a discussion of biblical text. This was not, however, my most serious offense: my proposal lacked merit because it did not explain the second person singular/plural changes throughout Deuteronomy. Thus I could not challenge the scholarly opinion that these alternations in Deuteronomy betray the presence of different authors.[12]

Now this criticism could be countered simply by noting that the scholar who thirty years ago had erected his theory of authorship on the singular/plural criterion had not applied it to the entire book either: in fact, he had explicitly omitted the section that I had examined! But let us say, for the sake of argument, that Minette had extended his hypothesis to *Nitzavim*; and let us also imagine that his theory is plausible (so long as one has no initial objection to the multiplication of authors on the basis of stylistic variation). How does this affect me? If it is incumbent upon us to refute the contending position, then we must either produce the comprehensive refutation or fall silent. If, however, our task is to forward our own interpretation, in accordance with the fundamental beliefs to which we are firmly committed, then I am free to advance

---

[9]For example, *Sanhedrin* 43b; my formulation avoids addressing the difference between Rabbi Yehuda and Rabbi Nehemia. On the function of "dotted letters" in rabbinic hermeneutics, see S. Lieberman, *Hellenism in Jewish Palestine* (New York: Jewish Theological Seminary, 1950), pp. 43–46.

[10]Whether "dotted letters" constitute a dimension of *peshat* in Rashi's methodology is discussed by Rabbi Menaham Schneerson, *Likkutei Sihot* 8:61ff.

[11]*Sheva Berakhot* for Rabbi Daniel and Hannah Katsman, 9/10/88.

[12]See G. Minette de Tillesse, "Sections 'tu' et sections 'vous' dans le Deutéronome," *Vetus Testamentum* 12 (1962): 29–87.

my reading, either as a local explication of *Nitzavim*, without any aim to explain other sections of the book, or as a provisional thesis, one that may, or may not, be successfully broadened to cover the other sections.[13]

To adopt the implicit outlook of my critic means that every thesis, every reading, every insight, to the degree that it deviates from the received position, must be pitted against the entire edifice of academic biblical scholarship. An idea that has not triumphed against the entrenched theories must be withdrawn from circulation. Autonomous Bible study by Orthodox Jews is thus frozen until the established views are decisively melted down. The alternative is to go our way, "calmly but persistently" seeking our own path to knowledge. Whether those outside our religious-intellectual community are curious, impressed, or dismayed by work firmly rooted in the fundamental beliefs to which we are firmly committed, whether they sit at our feet or relegate us to the outer darkness or pick up something from us even while keeping a safe distance —all this is, and should remain, their business.

Please don't get me wrong. I am not oblivious to the fact that many individuals who were taught Orthodox beliefs, and many more who were not, have learned something about conventional academic objections to those basic tenets, and consequently harbor doubts about, or reject outright, the fundamental doctrines of Orthodox Judaism. In my youth I tried very hard, though fruitlessly, to become such an individual myself, and my subsequent career as student and educator has brought me in contact with others similarly motivated. Clearly such individuals need to be supplied with some adequate warrant for Orthodox Judaism (which may, or may not, focus on the problems directly posed by biblical scholarship) before they devote themselves wholeheartedly to the *derekh ha-limmud* we propose. Surely it is desirable that there be advocates of Orthodox Judaism who can incline the disaffected in the direction of belief. But the justification of Orthodox doctrines pertinent to the study of Bible, though it sometimes draws attention to important questions previously neglected, is not necessarily a contribution to that study. A

---

[13]Naturally a well-established hypothesis is superior to a provisional one, as a theory of greater explanatory scope is preferable to a more limited one. My point is that a provisional and limited proposal is better than none at all, both because of the truth it contains and the truth its elaboration may lead to.

derekh ha-limmud must build, it must provide positive content and insight; a purely apologetic stance, however sophisticated and persuasive, is not the same thing.

Let me add that the constructive endeavor, independent of apologetic motives, is, in the final analysis, the most satisfactory defensive posture as well. After all, the considerations that lead an individual to offer, or withhold, his assent to Orthodox Jewish doctrine regarding the Bible are both complex and mysterious. What Ramban said about talmudic dialectic[14] is true of the reasoning that comes into play here: it does not aspire to mathematical precision, and therefore does not allow of knockdown arguments. In these circumstances, something will almost always beat nothing. If Orthodox writers limit themselves to parrying attacks, however competently, and exposing weak points in their opponents' theories, they will never seize the initiative; the ball, so to speak, will forever remain in the other team's possession. When Rabbi Kook extols the unblemished saints who, instead of carping about heresy and ignorance, increase faith and wisdom, he is not only commending an irenic disposition, but affirming the radical primacy of construction over defensive tactics.[15]

The Indivisible Mansion of Jewish Thought

No discipline is an island. Every facet of Torah is intimately related to the others. If we think of Torah as a mansion, each discipline within Torah can be compared to one of the rooms. The Orthodox explorer in the realm of *Tanakh*, whether he or she is a producer of original work or an active user of insights and research worked out by others, cannot be a mere tourist in the adjoining estates. Each student of Torah has his own interests and orientation; every attempt to do justice to all aspects of a *sugyah* will fall short; the hermeneutical horizon will ever recede. Nevertheless the development of a *derekh ha-limmud* in Bible, for the individual and for the community, is inextricably bound up with our ambition and achievement as students of Torah. The briefest overview must distinguish, with respect to Bible, three areas of activity:

---

[14]Introduction to *Milhamot haShem*.
[15]See Rabbi Kook, note 1 above.

1. *Torah she-be'al peh* has always been the "meat and potatoes" of Torah study. We believe that the Oral Torah transmits authoritative traditions with respect to *halakhah* and, to a lesser extent, *aggadah*; it thus constitutes an authoritative source for the study of Bible. To resume the image we introduced in the preceding paragraph, *Torah she-be'al peh* is a central chamber in the house of Torah: it communicates with all the other rooms. If the study of *Torah she-bi-Ktav* is not to become (or remain) marginal to our religious-intellectual enterprise, the comings and goings between the two neighboring and allied domains must reinforce their close cognitive and experiential proximity.

There are more specific reasons for intensifying the ties between Bible study and the traditional Talmud-oriented curriculum. In theory one may, following the great medieval and modern commentators, distinguish between the two levels of *peshat* and *derash*, and by asserting the autonomy of the former, free it of its dependence on the *derash* level (identified with the Oral Torah). In practice, however, the connection between the two dimensions of study is so intimate that one cannot hope to contribute to *peshat* in the legal portions of the Torah without observing and reflecting on the close interaction between the two. It is not accidental that those *Rishonim* and *Aharonim* who most magnificently explored the *peshat* level of the legal sections were equally renowned as talmudists: Rashi, Rashbam, Ramban, among the medievals; the Vilna Gaon, Netziv, *Meshekh Hokhmah*, and Rabbi David Zvi Hoffmann, to name but a few of their modern heirs.[16]

Nor is it fortuitous that one of the most influential strategies in contemporary Orthodox biblical analysis originates in the techniques of halakhic analysis. The idea closely associated with Rabbi Mordechai Breuer,[17] that different sections of the biblical text provide contrasting but complementary aspects of the divine message, corresponds to the *lomdish* analytic phrase "two *dinim*" popularized by Rabbi Hayyim Brisker to discriminate the multiple meanings of superficially uniform concepts.

Finally, the halakhic corpus occupies a position of primacy in Jewish theology. If the basic concepts, institutions, and imperatives taught in

---

[16]For an overview, see my article, "Biblical Exegesis, Jewish," *Encyclopedia of Religion* 2 (1987): 136–142.

[17]See Chapters 6, 7, and 8 in this volume.

the Bible are to be viewed in the context of a complex, comprehensive Jewish synthesis, the *halakhah* has a great deal to say about the nature of that synthesis.[18] Therefore an approach to biblical study that exploits the resources of *halakhah* is boundlessly richer than one that ignores these vital dimensions.

2. The relevance of traditional Jewish biblical exegesis, especially those trends identified with the method of *peshat*, is widely recognized today. Thanks in part to the remarkable lifework of Dr. Nechama Leibowitz, the giants of Jewish exegesis are routinely cited by Israeli Bible scholars with no rigid correlation to their own presuppositions, and research on classical *parshanut* has become a respectable subspecialty at the universities.

Current fashions in the study of literature have moderated the in-grained academic distaste for *derash* and for *peshat* approaches not easily distinguishable from *derash*. This broadening of perspective has helped legitimate a more generous selection from the traditional exegesis. When the quasitraditionalist M. Z. Segal, half a century ago, included a small monograph on the history of exegesis in his *Mavo ha-Mikra*, he inter-preted that history in terms of the conservative critical orientation that was his own, and ended his story, for all intents and purposes, with Abarbanel, after whom Jewish commentary retreats into the ghetto, leaving the banner of *peshat* in the hands of the gentiles. The fairly re-cent articles on exegesis in the *Encyclopedia Mikrait*, assigned to several authors, pursue the subject into the modern era, and do not recoil from treating such characteristic "ghetto" figures as the Vilna Gaon, the Netziv, and their like.[19]

3. Most people, when allusion is made to Jewish thought, think of what is customarily called Jewish philosophy, and/or ethical literature (Musar) and/or mystical works (including Hasidism). Much of the medieval lit-erature has enjoyed the same renewal of academic interest among Bible scholars that promoted the exegetical compositions discussed above: thus, to take a straightforward example, it's a good bet that whoever

---

[18]This is, of course, a fundamental postulate in the thought of *maran haRav* Soloveitchik, most explicitly in *The Halakhic Mind*.

[19]Even *Encyclopedia Mikrait* omits discussion of the classical supercommen-taries on Rashi, who are thus included only in my *Encyclopedia of Religion* article, "Biblical Exegesis."

would devote attention to Ibn Ezra or Radak will likewise spend time on the biblical exegesis of Maimonides' *Guide*. The literature of the modern period has not been so favored, whether because of *Wissenschaft des Judentum*'s built-in antiquarian bias or because the scholars knew too much about hasidic Jews, Musar preachers, and their attitude toward the scholars, making it impossible to take comfort in visions of imagined affinity.

From a contemporary vantage point, it is unfortunate that classic hasidic and Musar literatures are banished from the framework in which *Tanakh* is studied. Their indefatigable, almost palpable, striving to come to grips, through vigorous reflection on biblical and rabbinic texts, with the ultimate religious realities of suffering and sanctity and the yearning for spiritual and worldly redemption, although sometimes arbitrary from a textual point of view, can illuminate our perception of those texts no less dramatically (and I daresay more accurately) than the Rambam's efforts to elucidate Genesis 1 in the light of medieval physics and metaphysics. Chapter 5, by David Berger, amply demonstrates the relevance of the questions raised by this literature and the importance of confronting the answers it furnishes.

There is a feeling abroad, and it is not an unwarranted one, that the indivisibility of Torah builds more bridges than barriers between Orthodox scholars and proponents of the regnant theories in biblical scholarship. Sharing an interest in rabbinic exegesis and a respectful regard for the legacy of the medieval *pashtanim* may happily conceal the bottomless conflicts that defy collegial rapprochement. At a practical level, involvement in *parshanut* or rabbinic interpretation can become an agreeable "city of refuge" enabling the Orthodox scholar to participate in the academic field without affronting the ancestral pieties.[20]

The elaboration of common ground between the Orthodox and some segments of the scholarly establishment is, in my opinion, beneficial to both sides, and not only because of the pragmatic calculations noted above. Yet quite apart from the crucial, ineradicable, unabated conflict over essential beliefs, it is easy to overestimate the significance of this ostensible meeting of the minds. For the underlying motives and

---

[20]See, for example, the recommendation of Moshe Greenberg, *Al ha-Mikra ve-al ha-Yahadut*, ed. A. Shapira (Tel Aviv: Am Oved, 1984), pp. 330–337.

orientations of the two partners in intellectual dialogue remain different in kind. To the academic Bible scholar, the history of biblical study supplements the elaboration of the academic methodology: valued as a tool, even appreciated as an object of scholarship in its own right, in the larger context of biblical learning it is dispensable. The Orthodox thinker, by contrast, even one who values the reading of the biblical text in its ancient context, encounters the rabbinic literature and "what the veteran disciple is destined to innovate" as an integral part of biblical study.

One component in our commitment to the exegetical tradition is the awareness that, willy nilly, the passage of millennia and the accumulated burden of hermeneutics thwarts any ambition to isolate the primitive, uninterpreted meaning of the biblical text. This awareness is not necessarily limited to Orthodox thinkers. But our response to the tradition's constitutive contribution is also dogmatic and normative: we read the Bible in the light of the exegetical literature not only because such reading is unavoidable, but because we believe it to be the right way to read. It is this deeper commitment, this radical at-homeness in the indivisible mansion of Torah, that sets us apart from those we superficially resemble.[21]

I have emphasized that our *derekh ha-limmud* is firmly rooted in a commitment to the intrinsic relationship between the study of *Tanakh* and the spheres of Torah that border upon it. But this should not be taken to obliterate any distinction between the spheres. It is one thing to insist that the doors in a house be unlocked, that they ought to link the rooms rather than segregate them; it is another thing to overlook the existence of separate rooms altogether, in order to postulate an undifferentiated one-room mansion.

In principle, this should be perfectly plain to anyone exposed to our *parshanut*, anyone (to take one of numberless examples) who has come across Rashi's programmatic assertion (on Genesis 3:8) that his commentary on the Torah expounds *peshat* rather than *derash*. Frequently, however, it is easier for Orthodox readers and writers to know this principle than to practice it creatively. There is a natural tendency to blur the boundaries, so that other areas of Torah effectively substitute for and supplant the study of *Tanakh* itself.

---

[21]These two elements are touched on in S. Carmy and D. Shatz, "The Bible as a Source of Jewish Philosophical Reflection," in *The Routledge History of Jewish Philosophy*, ed. D. Frank and O. Leaman (London: Routledge, 1996).

In working toward our own *derekh ha-limmud*, there is little profit in lamenting the manifestations of this phenomenon in popular Orthodox culture. It is more enlightening to examine critically a justly admired example of contemporary Orthodox exegesis. The direct encounter with *Tanakh*, we shall discover, can take an interesting analysis based on later authorities, and endow it with even more significant implications.

Rabbi Moshe Eisemann's thorough, painstaking commentary on Chronicles, that most neglected of biblical books, is one of the high points of Orthodox Bible study in America. The "overview" advances the remarkable thesis that *Divrei ha-Yamim* is an eschatological book.[22] Argument for this position runs as follows: according to the Gemara (*Megillah* 3a) Yonatan b. Uzziel was forbidden by a heavenly voice from composing an authoritative translation of the Hagiographa (*Ketuvim*) because "the end of days" is hidden there. Rashi identifies the "end of days" with the visions in the book of Daniel. Maharal of Prague, however, infers that all the *Ketuvim* are included in the prohibition, and that therefore all *Ketuvim* contain eschatological material. Since Chronicles is part of *Ketuvim*, adopting Maharal's view (as opposed to Rashi's) entails that Chronicles contains eschatological material. This is a short step from the conclusion that the eschatological theme defines the unique character of Chronicles. Having secured this conclusion, the author appeals to it in explaining some salient features of the book. Where the portrait of King David in Samuel differs in emphasis from that of Chronicles, for example, it is because the former depicts David as a man, while Chronicles treats him as the messianic figure.

To be sure I am pleased to see Maharal's comments brought to bear on the issue at hand. But is the logic indeed compelling that would put so much weight on an inferred generalization from a comment by Maharal that is itself an inconclusive inference from a talmudic statement? Would it not be more responsible to submit this line of reasoning as no more than one possible overture to the book? By the same token, one might propose alternative explanations of the variations between Chronicles and Samuel. It might be suggested (and I am merely sketching the possibility) that Chronicles devotes more attention to David the king (and,

---

[22]*Divrei Hayamim 1* (ArtScroll), (Mesorah Publications, 1987), xvii–xix and xlii–l. Rabbi Nosson Scherman collaborated on the Overviews.

incidentally, to the Levitical genealogies and Temple cult) in order to reestablish, for the generation returning to Jerusalem, a sense of institutional continuity with the pre-Exile period.

The conventional academic critique of Rabbi Eisemann would stop here: taking him to task for overexploiting his Maharal text, one could, with a sniff of scholarly superiority and a sigh of relieved dismay, dismiss his work from further consideration. But the curious individual who continues to think along with Rabbi Eisemann's theory might eventually stumble across an obvious literary-historical question implicit in his approach. If Chronicles contains eschatological themes, why were these brought to the fore by an author living in the early Second Temple period, writing for an immediate audience of his contemporaries? Are we to judge the coincidence of historical situation and revelation as an accident without import for the theological message?

Let me add another problem to the last one, in the hope that the two difficulties will resolve each other. A famous conundrum, not addressed by ArtScroll: why doesn't Chronicles narrate the exodus from Egypt?[23] The question is too important to be shrugged off, and yet, to the best of my knowledge, it is not discussed by traditional commentators. It troubled me for many years.

Why should the story of our redemption from Egypt be omitted from a review of biblical history? The answer, I submit, is found in a prophecy of Jeremiah (16:14–15): the days will come, when people no longer swear by "God who brought up the children of Israel from the land of Egypt," but by "God who brought up the children of Israel from the land of the north, and from all the other lands where He had driven them. . . . "[24] The redemption from the Babylonian captivity will become more memorable than that of the first redemption from Egypt. Ramban, among others, picked up on this passage: he justified thereby the substitution of Babylonian names of months for the ordinal numbers of the First

---

[23]For a discussion with references to earlier literature, see Sara Japhet, *Emunot ve-Deot be-Sefer Divrei ha-Yamim* (Jerusalem: Bialik Press, 1977), pp. 322–327.

[24]Cf. Jeremiah 23:7–8. This does not imply that commemoration of the Egyptian Exodus will be obliterated. See *Berakhot* 12b (parallel in *Mekhilta of R. Ishmael* to Exodus 13:2). On the Talmud's use of the Jeremiah 23 instead of chapter 16, see note of Rabbi Zvi Hirsch Chajes, Chajes to *Berakhot*, elaborated in *Kol Kitvei Maharatz Hayyot*, I 74.

Temple era.[25] Jeremiah's prophecy thus articulates the consciousness of the returning exiles so strongly that it explains their adoption of a new vocabulary. Is it not reasonable that Chronicles would paint a picture of Jewish history expressing the same keen awareness of redemption?

I hold no particular brief for Rabbi Eisemann's thesis about the eschatological content of Chronicles. But if one is inclined to endorse that position, then my proposed solution to the problem of the missing exodus offers it support. By bringing to bear the eschatological prediction from Jeremiah one can at least suggest why Chronicles, written in the aftermath of the return from the Babylonian exile, might place special emphasis on the messianic theme.

What general lessons can we derive from this case? One result is to be dissatisfied with a methodology that relies exclusively on the exegetical and homiletical literature, at the expense of direct, unmediated encounter with the biblical text. But in the course of thinking through the example, paying attention not only to the results but also to the process by which we earn those results, we arrived at an insight that appears, at least superficially, to run in the opposite direction. For my own attempt to get to the bottom of the silent exodus problem was nurtured not only by the unadorned biblical text; it was fueled by my study of Ramban and other *Rishonim*, and my thinking was brought to a head by my critical encounter with Rabbi Eisemann's discussion.

Thus we draw a paradoxical moral: on the one hand, to beware of interpretation that substitutes for the primary source; on the other hand, to recognize the benefits that accrue from thinking along with our partners in the search for Torah understanding. You could put the fundamental question of this essay as follows: who are the interlocutors with whom we can best develop our authentic *derekh ha-limmud*? Who are the *havrutot* in whose company we may best fulfill our goals? With the academic world we recognize the potential value of new historical and geographical information, something that many Orthodox writers tend to ignore or downplay. Like the academicians we are wary of approaches that blur the borderlines between different facets of Torah. With our Orthodox colleagues we share a firm belief in the fundamental teachings of Judaism, with all their comprehensive implications for the study of

---

[25]Commentary to Exodus 12:2. See also Rabbi Yosef Albo, *Sefer hakkarim* 3:16.

Tanakh. And it is with our Orthodox brethren that we can unfold our understanding of *Tanakh* as part of the indivisible empire of Torah. In our quest for a unified, integrated way of studying and teaching, it seems to me that we will do best to cast our intellectual lot in this world with those colleagues with whom we hope to share our spiritual portion in the next. Despite divergence about method and procedure, substance and style, the place for thinking religious individuals is with each other, to learn and to teach, to question and to answer, to challenge and to refine.

The Confrontation of Cultures

Theological reflection and textual analysis do not happen in a cultural vacuum. To our study of Torah we bring ourselves, our presuppositions and prejudices, our experience of life, our hopes and fears. To be honest in our work, and honest with ourselves, we dare not shirk the duty of self-examination, the ruthless scrutiny of our cultural baggage, the careful inventory of its virtues and deficiencies, both moral and intellectual. The imperative of self-understanding and the collateral impulse to articulate and criticize our outlook, and that of our society, as precisely as possible ("to get the better of words") constitutes the major justification for liberal arts education, quite apart from any possible relevance to the study of Bible.[26] There is no alternative to serious, disciplined reflection on the language we make ours and the ideas embodied in that language. Failure to do so will impoverish and vitiate our intellectual-religious life. Yet nowhere is this more true than in the study of Bible. This is due to the enormous philosophical and psychological sensitivity of the texts and ideas, as well as the direct and indirect infiltration of concepts and habits of thinking of secularist and Christian origin.

We may get better purchase on this critical activity by exploring an instance from the literature. We shall examine a recent article on the binding of Isaac by Phyllis Trible, a highly respected feminist Bible scholar.[27] My choice is deliberate: unlike many feminist authors, Trible

---

[26]See my articles, "To Get the Better of Words," and "Why I Read Philosophy, etc.," *Commentator,* 1982, reprinted in *Torah uMadda Reader,* ed. S. Carmy (Yeshiva University Community Services Division, 1984).

[27]Phyllis Trible, "Genesis 22: The Sacrifice of Sarah," in *"Not in Heaven": Coherence and Complexity in Biblical Narrative,* ed. Jason Rosenblatt and Joseph

is unfailingly stimulating, relatively plausible, and responsible in her use of sources; many of the observations here presented, while open to question, are not unlike the ideas that might occur to us too. Thus we shall be able to evaluate both her approach and our possible responses to it.

According to Trible, the story of the *Akedah* "purports to be . . . a narrative of nonattachment." "To attach one's self to another is to negate love through entrapment. In surrounding Isaac, Abraham binds himself and his son. To attach is to know the anxiety of separation. In clinging to Isaac, Abraham incurs the risk of losing him—and Isaac suspects it. To attach is to practice idolatry." The use of the term *na'ar* (young man) shows that Abraham "distanced himself from Isaac[28] while affirming their unity. . . . Fear of God severs the link between detachment and attachment to save both Abraham and Isaac."

Trible goes on to argue that if Abraham requires the test of the *Akedah* in order to transcend the "entrapment of attachment," Sarah is even more in need of such purification. It was Sarah, after all, who insisted that Abraham expel Hagar and Ishmael because they threatened Isaac's position and destiny. "[S]he, not Abraham, ought to have been tested . . . that she learn the meaning of obedience to God, that she find liberation from possessiveness, that she free Isaac from maternal ties, and that she emerge a solitary individual, nonattached, the model of faithfulness." Because Sarah was not called upon to sacrifice her son, she was denied the opportunity for a final reconciliation with Hagar, which presumably would have come about once she had attained the heights of nonattachment.

These intriguing remarks proceed to an unfortunate and unacceptable conclusion. Trible decides that something has gone wrong with the narrative, and that Sarah has been replaced by the "ill-fitted" Abraham. This supposed deficiency of the biblical text is attributed to the "patriarchal" partiality of the author, fostering "a bias for father–son bonding" that overcomes "the logic of the argument."

Sitterson, Jr. (Indiana 1991), pp. 170–191; quotations are from pp. 178–182, 187–189. See also the comments on the *Akedah* in Carmy and Shatz, "The Bible as a Service of Jewish Philosophical Reflection."

[28]Trible does not remark on the possible relevance of a similar strategy of distancing in the next chapter. From the time he mourns Sarah until he accomplishes her burial, Abraham speaks of her as his "dead person" (*meti*).

We meet this kind of analysis, and this kind of conclusion, not only in academic journals, but in common educated discourse.[29] Some of the observations formulated by Trible are not alien to us: if reject them we must, then we must stand ready to criticize and refine our own conceptions and interpretations. And some of her insights may even be true, in which case they may still want unpacking, improvement, and distillation before they can become part of our intellectual property.

A full assessment of Trible's article cannot be undertaken short of a comprehensive study of the *Akedah*. My purpose here is to show how we must proceed with our work if we intend to be equal to the task. My precis of Trible's article highlights three elements: (1) a thesis about the purport of Genesis 22; (2) an ethical-psychological judgment about the situation described in the chapter; (3) an answer to the question "why Abraham rather than Sarah?" Let me comment on them in turn:

1. Trible takes it for granted that the section purports to be a "narrative of nonattachment." Abraham is indeed required to transcend normal human reactions for the sake of his exclusive commitment to God. Are these normal human reactions identical with the feelings of a father for a son, a father who gained that son only in his old age, after many tribulations? The Rambam[30] thought so, and God's speech at the beginning of the chapter, with its fourfold repetition "your son, your only one, whom you love, Isaac" lends his view support. But many readers have located part of the drama of the test elsewhere, not in the overcoming of Abraham's attachment to Isaac, but in the surmounting of Abraham's deep-seated allegiance to a Kantian conception of universal moral law (a central theme in Kierkegaard's *Fear and Trembling*), or in the demonstration of Abraham's unshakable certitude in the authenticity of his prophetic encounter (Rambam's second explanation) or even in the testing of Abraham's faith in life after death, since, according to this argument, Abraham would not have offered Isaac up had he not been

---

[29]Even as I write this paragraph, the August 1993 *Atlantic* arrives with a long cover essay by Cullen Murphy, "Women and the Bible" (pp. 39–64).

[30]*Guide* 3:24. Note, however, that Rambam does not locate the purpose of the chapter in a lesson learned by Abraham, but rather in the lessons taught through Abraham's exhibition of virtue.

assured that Isaac would return to life (Abarbanel following Saadia, both preceded by Paul's Epistle to the Hebrews). Despite my sympathy with this thesis of Trible's, her single-minded concentration on the interpersonal dimension runs the risk of oversimplification.

2. Trible states that her "interpretation plays with three concepts: attachment, detachment, and nonattachment. . . . In addition to scriptural foundations, this interpretation builds on Zen Buddhism and Metapsychiatry."[31] Whatever might be said of the ideas in her paper, the terminology certainly does not derive from the Bible. I don't mean this as a reproach. As noted above, we cannot avoid bringing ourselves to the act of study, and the only way we could eschew our own vocabulary would be to parrot a vocabulary that is not ours, and that consequently cannot express whatever it is that we want to say. If Trible finds that the categories of Zen Buddhism and Metapsychiatry illuminate the subject and permit her to say what she wishes to say, then she should, by all means, play with that terminology.

What about us, trying to bring our *derekh ha-limmud* to bear on the *Akedah*, or on any other *sugya* in *Tanakh*? Do we consider the categories of Zen Buddhism and Metapsychiatry adequate to our apprehension of the multifaceted *devar ha-Shem*? If we do not, it is not Professor Trible's fault. It is our responsibility to discover our own voice, and in the process to unfold our own unique insight.

Where shall we seek our own authentic voice? To begin with, in the careful, disciplined, alert, but emphatically not slavish, emulation of our predecessors and role models, keeping in mind what we have already seen regarding the interaction of different branches of Torah. Second, by plundering the ideas and language of culture, tirelessly trying them out, struggling against all odds "to get the better of words" for the task at hand. Last, but not least, by examining critically the ideas and language of culture, holding them at arm's length, making them recite their story like a lesson, till we put our finger on the point where things went wrong, and resolve, undeceived and enlightened, to go our own way and try to do better.

I know that many studious readers will balk at the suggestion that defective language, or the uncritical borrowing of categories from various

---

[31]Trible, "Genesis 22," p. 251, n. 20.

fashionable academic modes of discourse, can undermine our efforts to study *Tanakh* as thinking religious individuals. They would regard style as a matter of taste rather than substance; in any event, as something that comes naturally. Our brief discussion of Trible should cure us of any such illusion. To receive our language passively, to purchase it cheaply, off the rack, as it were, is to assume challenging intellectual responsibilities, replete with religious import, blithely oblivious to the shoddiness of our equipment. In a secular society, one becomes a sitting duck for every species of educated (or semieducated) jargon.

3. Finally, a word about the most controversial element of Trible's essay, her logical leap from the reasonable suggestion that Sarah was more "attached" to Isaac to her theory that the author of the Torah distorted the "true" story as a result of pervasive male chauvinism. Not a few scholarly people will, like one of my colleagues at Yeshiva, dismiss the question "why Abraham and not Sarah?" as an invitation to unwarranted speculation. Those who dispute Trible's reduction of the *Akedah* to its purely interpersonal aspect will be similarly skeptical of her conviction that everything about the story must be connected to resolution of the interpersonal issue.

But what if we are sufficiently impressed with Trible's account of attachment and detachment to place it at the center of Abraham's test? And what if we are convinced by her tenable claim that, of Abraham and Sarah, the one most attached to Isaac, and therefore the one who would profit most from withstanding the test of the *Akedah*, is Sarah? Does this support the hypothesis that the text in our *Humash* screens an original narrative deformed by an author who sacrificed his sense of psychological reality to the dictates of patriarchal ideology?

A moment's reflection may lead us to the opposite conclusion. When an individual is tested, God calls upon him or her to exercise extraordinary virtue. The Rabbis teach that God subjects those individuals to the test who are best able to respond: all things being equal, it is unfair to make an extraordinary demand of an individual that he or she cannot meet.[32] By Trible's own analysis, Sarah is more attached to Isaac. Hence the fact that Sarah is not the active participant in the *Akedah* is more consistent with the psychological reality depicted in the earlier narratives about Sarah and Abraham, Sarah and Hagar, Sarah and Ishmael, than is

---

[32]See *Genesis Rabbah* 55:2 (Theodor-Albeck edition) pp. 585–6.

the revised edition envisioned by Trible. (Unless, of course, you insist that the previous clashes between Sarah and Hagar are the product of patriarchal bias. But in that case the evidence of Sarah's attachment to Isaac can also be revised away, nor is there reason to lament the fact that Sarah and Hagar are denied the opportunity for reconciliation. . . .)

No doubt Trible brings her own presuppositions and hopes to the study of the text. Throughout her published work she has sought to bring biblical women and female imagery closer to the center of the text, and this motivation, which has enabled her to notice much that has previously been ignored, can also lead one to see what is not there. Because she is more preoccupied with theme than with character, she also finds it easy to treat Abraham and Sarah as figures in an allegory rather than as flesh and blood individuals whose destinies transcend the theory of gender conflict. Her approach, furthermore, betrays a too facile optimism: for Sarah to have taken Abraham's place at the *Akedah*, passed the test with flying colors, and triumphantly reconciled with Hagar would seem to require no more than a modicum of good will on the part of the author. Human reality is often more tragic: if, as Ramban held, Sarah's conduct toward Hagar was sinful,[33] it is not at all clear that the injury could be undone by nothing more than a meeting of reconciliation.

I make these criticisms, not to discredit the work of an intelligent and thought-provoking religious thinker, but to stress the need for vigilance in evaluating current ideas and formulations. The vigilance ought to be self-directed as well, for our thinking and writing may not be completely free of irrelevant or misleading preoccupations and motivations, even the very same vices observed a moment ago. And if so, it would be a pity if our *derekh ha-limmud* suffered from our reluctance to turn on ourselves the kind of critique it is incumbent upon us to apply to others.

A CONCLUDING COMMENT ON CULTURAL CONFRONTATION

Our discussion so far has alluded to essential beliefs, held firmly by Orthodox Jews, doctrines that play a central role in defining the content and the contours of our study of *Tanakh*. I have not felt the need to define

---

[33]See his Commentary to 16:6 and Chapter 5 in this volume, by David Berger.

those beliefs precisely, for the simple reason that our discussion has been concerned with the unbridgeable gaps between our beliefs and those of scholars who do not subscribe to our beliefs. These differences are visible to the naked eye, so to speak, and do not need fine-tuning: just think of the authorship of the Torah, the reliability of the biblical canon, the authenticity and authority of the Oral Law, and so forth. But cultivating a *derekh ha-limmud* sooner or later entails getting down to details, and that includes investigating the nuances of spiritual orientation and theological formulation.

We must recognize that an honest, informed, and sophisticated approach to *Tanakh* can be expected to arrive at, and subsequently to employ, results and procedures that will not always show a familiar and reassuring face to the man in the street, and that may even shock people who deem themselves reasonably learned. Determining the right path to follow will not always be self-evident. Part of our responsibility as students, teachers, and custodians of a *derekh ha-limmud* is to serve as a living laboratory in all areas belonging to our vocation. The problems that confront us as we seek to work through these issues can only be tackled in a forum where the fundamental beliefs underlying our learning are shared, where the goals of learning are held in common, and where, consequently, there is hope for a degree of consensus on the relative weights of various factors.

The reader to whom this sounds overly abstract will find many exhibits in Barry Levy's survey (Chapter 2) in this volume, and a thorough treatment of a narrow but important area—the stability of the Masoretic text in the light of rabbinic literature—in Yeshayahu Maori's study (Chapter 4). The focus of these discussions is what I would call the objective problem, by which I mean the problem of determining the truth or falsity of a particular proposition. The work of forging a *derekh ha-limmud* also has a subjective aspect—how we incorporate a proposition or procedure into our individual and communal intellectual-religious frames of reference is not a matter of indifference and not something to be left to nature, as it were. Let us look at an instance of each type of challenge.

Mishnah *Taanit* 4:5 states that the walls of Jerusalem were breached on the seventeenth of Tammuz; Jeremiah 39:2 gives the date as the ninth. Rabbi Tanhum b. Hanilai (*Taanit* 4:5) answers that the biblical text reflects a confused calculation (*kilkul heshbonot*). The Talmud discovers a similar confusion in Ezekiel 26:1, where (for reasons worked out in the *sugya*) the first of the month really refers to the ninth. Apparently the shock of disaster caused the messengers to get the date wrong, *and* the biblical text perpetuates the error.[34]

This passage attracted the attention of Rabbi Kook, at the turn of the century, when he addressed some of the putative conflicts between science and religion. Every intelligent person, he maintains, knows that whether one accepts the older or newer theories of astronomy or geology has no relation to the Torah. It is also well known that prophecy adapts itself to human language and to the contemporary human situation, "what the ear can hear in the present." Rabbi Kook then refers to the Yerushalmi cited above, "according to its simple meaning," before blaming contemporary heresy on the moral corruption of the Catholic church, as a result of which modern people are easily duped by newfangled suppositions.[35]

Now most religious readers of the Bible assume that the narrative is reliable, that when Jeremiah's account refers to the ninth of the month, it means the ninth, not the seventeenth. As readers of literature, however, we know that authors sometimes employ an "unreliable narrator," who may utter statements that the reader ought not to accept. The Talmud appears to be saying that, in order to commemorate the atmosphere of devastation and confusion, the Author of the Bible permitted several unreliable statements to creep into the biblical texts. Rabbi Kook implies that this example can be generalized and might resolve other apparent problems.

It seems obvious that Rabbi Kook doesn't advocate wholesale rejection of biblical statements. To do so would render *Tanakh* useless as a source of history. Under what circumstances would he countenance "deconstruction" of the text? Only where biblical texts contradict each other or rabbinic statements? Whenever the text appears to contradict well-attested Near Eastern documents? When the exact historicity is

---

[34]See commentators, including Hatam Sofer on the Yerushalmi margin. Note that Maharsha's puzzlement induced him to offer a strained interpretation of this statement (*Taanit* 28b, s.v. *Ba-rishonah*).

[35]Rabbi A. I. Kook, *Eder ha-Yekar* (Jerusalem: Mosad haRav Kook, 5727), pp. 37–38.

immaterial, in the judgment of the exegete, to the import of the text? When the exegete detects rhetorical elements in the biblical text itself that point toward such interpretation?

Most academic Bible scholars are not bothered by these questions and can hardly be expected to take our problem seriously. For them the biblical narrative enjoys no presumption of reliability at all. Our struggle to get Rabbi Kook right would earn us a silky "contempt for our fixations," sugarcoated in avuncular congratulations upon having at last taken one small step toward the progressive light.[36] Only at home, in our own theological clearinghouse, sensitive to all that we value, can these principles be embodied, seamlessly and unself-consciously, in our *derekh ha-limmud*.

My second example illustrates the challenge posed to healthy religious subjectivity by the introduction of an unsettling proposition. It is beyond the scope of our discussion to offer an exhaustive account of the debate over the provenance of the book of Isaiah. Most of those who date the second half of the book (40–66) to the later part of the sixth century B.C.E. operate with false theological presuppositions, such as the denial of prophecy *ante eventum*. One might, however, embrace the late dating on other grounds, without believing that this position is inconsistent with fundamental Jewish tenets.

Among Orthodox scholars who favored the divided Isaiah was Dr. Jacob Barth, who taught this view at the Hildesheimer Rabbinical Seminary in Berlin in the late nineteenth and early twentieth centuries.[37] One may question Barth's literary arguments and one may dispute his assessment of the theological considerations involved. Our interest here, however, is to record the subjective reaction of one prominent layman.

---

[36]The phrase in quotes is from Michael Rosenak's poignant lament for the infirmity of modern Orthodoxy and right-wing Conservatism, "In (Not Such) Splendid Isolation," *Forum* no. 50 (Winter 1983/4): 37–40.

[37]See Zvi Weinberg, "Jacob Barth's Lectures on Isaiah at the Berlin Rabbinical Seminary," in *Iyyunei Mikra u-Parshanut* [Toeg Memorial Volume], ed. U. Simon and M. Goshen-Gottstein (Bar-Ilan University, 1980), pp. 229–241, for Barth's lecture notes; and M. Breuer, *Modernity within Tradition*, trans. E. Petuchowski (New York: Columbia University Press, 1992), pp. 186–188, 205–207, for an account of the controversy.

As a young man, Jacob Rosenheim, a leading lay representative of Frankfurt Orthodoxy, visited Berlin, where he formed the following impression of Barth's activity:

> Professor Barth, in spite of his Southern German origin, and despite the fact that he was the son-in-law of Rabbi Ezriel Hildesheimer and indubitably lived as a devout Jew, both in thought and in action, endangered the faithfulness of the Seminary's students to the principles of Judaism. He had a completely *rationalistic, unphilosophical* mind, totally oriented to philological investigation, and it was he who accepted the view of the Bible critics about the two Isaiahs . . . , without realizing that this would necessarily undermine his young students' faith in the truth of the tradition concerning the composition of Scriptures. Indeed, all students of the Seminary who chose to study Orientalism or Hebrew at the university, were *required* to know the basic works of biblical criticism before taking their doctoral examinations, so that pure faith, nay elementary *respect* for divine revelation, was necessarily undermined.[38]

Presumably Rosenheim did not accept the multiple authorship of Isaiah. No scholar himself, his animadversions may well play out the Frankfurt–Berlin tensions that divided modern German Orthodoxy. Yet his complaint deserves to be read carefully within its own limits. He does not here castigate Barth as a heretic *malgré lui*. Instead he bemoans the *consequences* of Barth's teaching. He alleges that Barth was intellectually one-dimensional (lacking philosophical depth), and that he failed to understand the effect certain results and modes of investigation would have on his students. The logical implication of this is that had Barth displayed a more comprehensive (philosophical) approach, had he more successfully engaged his own piety in the act of teaching, had he better understood his students' mentality, Rosenheim would not have minded quite as much the raising of potentially unsettling theories. In fact, although Rosenheim is clearly unhappy with any exposure to heretical theories, he goes on to praise Rabbi David Zvi Hoffmann as a more satisfactory role model who injected a more tangible quality of fervor into his teaching.

Let me pose a problem to those who believe that the future of serious creative Orthodox *Tanakh* study passes through the academic

---

[38]Jacob Rosenheim, *Zikhronot* (Tel Aviv: Shearim, 1955), p. 50; italics in the original.

establishment. I presume that you, like me, want *Tanakh* to occupy an important place in Jewish education. Perhaps I have not convinced you that only a comprehensive, philosophical *derekh ha-limmud* can serve as our ultimate goal. Perhaps you believe that my conception of study suffused by and integrated with theological reflection is one more specialty, no better and no worse than a single-minded devotion to philology. But if you get your way, if the university orientation becomes the paradigm and pattern for our study, then the quasicritical and speculative subjects peripheral to the study of *devar Ha-Shem*—issues of authorship, dating, historical background, and the like—will inexorably work their way to the top of our syllabi. And if that is the case, then the marginality of Bible in the curriculum will necessarily be reinforced, as student and layman come to experience *Tanakh*, not as the occasion for confrontation with God and with ourselves, but as a complex of preoccupations, a sideshow of "problems," a vermiform appendix in the body politic of Torah, useless in itself, worthy of attention only when it causes pain or becomes infected.

III

Many arguments have been offered to urge a greater willingness, on the part of Orthodox Bible students, to participate in the professional culture of academia. Let us comment on some of them:

1. *Nonparticipation is intellectually dishonest.* In particular it is held that failure to apply to Torah the same methods used in other academic disciplines, and in the exact manner advocated by the upholders of greater participation, constitutes an inconsistency. This argument is specifically deployed against "highly regarded centrist *rashei yeshivah*" who advocate the study of Western literature, philosophy, and the like. When they insist that Torah is different from other disciplines, they are accused of coming close to making a mockery of the entire enterprise.

Many of us, especially those whose judgment of the aforementioned *Gedolei Yisrael* and their intellectual integrity or lack thereof is based on firsthand experience, would lack the equanimity to further discuss the imputation. But the argument makes sense if it means that what counts as truth and what counts as evidence is determined by the gatekeepers of a discipline, and that intellectual honesty requires us to forsake all knowledge that is not certified a part of the discipline we are studying at the moment. From a common-sense perspective, however, inquiry that systematically ignores everything else we know (including the knowledge given us through revelation), is not honest. On the contrary: it is the height of perversity![39]

We are fortunate to have a pertinent letter, dated August 11, 1953, by *maran ha-Rav* Soloveitchik *zt"l*, counseling against RCA participation in the planned JPS Bible translation.

> After all, we live in an age which admires the expert and which expects him to tell how things are and how they ought to be done. The expert, on the other hand, does not tolerate any opposition; all we ought to do is listen to him and swallow his ideas. I am not ready to swallow the ideas of the modern expert and scholar on our *Tanakh*. . . . [40]

---

[39]Cf. the remarks of a Christian philosopher that "we should declare the impossibility of pursuing Critical Studies that are neutral on important questions such as the nature and authority of the New Testament and should argue instead that Christian biblical scholars ought to work out of basic Christian presuppositions regarding the nature and purpose of Scripture. Christian biblical scholars ought not, therefore, to pretend to hold a methodological neutrality about the nature, authority, and purpose of the biblical texts. . . . Why should they deny themselves access to truths they already accept as they press onward in the pursuit of truth? Affecting a methodological neutrality toward Scripture should be recognized, then as neither possible nor desirable." Ronald J. Feenstra, "Critical Studies of the New Testament: Comments on the Paper of Peter van Inwagen," in *Hermes and Athena: Biblical Exegesis and Philosophical Theology*, ed. Eleonore Stump and Thomas P. Flint (Notre Dame University, 1993), p. 196. This volume seeks to open a dialogue between Christian philosophers and biblical scholars, an attempt that recapitulates many of the conflicts described here. John McIntyre, "Historical Criticism in a 'History-Centred Value System,'" in *Language, Theology and the Bible*, ed. Samuel Balentine and John Barton (Oxford University, 1994), pp. 370–384, explains that theology constitutes a "field-encompassing field" standing in relation to a multiplicity of disciplines within theology and the large number of methods and data often identified monolithically as "historical method."

[40]Copy in Louis Bernstein, "The Emergence of the English Speaking Rabbinate" (Ph.D. diss., Yeshiva University, 1977), pp. 561ff. The Rav's classic

2. *Nonparticipation is a sign of weakness.* It is held that refraining from participation in the academic enterprise projects to the external observer an image of weakness, not strength.

Imagine you have come to believe that a wonderful life-giving treasure is hidden in your backyard. Your neighbor, whether because he lacks access to your information or for some other reason, scoffs at your belief. You stop digging for the treasure; you will not get back to work until you have brought your neighbor around to your belief. Your neighbor reasonably concludes that since you don't pursue your commitment single-mindedly you either lack certitude in your own belief or that you don't really value the treasure. I would call this a projection of weakness, not strength. And the worst thing is that your belief may eventually ape your actions, so that you end up confirming his suspicion.

External observers are not all of one cloth, and not all of our skeptical neighbors will react like the one here invented. But I submit that being distracted from one's mission for fear of being perceived as weak is itself the most dramatic exhibition of weakness. A similar observation animates the Rav, in the letter just quoted:

> I noticed in your letter that you are a bit disturbed about the probability of being left out. Let me tell you that this attitude of fear is responsible for many commissions and omissions, compromises and fallacies on our part which have contributed greatly to the prevailing confusion within the Jewish community and to the loss of our self-esteem, our experience of ourselves as independent entities committed to a unique philosophy and way of life.

3. *The missionary position.* Orthodox scholars should enter academic Bible studies in the hope of attracting their errant colleagues to the true faith.

To make this claim ingenuously requires almost unbelievable naïveté. Each story of a human being assenting to the fundamental principles underlying either traditional Jewish belief or entrenched academic belief is both complex and mysterious, rich in implicit premises and barely

---

published statement on interfaith dialogue is "Confrontation," *Tradition* 6:2 (Spring-Summer 1964): 5–29.

avowed motivations. The vast majority of people, even thinking people, once having opted for a general network of beliefs, are unlikely to reconsider at the drop of an argument. When a sympathetic historian of the Graf-Wellhausen Hypothesis grudgingly acknowledges of Rabbi David Hoffmann, from the safe distance of several generations, that "[h]is work was well done and remains one of the best statements of scientific Conservatism,"[41] we do not expect him to adopt Hoffmann's views; we expect the author to move to the next item, and we are not disappointed. This is no different from what we do when a truth to which we were firmly committed collides with some particularly knotty problem. The gap is too wide to be bridged by reason alone, especially when our side is in the minority and, by the very definition of the game, forced to concede the home court advantage and use the vocabulary and conceptual matrix of our opponents.

4. *Light unto the professors.* There is so much that we can contribute to the scholarly world. If we persist in using our own parochial language and categories they won't listen to us.

It is difficult to judge how great an obligation, if any, we have to export biblical research to the world. Assuming that we want to, the question is why we can't be ourselves and speak in our own voices. The answer is either connected to the content—if we travel under our true colors, our message will be dismissed; or it is aesthetic—the kernel of truth, encased in the husks of Orthodox particularism, is harder to assimilate.

Both of these obstacles are real. I know this, because it is tiresome to "translate" the jargon of modern biblical scholarship into my own idiom, and irksome to separate the data that may be useful to me from the host of presuppositions I don't accept. But like it or not, not all jargon is obfuscation. The accretion of specialized concepts often reproduces authentically a network of systematic connections, subtle nuance, and the interaction of a discipline with its past, that cannot be encoded as well in any other way. Forthright intellectual relations, motivated by an honest desire to understand and appreciate, will survive the sometimes insurmountable imaginative challenge of translation.

---

[41]R. J. Thompson, *Moses and the Law in a Century of Criticism since Graf* (Leiden: E. J. Brill, 1970), p. 81.

5. *The only impediment to full participation is academic anti-Semitism.*
Jewish opposition to biblical scholarship has often been rallied by reference to the anti-Jewish ideology purportedly inspiring the academic
enterprise. Who doesn't know Solomon Schechter's jibe that the higher
criticism is the higher anti-Semitism? Most contemporary scholars are
not card-carrying anti-Semites; it is not even clear that they come
under the halakhic prohibition of "learning from a sorcerer [*magosh*]"
whom Rashi defines as one fervently committed to leading Jews astray.[42]
It is therefore argued that our traditional revulsion toward Bible scholars is outmoded.

I don't know the prevalence of anti-Semitism or violent hatred of
Torah among present day biblical scholars (my own limited experience
having been uniformly benign).[43] Leftist and/or feminist academic ideologues are disposed to the doctrinaire slur, and occasionally you come
across something genuinely nauseous.[44] It happens that the university
career of a Bible scholar is sidelined or smashed because someone in
power (usually a Jew) cannot brook the presence of a believing Jew in

---

[42]Rashi *Shabbat* 75a, s.v. *ve-ha-lomed*. See Rabbi Ahron Soloveichik, *Logic of
the Heart, Logic of the Mind* (Jerusalem: Genesis Jerusalem Press, 1991), pp. 45–
46, and compare to his *Od Yisrael Yosef Beni Hai* (Chicago: Brisk Yeshiva of
Chicago, 1993), p. 11.

[43]Cf. the judgment of a distinguished philologist and biblical scholar: "But,
in so far as this criticism was at all valid, it was not at all specific to the critical
approach. It derives rather from general structures within nineteenth century
Christianity. . . . Regrettable as this teaching was, there was never any proper
justification for the deplorable remark 'Higher criticism—higher anti-Semitism,'
a remark which would never have been made by a great scholar, and yet is sometimes repeated." James Barr, *Fundamentalism* (London and Philadelphia: Westminster Press, 1977), p. 286. I doubt Barr's claim that liberal Christian scholars
are less prone to anti-Judaic bias than theological conservatives: militant re-
sentment of Jewish particularism in the name of "third world" liberation and
feminist hatred toward the "phallocentric" ethic of the commandment are not
conservative theological positions.

[44]R. J. Thompson, in "Moses and the Law," upon mentioning the venerable
German-Jewish periodical *MGWJ* which had predicted the fall of the Graf-
Wellhausen hypothesis, cannot restrain an unpardonable sneer: "*MGWJ* . . .
relapses into critical silence, broken only by another "demise" article on Wellhausen, a year before its own final demise in 1939" (p. 84 n. 4).

the profession, but these episodes are infrequent, if only because the profession's tolerance is so rarely tested.

But the entire attempt to judge academic Bible study by the personal ethics of its practitioners is inherently misguided. Even if it were true that each and every member of the regiment that liberated Dachau were an unreconstructed follower of Wellhausen, I would not expect these valiant and humane professors to nominate an Orthodox Jew to a tenured chair in their department. The insuperable gap is not academic politics, but belief, presumably sincere and deep-seated belief.

6. *The increased popularity of "neutral" specialties breaks down the barriers.* Earlier we noted the recent respectability of history of exegesis and similar safe havens. Methodological fragmentation in the humanities has led to greater tolerance for pluralistic approaches, which may open a crack in the door through which our own people can gain a foothold, if not in Jewish studies, then at least in departments of literature.

This is true up to a point. That a lifework encompassed by such an intellectual agenda would fall short of the literary-theological comprehensiveness we have described needs no repetition. But another caveat is in order. When we think of elements incompatible with Judaism in academic ideology, we are quite alert to themes deriving from Christian sources. We often let our dukes down when the ideology is secular, and hence nominally neutral. Moreover, we must not forget that secular neutrality manifests itself in more than the adoption, rejection, or bracketing of specific beliefs or methods. Let me explain by way of reference to the "Bible as literature" movement that has generated so much enthusiasm in recent years.

For Orthodox Jews, there are obvious attractions in applying to the Bible the methods that have been successfully developed for the study of great literature: literary close reading shares affinities with the insights of *parshanut*, sometimes by dressing them up in a more contemporary and systematic garb,[45] sometimes by providing a theoretical framework that deepens the meaning of the midrashic enterprise[46]; the literary approach

---

[45]The early essays of Robert Alter stimulated interest among English readers partly for this reason. See his *Art of Biblical Narrative* (New York: Basic Books, 1981) and *Art of Biblical Poetry* (New York: Basic Books, 1985).

[46]I am thinking of Meir Sternberg's *Poetics of Biblical Narrative* (Indiana

tends to uncover the unity of the text; most (though not all) literary readers do not presuppose the Documentary Hypothesis in their analysis. Last but not least, the literary understanding of biblical narrative and poetry is a potential ally in the cause of existential truth as most academic scholarship is not.

Of course the literary critics carry presuppositions of their own, and not every approach suitable to the study of some genre or period can be transferred to Bible. It makes an immense difference, for example, that the biblical narratives contain historical information and moral instruction of the utmost importance for the original audience. Thus the modern literary reading of Genesis, for example, often combines keen attention to character development with indifference to the passages in which God speaks of the destiny of the Jewish people, ignoring the fact that the ancient Jews were at least as interested in God's promises to them as in those narrative units that still allure the modern literary sensibility. Most literary analysis has nothing to say about the vast amount of legal material, or even about its connection to the adjacent narrative. We know that scholars who do not share our beliefs are prone to miss these points, and that they may even consciously utilize the rubric "as literature" to prescind from the theological claims made by the Bible.[47] Despite these pitfalls and shortcomings, we (I and many of my friends) look forward to the publications of Robert Alter, for example, and are not much perturbed by the complaint of an eminent non-Jewish student of literature, that "'Our' and 'we' are accurate only if Alter is addressing atheists, Low Church Protestants, and Jews who don't believe or practice the faith."[48] We can benefit from Alter's shrewd insights without imagining that we are part of his "we."

University, 1985) and similar works. By exhibiting the ubiquity of narrative gaps in the biblical story, Sternberg both demonstrates the demands made by the Bible on its readers and encourages us to understand why, and how, Hazal respond to those demands.

[47]Harold Fisch has made an important contribution by contrasting the theological poetics of the Bible with the ingrained assumptions underlying modern responses to literature. See his *Poetry with a Purpose* (Indiana University, 1988), in particular the essays on the Song of Songs and Job.

[48]Denis Donoghue, "Book of Books Books," *New York Review of Books*, 5 November 1992, 46–50 (p. 47).

But the secular orientation that excludes us from Alter's "we" is not merely a matter of disputed doctrines. The secular approach often betrays a completely different conception of what is at stake in the quest for truth. This judgment is confirmed by an almost trivial throwaway comment in Alter's largely negative review of Harold Bloom's *Book of J*, with its "fiction or fantasy, and not necessarily a helpful one" that the so-called J document of *Humash* was written by a woman.[49] His disapproval of Bloom's book does not prevent Alter from extending the following faint praise: "The decision about her gender, of which Bloom says he is intuitively convinced, is a fine way to *épater les fidèles;* every time the pronoun 'she' occurs, readers are likely to find themselves shaken out of their preconceptions about the Bible, *and that is all to the good.*"[50]

The breezy epistemology of the last phrase can be accepted only if we assume that all traditional preconceptions are untrustworthy until proven true, or that the truth of those preconceptions doesn't much matter, so that shaking them up is nothing but good clean American fun, like giving your stuffy neighbor a hotfoot at the baseball stadium. Such frolics may indeed be appropriate in dealing with literature that invites playful ambiguity, from Conan Doyle to Nabokov. *Tanakh* does not fall in the same category. Hence, the committed Orthodox scholar who can pass a pleasant and profitable hour in the company of his secular counterpart, as one would with an amiable acquaintance at a well-appointed bar, will return to his own home when the time comes for work and sleep. It is like a wartime encounter in a neutral city. Were someone to declare that he or she had come there to find a source of living water, they would either be joking or misinformed.

7. *Bold scholar to the rescue.* It is conceded that those who participate, for whatever reasons, in academic biblical studies will not be able to solve many of the most important questions, within the framework of the current academic establishment. These major questions remain disturbing and unanswered and the professional response of these scholars, whatever their "private" beliefs might be, will again and again be *tzarikh iyyun.* This unfortunate state of paralysis can only be remedied when a bold scholar takes the initiative and solves one of these fundamental problems.

---

[49]Robert Alter, *The World of Biblical Literature* (New York: Basic Books, 1992): "The Quest for the Author" (153–170), 168.

[50]Alter, "The Quest for the Author" p. 161; italics in last sentence are mine.

To the extent that this argument describes the dilemma of those en-gaged in academic scholarship rather than defining a comprehensive *derekh ha-limmud*, it has more to do with the topic of the next section. Yet I believe that the appeal to the bold scholar highlights one of the problems with our affiliation to the academic establishment. The genu-inely creative literary-theological thinker, whatever the scope of his or her interests, must be firmly and persuasively rooted in his own vocabu-lary and weltanschauung; he must operate in the name of a rich, authen-tic *derekh ha-limmud*. Success in the academic world, however, is pre-dicated on one's ability to distance one's religious identity from his professional activities. The bold scholar, if she is to appear, is thus unlikely to be clad in academic raiment. Meanwhile piecemeal solutions, the kind that can be cultivated by less prodigiously gifted individuals operating within the autonomous framework of a *derekh ha-limmud*, are deferred because many of those individuals, exiled in academia, are not in con-trol of their own intellectual-religious vocations. A passenger cannot guide the carriage by holding on to the seat in front of him; he must get out of the carriage and at least guide himself. This is true, not only of the exceptional scholar, the *deus ex machina*; it is true for every thinking religious individual.

IV

I could make a more unified presentation by omitting the next section. I could then conclude that Orthodoxy would create a self-sufficient sys-tem of biblical studies. Not only would we produce our own theology, our own integration of *Torah she-be'al peh* and *Torah she-bi-Ktav*, our own perspective on history of exegesis and its relation to other dimensions of study, and so forth; we would also conduct an autonomous archaeology, Assyriology, Egyptology, Semitics, and the like. Unfortunately this vision is utterly unfeasible at present. Any consideration of Orthodox Bible study and its relation to the secular university must make room for this fact.

At a practical level I would suggest a rough distinction between two domains pertinent to biblical scholarship. The first includes archaeol-ogy, Near Eastern history, and, to a lesser degree, Semitic languages. The second covers those areas where theological doctrines are more explic-itly involved and where the results and formulation of one's study more directly influence theological experience.[51] Three factors lead me to place the first set of disciplines in a class of their own:

1. They can be practiced actively only by individuals who have undergone complicated, sophisticated, specialized training.
2. These disciplines generally do not supply the content of Torah study, but rather background information for Torah study.
3. Partly as a result of the second factor, conflict in these disciplines is less likely to interfere with Talmud Torah.

The first factor suggests that, where the critical mass (in both senses of the term) is lacking, it is just as well if these areas become the possession of the few. The second factor implies that lack of training in these areas does not impoverish the individual's *derekh ha-limmud*. His needs can be met by consulting the experts. The third factor implies that there is less of a risk that the *derekh ha-limmud* will be distorted if we make common cause with scholars outside our camp.

The last point may seem a bit puzzling at first blush. An example may be helpful. We all know that it has so far proven impossible to harmonize completely the biblical stories about the conquest of the land with the prevalent interpretations of the available archaeological evidence. Twenty years ago it was widely believed that much of this tension could be resolved if the conquest were dated to approximately 1300 B.C.E. But this contradicted 1 Kings 6:1, which places the beginning of Solomon's reign 480 years after the Exodus, yielding 1400 B.C.E. as the approximate date of the conquest. I recall one of my college teachers quipping that if the power were bestowed upon him to emend one, and only one, biblical verse, he would choose to reduce the number to 380. In a more sober vein, a work professing to reconcile the various sources retreated before this problem, conceding "an abyss between the two [Bible and archaeology] as to chronology, a gap that cannot be passed over in any manner, that is distressing and unrelenting."[52] With John Bimson's *Redating*

---

[51]Some areas straddle the border between these categories. Dead Sea Scroll exegesis, for example, is a fairly specialized pursuit, yet it has direct implications for literary-theological investigation.

[52]Israel Ben-Shem, *Kibbush Maarav ha-Aretz* (Ph.D. diss., Tel Aviv University, 1978), p. 108. The sponsor was Y. M. Grintz.

the Exodus[53] the 480 years found a defender, but his view raised other difficulties. What is interesting for our purposes is that the correct historical solution to this puzzle, so long as we believe that there is a solution, need not affect the way we study Bible day by day.

To be sure the situation is not as neat as I have depicted it. As Barry Eichler shows in Chapter 3, the scholar of Mesopotamian civilization is more than a mechanical resource for background information to be made available to students of Bible; he or she also interprets the Bible in its relation to the nonbiblical cultural context. Shaping our conception of biblical history, its continuity and discontinuity with the surrounding culture, is as much a theological as it is a purely historiographical task. So too my example in the last paragraph can be challenged by counterexamples: dating an incident, tracing the trajectory of a battle, and certainly ascertaining the truth of a new explanation based on cognate languages, often do alter theological interpretation. The reader of Isaiah, chapter 36, for instance, wonders why Hezekiah's stance toward Assyria moves from compliance to defiance. *Rishonim* already debated whether the two phases are reactions to two Assyrian campaigns, or a shift in the course of one.[54] The modern debate on this question includes the Prism of Sennacherib: what conclusion we draw from the aggregate evidence affects our entire conception of Hezekiah and his age. Lastly, of course, the archaeologists and philologists, despite the apparent objectivity of their data, are not free of their own presuppositions, reflecting their religious inclinations and intellectual biases.

Nevertheless, I think it unwise for us, at this time, to erect a "Jewish" archaeology or biblical geography. In practical terms, I recommend that we refrain from putting weight on hypotheses in these areas, however congenial to our own firmly held beliefs, so long as these hypotheses have not passed muster in the conventional academic literature. This means that Orthodox scholars engaged in these disciplines will have to regard

---

[53](Sheffield, 1982). A heated exchange between Bimson and David Livingston ("Redating the Exodus," *Biblical Archeology Review* (BAR) 13:5 [September–October 1987]: 40–53) and Baruch Halpern, "Radical Exodus Redating Fatally Flawed," *BAR* 13:6 (November–December 1987): 56–61, was followed by a volley of excited letters: see 14:1 (January–February 1988): 14–15 and 14:2 (March–April 1988): 12–13; 58.

[54]See Gersonides (2 Kings 18:19) and Abarbanel (Isaiah 36:1).

their academic colleagues as their primary peer group, even though this may diminish their ability to contribute to a *derekh ha-limmud* in the manner discussed here. The intellectual (perhaps even religious) sacrifice entailed can be compared to that of a diplomat posted to the capital of a hostile neighbor: he is doing his patriotic duty, but he risks losing touch with the life of his nation. The ideal of splendid autonomous isolation, "calmly and persistently" navigating toward the truth must give way to *tzarikh iyyun*. Such a policy may be frustrating to us. It is also inapplicable to the Orthodox scholar whose own attainments in these fields permit him or her to buck the consensus. But, for most of us, selective theorizing in these areas smacks of propaganda and reinforces haphazard intellectual hygiene.

V

And in general, this is an important rule in the struggle of ideas: we should not immediately refute any idea which comes to contradict anything in the Torah, but rather we should build the palace of Torah above it; in so doing we are exalted by the Torah, and through this exaltation the ideas are revealed, and thereafter, when we are not pressured by anything, we can confidently also struggle against it.[55]

This essay can be read as an extended commentary on these inspiring words of Rabbi Kook. Our immediate, and primary, goal in confronting unsettling ideas is neither impatient or anxious refutation, nor is it paralyzed silence. We are to get on with our learning, to integrate the challenging ideas, insofar as this is warranted, into the seamless fabric of our *derekh ha-limmud*. The group around the Yaakov Herzog Institute at Yeshivat Har Etzion, who are responsible for the journal *Megadim*, have made a good start at making this ideal a reality.[56]

If we wish to do the same, we must bear in mind the memorable formulation of Rabbi Kook's close disciple-associate, Rabbi Yaakov Moshe

---

[55]Rabbi Kook, *Iggerot ha-Reiyah* I no. 134, translated by Tzvi Feldman in *Selected Letters* (Ma'aleh Adumim: Ma'aliyot Publications of Yeshivat Birket Moshe, 1986), p. 14.

[56]For a recent statement of their shared outlook, see Rabbi Yoel Ben-Nun, *Megadim* 15 (Marheshvan 5752): 99–102.

Charlop, who taught that Jewish thought appropriates foreign ideas, not by adopting them, but by converting them, as it were, to Judaism. We must eschew the collective intellectual paralysis of the intellectual Marrano. We cannot become fixated on how we are perceived by others, whether this means caring too much how we are regarded by scholars at other institutions, or caring too much what our neighbors think of us in *shul*, whether we lower our standards to play the galleries or lower our eyes with the humility of the feckless. We must be wary of being more preoccupied with what we say to others than we are occupied in thinking about what we say to ourselves. We must abjure the interminable hand-wringing over acceptable method that confirms Rabbi Joseph Wanefsky's observation to the effect that richness of content in a presentation often stands in inverse proportion to the frequency with which the word "methodology" is invoked.[57]

I return to Rabbi Kook's fascinating image of the palace of Torah that expropriates the challenge of ideas contradicting Torah. I wonder if these words do not intimidate us as much as they spur us on to greater and more authentic achievement. Unable to build a palace in one fell swoop, we build nothing and call for a *deus ex machina* to fill the void and get us off the hook. Our *derekh ha-limmud* must be built example after example, brick on top of brick. Before we build the palace we need a place where we can unpack our trunk, get our books out of storage and back into our hands. We want a room with a view, since there is knowledge to be had that we want to have for our enhanced study of Torah. But we cannot do our work, we cannot prepare to build the palace, unless we do it in a room of our own.

---

[57]According to his biographer, Professor Ephraim Urbach was wont to make a pungent observation in the same spirit: *"Über Methode spricht nur wer von der Sache nichts versteht"* (Y. Zusman, "The Scholarly Achievement of Prof Urbach," in *E. E. Urbach: Bio-Bibliographia Mehkarit*, Supplement to *Jewish Studies* 1993, p. 26.

2

The State and Directions of Orthodox Bible Study

B. Barry Levy

Orthodoxy and the Bible is an overwhelming topic that intimidates merely as a bibliographic exercise requiring one to list the appropriate exegetical texts; it must humble anyone who attempts to digest it *en masse*.[1] Yet, despite the difficulties inherent in discussing this vast and complex subject at all, much less in a very limited space, I have been asked to undertake the task and to consider, as well, the prescriptive value of my observations. I begin by describing the subject and by sharing some of the choices I have been forced to make in treating it, and then move to some of the more complex considerations.

---

[1]Many aspects of this presentation are related to my "On the Periphery: North American Orthodox Judaism and Contemporary Biblical Scholarship," in *Students of the Covenant: Jewish Bible Scholarship in America*, ed., D. Sperling (Atlanta: Scholars Press, 1992). I thank Professor Sid Leiman and Rabbi Shalom Carmy for their comments on that essay, which contributed to this one, and both Mr. Joel Linsider and Dr. Baruch Schwartz for their editorial suggestions. The interested reader is encouraged to examine the original study and the accompanying documentation, as the present one is broader and less detailed in some of its treatments.

WHO OR WHAT IS ORTHODOX?

Historians of Orthodoxy regularly date the movement's beginning to the first known application of the term "orthodox" to Jews in 1795,[2] which effectively limits our present concern to the last two centuries. But Orthodox writers have done many different things with the Bible, which forces us to choose from, or to combine, how it has been treated by any and all of Orthodoxy's constituent subgroups, rather than by Orthodoxy as a whole. Great differences emerge when one considers only the attitudes of *Haredim*, or of Musarites, or of the individual hasidic groups, or of Centrists, or when one attempts to find some small plot of ideological ground they all share.[3] Moreover, Orthodox Jews are found not only in North America and in Israel, but also in Central and South America, in North and South Africa, and in parts of Europe and Asia. They have all shared in the enterprise of Orthodox Bible study; some have published their ideas. Which of them deserve a share of our attention?

Must a publication aspire to acceptance as an Orthodox religious work to qualify, or is it sufficient for it to have been written by an affiliate of an Orthodox synagogue? Should all studies by the halakhically committed be included, or does employment by a non-Jewish institution, or a non-Orthodox one, pose an obstacle? Must authors be ordained Orthodox rabbis? Must their books be endorsed by unquestionable rabbinic authorities?[4] May we, dare we, judge only the books and their contents,

---

[2]For example, *Encyclopaedia Judaica,* s.v. "Orthodoxy"; note, also, Moshe Samet, "The Beginnings of Orthodoxy," *Modern Judaism* 8 (1988): 249–270.

[3]The mélange of extant Orthodox positions and sharp polarizations, especially in matters related to Bible study, suggests that Orthodoxy is not a coherent movement and cannot be described accurately unless subdivided. This is not the place to consider this problem, and I am surely not encouraging a political split; but were it to happen, the issues of Bible study would suggest that it be done by recognizing two groups—an intellectual elite and the masses—in place of the seemingly more natural and popular divisions that separate the movement into factions often identified in popular conversation as liberal Orthodox, centrist Orthodox, really Orthodox, rightist Orthodox, sectarian Orthodox, and ultra-Orthodox, or in Israeli political terms as Mizrachi, Aggudah, hasidic, Haredi, and so forth.

[4]Compare my "The Orthodox Publication Explosion," in *Jewish Book Annual* 44 (1986–1987): 6–17.

or must we also scrutinize their authors' personal lives; can the propriety of religious teachings be determined solely with respect to what they contain, or must one also ask who said them? Does this essay—by virtue of its goals, its author's identity, and/or the nature of its audience—qualify as a part of our concern, or does its attempt to look at the subject from a distance, however short, preclude such consideration?

To clarify the question, at the risk of reducing it to ad hominem considerations: Can or should the early discussions of Bible-related issues by Louis Jacobs,[5] the text-critical efforts by Moshe Goshen-Gottstein,[6] the recent book on *peshat* and *derash* by David Weiss Halivni,[7] or the many potentially relevant books by Nehama Leibowitz,[8] Nahum Sarna,[9] Umberto Cassuto,[10] James Kugel,[11] Jon Levinson,[12] and Lawrence Schiffman[13] (and numerous others of whose personal lives I have no knowledge) be considered Orthodox?

---

[5]For example, Louis Jacobs, *Principles of the Jewish Faith* (New York: Basic Books, 1964), especially chapters 8–9.

[6]For example, the various editions of all or part of Isaiah published by the Hebrew University Bible Project between 1965 and 1981.

[7]David Weiss Halivni, *Peshat and Derash: Plain and Applied Meaning in Rabbinic Exegesis* (New York: Oxford University Press, 1991).

[8]Including the many volumes of her *Iyyunim*, which have appeared in both Hebrew and English, the latter beginning in 1972; *Limud Parshanei ha-Torah u-Derakhim le-Horaatam* (Israel: World Zionist Organization, 1975); and *Peirush Rashi la-Torah: Iyyunim be-Shitato*, 1–2 (Ramat Aviv: The Open University, 1990).

[9]Nahum Sarna, *Understanding Genesis* (New York: McGraw Hill, 1966); *Exploring Exodus* (New York: Schocken, 1986); *The Jewish Publication Society Torah Commentary*, Genesis, Exodus (Philadelphia: Jewish Publication Society, 1989 and 1991).

[10]A bibliography of Cassuto's work is available in *Studies in Bible Dedicated to the Memory of U. Cassuto on the 100th Anniversary of His Birth* (Jerusalem: Magnes, 1987): 9–42.

[11]For example, James Kugel, *The Idea of Biblical Poetry: Parallelism and Its History* (New Haven: Yale University Press, 1981); *In Potiphar's House: The Interpretive Life of Biblical Texts* (San Francisco: Harper, 1990); and with R. A. Greer, *Early Biblical Interpretation* (Philadelphia: Westminster Press, 1986).

[12]Jon Levenson, *Creation and the Persistence of Evil* (San Francisco: Harper and Row, 1988) and *Sinai and Zion* (New York: Winston Press, 1985).

[13]For example, Lawrence Schiffman, *From Text to Tradition: A History of Second Temple and Rabbinic Judaism* (Hoboken: Ktav, 1991).

Many who identify themselves as Orthodox might find something objectionable in most of these works and in others of their ilk, suggesting, perhaps, that the authors of un-Orthodox books cannot be Orthodox, or that some Orthodox authors sometimes write un-Orthodox books, or that a book is not rendered un-Orthodox because some people object to it. Perhaps, in addition to being written by an Orthodox Jew, usually for Orthodox Jews, an Orthodox book must have the obvious goal of furthering Orthodox religious or political interests. If not, it might not be Orthodox, regardless of its contents, the author's lifestyle, or the book's value to Orthodox readers. On the other hand, some might suggest that an Orthodox Jew cannot write (and therefore should not attempt to write) a fully objective, academic book about any religious subject; but this assumption can have very severe implications for those who disagree, as evidenced by its use to exclude more than a few observant Jews from university positions in Religion departments.[14]

Whether or not history ultimately finds for their Orthodoxy or for that of their books, the borderline cases help define the outer limits of Orthodox Bible study. Either from within or from without, they let us explore how far Orthodox writers can go in their work, and they help sharpen our understanding of what Orthodox Jews may think about the Bible, what they may accept as its legitimate meanings, and how they may teach it. Often these limits are challenged, refined, and even redefined in precisely those marginal books that are acceptable to less than the entire community. They are worthy of attention, but this is neither the time nor the place; fellow travelers, well-wishers, and impostors cannot play a role here.

If so, my questions may appear trivial and designed to confuse or to distract us; they are not. It is substantially easier to identify an Orthodox rabbi than an Orthodox Bible scholar. Not only are the former in much greater supply and much better known, the latter are an endangered species (at least in North America) that is not only less visible, but less influential, and, one might conclude, less necessary.

Some senior rabbis have tried to assist in identifying potential spokesmen for Orthodoxy by adding personal letters of introduction to their students' and colleagues' books. In fact, ours is a time when rabbinic

---

[14]See, for example, D. A. Oren, *Joining the Club* (New Haven, CT: Yale University Press, 1985): 330, the entry for 1978.

approbations have grown in importance, primarily, I suspect, to help sort through the diverse range of works that legitimately claim our attention and potential commitment, and secondarily to certify the acceptability of certain works for specific Orthodox subgroups. But approbations seldom spare the movement at large from the inappropriate teachings of outsiders; they only identify approved books (not those to be avoided) and virtually never endorse the contents of the books in which they appear, because they are almost always about the authors, not their work.

Orthodoxy identifies with all of the vast and varied pre-Orthodox rabbinic tradition and theoretically takes seriously its range of ideological positions (and is the only contemporary Jewish religious movement to do so); therefore it needs to show little concern for the credentials of those whose work might speak for it. Being broad-based and wide-ranging, it should be able to absorb almost any work of potential value and either grant it status as an influential contribution or consign it to oblivion (as erroneous or peripheral), or both. Philosophical correctness is hardly *de rigueur*, unless one speaks of a particular branch of the movement that espouses a much more limiting ideology. Given the extent to which some areas of Bible study have been neglected by Orthodox writers and the amount of attention they have received from others, perhaps there is reason to cast our net as widely as possible. Even so, some measure of commonality must exist among all of the different types of Orthodox contributions to Bible study, and the rabbinic tradition is clearly its major component.

For most Orthodox Jews, this rabbinic tradition, with its suggestive interpretations and binding applications, is in many ways more a part of Bible study than are many scriptural books. The definition of that tradition and its theoretical and practical roles in Bible interpretation are quintessential considerations. Whether its influence is minimized or maximized, its importance for Orthodox Bible study can hardly be overstated.[15] Because the rabbinic writings of the past two millennia ever lie open, ready to enrich, to guide, to redirect, and to correct what presently

---

[15]In this context, it is interesting to examine Moshe Greenberg's unfinished *Understanding Exodus* (New York: Behrman House, 1969), which may be the most rabbinic scholarly work on the Bible not produced by an Orthodox Jew. It is quite different from Nahum Sarna's *Understanding Genesis*, a part of the same Jewish Theological Seminary project. Also important are Jacob Milgrom's

exists, Orthodox Jews cannot open the Bible *de novo* and begin to make their way. They may choose not to set their own sights from the shoulders of the giants who preceded them, but they cannot ignore what they saw. Therefore, it is difficult to imagine an Orthodox contribution to Bible study that does not derive from, depend on, relate to, or receive inspiration from the vast legacy of pre-Orthodox, rabbinic Bible interpretation; however, the Orthodox contribution should not be misconstrued to consist solely of copying, repeating, explaining, or defending it.

Even if we limit our discussion to the past two centuries and to their unique directions and contributions, we still cannot assume that the original Orthodox contribution to Bible study is only that which differs from what was taught by the preceding generations of rabbinic writers, though it is a major part and of significant size. The visibility of the individual elements of this pre-Orthodox rabbinic tradition—how and to what extent they have been studied, taught, preached, published, annotated, translated, anthologized, reinterpreted, disavowed, or simply ignored (one of the most significant treatments)—is as much a part of Orthodox Bible study as whatever new ideas have been expressed directly or indirectly about Scripture. The Orthodox reader must choose carefully the shoulders on which to stand, and there are many from which to pick. I have limited consideration here to a selection of the more prominent contemporary groups and individuals, and to their publications; many more are worthy of attention.

WHAT IS BIBLE STUDY?

Treatment of the Bible comes in many forms, and we must arrive at some general agreement on what is meant by Bible Study. Does the term refer to only the academic discipline, and then as practiced only in Orthodox institutions, or are faculty members of other institutions, or others at large, eligible for consideration? Should equal weight be given to Bar-

---

interpretations of Leviticus in the Anchor Bible series and of Numbers in the Jewish Publication Society Torah commentary. While the extensive use of classic Judaic exegetical material is perhaps not unexpected in the latter, its appearance in the former is quite noteworthy.

Ilan's Bible department and to Yeshiva University's; to YU's Bible professors, and to its *rashei yeshivah?* Must any Bible-related contribution
by an Orthodox rabbi be considered, including the taped homiletical
presentations to isolated American communities, on the one hand, and
to the *shtiblakh* of Brooklyn, on the other, or must some inchoate standard be applied?

If one can settle these issues, what is to be made of the popular beliefs
and Bible study habits of Orthodoxy's many and vastly different laities?
In previous centuries, their opinions could not be taken into account,
but we are more able to obtain a representative sample of them. Should
we? If our concern is Orthodoxy at large, can we treat only the ideas of
the leaders? If Orthodox Jews express most of their commitment to Bible
study through review of the weekly Torah reading and never open the
books of Job, Daniel, or Chronicles, or believe erroneously that their
ancestors built the pyramids or that Mordecai was Esther's uncle, should
these data not play a role in our evaluation?

Bible Study—including both the academic and nonacademic fields—
can be described under four headings: Text, Texture, Context, and Pretext. *Text* deals with what the Bible text is and what it says. *Texture* is
concerned with its literary qualities. *Context* focuses on the Bible's geographic, historical, and cultural settings. *Pretext* is the use of a passage
for intentions other than those outwardly expressed in it. All four are
important parts of both classical and modern Bible study, but they have
not received equal weight in all times and places. Much—but very, very
far from all—of what the rabbinic tradition has done with the Bible falls
under the heading of Pretext, and unfortunately this constitutes the
major type of Bible study with which synagogue-goers are most familiar.
The talmudic teaching that only those portions of the prophetic legacy
needed forever were preserved in the Bible suggests that all parts of Scripture are always relevant. The search for this relevance stimulates the
Bible's use as a pretext for what is not clearly stated in it and both accounts for a large part of the practicing Jew's interest and explains why
knowledge of its other aspects is relatively limited.

The impact of this one-sided interest in the Bible has been profound.
We can count on the fingers of one hand the Orthodox North Ameri-
can scholars who regularly write about one or more of the first three areas
—Text, Texture, and Context—the primary concerns of the academic

field of Biblical Studies.[16] The inclusion of the study of Semitic Languages and the concern for the history of Jewish Bible interpretation augments the number of contributors substantially, but hardly to the critical mass needed to support one learned society or one academic journal devoted solely to it. Thus, to limit ourselves to an academic definition of Bible Study and to admit only those who publish relevant books or articles would effectively eliminate North America from consideration, despite the fact that some fine Orthodox Bible professors are found here. And while Israel would fare much better, this decision would thwart our attempt to understand what is happening here. Accordingly, I opt for a broader definition of Bible Study, which includes learned contributions of many types and is not limited to the academic field of the same name.

PRE-ORTHODOX AND EARLY ORTHODOX RABBINIC BIBLE INTERPRETATION

By the time Orthodoxy began to be recognized as an organized movement, Judaism had experimented with, developed, and, in a few cases, discarded, many types of Bible interpretation. In this way, allegorical, midrashic, philological, philosophical, kabbalistic, scientific, and other approaches were explored, and their contributions to the fiber of rabbinic Bible interpretation were insured.[17] The four exegetical literatures associated with philology, philosophical allegory, midrash, and Kabbalah (*PaRDeS*) seemed to represent the totality of Jewish Bible interpretation, but they are essentially medieval categories. During Orthodoxy's appearance at the turn of the nineteenth century, others were more evident. Relying on the types of sources from which they drew their primary sus-

---

[16]See my "On the Periphery . . . " for details.

[17]I would digress too much by discussing these developments, or even the integration of science into Torah study, but interesting examples of including scientific concerns in a Torah commentary merely to have them considered as a part of it can be found in the illustrated portions of Moses ben Gershom Gentili's *Melekhet Mahshevet* (Venice, 1710). See, further, my *Planets, Potions and Parchments: Scientifica Hebraica from the Dead Sea Scrolls to the Eighteenth Century* (Montreal: McGill–Queens University Press, 1990).

tenance, which also suggest the general tones of the resultant works, we can identify three such literatures and approaches among Ashkenazi writers.

The first is Midrashic-Kabbalistic. Midrashic interpretation was rarely practiced in isolation from the Talmud and generally considers it an essential ingredient, but the surge of kabbalistic thinking and influence in the sixteenth and subsequent centuries greatly increased the importance of the Zohar as an exegetical text, revived the midrashic mindset of earlier centuries, and reasserted the centrality of midrashic Bible interpretation.[18] Midrashic-Kabbalistic writers were rarely hostile to the Talmud; they simply chose their interpretative materials and approaches primarily from the kabbalistic and midrashic realms, including the talmudic *midrashim*. Creative and influential, the attitudes of these people differed from those of two other learned groups, who sometimes criticized them and their positions.

The second approach is Talmudic-Midrashic. Writers of this type gradually allowed the Zohar and its speculative, other-worldly interpretative focus to dissipate. Nonzoharic rather than antizoharic, they preferred to base their Bible interpretations on the *midrashim* and the Talmud, and on the latter's own interpretative literature, the medieval and postmedieval commentaries and codes. In effect, this position was a compromise that defended the unity of Scripture (especially the Torah) and the oldest rabbinic traditions, which became the almost exclusive key to scriptural interpretation. The newly developed strength of this idea's supporters challenged the time-honored and reemerging claim that the rabbinic tradition distorted the true meaning of the text. Simultaneously, it allowed the talmudist's literary world to dominate the biblicist's.

The third approach is Rational-Scientific (including what we might call aspects of the humanities and sciences). Writers in this group preferred philological accuracy and historical credibility to midrashic and zoharic alternatives. Often hostile to what they perceived as mystical distortion but sympathetic to other forms of rabbinic interpretation (at least in the earlier days), these writers tried to break new ground by adopting more open approaches to the Bible. Some of them even sought out and published unavailable or previously unknown medieval works that supported

---

[18]See G. Scholem, *On the Kabbalah and Its Symbolism* (New York: Schocken, 1965), chapter 3, "Kabbalah and Myth."

their beliefs, thereby contributing much to understanding the evolution
of Jewish Bible interpretation, not only to their preferred position.

These three groups of writers, who are often counted respectively
among the *hasidim*, the *mitnagdim*, and the *maskilim* in other contexts
but are not identical to them in all respects, divided up the legacy of
earlier Bible interpretation into three complementary but not totally
exclusive realms from which they derived their exegetical sustenance and
support. In following the sixteenth-century's fascination with mystical
interpretation, the Midrashic-Kabbalistic writers continued the most
recent of the traditional exegetical literatures. The Rational-Scientific
types threw their lot in with the earlier, medieval thinkers, and based
much of their work on the writings of the philologists—authors committed to *peshat*—and the philosophers, especially Maimonides, who
anticipated some modern interpretative attitudes and was credited with
others; they also shared much with some Renaissance writers. The Talmudic-Midrashic approach was supported by strongly committed rabbinic
writers, including some *hasidim* (which is one reason these new designa-
tions are preferable in this context). In fact, it reformed traditional Bible
interpretation by avoiding (or, in the case of its participating *hasidim*, by
downplaying) the kabbalistic literature and even most of the medieval
Bible interpreters, while working closely but selectively with the talmudic
and midrashic literatures, the oldest rabbinic texts.

To be sure, few writers fit perfectly into one category. Some were 90
percent Talmudic-Midrashic and 10 percent Midrashic-Kabbalistic or
Rational-Scientific; others exhibited different mixes, and a few even
utilized all three. But even when these terms fail to describe accurately
an actual interpretative text—and the identity of the first "pure" Rational-Scientific work by a Jew is an interesting question in itself—they still
serve as useful markers from which to measure their authors' positions.

If asked to identify the leading figures in Bible study during the nine-
teenth and early twentieth centuries, different Orthodox Jews might choose
Rabbi Meir Leibush Malbim, Rabbi Samson Raphael Hirsch, Rabbi Jacob
Zvi Mecklenberg, Rabbi Naftali Zvi Yehudah Berlin, Rabbi Meir Simhah
HaKohen, Rabbi David Zvi Hoffman, or Rabbi Hayyim Heller.[19] Regard-

---

[19]It is quite unnecessary to add that none of these commentators would appear
in any list of the leading nineteenth-century and early–twentieth–century critical
Bible scholars; but it is interesting to note how few of the books by those who
would are still read by most contemporary critics. For information about them,

less of who might be picked as best or why (all made important, creative contributions), one immediately senses a few of the many ways in which their approaches differed from each other regarding, for example, the extent to which they expressed themselves only in the form of commentaries, or the degrees to which they dealt only with the Torah, or were, in turn, more or less apologetic, linked to the Talmud's exegetical agenda, independent of the medieval interpretative literature, or open to the scientific knowledge of their time. Nonetheless, the fact remains that all were largely Talmudic-Midrashic in approach.

Additions might include more of the same types and stronger Midrashic-Kabbalistic influence, perhaps the likes of Rabbi Meir Dan Plotzki (author of *Keli Hemdah*),[20] Rabbi Joseph Patsanovsky (who completed three of his projected five volumes of *Pardes Yosef*),[21] and Rabbi Joseph Rozin (the Rogachover).[22] Many other hasidic leaders, *rashei yeshivah*, halakhic authorities, and writers from many different parts of the Orthodox world could be added, but few respondents would be apt to suggest Rabbi Samuel David Luzzatto[23] or Rabbi Moshe David (Umberto) Cassuto,[24] and some might be troubled by the inclusion of Rabbi David Zvi Hoffman.[25] Of course many factors contribute to these preferences, including the use of Italian and German for many of their works and the obviously dated contents of some of their discussions, but

---

see T. K. Cheyne, *Founders of Old Testament Criticism* (London: Methuen, 1893); R. J. Thompson, *Moses and the Law in a Century of Criticism since Graf* (Leiden: Brill, 1970); and J. Rogerson, *Old Testament Criticism in the Nineteenth Century: England and Germany* (London: SPCK, 1984).

[20]Vols. 1–3 (Piotrkow: 1927–1935; reprint, Brooklyn, NY, 1986).

[21]Vols. 1–3 (Piotrkow, Lodz: 1929–1939; reprint, Israel, 1975). Note also Yom Tov Lipmann Freedman's new annotated edition, the first several volumes of which appeared in Bnai Berak, 1993.

[22]*Zafnat Paneah*, 1–5, edited by M. M. Kasher (Jerusalem).

[23]The fullest treatment of his work is M. B. Margolies, *Samuel David Luzzatto: Traditionalist Scholar* (New York: Ktav, 1979).

[24]The fact that Cassuto wrote in Italian and later in Hebrew cost him potential followers among many scholars of this century's middle decades, but learned Jews have been aware of his contributions nonetheless. Despite his many devoted followers in Israel, one senses that he has had relatively little impact on the American Orthodox community.

[25]See A. Marx, *Essays in Jewish Bibliography* (Philadelphia: Jewish Publication Society, 1947): 185–222.

the impression of ideological disapproval cannot be ignored, especially given the existence of some English or Hebrew translations or paraphrases. In general, contemporary Orthodox preferences in Bible interpretation rank Talmudic-Midrashic interpretation first, Midrashic-Kabbalistic second, and Rational-Scientific third.

A GLANCE AT SOME CONTEMPORARY ORTHODOX WORKS ABOUT THE BIBLE

Despite the difficulties in identifying all potential contributors, some unquestionably Orthodox projects have been devoted to the Bible, and they provide valuable samples of what Orthodox writers are actually saying about it and doing with it.

1. *Da'at Mikra'* combines traditional values about Bible study with great concern for philological precision and gleanings from the fields of archaeology, geography, and history. The volumes regularly include a section on Masoretic variations, but generally ignore thornier scholarly problems. By leaving the Torah volumes for last, *Da'at Mikra'* established its editorial policies and reputation in less controversial areas, and by including Rashi's commentary on the Torah, it affirmed a link with traditional interpretation that was less apparent in the earlier volumes. It is the best twentieth-century Orthodox commentary approaching coverage of the complete Bible.[26]

2. ArtScroll's Bible commentaries contrast sharply with *Da'at Mikra'*. Aside from being written in English, with French and Hebrew translations on the way, this American project eschews interest in the potential contributions of modern scholarship and tries to cull its materials solely from classical rabbinic works. Ideologically, *Da'at Mikra'* and ArtScroll represent vastly different and far from complementary positions within the Orthodox world. The latter exhibits much stronger influence from the midrashic, mystical, Musar-based, and hasidic literatures, and is far less interested in matters related to the Bible's text, texture, and context than the former, which actively but sometimes surreptitiously appropriates from contemporary scholarship.[27]

---

[26]See my review of *Da'at Miqra': Bamidbar* in the *AJS Review* (1992).

[27]See, further, my "Our Torah, Your Torah and Their Torah: An Evaluation of the Artscroll Phenomenon," in *Truth and Compassion: Essays on Judaism*

3. *Torat Hayyim*, Mossad HaRav Kook's new Humash edition, complements *Da'at Mikra'*.[28] Containing reworked and improved editions of virtually everything in it and printed entirely in square letters, it offers a major improvement over the editions of many texts found in the regularly used *Humashim*, but its most important change is the limitation of its commentaries to those produced in medieval times. By omitting the work of all *aharonim*, especially Rabbi Hayyim Ibn Atar's *Or ha-Hayyim* and Rabbi Solomon Ephraim Luntshitz's *Keli Yakar*, it holds up the medieval traditions of Bible study as the appropriate contemporary model and thereby suggests the propriety of both commitment to the quest for *peshat* and serious appreciation of nonrabbinic learning.

4. Hertz's Torah commentary,[29] which long served as the pew Bible for English-speaking synagogues, is dropping from fashion. To be sure, Reform and Conservative groups have replaced it, or are replacing it, with more modern interpretations, but the Orthodox tendency to allow it to slide into disuse generally reflects dissatisfaction of a different sort,

---

and Religion in Memory of Rabbi Dr. Solomon Frank, ed. H. Joseph et al. (Waterloo, Ontario: Wilfred Laurier University Press, 1983): 137–190; "Judge Not a Book by Its Cover," *Tradition*, 19 (1981): 89–95; and "ArtScroll: An Overview," in *Approaches to Modern Judaism*, ed. M. L. Raphael, vol. 1 (Chico, CA: Scholars Press, 1983): 111–140, 157–162.

[28] On the history of rabbinic Bibles in general and the position of *Torat Hayyim* within it, see my "Rabbinic Bibles, *Mikraot Gedolot*, and Other Great Books," *Tradition* 25 (1991): 65–81. Since the appearance of that article, several other related projects have begun to appear, notably the *HaMaor* edition of the Torah with commentaries, the first volume of the Bar-Ilan University edition of *Mikraot Gedolot* on Nakh, and several volumes of a new edition of Nakh entitled *Ha-Keter*. The first volume of the last project, which contains newly edited texts of the Bible (based on the Aleppo Codex), Targum Jonathan, and the commentaries of Rashi, Radak, and Ralbag, and the *Metzudot*, appeared under the general editorship of Joseph Dayyan, *Yeshoshua* (Jerusalem: R. Mass, 1991). Among the most immediately apparent contribution of all these publications is improving the readability of the texts. Evaluation of their other aspects must await another occasion.

[29] Originally published in five separate volumes as *The Pentateuch and Haftorahs* (London: Oxford University Press, 1929–1936), Hertz's work has been revised and reissued in both two-volume and one-volume formats. It has been studied in detail by H. W. Meirovich in his JTS dissertation, *Judaism on Trial: An Analysis of the Hertz Pentateuch*.

a rejection of Hertz's modernizing tendencies and a desire for deeper and more classically rabbinic interpretation. Perhaps it is most significant that this is happening even though no obvious replacement has appeared.

The ArtScroll commentary (more correctly the six volumes of Genesis and two of Leviticus, plus whatever else might be added) are too large to be a pew Bible, (though reprints keep packing more material into single volumes). And the new one-volume commentary, though planned with this market in mind, has yet to control it. Aryeh Kaplan's *The Living Torah*,[30] despite being worthy of attention, is too brief in its commentaries; the Soncino Humash[31] is too limited in scope. While popularizations and translations of classical writers are frequently seen in the hands of synagogue goers, the need for a good portable commentary is very apparent, though it may be impossible to treat both the Torah and its rich exegetical literature (which is essential for contemporary Orthodox acceptance) in one volume.

5. The publication of the Soncino Bible commentaries in the 1940s marked an important attempt to present a modern, traditional interpretation of the Bible. However one evaluates its impact—which probably was substantial, because for many years it was virtually the only traditional work in English on many biblical books—it is now being reissued with midrashic additions. This change responds to significantly altered market conditions: competition from ArtScroll (whose effort I believe to have been motivated in large part by dissatisfaction with the Hertz and Soncino efforts) and a reading public oriented more toward the rabbinic tradition than away from it, more sympathetic to a midrashic mindset, and more observant.

6. The Hebrew and English translations of *Me-Am Loez*,[32] an essentially eighteenth-century encyclopedic anthology of interpretations and applications of the Bible, are also important, because their size (twenty volumes of the English translation of the Torah commentary alone) bespeaks a strong commitment to its contents. A vast collection of clas-

---

[30] Aryeh Kaplan, *The Living* Torah (New York: Maznaim, 1981).

[31] A. Cohen *Soncino Humash*, (London: Soncino, 1956).

[32] The first volume of the Hebrew translation of Genesis appeared in 1967; the first volume of the English translation of Genesis, which carries the title *The Torah Anthology*, appeared in 1977. Both series have published over two dozen volumes.

sical law and lore, its popularity today reflects the contemporary commitment to homiletical and midrashic interpretation.[33]

7. Rabbi Menaham Kasher's magnum opus, *Torah Shelemah*,[34] marks
a high point in the modern treatment of midrashic Torah interpretation.
The discussions of classical rabbinic texts and the learned notes are
complemented by extensive essays on many important issues and offer
both the learning and the learned reader a wealth of seminal material.
Disappointment is the only way to respond to the absence of these features from most of the recent volumes prepared under his successor's
editorship. Rabbi Kasher's death caused an irreplaceable loss, but one
must wonder whether the editorial decision to abandon some of his
efforts was motivated, at least in part, by a reversal of priorities, which
now favor merely anthologizing the midrashic sources, to the virtual
exclusion of their scholarly treatment.

8. Nehama Leibowitz has become a household name in much of the
Jewish world, and thousands of Bible enthusiasts, including many who
never met her, consider themselves her students. Professor Leibowitz's
classes and writings have had a profound impact on the Israeli educational establishment, and, in turn, on the global teaching of the Torah.
Her approach, which generally combines a close reading of the biblical
text with careful comparison of several interpretations, highlights the
multifaceted richness of both Scripture and its classical interpreters, and
helps to clarify the ambiguities and possible nuances in the former and
the interpretative sensitivities of the latter.

9. Rabbi Joel Teitelbaum's *Divrei Yo'el*[35] continues the tradition of
hasidic homiletics applied to the Torah, but, unlike some of its predecessors, it is of monumental size and displays a very impressive mastery

---

[33]In addition to the introductory material about the author and his work found
in the translations, see M. Angel, *Voices in Exile* (Hoboken, NJ: Ktav, 1991):
103–109.

[34]The first edition of volume 1 appeared in 1927, the third in 1949; since
that time, the series has averaged about one volume per year for half a century.
For background on Kasher himself, see A. Greenbaum, "Architect and Builder:
The Life of Harav Menachem M. Kasher," in *Sages and Saints*, ed. L. Jung
(Hoboken, NJ: Ktav, 1987): 231–272.

[35]Rabbi Yoel Teitelbaum, *Divrei Yoel*, Parts 1–9 (Brooklyn, NY: Jerusalem,
1981).

of classical rabbinic learning. It is complemented by a whole library of Torah-related publications issuing from other hasidic groups in both Hebrew and English.

10. Rabbi Shimon Krasner of Baltimore continues the publication of his *Nahalat Shimon*, thus far five volumes on the Former Prophets.[36] His well-researched essays treat serious issues in Bible study that have been discussed in the classical exegetical and halakhic literatures and are an important (and, as far as I can tell, a generally neglected) model for how to integrate this vast rabbinic corpus into the study of the non-Pentateuchal books.

11. Other efforts vary in quality and lasting value. Rabbi Joseph B. Soloveitchik's writings, though not devoted primarily to Bible interpretation, include many observations of importance to it.[37] Valuable mate-

---

[36]Shimon Krasner, *Nahalat Shimon* (Brooklyn, NY: S. Krasner, 1982 ff).

[37]His published writings include "*Ish ha-Halakhah*," *Talpiyot* 1 (1944): 651–735, translated as *Halakhic Man* (Philadelphia: Jewish Publication Society, 1983); "Confrontation," *Tradition* 6 (1964) [also reprinted in *Studies in Judaica in Honor of Dr. Samuel Belkin as Scholar and Educator* (New York: Ktav, 1964): 45–133]; "Lonely Man of Faith," *Tradition* 7 (1965) [also reprinted in *Studies in Honour of Dr. Belkin*]; *Ish ha-Emunah* (Jerusalem Mossad HaRav Kook, 1968) [containing: "*Ish ha-Emunah ha-Boded*" and "*Kol Dodi Dofek*"]; *Hamesh Derashot* (Jerusalem: Tal Orot Institute, 1974), translated as *Five Addresses* (Jerusalem: Tal Orot Institute, 1983) [addresses delivered to conventions of the Mizrachi movement between 1962–1967], compare *Fier Droshos* (New York: Machon Tal Orot, 1967); *Shiurei HaRav: A Conspectus of the Public Lectures of Rabbi Joseph B. Soloveitchik* (New York: Yeshiva University, 1974) [summaries of twenty *shiurim* delivered by the Rav, with an introduction by Rabbi Aharon Lichten-stein]; *Al ha-Teshuvah*, edited by Pinhas Peli (Jerusalem: World Zionist Organization, 1975), translated as *On Repentance* (Jerusalem: Orot, 1980); *Be-Sod ha-Yahid ve-ha-Yahad*, edited by Pinhas Peli (Jerusalem: Orot, 1976) [six essays, including *Ish ha-Halakhah*, *Mah Dodekh mi-Dod*, *Peleitat Sofreihem*, *Ba-Seter u-va-Galui*, *Kol Dodi Dofek*, and *Al Ahavat ha-Torah u-Geulat Nefesh ha-Dor*]; "Sacred and Profane: *Kodesh* and *Chol* in World Perspectives," *Gesher* 3 (1966): 5–29; [A special issue of *Tradition* containing five of his essays: "The Community," "Majesty and Humility," "Catharsis," "Redemption, Prayer, Talmud Torah," and "A Tribute to the Rebbitzen of Talne," *Tradition* 17 (1978); *Mi-Beit Midrasho shel ha-Rav* (Jerusalem, 1978) [*shiurim* on *Hilkhot Keriat ha-Torah*, *Hilkhot Tzitzit*, and *Hilkhot Tefillin* published by his students].

Also *Reflections of the Rav*, ed. A. Besdin (Jerusalem: World Zionist Organization, 1979) [summaries of twenty *shiurim*, with a bibliography of both primary

rial can be culled from *Pahad Yitzhak*, Rabbi Isaac Hutner's collected essays;[38] from *Pirkei Emunah*, Rabbi Mordecai Gifter's similar but smaller collection;[39] from *Darash Mosheh*, the homiletical presentations of Rabbi Moshe Feinstein, and from some of his many responsa.[40] Rabbi Aharon Kotler's English pamphlet, "How to Teach Torah," also available in several volumes of his collected Hebrew writings, displays and encourages

---

and secondary materials], also published in Hebrew as *Perakim be-Mahshevet ha-Rav Y[osef] D[ov] ha-Levi Soloveitchik* (Jerusalem: Ha-Mahlakah le-Hinukh u-le-Tarbut Toraniim ba-Golah, 1984); *Ish ha-Halakhah—Galui ve-Nistar* (Jerusalem: World Zionist Organization, 1979) [reissues of the essays "*Ish ha-Halakhah*," *Talpiyot* 1 (1944) and "*u-Bikashtem mi-Sham*" and "*Raayonot al ha-Tefillah*," *Ha-Darom* 47 (1979)]; *Divrei Hagut ve-Ha'arakhah* (Jerusalem: World Zionist Organization, 1982) [twelve essays, including four that appeared in *Be-Sod ha-Yahid ve-ha-Yahad*]; *Shiurim le-Zekher Abba Mari, ZaL*, 1–2 (Jerusalem: Makhon Yerushalayim, 1983–1985) [collections of twenty-seven discourses delivered in memory of his father]; *Kovetz Hidushei Torah* (Jerusalem: Makhon Yerushalayim, n.d.) [eight essays by Rabbi Moshe Soloveichik and eighteen of Rabbi Joseph Soloveitchik reprinted from various earlier sources]; *Yemei Zikaron* (Jerusalem, 1986) [twelve memorial essays translated from Yiddish]; *Kuntres be-Inyan Avodat Yom ha-Kippurim* (Jerusalem, 1986); *The Halakhic Mind* (New York: Free Press, 1986) [written in 1944 but first published in 1986]; *Man of Faith in the Modern World: Reflections of the Rav*, 2, (Hoboken, N.J.: Ktav, 1989) [summaries of sixteen *shi'urim*]; all issues of *Mesorah*, ed. H. Schachter and M. Genack (1989–present) [A journal published by the Kashruth Division of the Union of Orthodox Jewish Congregations of America that includes summaries of many of the Rav's teachings]. A. A. Y. Blau, *Efneh ve-Eshneh* (New York: Yeshiva University, 1993); *Hidushei ha-GRaM ve-ha-GrYM*, ed. H. Soloveitchik (Riverdale, NY: Morasha Foundation, 1993); H. Schachter, *Nefesh HaRav* (Jerusalem: Reishit Yerushalayim, 1994). Note also the partial bibliography found in Z. E. Klein, "*Benei Yosef Dovrim*: Rabbi Joseph B. Soloveitchik, *zatzal*: A Bibliography," *The Torah U-Madda Journal* 4 (1993): 84–147.

[38]Rabbi Yitzchak Hutner, *Pahad Yitzchak*, 1–8 (Brooklyn, NY: Gur Aryeh, 1983–1991).

[39]Rabbi Mordecai Gifter, *Pirkei Emunah*, 1 (Jerusalem: Feldheim, 1969); 2 (Jerusalem: Messorah, 1978).

[40]Rabbi Moshe Feinstein, *Kol Ram*, 1–3 (New York: 1978–1980); *Darash Mosheh* (Beni Berak: Estate of R. Moshe Feinstein, 1988). See, also the relevant responsa, conveniently indexed in D. Eidensohn, *Yad Moshe: Mafteah Kelali LaSh[e'eilot] uT[eshuvot] Shel HaR[av] HaG[aon] Rabbeinu Moshe Feinstein* (Brooklyn, NY, 1988).

the devotion to midrashic interpretation that one meets in some Orthodox circles, a popular but unnecessarily extreme position.[41]

Also noteworthy are Rabbi Isaac Sender's *Mahazeh Elyon*, a study of prophecy and prophet-related subjects in the halakhic literature;[42] Rabbi Jacob Kamenetsky's *Emet le-Yaakov*, relatively brief treatments of individual phrases, issues, or themes from the Torah;[43] and a host of notes, comments, bons mots, and anthologies on the weekly Torah reading produced by local synagogues, schools, community organizations, and other active religious and political groups.[44]

Attention should also be called to the dozens of English books on related subjects. An early and frequently overlooked one is Eliezer Berkovits's *Man and God: Studies in Biblical Theology*.[45] Two recent volumes are *In the Beginning*, Nathan Aviezer's effort to juxtapose Genesis 1 and contemporary scientific cosmologies,[46] and *Genesis and the Big Bang: The Discovery of Harmony between Modern Science and the Bible*, Gerald Schroeder's attempt to integrate them.[47] Others include Jose Faur's *Golden Doves with Silver Dots*;[48] *Emunah, Dat u-Madda*[49]; the various publications of Chaim Zimmerman;[50] *Challenge: Torah Views on Science*

---

[41]"How to Teach Torah" (Lakewood, NJ: Oraysa, 1972), known in Hebrew as "*Ha-Havanah Ha-Amitit Shel Sippurei Ha-Torah*" in *Osef Hidot HaGra Kotler* (Jerusalem: Oraysoh, 1983): 402–411, and as "*Be-Darkhei Hora'at Torah She-bi-Khtav*" in *Mishnat Rabbi Aharon*, 3 (Lakewood, NJ: Makhon Mishnat Rabbi Aharon, 1988): 177–187.

[42]Rabbi Isaac Sender, *Mahazeh Elyon* (New York: I. Sender, 1987).

[43]Rabbi Jacob Kamenetsky, *Emet le-Yaakov* (New York: A. Kamenetsky, 1986).

[44]See, further, "Shabbat Shul Sheets," *Jerusalem Post International Edition*, July 4, 1992, p. 14.

[45]Eliezer Berkovits, *Man and God: Studies in Biblical Theology* (Detroit, MI: Wayne State University Press, 1969).

[46]Nathan Aviezer, *In the Beginning* (Hoboken, NJ: Ktav, 1990).

[47]Gerald Schroeder, *Genesis and the Big Bang: The Discovery of Harmony Between Modern Science and the Bible* (New York: Bantam, 1990).

[48]Jose Faur, *Golden Doves with Silver Dots* (Bloomington, IN: Indiana University Press, 1986).

[49]*Ha-Kinus ha-Shenati le-Mahshevet ha-Yahadut*, no. 11, second edition (Jerusalem: Minstry of Education, 1973).

[50]E.g., Chaim Zimmerman, *Torah and Existence: Insiders and Outsiders of Torah* (Jerusalem: C. Zimmerman, 1986).

and its Problems, edited by Aryeh Carmell and Cyril Domb;[51] and *Fusion: Absolute Standards in a World of Relativity—Science, the Arts and Contemporary Life in the Light of Torah,* edited by A. Gotfryd, H. Branover, and S. Lipskar.[52] All may not belong in the same paragraph, but they are all part of our present concern.[53]

Also, the thoughtful and provocative publications of Professor Yeshayahu Leibowitz,[54] the *midrash*-based commentaries of Yehoshua Bachrach,[55] collections of brief presentations on the weekly Torah reading by dozens of people, including Yeshayahu Leibowitz[56] and Pinhas Peli,[57] and the fascinating essays, *Pirkei Mo'adot,* by Mordecai Breuer.[58] New commentaries (or commentarylike works) include *Ohel David,* three volumes of notes on the non-Pentateuchal books by Rabbi David Cohen, which contain many interesting and informative observations;[59] *Nahalat Avot* (on Joshua and Judges), by Abraham Blau;[60] *Parshiot be-Sifrei ha-Neviim: Yehoshua,* by Yitzhak Levi;[61] and *Samson's Struggle: The Life and Legacy of Samson Reflecting 2,000 Years of Jewish Thought,* by Rabbi

---

[51]*Challenge: Torah Views on Science and its Problems,* ed. Aryeh Carmell and Cyril Domb (Jerusalem: Feldheim, 1976).

[52]*Fusion: Absolute Standards in a World of Relativity—Science, the Arts and Contemporary Life in the Light of Torah,* ed. A. Gotfryd, H. Branover, and S. Lipskar (Jerusalem: Feldheim, 1990).

[53]Many additional items, particularly in the area of Torah and science, could be listed, but this seems unnecessary.

[54]In particular, *Yahadut, Am Yehudi, u-Medinat Yisrael* (Jerusalem: Schocken, 1975) and *Emunah, Historiah va-Arakhim* (Jerusalem: Akademon, 1982). Note also *Judaism, Human Values, and the Jewish State* (Cambridge: Harvard University Press, 1992).

[55]In a series of books, midrashic treatments of biblical characters and texts, including Ruth, Jonah, Esther, and David.

[56]Yeshayu Leibowitz, *He'arot le-Parshiot ha-Shavu'a* (Jerusalem: Akademon, 1988).

[57]Pinhas Peli, *Torah Today* (London: Bnei Brith Books, 1987).

[58]Rabbi Mordechai Breuer, *Pirkei Mo'adot,* 1–2 (Jerusalem: Horev, 1986).

[59]Rabbi David Cohen, *Ohel David,* 1–3 (Brooklyn, NY: Mesorah / Biegeleisen, 1980–1983).

[60]Abraham Blau, *Nahalot Avot, Yehoshua* (Benei Berak: Ha-Mahlaqah le-Hinukh u-le-Tarbut Toraniim, 1985); *Shoftim* (Benei Berak: Ha-Mahlaqah le-Hinukh u-le-Tarbut Toraniim, 1986).

[61]Yitzhak Levi, *Parshiot be-Sifrei ha-Neviim* (Jerusalem: Feldheim, 1988).

Gershon Weiss.[62] The last is a very unusual treatment of the Samson narratives, which, among other things, presents them as a model for the proper relationship between a young husband and his wife. While the author acknowledges in a Hebrew footnote on page 155 that the tradition admits of interpretations other than his, the volume is more useful as a sample of what can be done to an unsuspecting text than as a serious treatment of it. And how can we omit Rabbi Adin Steinsaltz's lamented *Biblical Images: Men and Women of the Book?*[63]

Never has any generation been inundated with anything approaching the number of new editions, reprints (including microfiche reproductions), translations, and treatments of classical exegetical texts that are available to us. Even the printing explosion of the sixteenth century cannot compare to the present publication revolution, and the potential contributions to Bible study from computerized databanks of rabbinic texts are only beginning to be realized. It is virtually impossible to keep up with the deluge of materials, and the quality of the editorial work continues to improve. New and important editions of many *midrashim*, the Mishnah, individual tractates of the Babylonian and Palestinian *Talmudim*; the commentaries of Rashi,[64] Ibn Ezra, Ralbag, and the Maharal (to name a few); and a host of additional rabbinic writings accompany improved printings and annotations and a constantly expanding collection of English translations.

In addition, we witness the daily growth of international and interdenominational interest in the history of Jewish Bible interpretation, a field in which Orthodox scholars are prominently represented but far from the only valuable contributors.[65] In fact, hundreds of books and articles are devoted partly or fully to this subject every year, and the level of discussion constantly improves as scholars become ever more sensitive

---

[62]Rabbi Gershon Weiss, *Samson's Struggle* (Staten Island, NY: Kol HaYeshiva Publications, 1984).

[63]Rabbi Adin Steinsaltz, *Biblical Images: Men and Women of the Book* (New York: Basic Books, 1984). Note, also, the furor that erupted in some Israeli quarters (reflected in the Israeli press of the summer of 1989) over some of the characterizations in this volume, especially that of Samson.

[64]For discussion of how this has affected study of Rashi's commentaries, see my "Rashi's Commentary on the Torah: A Survey of Recent Publications," *Tradition* 22 (1988): 102–116.

[65]It is impossible to list the many Orthodox scholars who have contributed to this field. Suffice it to say that the number of important contributions grows almost daily.

to the nuances of the exegetical documents and to the reasons why interpreters said what they did. Moreover, our knowledge is constantly enriched by many important studies on related subjects, including the rabbinic sources related to the canonization of the Bible;[66] the *Massorah* and the Tiberian and non-Tiberian vocalization and cantillation systems[67]; and, of course, an endless stream of studies of prerabbinic and nonrabbinic interpretative texts, including the Apocrypha and Pseudepigrapha,[68] Philo,[69] Josephus,[70] the Septuagint,[71] and the Dead Sea

---

[66]On the canon, see S. Z. Leiman, *The Canonization of Hebrew Scripture: The Talmudic and Midrashic Evidence* (Hamden, CT: The Connecticut Academy of Arts and Sciences, 1976) and the further discussion in Roger Beckwith, *The Old Testament Canon of the New Testament Church* (Grand Rapids, MI: Eerdmans, 1985), and in J. Barton, *Oracles of God: Perceptions of Ancient Prophecy in Israel after the Exile* (Oxford: Oxford University Press, 1986). Also important in this area and others is *Miqra: Text, Translation, Reading and Interpretation of the Hebrew Bible in Ancient Judaism and Early Christianity*, ed. M. Mulder (Minneapolis, MN: Fortress Press, 1990).

[67]See I. Yeivin, *Introduction to the Tiberian Masorah* (Missoula, MT: Scholars Press, 1980); on the cantillation system, M. Breuer, *Ta'amei ha-Miqra' be-Khaf Aleph Sefarim u-ve-Sefarim Emet* (Jerusalem: Michlalah, 1982). On vocalization, see M. Dietrich, *Neue Paläestinisch Punktierte Bibelfragmente* (Leiden: Brill, 1968); E. J. Revell, *Hebrew Texts with Palestinian Vocalization* (Toronto: University of Toronto Press, 1970); I. Yeivin, *Massoret ha-Lashon ha-Ivrit ha-Mishtaqefet ba-Niqud ha-Bavli*, 1–2 (Jerusalem: Ha-Akademiah la-Lashon lha-Ivrit, 1985). Mordecai Breuer has also contributed a series of publications on Massorah and related matters. Most important are *Keter Aram Tzovah ve-ha-nusah ha-Mequbbal Shel ha-Miqra'* (Jerusalem: Mossad HaRav Kook, 1976) and *Ha-Massorah ha-Gedolah la-Torah* (New York: Lehmann Foundation, 1992); a complete bibliography appears in *Sefer Ha-Yovel la-Rav Mordecai Breuer*, 1 (Jerusalem: Academon Press, 1992): 9–12.

[68]J. J. Charlesworth, *The Pseudepigrapha in Modern Research, with a Supplement* (Chico, CA: Scholars Press, 1981).

[69]L. H. Feldman, *Scholarship on Philo and Josephus (1937–1962)* (New York: Yeshiva University, 1963); R. Radice and D. T. Runia, *Philo of Alexandria: An Annotated Bibliography (1937–1986)* (Leiden: Brill, 1988).

[70]See, further, L. H. Feldman, *Josephus and Modern Scholarship (1937–1980)* (Berlin: W. de Gruyter, 1984).

[71]Two excellent books about the Septuagint with bibliographies are S. Jellicoe, *The Septuagint and Modern Study* (Oxford: Oxford University Press, 1968) and E. Tov, *The Text Critical Use of the Septuagint in Biblical Research* (Jerusalem: Sinor, 1981).

Scrolls;[72] the writings of the Samaritans,[73] the Karaites,[74] and the Fala-
shas;[75] the interpretative murals found in the Dura Europos Synagogue;[76]
Kurdistani *midrashim* and *targumim* in modern Aramaic (actually rabbinic, though not generally perceived as a part of the rabbinic tradition);[77]
seventeenth-century Spanish ballads about biblical characters;[78] and
Bible-based Yiddish drama.[79]

SOME OBSERVATIONS

Notwithstanding the more controversial or peripheral authors alluded
to above, the three premodern exegetical trends continue as living
Orthodox phenomena, two of them far more actively than in the other

----

[72]A useful bibliography of the scrolls was produced by J. Fitzmyer, *The
Dead Sea Scrolls: Major Publications and Tools for Study* (Missoula, MT:
Scholars Press, 1977), but the recent rush of publications has left it somewhat
outdated.

[73]A. D. Crown, *A Bibliography of the Samaritans* (Metuchen, NJ: American
Theological Library Association, 1984).

[74]Still very helpful is L. Nemoy, *Karaite Anthology* (New Haven, CT: Yale
University Press, 1952).

[75]S. Kaplan and S. Ben-Dor, *Ethiopian Jewry: An Annotated Bibliography*
(Jerusalem: Ben Zvi Institute, 1988), to which may be added M. Corinaldi,
Yahadut Itiopiah (Jerusalem: Rubin Mass, 1988).

[76]For a bibliography, see C. Hopkins, *The Discovery of Dura-Europos* (New
Haven, CT: Yale University Press, 1979).

[77]For example, *Sefer Bereishit be-Aramit Hadashah ba-Niv shel Yehudei Zakho*,
ed. Y. Sabar (Jerusalem: Magnes, 1983) and *Midrashim be-Aramit Yehudei
Kurdistan* (Jerusalem: HaAkademiah LaLashon HaIvrit, 1985). In general, see
Y. Sabar, *The Folk Literature of the Kurdistani Jews: An Anthology* (New Haven,
CT: Yale University Press, 1982).

[78]T. Oelman, *Marrano Poets of the Seventeenth Century* (Toronto: Associated
University Presses, 1982) and S. G. Armistead and J. H. Silverman, *Folk Literature of the Sephardic Jews*, vol. 1 (Berkeley, CA: University of California Press,
1971), pp. 116–133 and bibliography.

[79]C. Shmeruk, *Mahazot Mikra'iim be-Yiddish (1697–1750)* (Jerusalem: Ha-
Akademiah la-Lashon ha-Ivrit, 1979).

contemporary Jewish movements. Midrashic-Kabbalistic literature is more fashionable today than at any point in recent memory, and the homiletical hasidic literature produced during the past two centuries, which, together with scholarly interests in Kabbalah, accounts for a large share of the trend, constantly grows in availability, attention, and influence. New books in the old homiletical style continue to appear, as do scholarly treatments of them, and extensive propagation of oral teachings have created (at least in Montreal, but I suspect far beyond) a virtually ubiquitous Midrashic-Kabbalistic impact.

Talmudic-Midrashic interpretation, the favorite approach of the *yeshivot*, also endures and thrives. The popularity of commentaries derived almost exclusively from the Talmud and its exegetical literature, and even the creation of new commentaries excerpted from individual rabbis' Talmud commentaries and other writings,[80] are signs of health (though Rabbi Baruch ha-Levi Epstein's *Torah Temimah* does seem less used than it was twenty-five years ago). ArtScroll's success in some circles and Soncino's midrashic addenda might suggest that the interest is limited to the English-speaking diaspora, but the popularity of other Hebrew works that share this attitude and editorial changes in the *Torah Shelemah* show that it is more widespread.

The Rational-Scientific approach also continues to be represented, but primarily in Israel, and I find it difficult to estimate its impact from here. Its success may result from the simple fact that the land of the Bible is more of a presence to Israelis than it can be to most outsiders, from the more numerous group of potentially interested followers, from the larger number of religious scholars who are able to specialize in ways that are simply impossible in North America, and from the very significant contributions of non-Orthodox Israelis, which gives Rational-Scientific Bible study a

---

[80]For example, the comments of the Hatam Sofer collected by M. Stern, *Sefer Tehillim im Peirush ha-Hatam Sofer* (Brooklyn, NY: M. Stern, n.d.) and I. Z. Bernfeld, *Megillat Shir ha-Shirim im Peirush Hatam Sofer* (Bnei Berak, 1977) and *Megillat Eikhah im Peirush Hatam Sofer* (Bnei Berak, 1982); A. A. Klein, *Sefer MaHaRaM Schick ha-Shalem al ha-Torah*, 1–3 (*Bereishit, Shemot, va-Yikra*) (Jerusalem: Benei Moshe, 1989,); M. Ibgui, *Sefer Hokhmat ha-Matzpun*, 1–5 (Bnei Berak, 1974); S. Greenman, *Hafetz Hayyim al ha-Torah* (reprint, Bnai Berak: Sifriyati, n.d.).

relatively high profile in Israeli culture. Commitment to this outlook is evident from the editorial policies of *Da'at Mikra'*, from the choice of medieval writers included in *Torat Hayyim*, and, most of all, from the important nonexegetical efforts that have been produced by Israeli scholars. Some Orthodox Americans identify with these books and teach from them, but their commitment has not been expressed through extensive involvement in any of the major projects noted above. In fact, one looks in vain for sustained, Bible-related publications by North American centrists, a shortcoming that surely must be addressed if they are to assert a position more worthy of universal attention and of historical significance.

In addition, one sees a groundswell of activities aimed at enhancing the accessibility and sophisticated appreciation of the entire literature of Jewish Bible interpretation. When this work has been developed more fully, it will be available to inform, and perhaps even to guide, the ongoing Orthodox reappraisals of the rabbinic interpretative tradition.

Globally, then, all seems to be fine. Orthodoxy continues to develop its interpretative literatures as it did several centuries ago. It appears true to its origins and traditions, faithful to its ideological commitments, and pluralistic to a degree that must amaze anyone who takes its range seriously. But . . .

POPULAR, CURRENT ORTHODOX HERMENEUTICS

I alluded above to the inherent difficulty in establishing a general Orthodox position on Bible study and to the potentially deleterious impact of selective use of the rabbinic tradition. Let us now examine some of the results of this highly controlled gleaning, particularly as it emerges in the popular Orthodox presentation of the Bible and its resultant tendency to drive a wedge between the traditional modes of Bible study and most of those practiced by modern scholars.

1. Orthodox teaching suggests that the patriarchs should serve as models of rabbinic-type piety and practice. Notions about marriage, honor due to parents, the origins of prayer and circumcision, laws of land acquisition, and virtually every other religiously significant theme are derived from the stories in Genesis. Even so, as far back as the Talmud, the rabbis recognized the possibility that the patriarchs' religious prac-

tices differed from those of Mosaic and post-Mosaic times. Some medieval interpreters assumed that the patriarchs followed only the rational commandments and that certain of their actions adhered to local societal norms, but popular Orthodox teaching has largely overlooked this position in favour of one that portrays the lives of the characters in Genesis according to later rabbinic worldviews.[81]

2. Orthodoxy teaches that the entire Torah was given on Sinai, and few beliefs are assumed by both traditionalists and nontraditionalists to be so basic to it. This position does reflect a well-developed rabbinic notion, but a key talmudic passage (*Gittin* 60a) suggests that the Torah was given either "scroll by scroll," presumably throughout the forty years of wandering in the desert; or "sealed," all at once. And while the latter alternative might suggest that the entire Torah was given on Sinai, many medieval interpreters understood it to mean that it was given at the end of the forty years in the wilderness.[82] Notwithstanding the status of its many laws and the rabbinic oral law—traditionally taken to have been given to Moses—rabbinic teachings acknowledge the legitimacy of the notion that the full text of the Torah was not Sinaitic.

3. Orthodoxy teaches that the Torah was composed by God and dictated to Moses. In fact, a number of rabbinic writers suggested that Moses had a personal impact on some aspects of the Torah. Most of those so inclined assumed that God put His final approval on the text, and that, in its present form, it represents His version; but the possible role of Moses is both acknowledged and used as a rationale for linguistic and

---

[81]The issue often centers on the interpretation of Genesis 26:5 in the Talmud and later commentators, as well as a series of other passages, in which the patriarchs seemed to be in violation of what later became normative expectations. See, for example, this verse's treatment in the commentaries of Rashbam, Ibn Ezra, Radak, and Ramban, in contrast to the more popular and more influential presentation of Rashi. Many related matters have been treated by Baruch Rakovsky in his *Birkat Avot* (Jerusalem, 1990). The development of this issue in the hasidic literature has been discussed by Arthur Green in *Devotion and Commandment: The Faith of Abraham in the Hasidic Imagination* (Cincinnati, OH: Hebrew Union College Press, 1989).

[82]See, for example, the many sources cited in "*Kuntres Seder Ketivat ha-Torah*," the fifty-page appendix to volume 19 of M. M. Kasher, *Torah Shelemah* (New York: American Biblical Encyclopedia Society, 1960): 328–379.

orthographic irregularities. A few rabbinic writers even suggested that people other than Moses contributed to the production of the Torah, a notion discussed in the Talmud and throughout later centuries.[83] It was

---

[83]See, for example, Jacob ben Asher, *Baal ha-Turim* to Leviticus 1:1, Hayyim ibn Atar, *Or ha-Hayyim*, to Numbers 33:2, and the sources cited in *Torah Shelemah*, as well as the passages in *Peirushei ha-Torah le-R[abbi] Yehudah he-Hasid*, ed. I. Lange (Jerusalem, 1975) that were censored with recommendations that they be burned by Rabbi Moses Feinstein, *Igrot Mosheh*, 4 (New York: Gross Brothers, 1981), pp. 358–361. Rabbi Feinstein cited the questionable passages in the course of his discussion, so they are readily available for all who are forced to use the later, expurgated edition of the commentary. Note also, Rabbi Hutner's *Pahad Yitzhak, Kuntres Yerah ha-Eitanim* (New York: Gur Aryeh, 1987) 8:2, pp. 185–186, and *Igrot u-Ketavim* (New York: Gur Aryeh, 1991) no. 270, p. 346.

Almost three decades old—but far from out of date and still important—are the responses of a group of prominent Orthodox rabbis to *Commentary's* 1966 questions in *Symposium on the Condition of Jewish Belief* (reprint, Northvale, NJ: Jason Aronson, 1989). The first of five paragraph-length questions—which began, "In what sense do you believe the Torah to be divine revelation?"—offered well known Orthodox rabbis and scholars, including Eliezer Berkovits, Marvin Fox, Immanuel Jakobovits, Norman Lamm, Aharon Lichtenstein, Emanuel Rackman, M. D. Tendler, and Walter Wurzburger, a brief opportunity to discuss the extent to which the Torah is still believed to be divine.

One senses in the introductory paragraphs to many responses misgivings about the space limitation and some of the other pressures under which the authors felt themselves to be working. Perhaps these have forced things to be expressed other than as they would have been in other contexts, but even so, several patterns of thought emerge.

Since the full question challenged the obligation to follow the Torah even more than its divinity, it is quite understandable that these respondents stressed the importance of the *Torah she-be'al peh* and the eternally binding quality of *halakhah*. But it is also significant that they made almost no attempt to use, or even to acknowledge the potential value of, anything that might pass for a "scholarly" look at the Bible. The divine origin of the Torah was accepted as binding, the need to provide a rational defense of divine revelation was generally eschewed, and discussion of it was conducted on a philosophical or mystical plane, but never on an historical one. In other words, revelation was primarily described as a philosophical concept, and if secondarily as an historical event, not one to be related to other historical realities of the ancient Near Eastern

never popular among the rabbis, but its persistent appearance suggests both legitimacy and potential compatibility with other rabbinic teachings.

4. One of the hallmarks of Orthodoxy is the relatively little attention given to many of the non-Pentateuchal books, but when their authorship is discussed, the talmudic and midrashic attributions, particularly those listed in *Bava Batra* 14b–15a, are dominant. However, the list of authors in *Bava Batra* has been subjected to much critical scrutiny by later rabbinic writers, who, following the lead of that same talmudic passage, offered their own suggestions and comments on the authorship of a number of books. In fact, virtually every attribution in this passage has been rejected by at least one respected rabbinic Bible interpreter, and the history of its interpretation leaves the impression that it was taken to have no greater authority than many other *midrashim* that could be accepted or rejected more or less at will.

5. Orthodoxy teaches that midrashic interpretations are binding.[84] This accurately represents rabbinic thinking insofar as halakhic behavior is controlled by the Talmud and codes, not by the Bible, but, in nonlegal passages and in the quest for the *peshat* of the legal ones, the situation is quite different. Rabbinic interpretation of these types of biblical passages is much more open than Orthodox spokesmen often acknowledge. In fact, the medieval and postmedieval positions on the authority of rabbinic *midrash* and *aggadah* were remarkably flexible. Although rabbinism did include staunch defenses of reading *midrashim* literally, it encompassed much more rational options, as well. The *geonim*, many medieval Bible commentators, and most medieval philosophers recognized fully the need to control, and to avoid being controlled by, the midrashic literature. Their suggestions that much of this material was conjectural, private, and subject to both radical reinterpretation and open rejection were a recognized part of the rabbinic responses to it. Its value was not globally challenged by rabbinic writers (that task was undertaken by Karaites, Christians, and

---

world. Only the response of Emanuel Rackman acknowledged the possibility of human contributions to the creation of the Torah, though these, too, were qualified; see, further, p. 180.

[84]In addition to the sources cited in note 11, see *Kovetz Igrot . . . Hazon Ish*, ed. S. Greeneman (Jerusalem, 1955), 1, nos. 15, 32, and 209; and the way the last has been excerpted in *Pirkei Emunah, Hashkafah ve-Hanhagah*, ed. S. Shulvitz (Israel, 1991): 68–69.

other opponents of rabbinic Judaism); but the presumption of its binding authority, especially when it posed problems for an interpreter, was not a major stumbling block. Dogmatic acceptance of its teachings was neither a necessity nor a universal priority.[85]

6. Complementing the strong commitment to traditional rabbinic interpretation is the popular Orthodox notion that nontraditional sources—including the potential contributions of non-Orthodox Jews, secularists, Christians, and scholars of the humanities—have no place in Bible study.[86] The notion is not a new one, and many of the late responses to medieval philosophy reflect a similar exclusivity; but it is not the only option that the rabbinic tradition respects. In fact, virtually all medieval philosophers and many Bible commentators actively supported the right, if not the obligation, to use nontraditional ideas as supplements (and even as replacements) for some of those preserved by the tradition. Linguistic, geographic, and historic explanations were frequently enriched by the contributions of nontraditional writers; and many whole literatures that had profound impacts on classical interpretative efforts—including philosophy, grammar, the natural sciences, and lexicography—owe serious debts to non-Jewish trends and sources. Approaches to interpretation and modes of thinking, not only new information, could be borrowed from whatever source offered them, if they seemed useful.[87]

---

[85]See, further, *Azariah De Rossi, Me'or Einayyim* (1866; reprint, Jerusalem: Makor, 1970), chapters 14–15; Z. H. Chajes, *Mavo ha-Talmud*, in *Kol Kitvei ha-MahaRaTz Hayyot*, vol. 1 (Jerusalem, 1958), chapters 18ff., English translation, *Students Guide through the Talmud* (New York: Feldheim, 1960); S. Lieberman, *Sheki 'in* (Jerusalem: Wahrman, 1970); and the first chapter of Marc Saperstein, *Decoding the Rabbis: A Thirteenth-Century Commentary on the Aggadah* (Cambridge: Harvard University Press, 1980).

[86]For example, Mordecai Gifter, *"Torah ba-Goyyim, Al Taamin,"* in his *Pirkei Emunah* (Jerusalem: Feldheim, 1969), pp. 141ff.

[87]On the use of foreign languages to explain biblical Hebrew, see E. Z. Melammed, *Mefarshei ha-Mikra*, 2 (Jerusalem: Magnes, 1975): 617–623; and Aharon Maman, *Hashvaat Otzar ha-Millim shel ha-Ivrit le-Aravit u-le-Aramit le-Min RaSaG ve-ad Ibn Baron* (Ph.D. diss., Hebrew University, 1985).

See, also, the Apocryphal Additions to Esther borrowed from the Vulgate into Yossipon; Nahmanides' reference to *Sefer Hokhmeta de-Shelomo* (the Wisdom of Solomon) in the introduction to his Torah commentary; and Maimonides,

7. Finally, and perhaps most poignantly, Orthodoxy teaches that the Torah has been transmitted in a letter-perfect manner, and that the plene and defective spellings of its words are of cognitive significance. In recent years, this belief and has been supported through the "discovery" of encoded messages and late historical references that can be meaningful to only modern readers in the Torah's consonantal text. This approach follows a popular notion with antecedents in the Talmud and *midrashim*, and surely reflects the ideal of the halakhic literature. Countless presentations are predicated on it, and unsuspecting audiences often transfer it to the entire Bible and to all rabbinic texts.[88]

However, the Talmud and the halakhic literature also acknowledge that the ideal of a letter-perfect Torah text has not been maintained, leading some rabbis to admit the virtual impossibility of determining the precise manner in which many of the words in the Torah should be spelled. Rules requiring replacement of erroneous scrolls during public reading were compromised, because no one knew what was correct; in some cases, the medieval presumption of a scroll's accuracy was replaced by the realization that, even if correct in one place, every scroll *would*

Guide for the Perplexed 3, 50, and *Sefer ha-Mitzvot*, Negative Commandments, no. 42. Abravanel's uses of Christian interpretations were collected by M. Segal in *Massoret u-Bikkoret* (Jerusalem: Kiryat Sefer, 1957): 255–257. Note also the extensive use of non-Jewish writers in Menasseh Ben Israel's *Conciliator*, trans. E. H. Lindo (reprint, New York: Hermon Press, 1972), in Azariah De Rossi's *Me'or Einayyim*, in Hertz's commentary on the Pentateuch, and the like.

[88]A full explanation is found in Doron Witztom, *Ha-Meimad ha-Nosaf* (Jerusalem: D. Witztom, 1989); see also Isaac Hirsch, *Yisrael, ha-Sod ve-ha-Takhlit* (Israel: I. Hirch, 1989) and *Discovery* (n.p.: Aish HaTorah, 1991). More recently, Joseph Furst has tried to demonstrate the antiquity of this approach, including its extensive use by Rashi (*Remazim ba-Torah be-Shitat Dillug* (Herzliah: Joseph Furst, 1994).

Norman Lamm has commented: "No amount of intellectual legerdemain or midrashic pyrotechnics—or even sophisticated but capricious computer analysis of sacred texts—can convince us that the Torah somehow possesses within itself the secrets of quantum mechanics, the synthesis of DNA, and the like" *Torah Umadda* (Northvale, NJ: Jason Aronson, 1990), p. 47. The application of this attitude to the many, many other notions forced into the Bible would clear the way for a much more philologically precise and historically realistic treatment of it.

contain (not merely could contain) errors elsewhere. The justification
for a scribe's not reciting a blessing when copying a Torah was sometimes based on the fact that no one really knew how to spell some of the
words properly, a notion found in the Talmud itself. Some halakhic
authorities admitted that it was altogether impossible to fulfill the commandment of writing a Torah Scroll, because the definitive spelling of
some words could no longer be determined.[89]

Each of these seven issues is debatable because the rabbinic tradition
allows for a range of responses, but contemporary Orthodoxy—at least

---

[89]See, for example, *Kiddushin* 30a; the commentary of Menahem Meiri, *Beit
ha-Behirah*, ed. A. Sofer, 3rd ed. (Jerusalem, 1963); Menahem *Meiri, Kiryat Sefer*,
ed. M. Herschler (Jerusalem, 1957); Jacob Barukh ben Judah Landau, *Sefer
ha-Agur ha-Shalem*, ed. M. Hershler (Jerusalem, 1960): 42ff; Moses Isserles,
glosses to *Shulhan Arukh, Orah Hayyim*, chapter 143; Judah Leib Saraval, note
at the end of Moses HaLevi Abulafia's *Massoret Seyyag la-Torah* (Florence, 1750;
reprint, Israel, 1969); Aryeh Leib Gunzberg, *Shaagat Aryeh, Hilkhot Sefer Torah*
(Warsaw, 1879; reprint, n.d.), no. 36; Moses Sofer, *She'eilot u-Teshuvot ha-Hatam
Sofer, Orah Hayyim* (Vienna, 1895; reprint, Jerusalem: Makor, 1970), no. 52;
Moses Schick, *She'eilot u-Teshuvot ha-Maharam Schick, Yoreh De'ah* (reprint,
Jerusalem, n.d.), no. 254; Ovadiah Yosef, *Yehaveh Da'at*, 6 (Jerusalem: O. Yoseph,
1984), no. 56.
Compare, for example, the presumption of accuracy attributed to Torah
scrolls by Solomon ben Adret, *She'eilot u-Teshuvot ha-Rashba ha-Meyuhasot
le-ha-Ramban* (Warsaw, 1883), no. 232 and *Teshuvot ha-Rashba*, ed. H. Z. Dimitrovsky (Jerusalem: Mossad HaRav Kook, 1990), no. 14, and by David ben
Solomon ibn abi Zimra, *She'eilot u-Teshuvot ha-Radbaz*, 2, pt. 4 (reprint, New
York: Goldman-Otzar Sefarim, 1967), no. 1172 (101), with the lack thereof in
the responsum of Yehezkel Landau, *Noda bi-Yehudah, Yoreh De'ah*, Second Series (reprint, New York: Otzar Sefarim, 1973), no. 178. I know of only one admission of this situation in a work intended for popular consumption, Rabbi
Yaakov Weinberg's *Fundamentals and Faith: Insights into the Rambam's 13 Principles* (Southfield, MI: Targum Press, 1991): 90–91, pointed out to me by Dr.
Moshe Bernstein. Much of Marc. B. Shapiro's "The Last Word in Jewish Theology? Maimonides' Thirteen Principles," *The Torah U-Madda Journal* 4 (1993):
187–242, also relates to the lack of a uniform rabbinic commitment to the belief in a letter-perfect text, but it is very recent and aimed at more scholarly
readers.

in the form popularly taught and preached to many adherents—has generally chosen the one less receptive to those traditional writers who prefer to give the Bible, or the allegedly improper position, an independent hearing. In fact, public discussion of these matters is almost systematically shunned, and private disclosure frequently engenders disbelief and suspicion of heresy. It is no accident that many of these examples potentially impinge on issues of religious authority, but authority and practice are not the only concerns facing the Orthodox world, and one of the others on which even these two depend is the proper treatment of its sacred literature.

Of course, this restrictive attitude is generally not shared by Orthodox Bible scholars. Their advanced students appear to benefit from a much more open and thorough presentation of the issues, many of which are also discussed in some of the more technical Israeli publications mentioned above. But since American Orthodox teachings of this type remain unpublished and almost secretive, we appear to be witnessing the creation of a new oral tradition, which, like the esoteric teachings of the Middle Ages, cannot be committed to writing—at least not yet. Interestingly, the Bible scholars are not alone in doing this, for it seems that a parallel phenomenon exists among halakhic authorities who, upon private consultation, permit practices they will not condone in print, even as rulings for individuals. This underscores the profound restraint of pious interests on Orthodox intellectual life, but also suggests the eventual rise of a new class of initiates, who one day will claim possession of the true teachings of our generation's scholars. Only the future will reveal whether or not, in the absence of written documentation, their claims will be heeded. In the past, access to mysticism was restricted in this way; it seems that now access to rationality is.

INFORMATION, NONINFORMATION, AND MISINFORMATION

Though I have no interest in dwelling on the textual problem, recent discussions of it in *Ten Daat* reveal how avoidance of proper education can lead to miseducation. When Rabbi Marvin Speigelman queried readers about the propriety of teaching high school students about the textual inconsistencies found in the classical rabbinic literature and in the

Bible, including the Torah, he received several learned and very carefully worded responses from Bible professors at Yeshiva University.[90] Without actually disclosing in print any information about the Bible-related part of the problem, they admitted its existence, referred to other discussions of it, and suggested both that the subject cannot and should not be taught in high school and that it is covered in their courses. They did allow for more extensive application to non-biblical texts, but did not offer any substantial suggestions about its handling.

The facts are clear, as all the parties readily admit; unfortunately, minor textual details are sometimes in doubt. The question is educational and relates to the proper time and way to deal with a potentially contentious issue. The suggestion to ignore it until college, meaning that those who do not enroll in a particular course at Yeshiva University will probably not even be aware of the problem, strikes me as grossly inadequate, even if possibly appropriate for the school in question.

This educational and ideological problem results, at least in part, from the fairly recent practice of having all students use identical editions of every text throughout their educations. Were they sometimes exposed to two or three different editions of the *Mishnah* and *Gemara* when they study them and to different recensions of Rashi's commentaries when they study them (as well as occasional manuscript copies of all three), they would rapidly realize that all copies of these texts are similar but not identical. When important, the differences could be discussed; but the presumption of textual perfection would disappear, thus eliminating the need to debunk it later.

Obviously there are fewer opportunities to explore this problem with the Bible—and the stakes are higher—but the traditional literature provides enough examples to more than justify the claim, and the same procedure should be followed. Those who fail to explore this matter with their students omit a legitimate aspect of Torah study from their educations and create a vacuum of correct textual information. This omission may seem no more serious than skipping any other important topic for

---

[90]M. Spiegleman, "The Truth of Torah: The Role of Textual Transmission," *Ten Daat* 3:2 (1989): 33–34; S. Carmy, "Teaching About Textual Transmission: How Important? How Necessary?" *Ten Daat* 3:3 (1989): 44; M. Bernstein, "Textual Transmission, Continued," *Ten Daat* 4:1 (1989): 35–36; and S. Carmy, "Textual Transmission: A Response," *Ten Daat* 4:1 (1989): 37.

lack of time, but it allows pious-sounding misinformation to direct public thinking about important issues. The creation of similar vacuums in other key areas, and the admission of the other misinformation or partial truths noted above, encourage particular choices (I use that word, for they seem to be conscious) that lead to the avoidance of Rational-Scientific thinking, widen the gap between biblical scholarship and Orthodoxy far beyond what it need be, and sometimes even engender fear of serious Bible study.[91]

Perceiving the potential impact of such ideas as erosive and modern intellectual influence as a threat, some Orthodox leaders have tried to discredit any doctrine that can be taken to suggest religious compromise and to passively (or sometimes actively) suppress discussion of any traditional writer who does not fit their model.[92] Thus, avoidance of the openness that typifies much of the rabbinic tradition actually seems to have had a significant impact on contemporary Orthodox interpretation, and has cut off many contemporary students of the Bible from important parts of the rabbinic tradition, not only from potentially deleterious nonrabbinic influences. It has probably fertilized the growth of Midrashic-Kabbalistic interpretation, as well.

In addition to their obvious implications for the use of recent books, these preferences have an impact of at least equal measure on the choice of classical rabbinic materials drawn into the contemporary exegetical picture. If Talmudic-Midrashic and Midrashic-Kabbalistic interpretation

---

[91]See, for example, the discussion of S. Baron, *A Social and Religious History of the Jews*, 16 (Philadelphia: Jewish Publication Society, 1976): 56ff. Perhaps more poignant, and surely more current, is Rabbi Hutner's perhaps playful but almost insulting *mikhtav berakhah* in the first volume of Rabbi David Cohen's *Ohel David*, p. 4, in which he wondered why the author published his notes on the Bible before his studies of more weighty rabbinic matters.

[92]Note the extent of censorship described by M. Carmilly-Weinberger in "*Sefarim [shel Mehabrim Yehudim] Muhramim [al yedei Yehudim] be-Meshekh ha-Dorot*," *Perakim* 4 (1966): 223–241; *Sefer ve-Sayif* (New York: Sura, 1966); and *Censorship and Freedom of Expression in Jewish History* (New York: Sepher-Hermon Press, 1977); as well as S. Leiman, "R. Israel Lipshutz and the Portrait of Moses Controversy," in *Danzig, Between East and West: Aspects of Modern Jewish History*, ed. I. Twersky (Cambridge: Harvard University Press, 1985): 51–63.

dominate contemporary preferences, *Midrash* and midrashic thinking (the common denominator) must, as well. And if Rational-Scientific interpretation receives less attention, it is likely that the same will be true of the contributions of the medieval rationalists and philologists, this approach's primary models.

To be sure, the Rational-Scientific outlook has never dominated rabbinic thinking about the Bible, but it has played an important role, especially through its antecedent, medieval elements. In some contexts, it ran a close third behind the Talmudic-Midrashic and Midrashic-Kabbalistic approaches, and it occasionally appeared in second position; frequently its impact on seminal issues was both profound and pervasive. Thus, it contributed to the thinking of some favorite Orthodox writers, and of many of their successors, including Rabbi Isaac Herzog and Rabbi Joseph B. Soloveitchik. It moved the founders, and continues to move many of the teachers, students, and supporters, of Yeshiva University and of Bar-Ilan University, as well as other Orthodox Jews. All of this suggests that the Orthodox world still holds a place for it, albeit one that is limited and localized.

On the other hand, many Orthodox Jews perceive an attraction to the Rational-Scientific aspects of Bible interpretation as unnecessarily risky. Rational-Scientific attitudes helped produce the *Haskalah*, contributed to the development of Reform, encouraged antihalakhic rebellion, and created the hostile postures against which a number of the favorite commentaries listed above polemicized. They also shared some common ground with contemporary non-Jewish trends in Bible study that were often driven by the desire to advance anti-Jewish biases or positions on inner-Christian debates. Solomon Schechter's now famous equation of higher criticism with higher anti-Semitism was neither incorrect nor overstated when he made it;[93] and it has analogues even today. But despite these legitimate concerns, not all Rational-Scientific inquiry is inherently hostile, and those who discount all of it in one motion misrepresent the teachings of the traditionalists who did not and insult those who rightly value it.

All of this brings us to what may be the major dilemma facing the contemporary Orthodox biblicist, one which addresses issues of identity

---

[93]At an address made in March, 1903, published in *Seminary Addresses and Other Papers* (Burning Bush Press, 1959): 35–39.

and self-definition and has always faced the religious biblicist, but which because of its frequent association with hostile challenges (from sectarian Jews, non-Jews, heretics, and critics) often receives a reflexive rather than a reflective response, especially in public: to what extent, in what spheres of inquiry, and in what ways should the existing rabbinic tradition control our attention to the Bible and our understandings, our presentations, and our applications of it; and to what extent, in what spheres, and in what ways should it not? The need to work out an appropriate response to the ever-changing world of modern scholarship—which cannot be minimized, for it, too, is very important—can be addressed only after a satisfactory resolution of the first problem has been achieved. I now offer a series of propositions that attempt to move in this direction.

TOWARD A CONTEMPORARY ORTHODOX HERMENEUTIC[94]

1. The entire Bible must assume primacy as a central religious text, and this must be evident in both the quantity and quality of attention it receives in all religious and educational institutions, including synagogues, elementary schools, secondary schools, *yeshivot*, and institutions of higher learning that train teachers or rabbis. The primary allocation of this attention must be directed to the Torah, and a secondary amount

---

[94]As the revising of my presentation drew to a close, I accidentally happened upon a secondhand copy of Rabbi Aryeh Kaplan's *Handbook of Jewish Thought* (New York: Maznaim, 1979), an approximately three-hundred-page listing of principles of Judaism, including several chapters (some sixty pages) devoted to traditional attitudes about the Bible. It has been impossible to incorporate or to evaluate this material here, but the interested reader may wish to examine it, especially the seemingly bold but very cautious treatment of textual accuracy, pp. 134ff.

One remarkable exception to the situation here described, which is very recent and perhaps in some ways even a response to the original presentation of this paper, is the brief but heavily annotated article of Marc Shapiro, "Maimonides' Thirteen Principles: The Last Word in Jewish Theology?" that appeared in *The Torah U-Madda Journal* 4 (1993), especially pp. 197–207. Some readers will recognize the issues from Louis Jacobs's work *Principles of the Jewish Faith*, but Shapiro's is much more detailed.

to all other biblical books of liturgical importance; but the parts of Psalms and the Prophets that are not excerpted for use in the *Siddur* and *haftarot*, and the five neglected books (Job, Proverbs, Daniel, Ezra-Nehemiah, and Chronicles), along with the issues that relate to their study, must emerge from the darkness that frequently envelops them.[95]

2. Bible study must be predicated on a sophisticated and precise knowledge of its original languages (primarily Hebrew, secondarily Aramaic). This knowledge must include an awareness of the contributions of cen-

---

[95]Although comments and criticisms have been solicited from the conference participants, this one paragraph has received virtually all of them, whether voiced publicly or privately. Only blissful naïveté would allow me to interpret this silence as total agreement with my presentation, but I am truly surprised that, of all the possible issues, only this one has become a focus of attention (at least thus far).

My statement recommends neither adopting a Karaite-like posture regarding the rabbinic tradition nor replacing all Talmud *shiurim* throughout the Orthodox educational system with Bible classes. (If done, this might make them resemble many schools for women, which, if nothing else, often do a better job of teaching the Bible, but this is not my plan.) However, I do believe that the Bible will never be taken seriously until the respect, the intellectual effort, and the allocation of time now reserved for studying only rabbinic literature is shared with it. Scripture cannot be the only primary text studied, for *Torah She-Be'al peh* is also a sacred trust that demands great devotion and curricular commitment. Indeed, the power of the Oral Torah has been so overwhelming that in common use (i.e., in Yiddish, in Yinglish, and in English) the word *Torah* has almost lost its earlier meaning of Pentateuch and now serves as the catch-all for all rabbinic learning. Even so, how can anyone who really thinks *Torah SheBiKhtav* possesses divine content—and the sanctity, and the potential to inspire and to guide that the Talmud itself attributed to it—allow it to be ignored or relegated to secondary or tertiary status? The Talmud recommended that one-third of one's study time be devoted to it; I would gladly support such an arrangement, though it would necessitate circumventing many popular rationalizations by great authorities who thought otherwise and correcting centuries of mishandling or neglect.

As well, I must note Moshe Bernstein's very interesting article "The Orthodox Jewish Scholar and Jewish Scholarship: Duties and Dilemmas," *The Torah U-Madda Journal*, 3 (1991–92): 8–36, the first published announcement of the first draft of the present paper and the first formal discussion of some of its contents.

turies of serious work in grammar and lexicography and also an appreciation of these subjects' creative dynamics.

3. The first obligation in presenting any Bible text is to clarify its simple meaning, which should become the starting point for discussion. Other needs never justify uncontrolled abandonment of this starting point, though they will often encourage distant travel from it.

4. Discussion of the text should always be predicated on defining the problem it presents—be it philological, legal, literary, philosophical, or historical—and then moving to the suggested solutions; interpretation should ever remain a dialectic process.

5. It is presumed that all of the Bible was relevant in ancient times and that it bore recoverable meaning in its historical contexts. These and other meanings, many never fathomed by the ancients, have been suggested to subsequent generations of readers by the text, and their study is valid in its own right, though often of only fleeting relevance. This search for meaning is legitimate and will continue into the foreseeable future.

6. Examination of the breadth, depth, and creativity of rabbinic Bible interpretation should be a high priority, and care should be exercised to insure that a full range of existing rabbinic solutions to any interpretative problem—not only those available in the few generally consulted commentaries or exegetical anthologies—is sought and made available.

7. The authority and sanctity of rabbinic interpretations, even those that may do violence to the simple meaning of a text, should always be taken seriously but should not replace the message of the Bible itself.

8. The strategies and dynamics of problem solving and interpretation should receive the attention due them as the essential building blocks of a proper approach to understanding the Bible. How one interprets, or should interpret, is a subject of profound significance and should be taught, discussed, and debated both as an integral part of presenting the Bible and as a natural adjunct to it.

9. Comprehensive study of the history of Bible interpretation should permeate the educational experiences of all who would teach or preach Orthodox Judaism. A sophisticated understanding of this history—its different periods, stages, and problems, and their influences on the creation of the interpretations themselves—should anchor presentations and evaluations of interpretations in the contexts from which they emanated. Concomitantly, the search for new and more satisfying interpretations

should be encouraged, and they should be submitted to the same exacting debate experienced by previous contributions.

10. Beliefs about the Bible should be subjects of serious concern, and their discussion should broaden general understanding of the issues related to them; except at the most elementary levels, they should not be presented as unchallenged or unsubstantiated facts.

11. No limit on knowledge, regardless of its source, or on its applicability to Bible study should be tolerated, but careful distinction must be made between confirmed facts and speculation.

12. Intellectual and spiritual welfare are quintessential outgrowths of the way the Bible is treated. Neither can be sacrificed out of concern for the other.

13. Whenever the Bible text and a suggested interpretation of it do not appear to be identical, a clear distinction must be made between what the text says and what it has been said to mean, and a serious attempt must be made to clarify and to evaluate the method by which the interpreter arrived at the interpretation and its inherent strengths and weaknesses. Attempts to determine what the author of a biblical text may have intended, if this is deemed different from what appears to have been expressed, are fraught with difficulty; they rarely result in certainty.

14. The Bible text has been subjected to extremely detailed scrutiny that takes all phenomena, however incidental they may appear at first glance, to be highly significant. In this context, it must be recalled that the rabbinic interpretative tradition recognizes the validity of both thee assumptions underlying this procedure and their opposites, for example, that synonyms can carry identical meanings and that biblical (even Pentateuchal) texts can repeat ideas in different words without intending to convey changes in meaning. Though potentially contradictory, both positions should be respected and applied where deemed most appropriate.

15. The perception of problems that lie in Bible texts, or that emerge from their close examination or from contradictions between them should not be allowed to deter their study. Such matters must be assigned priorities with respect to other religious concerns, but this should not consign any major textual issue to oblivion.

16. The initial assumption of the reader of a biblical narrative should be that it describes past reality. When that possibility is challenged by facts or logical considerations, other readings must be considered. Where

the literal meaning of a passage seems untenable, one should search for potential truth in a nonliteral interpretation or in one that assumes something other than the presentation of historical or scientific fact to have been the text's primary intention.

17. The Bible's messages and imperatives are presented through literary media, and one must take seriously the proper appreciation of these media, their different subtypes, and the implications of using them as the vehicles for communicating divine messages. Modern writers sometimes use terms like legend, fiction, and myth (and others that are no less foreign to the vocabulary of traditional rabbinic Bible study) to characterize some Bible texts. Some medieval rabbis characterized these passages as parables or prophetic visions.

18. The biblical books must be read and appreciated in their individual and collective literary entireties. They cannot be treated merely as sources from which to draw detached passages for educational or exhortative purposes, and efforts directed toward the latter aim should be prefaced by consideration of the former.

19. The potential contributions of contemporary scholarly research about the Bible and the people, places, or events described in it should be sought and integrated into the fiber of Orthodox Bible study without allowing positions of questionable validity to assert undue influence. This requires the continuous support of a broad-based, respectful effort to study, to monitor, and to evaluate the Bible-related activities of Jewish and non-Jewish scholars of both the humanities and the sciences.

20. Commitment to the importance of reconstructing the historical contexts of individual Bible passages suggests the need to explore the potential contributions of the physical and literary remains of the ancient Near East. The proper understanding of these discoveries requires that attention be devoted to mastering their languages, to reconstructing their cultural contexts, to understanding the dynamics of the academic fields that are devoted to them, and to allowing the results of this work to percolate through Orthodox Bible study at appropriate times and places.

21. The search for the contexts of biblical stories should not be discouraged by the seemingly unimportant or irrelevant role attached to many events by related ancient civilizations and the paucity of recovered materials that relate directly to them; much can be learned from the Bible's unconfirmed reports.

22. A notion expressed in a biblical text presumably suggests what the author of that text wished the reader to believe at a certain moment, not necessarily the complete, independently validated truth. In other words, the Bible's message may lie in the interpretation of the reality it describes, not in the description. The Bible does not contain the only possible presentation of the events; it chose and limited its presentations, and it interpreted reality while doing so. Different perspectives on a single event are sometimes available in two or more biblical passages; they suggest the obligation to develop a sensitivity to the varied perspectives in the text and also provide the opportunity to do so.

23. Reconstructions of ancient events, or of the lives of biblical characters, will always reflect something of the one who does the reconstruction. This subjective process should be encouraged, though readers should be sensitized to the pitfalls inherent in it and should be made self-conscious about their results.

24. Serious commitment must be given to the notion that God communicated with people in biblical times and that the Bible contains the best available record of that communication, the one deemed binding on subsequent generations.

25. Where recoverable, the historical context of every biblical passage should play a major role in understanding its primary message. However, the Bible's sanctity and compelling messages, as well as the tradition of applying it to all types of postbiblical situations, also suggest its relevance to continuous generations of readers and the necessity of exploring its transfer and application to contemporary situations.

26. The application of the Bible must take seriously both the simple meaning of the text taken in its historical context and the continually unfolding understanding of its potential meanings. In the final analysis, it must be controlled by the halakhic literature as evaluated by each generation's halakhic authorities.

27. There is no requirement that application of a passage follow its literal meaning and, consequently, no necessity to force into it meanings derived tangentially from it or associated with it. Therefore, the obligation to follow biblical law as interpreted by generations of authoritative rabbinic writers need not be sacrificed to other philosophical, historical, or philological considerations, nor should these considerations necessarily be altered for the sake of consistency with *halakhah*.

28. Hermeneutical assumptions and interpretative conclusions must be reasonable and defensible. The popularity and persuasive powers of some demonstrably erroneous notions cannot validate them, and this must be recognized and publicly acknowledged.

29. Place for considering nonrabbinic Bible interpretations (for example, those of Samaritans, Karaites, and Christians) should be provided in the course of an Orthodox education, in order to allow students to appreciate their contributions to the polemics surrounding exegetical debates. Appreciation of their premises and postures can contribute to a finer understanding of rabbinic responses to them and to their representative spokesmen.

30. Determinations of the validity of historical reconstructions, or of any suggested interpretations, will reflect the changing thoughts, experiences, and beliefs of the educated reader. Commitment to a lifelong program of Bible study must be a priority of every educated Jew.

IN CONCLUSION

The Torah and all or part of some other biblical books have a well-established and well-developed place in Orthodox liturgical and homiletical contexts where they serve as a medium for expressing devotion to God and aid in recalling the ancient past, in teaching the oldest and most seminal parts of Jewish sacred literature, and in anchoring later beliefs and practices. Orthodoxy is also heir to an almost indescribably rich and multifaceted heritage of rabbinic Bible study that it does not fully appreciate, and it is challenged to respond to a powerful and enticing literature of modern scholarship whose value it does not really recognize, much less fully understand. While neither can offer it an ideal contemporary approach to Scripture, both deserve more serious consideration as contributing components to contemporary Orthodox thinking about the Bible, which must transcend the liturgical and homiletical uses to which it has been put. In order to explore and exploit them more fully, a firm and permanent resolve to avoid superficiality—in the treatment of the Bible, in the treatment of the classical interpretative literature, and in the treatment of the potential contributions of modern scholarship—must be forthcoming from both Orthodoxy's individual leaders and the movement as a whole. This, in turn, will provide or suggest new or unanticipated types of solutions to problems that confront the serious Bible student, many of which will facilitate forging links between the classical rabbinic and the modern scholarly outlooks.

The perspective that derives from comparing and contrasting these two universes of thought and leads to fashioning these links should also offer the most sophisticated and intellectually satisfying religious approach to Bible study that is possible at this time, which must become the primary standard for all contemporary Orthodox treatment of it and the model of the next generation's attempts at improvement. This approach must be pursued vigorously in the name of those hallowed writers of previous generations whose ideological commitments reflected its legitimacy and necessity, and in the name of intellectual honesty and the universal pursuit of truth. Its value must be pressed over the objections of those whose vision of Orthodoxy insists on isolation of rabbinic learning and in opposition to that element of the rabbinic tradition on which the isolationist position is based; and it must be shared with all Jews who derive spiritual and intellectual sustenance from the Bible, including Orthodox laymen and students. Simply stated, we must assert boldly, emphatically, and unequivocally that any narrower position is a distortion of Judaism and possesses no value as an ideal model; and there is no area in which it is a greater distortion than Bible study.

Rabbinic writers continually looked inward to Jewish sources in the hope that their search for truth would be enriched by the virtually infinite realm of rabbinic learning; others looked elsewhere, hoping that theirs would be enriched by the virtually infinite corpus of knowledge available in the nonrabbinic world. Carried to extreme, both approaches have produced highly specialized devotees, who are correct regarding the value of what they know, but incorrect when confidence in their area of specialization suggests to them that little of value exists outside it. Only a unique blend of the best aspects of both rabbinic tradition and nonrabbinic scholarship—the model provided by a significant portion of the premodern rabbinic elite—can honestly claim to satisfy the contemporary Orthodox thinker's quest to understand, to appreciate, and to apply the Bible as best he or she can—things that, after all is said and done, rabbinic Jews like us have been doing for thousands of years.

3

Study of Bible in Light of Our Knowledge of the Ancient Near East

Barry L. Eichler

Today with the advent of archaeology as a full-fledged discipline and the subsequent rediscovery of the pre-Classical ancient world, the opportunity now exists to gain a richer appreciation of the content, nature, and message of the Bible in relation to this ancient world. Knowledge of the ancient Near Eastern context in which the Bible may now be studied has resulted mainly from the disciplines of Egyptology and Assyriology.

Assyriology is the study of the civilization created by those people who inhabited the fertile crescent of Mesopotamia—the lands of the Tigris and Euphrates rivers, corresponding to modern-day Iraq. Although this area had been inhabited by many different peoples, including the Sumerians, Akkadians, Assyrians, Babylonians, Amurrites, and Arameans, these people created and shared a common cultural heritage, which may be called Mesopotamian civilization. This civilization played a vital role in the formative period of the history of the Jewish people during the biblical period. Abraham was born there. It gave Isaac Rebecca, his wife. Jacob fled there to escape the wrath of Esau and he married Mesopotamian women, Leah and Rachel. During the period of the Divided Monarchy, both the kingdom of Israel and the kingdom of Judah interacted

81

with Mesopotamian political, cultural, and religious influences. The kingdom of Israel paid heavy tribute to the Mesopotamian political state of Assyria which eventually destroyed that kingdom, deporting and dispersing the Ten Tribes within its far-flung empire. The kingdom of Judah fell to the Mesopotamian political state of Babylonia and with the destruction of the First Temple and exile, Jews found themselves again in Mesopotamia. And it was from Mesopotamia under the leadership of Ezra and Nehemiah that Jews returned to the land of Israel.

Mesopotamian civilization flourished for more than 2,500 years until the rise of Hellenism a few centuries before the beginning of the Common Era. The task of the Assyriologist is to reconstruct Mesopotamian civilization on the basis of clay tablets inscribed with cuneiform writing, which have continued to be unearthed by archaeologists for the last one hundred years. The major Mesopotamian languages written in cuneiform are Sumerian (a non-Semitic language) and Semitic Akkadian with its Babylonian and Assyrian dialects. With the discovery and decipherment of these and other ancient Semitic languages such as Ugaritic, Amurrite, and Eblaic, new insights have been gained in Hebrew grammar and lexicography which help elucidate the biblical text. The nearly 500,000 cuneiform tablets now housed in museums around the world have also brought to light the history and culture of ancient Mesopotamia and its surrounding civilizations. With the illumination of this historical backdrop against which the Torah was given, the relationship between ancient Israel and its neighbors, as well as the cultural and social institutions of the Bible, can now be viewed from new perspectives.

At the very onset, we should bear in mind that the use of such disciplines as comparative Semitic linguistics, ancient cultures, and even archaeology, for the study of the Bible is neither foreign nor really new to traditional Jewish scholarship. Throughout the long history of Jewish biblical exegesis, many of our *Rishonim* utilized these disciplines in their attempt to fathom the plain sense of the biblical texts and to interpret the message of Scripture. We need pause only to mention a few examples:

Rabbi Saadya Gaon of the eary tenth century is considered by many to be the father and founder of Hebrew philological science. His treatises in the field of Hebrew grammar and lexicography make use of his knowledge of other Semitic languages, chiefly Arabic. To Rabbi Saadya, Hebrew philology was the necessary scientific apparatus for the main objective of interpreting Scripture. Subsequent Spanish Jewish grammarians and exegetes further refined this discipline.

Maimonides in the twelfth century was one of the first to advocate the study of ancient cultures for a deeper appreciation of biblical truths. In Part III of his *Moreh Nebuchim*, in his discussion of the Divine Commandments, the Rambam utilized the ancient chronicles of the idolatrous tribes known as the Sabeans, which were extant in Arabic translations, in order to gain insights into biblical precepts. Maimonides believed that many of the laws of the Torah were given to cure mankind of idolatrous practices. Thus, for example, the Rambam sought to comprehend the Torah's injunction against the eating of blood (Leviticus 17:10) by referring to the Sabean practice of eating blood in order to commune with the spirits. This practice was based on the Sabean belief that blood was the food of the spirits. In his *Moreh Nebuchim* (Part III, end of chapter 49), the Rambam lamented the fact that his knowledge of Sabean doctrines was not complete since they had been extinct for almost 2,000 years. The Rambam then went on to assert that if the rules of the Sabeans and the events of those days were better known, it would be possible to see plainly the reason for most of the practices mentioned in the Torah.

Nachmanides (Ramban) of the thirteenth century gives testimony to the use of archaeological survey, albeit primitive, as a means of ascertaining the correct interpretation of biblical texts. Genesis 35:16 states that Benjamin's birth and Rachel's tragic death took place while Jacob and his family were still *kibrat ha-aretz* from Ephrat. Does this expression denote that the tragedy occurred at a great distance from Ephrat and hence Jacob could not bring her into the city for burial; or does the expression denote a short distance from Ephrat regardless of which Jacob chose not to bury her within the city? In his commentary the Ramban addresses this problem, cites the opinions of Menahem ben Saruk, the Midrash, Rashi, and Radak, and accedes to the opinion of the Radak. But subsequently he adds the following remarks: "This I originally wrote while still in Spain, but now that I was worthy and came to Jerusalem . . . I saw with my eyes that there is not even a mile between Rachel's grave and Bethlehem. This explanation of R. David Kimchi has thus been refuted as have the words of Menachem. . . . " The Ramban also realized that archaeological data may answer certain queries while at the same time giving rise to other problems. He therefore goes on to state,

I have also seen that Rachel's grave is not in Ramah nor near to it [as the plain meaning of the verse in Jeremiah 31:15 would seem to indicate: "A voice is heard in Ramah . . . Rachel weeping for her children"]. Instead, Ramah which is in Benjamin is about four Persian miles distant from it, and Ramah of the hill-country of Ephraim is more than two days' travel from it. Therefore, I say that the verse stating "A voice is heard in Ramah" is a metaphor, in the manner of rhetorical expression, meaning to say that Rachel wept so bitterly that her voice was heard from afar in Ramah, which was on top of the mountain of [the territory of] Benjamin.

From the above references, it is clear that the study of Torah in light of our knowledge of the ancient Near East is definitely in keeping with the spirit of traditional Jewish exegesis. And if so, the imperative to such study should not be limited to the category of *daʿmah shetāshiyv* but rather include the positive aspect of providing new opportunities to appreciate the biblical text and its message.

In an attempt to give tangible expression to the positive results which can be achieved through the application of new data gleaned from the world of the ancient Near East to the biblical text, brief examples will be cited below from the areas of grammar, lexicography, history, and culture:

1. Grammar

It is commonly recognized that the *hitpaʿel* verbal form imparts a reflexive meaning (*hitqaddesh* "sanctify oneself"), middle meaning (*hithannen* "implore favor for oneself"), or reciprocal meaning (*hitraʾah* "look at one another") to the verb. However, there are a number of *hitpaʿel* forms in biblical Hebrew in which the infixed *t*-morpheme does not impart a reflexive, middle, or reciprocal meaning. These atypical forms appear to have the same meaning as their corresponding stems without the *t*-morpheme (cf. *ʾbl* "to mourn" in Amos 9:5 with *htʾbl* in 1 Samuel 15:35; *ʾwh* "to desire" in Deuteronomy 12:20 with *htʾwh* in Proverbs 21:26; *hlk* "to walk" in Genesis 12:4 with *hthlk* in Genesis 5:22). On closer examination of the biblical contexts, all the atypical *hitpaʿel* forms seem to connote repeated, continuous, or habitual action. Knowledge of Akkadian grammar has allowed a verification of this observation concerning the meaning of these atypical *hitpaʿel* forms. Akkadian, unlike Hebrew, exhibits a more extensive class of infixed *t*-morphemes, including a *tn*-morpheme which at times is reduced to a *t*-morpheme. The *tn*-morpheme imparts an iterative, habitative, or durative meaning to the verbal form. Thus in Akkadian, the *tn*-forms of the verb *alāku* "to walk" bear the meanings: "to walk about, to walk to and fro, to wander, to walk with on a regular basis or to commune with." Hence it seems proper to separate the atypical *hitpaʿel* forms in Hebrew from the normal *hitpaʿel* forms and to identify the former with the Akkadian *tn*-forms. A further appreciation of the biblical use of *hithallek* as an expression of man's intimate association with a deity (for example, Genesis 5:22 *wayyithallēk hanok ʿet-ha ʾelokim*) is gained from the following Akkadian passage which uses the *tn*-form of the verb "to walk": "[If he rejected sin,] his god will continually walk with him (*ilšu ittišu ittanallak*)."[1]

2. Lexicography

In Semitic languages, the basic semantic unit is a root, usually comprised of three sounds, or radicals, whose meaning is modified by the various verbal and nominal patterns into which it is formed. Semitic lexicography attempts to determine the common semantic denominator of a particular root in a particular language in order to understand the semantic development of the root and its full range of meanings. In Hebrew, the common semantic denominator of the root *špt* is usually understood to be "judging," with the verb meaning "to judge" and its nouns, *šopēt* "a judge" and *mišpāt* "judgment." A close analysis of all the biblical occurrences of this root indicates that a judicial meaning is too limited in scope to allow for a semantic development which would encompass its occurrence in such phrases as *mišpat hammelek* in 1 Samuel 8:11 and *mišpat haggoyim* in 2 Kings 17:33 where a translation "judgment" is contextually inappropriate, and in the occurrences of *šopetim* in the Book of Judges, designating leaders whose main activities described therein were not primarily judicial. Based on the use of the verb in 1 Samuel 8:5 (*simah-lānu melek lešāptēnu kekāl-haggoyim*) in which the people demand a king who will govern them, the semantic denominator "to exercise authority" suggests itself. The noun *šopet* would thus be understood as "the one who exercises authority" and the term *mišpat* would thus denote "an authoritative procedure." The judicial aspect would represent a secondary and tangential development based on the fact that a judge does exercise authority in rendering decisions. The use

---

[1] E. A. Speiser, "The Durative *Hitpaʿel*: A *tan* Form," reprinted in *Oriental and Biblical Studies: Collected Writings of E. A. Speiser*, ed. J. J. Finkelstein and M. Greenberg (Philadelphia: University of Pennsylvania Press, 1967), pp. 506–514.

of the term *mišpāṭim* in a legal sense may not necessarily be rendered "judgment" but may rather indicate the authoritative or prescribed mode of behavior and thus best translated as "norms, regulations." The occurrences of the root *špṭ* in Akkadian supports such a semantic understanding. In the Akkadian texts from Mari, the term *šāpiṭu* (cognate of Hebrew *šopēṭ*) designates the highest functionary in the regional administrative bureaucracy and is translated as "governor." He issues *šipṭū*, disciplinary warnings and punitive measures designed to enforce his authority over the governed territory. This term is a cognate of Hebrew *šāpeṭ*, (pl. *šepāṭim*) describing the plagues in Exodus 6:6 and 7:4, and allows the translation of the Hebrew term as "disciplinary or punitive measures" rather than "judgments."[2]

3. History

The last years of the Assyrian empire are documented in the Mesopotamian cuneiform sources. Within a decade after the death of Assurbanipal in 627 B.C.E., Nabopolassar, founder of the Neo-Babylonian dynasty joined with the Medes in a final offensive against Assyria. He devastated Nineveh in 612 B.C.E. and defeated the Assyrian forces which had regrouped at Harran in 609 B.C.E. His son, Nebuchadrezzar who had been appointed coregent, was responsible for the final victory over Assyria at the Battle of Carchemish in 605 B.C.E. The Egyptian army under the leadership of Necho II marched through Israel and Syria in an attempt to aid Assyria in its fateful confrontation with Babylonia. Against this historical backdrop, one is to read 2 Kings 23:29, which states that Pharaoh Necho *ʿalah ʿal melek ʿaššur*. The parallel passage in 2 Chronicles 35:20 correctly connects this episode with the Battle of Carchemish but does not indicate on whose side Necho would fight. Radak as well as most exegetes translate *ʿalah ʿal* "to march against" Assyria. However, in light of the above historical realities, one must translate this expression as "set out to" the king of Assyria. Note that *ʿal* may interchange with *ʾel* in these texts as evidenced by comparing the text of 2 Kings 18:27 with the text of Isaiah 36:12. Thus, the correct meaning of the biblical verse is firmly established through an awareness of Mesopotamian history.

---

[2]E. A. Speiser, "The Manner of the King," in *Judges: The World History of the Jewish People,* ed. B. Mazar, vol. 3 (New Brunswick, NJ: Rutgers University Press), pp. 280–287.

4. Sociolegal Institutions

The ancient city of Nuzi has yielded thousands of Akkadian legal texts, dating to the second half of the fifteenth century B.C.E., which document many sociolegal institutions of ancient Mesopotamian society. Among these institutions is the sale of freeborn daughters which can be reconstructed from over forty legal contracts that bear the superscription *tuppi martūti u kallatūti* "documents of daughtership and daughter-in-lawship." According to these contracts, a father or a mother and brother (presumably upon the death of the father) may sell a daughter to another person for the eventual purpose of matrimony. The sold daughter becomes a member of the purchaser's household and she is subject to certain conditions, depending upon the stipulations of the specific contract. The documents specify that, under such an arrangement, the purchaser may have the right to take her as his own wife or to give her in marriage to a natural son, an adoptive son, or an outsider, or to designate her as the wife of one of his slaves. In the latter case, she remains permanently bound to the purchaser's household, and upon the death of her husband-slave, she is to be redesignated as the wife of another slave. Any children of these slave unions remain the property of the purchaser as does any property which the sold daughter may eventually acquire. These Nuzi documents allow us to view a social practice in which an indigent parent may provide for the welfare of a young daughter by attaching her to the home of a more prosperous patron who will secure her well-being by obligating himself to arrange for her future marriage in accordance with certain contractual stipulations. This Mesopotamian practice is reminiscent of the biblical law of *'amah 'ivriyah* in Exodus 21:7–11: "When a man sells his daughter as a slave, she shall not be freed as male slaves are. If she proves to be displeasing to her master, who designated her for himself, he must let her be redeemed; he shall not have the right to sell her to outsiders, since he broke faith with her. And if he designated her for his son, he shall deal with her as the practice of free maidens. If he marries another, he must not withhold from this one her food, her clothing, or her conjugal rights. If he fails her in these three ways, she shall go free, without payment." In viewing this biblical law against the backdrop of the Mesopotamian sociolegal institution of the sale of freeborn daughters, it is apparent that slave laws in the ancient Near East were in part a response to pressing economic distress and which in many ways served

as an ancient form of welfare. An indigent father who sold his daughter
in a *martūti u kallatūti* arrangement could not only receive needed cash
but also could save his daughter from present deprivation and secure
her future economic well-being by ensuring her eventual marital status.
The biblical legislation also allows the Israelite father this right but,
when contrasted with the Mesopotamian legal documents, seems to limit
the specific contractual stipulations which are allowable. The sold daughter explicitly may not be sold to an outsider and implicity may not be
married to the purchaser's slave. Furthermore, the Torah legislation
is concerned also with her rights subsequent to her marriage.[3] This is
but one example of the way in which the biblical message can be newly
appreciated by studying the Bible in the light of ancient Near Eastern
culture.

If, from the above discussion, one is convinced that such scholarship
is in keeping with traditional Jewish exegesis of the Bible and that the
scholarly results of the application of newly acquired knowledge from the
ancient Near East positively enhances our understanding of the Bible,
it then behooves us to comprehend fully the nature of the challenges
that such knowledge presents to Orthodox Judaism and to confront these
challenges forthrightly.

Even without the application of knowledge recovered from the
ancient Near East, any serious study of the Bible will arouse certain
tensions. These tensions are inherent tensions within the biblical text
which for the most part result from seeming inconsistencies and contradictions. *Ḥazal* and traditional Jewish exegetes have noted and discussed such tensions, offering various interpretations in an attempt to
resolve them, usually by harmonizing the texts. In bringing ancient Near
Eastern archaeological and epigraphic knowledge to bear on the biblical text, it is inevitable that new tensions will arise. Some of this new
knowledge will result in the need to reassess previously held interpretations which no longer seem plausible in light of new awareness. As
the Ramban noted above, "archaeological" determination of Rachel's

---

[3] I. Mendelsohn, "The Conditional Sale into Slavery of Free-Born Daughters in Nuzi and the Law of Exodus 21:7–11," *Journal of the American Oriental
Society* 55 (1935): 190–195.

burial place necessitated a new understanding of Jeremiah's use of the place name Ramah. More serious tensions stem from historical and chronological issues. Seeming anachronisms, such as the use of the term "Philistines" in the Patriarchal Period, and seeming contradictory historical reconstructions, such as archaeological data associated with the Israelite conquest and settlement of Canaan that do not corroborate certain accounts in the Book of Joshua, may be viewed as challenging the historicity and validity of the biblical account. By and large, however, knowledge gleaned from ancient Near Eastern sources tends to support the biblical accounts in general terms and most of the existing discrepancies can be tolerated.

Furthermore, one should not lose sight of the fact that, despite great advances in the field, interpretation of ancient finds is still and will always be more of an art than a science. Current scholarly knowledge will always be dependent upon the accident of the spade and new discoveries and new perceptions are constantly forcing reevaluations of currently held positions. It is this state of flux which helps alleviate such tensions to a certain degree by allowing discrepancies and contradictions to stand while awaiting further clarification and future reassessment. However, the most serious tensions to be faced stem from the undeniable commonality of cultural and literary motifs that the Bible shares with the civilizations and literatures of the ancient Near East. To be sure, these tensions are not unlike those found stemming from such disciplines as anthropology, sociology, and folklore, in which cultural norms of primitive and ancient societies, similar to those of the Bible, are understood in purely humanistic terms. In the case of biblical and ancient Near Eastern parallels, however, it is not only the uniqueness of biblical norms which is brought into question but also the willingness and tolerance of Orthodox Judaism to comprehend "divine texts" in the context in which they were given. In order to appreciate these tensions by removing them from the abstract level of thought to a concrete level of empirical reality, one example of parallel texts will be presented in great detail. The parallel chosen for discussion stems from the realm of law since Torah law is the very foundation and source of authority of Jewish religious and legal practices. The most closely related and widely discussed Mesopotamian parallel to the laws of the Torah are those rules concerned with the case of an ox goring a person to death.

THE LAWS OF ESHNUNNA (C. 1800 B.C.E.)

54. If an ox was a habitual gorer, the local authorities having so duly notified its owner, yet he did not keep his ox in check and it then gored a man and caused his death, the owner of the ox shall pay two-thirds of a mina of silver.

55. If it gored a slave and caused his death, he shall pay fifteen shekels of silver.[4]

THE LAWS OF HAMMURAPI (C. 1750 B.C.E.)

250. If an ox, while walking in the street, gored a person and caused his death, no claims will be allowed in that case.

251. But if someone's ox was a habitual gorer, the local authority having notified him that it was a habitual gorer, yet he did not have its horns screened nor kept his ox under control, and that ox then gored a free-born man to death, he must pay one-half mina of silver.

252. If [the victim was] someone's slave, he shall pay one-third mina of silver.

THE BIBLICAL LAWS (MOSAIC PERIOD C. 1300 B.C.E.)

i. If an ox gores a man or woman to death, the ox shall be stoned to death, its flesh may not be eaten, but the owner of the ox is innocent.

ii. But if the ox was previously reputed to have been a habitual gorer, its owner having been so warned, yet he did not keep it under control, so that it killed a man or a woman, the ox shall be stoned to death and its owner shall be put to death as well. Should a ransom be imposed upon him, however, he shall pay as the redemption of his life as much as is assessed upon him. Whether it shall have gored a son or daughter [i.e., a minor], this same rule shall apply to him.

iii. If the ox gore a slave or slavewoman, he must pay thirty shekels of silver to his owner, but the ox shall be stoned to death. [Exodus 21:28ff.]

---

[4]Translations of the Ancient Near Eastern legal material render my understanding of the cuneiform texts. Useful translations of the law collections in their entirety may be found in J. B. Pritchard, ed., *Ancient Near Eastern Texts Relating to the Old Testament* (2nd ed., Princeton, NJ: Princeton University Press, 1955), pp. 161–180.

Apart from the obvious similarities in content, style, and phraseology that exist between the laws of the Torah and the Mesopotamian law corpora, the following legal comparison may be noted:

1. Where there is no premonition of existing danger—the ox is not known to be a gorer—there is no liability in both the Mesopotamian and biblical rules. However, in the Torah, the ox is to be stoned.

2. Where liability exists—the owner of the ox was forewarned but he did not take the necessary precautions to guard against the existing danger, the Mesopotamian sanction for such culpable negligence is pecuniary, while the Torah views the case as criminal and capital, but allows for the acceptance of ransom instead. Again the Torah demands that the ox be stoned.

In both the Mesopotamian rules and the Torah, recognition of the category of negligent homicide is clearly reflected. But how does one view the relationship between the Mesopotamian and Biblical rules, accounting for both their similarities and divergencies?

Many of the readers may be familiar with some of the scholarly literature written on this subject, and especially with the articles of M. Greenberg.[5] Professor Greenberg, understanding that law is an aspect of culture, sought to understand the Mesopotamian and biblical rules within the context of their own cultural value-systems, which reflect their differing cosmological ideologies.[6] The fundamental differences between the Mesopotamian and Biblical cosmological views stem from differences in the very conception of the nature of divinity and the definition of the godhead. Mesopotamian polytheism defines the gods as having emerged from a preexistent primordial realm which preceded them in time and transcended them in power. Hence, the Mesopotamian gods are not

---

[5]Moshe Greenberg, "Some Postualtes of Biblical Criminal Law," *Yehezkel Kaufmann Jubilee Volume*, ed. M. Haran (Jerusalem: Magnes Press, 1960), pp. 5–28; "Crimes and Punishments," *Interpreter's Dictionary of the Bible*, vol. 1 (Nashville: Abingdon), pp. 733–37; "More Reflections on Biblical Criminal Law," *Scripta Hierosolymitana* 31 (1986): 1–17.

[6]Y. Kaufmann, *The Religion of Israel*, trans. and abridged by M. Greenberg (Chicago: University of Chicago Press, 1960), pp. 21–101. Cf. J. J. Finkelstein, "Bible and Babel," *Commentary* (1958): 431–444.

ultimately sovereign or all powerful. Man was created from a god and thus the primordial watery mass, the gods, the earth, and man are part of an unbroken continuum. The task of man is to be a slave of the gods, providing the gods with their daily needs.

In contrast, the biblical God did not emerge from a preexistent primordial realm and hence God is free from all the primordial forces of the cosmos—both natural and supernatural, and His will is transcendent and sovereign over all. Thus, the essence of the biblical conception is not merely the belief in the existence of one God but rather in the absolute freedom of the godhead. Man was formed from the dust of the earth and received the breath of life from God. Man is discontinuous from the rest of nature in that he was created in the image of God, yet he is in no way comparable to God who is wholly other. His task is to be fruitful and to inhabit the earth. Man is to exploit nature for his own benefit. Yet despite his mastery of the earth, man is to be ever mindful of his true status as a creature of the Creator whose command he must obey.

From each of these contrasting cosmological ideologies stems a different series of implications and corollaries, which are reflected in each society's culture and are intrinsic to each of their value-systems. Recognizing this premise, Greenberg distinguished fundamental differences between the biblical and Mesopotamian conception of law. In Mesopotamia, law is an aspect of the cosmic order—one of the forces of the universe, which existed prior to the creation of the gods, the earth, and mankind. Law as the embodiment of this cosmic principle is called *kittum*, "truth." Since *kittum* is eternal and universal, it could never originate with the gods or man. Shamash, the Mesopotamian god of justice, was not the source of *kittum* but only its patron or guardian. In order to enable the Mesopotamian king to fulfill his obligation to establish equity within his realm, Shamash inspired the king with the perception of *kittum*. Thus the function of the king was confined to the just and equitable implementation of *kittum*. Although the Mesopotamian king was not the source of law—*kittum*—but only its agent, he nevertheless claimed the actual authorship of the laws in his law corpora and rendered the final decision as to their applicability.

This idea of the transcendence of the law expressed in terms of a cosmic principle that is above the gods as well as man is incompatible with the biblical cosmological ideology. According to the Bible, law is the command of God. God is not merely the custodian of justice but the ultimate source of the law, which is a statement of His will. Violation of the law is a rebellion against God's will, an absolute wrong, transcending the power of man to pardon.

In light of these basic differences between the Mesopotamian and biblical conceptions of law, Greenberg sought to explain the divergent elements existing between the Mesopotamian and biblical rules of the goring ox as arising from very different underlying principles, which stem from their contrasting cosmological ideologies and conceptions of law.

In Mesopotamia, the king was entrusted with the implementation of justice and establishment of equity in his realm. This obligation was conceived basically in terms of the economic security and well-being of his subjects. The economic foundation of the law is evident from the concern of Mesopotamian law with safeguarding property rights and compensating for loss of property. The sanctity of private property is a pervading consideration within Mesopotamian law and an offense against private property can escalate to a capital crime. In Mesopotamian law there is evidence of an economic valuation of human life which reflects the Mesopotamian conception of man's place and role in the cosmos. Even the intentional killing of a human being is viewed as an economic loss for which monetary compensation may be paid, with the consent of the aggrieved family.

However, in the Bible, it is God who promulgates the law and thus a religious evaluation permeates biblical law. One of its basic postulates is the invaluableness of human life. Murder is viewed as an absolute wrong, a sin committed against God, which is not subject to human arbitration. Hence for murder there is only the death penalty. According to the rule in Numbers 35:31: "You shall not take a ransom for the life of a manslayer who is guilty of death; he shall surely be put to death." Ransom may be accepted only for negligent homicide not personally committed, as in the case of the goring ox.

The biblical postulate of the invaluableness of human life is set forth in Genesis 9:5 ff.: "For your own life-blood I shall require a reckoning: of every beast I shall require it; of man, too, will I require a reckoning for human life, of every man for that of his fellow man. Whoever sheds the blood of man, by man shall his blood be shed, for in the image of God, did He make man." Note the cosmological reference to the biblical conception of man. Because of this sanctity of human life, the Bible views every innocent shedding of human life as a criminal act. Even a beast that kills a man destroys the image of God and must give a reckoning for it. Thus in the case of a goring ox, the ox must be stoned.

The prohibition of eating the flesh of the ox is a clear indication of the religious rather than utilitarian evaluation inherent in the law which requires the destruction of the ox. Another principle evident in biblical law is that of individual culpability, which does not recognize the Mesopotamian practice of vicarious punishment. Hence should the ox gore a minor to death, the owner of the ox and not his son or daughter is to be punished. In this way, Greenberg argues, the divergence of law between the Mesopotamian and biblical rules of the goring ox "reflects a basic difference in judgments of value, rather than stages in a single line of development."[7]

Although one may agree that Greenberg's approach prevents the application of extrabiblical parallels from becoming superficial or tendentious, nevertheless the important issue of the interrelationship of Mesopotamian and biblical law has not been resolved. Are the similarities of stylistic formulation and categorization in the biblical and Mesopotamian rules concerning an ox that gored a person to death to be understood as signs of borrowing or interdependence? Or, are their divergencies to be taken as proof of their unrelatedness?

In order to bring the issue into sharper focus, the Mesopotamian and biblical rules of an ox goring an ox need be compared.

Laws of Eshnunna (c. 1800 B.C.E.)

53. If an ox has gored another ox and caused its death, the owners of the ox shall divide between them the sale value of the living ox and the carcass of the dead ox.

The Biblical Laws: Exodus 21:35–36
(Mosaic Period c. 1200 B.C.E.)

i. If an ox belonging to one man gores to death the ox of his fellow, they shall sell the live ox and divide the proceeds and they shall divide the dead one as well.

---

[7]Greenberg, "Some Postulates of Biblical Criminal Law," 5–28.

ii. But if the ox was previously reputed to have been a habitual gorer and its owner has not kept it under control, he shall make good ox for ox, but will keep the dead one for himself.

In the laws of an ox goring an ox where there is no awareness of a vicious predisposition on the part of either animal, the Torah rule is identical with the Mesopotamian rule in legal substance and formulation. In such a case where neither owner is at fault, both the Mesopotamian and biblical rules invoke the principle of "equitable distribution of loss," which both phrase in an identical manner. How is this similarity to be understood? Is the biblical rule of an ox goring an ox an example of direct borrowing from the Mesopotamian law corpora?

The determination as to whether a given parallel found in two sources represents either a direct borrowing, a mediated connection, or a codependency upon a specific common source or more general common cultural tradition is based on probability and hence will always be a subjective judgment. Nevertheless, certain principles of the comparative method have been enunciated to help determine a high probability of relatedness.[8] First and foremost, one must be able to establish the possibility of both a chronological and geographic linkage between the two parallels. The Bible attests to strong linkage between Mesopotamia and Israel during the biblical period, from Patriarchal times to the end of the Babylonian exile. Throughout this period, Mesopotamian civilization was a potent cultural force in the ancient Near East. Its language was the lingua franca of the civilized world as attested by the diplomatic correspondence and international treaties found in Egypt, Syro-Palestine, Asia Minor, and Elam. The influence of Mesopotamian law and its scholastic traditions was also widespread. Certain ethnolinguistic groups including the people of Ugarit in Syria, who had their own native language and script, nevertheless chose to write their legal documents in Akkadian, using Mesopotamian legal formulary. Others such as the Hittites wrote their law in their own native language but closely followed Mesopotamian literary-legal traditions.

As for the chronological issue, the Mesopotamian scribes preserved Mesopotamian legal literature within the scholastic traditions of its

---

[8]M. Malul, *The Comparative Method in Ancient Near Eastern and Biblical Legal Studies* (Alter Orient and Altes Testament, 227), (Neukirchener-Vluyn: Butzon & Bercker Kevelaer, 1990).

cultural legacy. Thus the Laws of Hammurapi, for example, were copied and recopied by Mesopotamian scribes for over a thousand years together with legal textbooks such as model contracts and legal formularies. Especially noteworthy is the discovery of Akkadian cuneiform tablets including diplomatic, literary, and scholastic texts found at archaeological sites in Israel dating from the second millennium B.C.E.

On the basis of the above, it is reasonable to conclude that there is good probability for possible linkage between Mesopotamian and biblical law. But in order to further strengthen the probability of linkage, one must ascertain uniqueness rather than coincidence. Is the parallel noted in the two sources unique to the two cultures involved, thereby suggesting a connection; or is the parallel also present in other cultures that fall outside of the sources' historic stream, thereby suggesting parallel yet independent development?

The legal solution of "equitable distribution of loss" in the case of an ox goring an ox is not found in either Roman or Germanic law where a beast which causes damage is surrendered in toto to the injured party. Today, the principle prevalent in common law in the realm of torts is that of "letting the losses fall where they may." The absence of this solution in other legal systems heightens the uniqueness of this principle and further strengthens the probability of linkage. The strongest argument for linkage, however, stems from identical terminology which would not only support a cultural linkage but a literary one as well.

In comparing the biblical terminology used in the cases of an ox goring an ox with that of the the biblical cases of an ox goring a person, a clear dichotomy is found. In the cases of an ox goring a person the verb *ngḥ* is used to describe the action of the ox and the verb *ʿwd* is used to describe the warning given to the owner; while in the cases of an ox goring an ox, the verb *ngp*, which does not bear the meaning "to gore" in Hebrew, is used to describe the action of the ox and the verb *ydʿ* is used to describe the warning given to the owner. In the Mesopotamian rules of an ox goring an ox and an ox goring a person, the Akkadian verb used to describe the action of the ox is *ngp*, which, unlike the Hebrew, has the primary meaning "to gore" in Akkadian; and the verb used to describe the warning given to the owner is *ydʿ*. A comparison of terms yields the following results: the biblical rule of an ox goring an ox uses the same verbs as the Mesopotamian rules, while the biblical rule of an ox goring a person uses a different set of verbs. Based on all the above observations one must conclude that there exists a very strong probability that the biblical rule of an ox goring an ox, which is identical in legal substance and formulation to the Mesopotamian rule, shares a common Mesopotamian literary tradition. How disconcerting is such a conclusion?

It needs to be said that, despite the identity of the Mesopotamian and biblical rules of an ox goring an ox, the biblical perception is markedly different from the Mesopotamian. To the Israelite, the rule is an expression of the divine will, while to the Mesopotamian, it is a human attempt to mirror the cosmic principle of truth. Furthermore, in the Laws of Eshnunna, the rule of an ox goring an ox immediately precedes the rule of an ox goring a person. Both rules in Eshnunna treat the injuries as private wrongs whose remedies are pecuniary. Thus in Mesopotamian law, whether the ox gores a person or another ox, the wrong constitutes an economic trespass against the kin of the victim or the owner of the dead ox. However, unlike the Laws of Eshnunna, the Torah separates the biblical rules of an ox goring an ox from the rules of an ox goring a person, despite the similarity of subject matter. The latter rules occur in the context of crimes against a person, while the former rules occur in the context of wrongs against property. This discontinuity in the biblical sequence of the laws of the goring ox eloquently underscores the disparity in ideological outlook that exists between the biblical and Mesopotamian rules of the goring ox in which the victim was a human being. Nevertheless, those similarities which the biblical rules do share with the Mesopotamian law corpora seem to attest to the simple fact that the Israelites, however much they departed from neighboring cultures in their ideological orientation, stood with them culturally speaking as members of an interrelated complex, which spanned almost all of Western Asia. The shared features, such as the laws of an ox goring an ox, seem to represent those common elements that are not inimical to the biblical worldview.

But can Orthodox Judaism tolerate the strong probability that the biblical rule of an ox goring an ox shares a common literary tradition with the Mesopotamian rule? To be sure, approaches may be found within Jewish tradition to accommodate such probabilities. These probabilities would add new dimensions to the rabbinic concept of *yeshivat shem ve'eber* or to the Ramban's position that

> the meaning of the "Laws" which the Rabbis have counted among the seven Noachide commandments is not just that they are to appoint judges in each

and every district, but that He commanded them concerning the laws of theft, overcharge, wronging, and a hired man's wages; the laws of guardians of property, forceful violation of a woman, seduction, principles of damage and wounding a fellowman; laws of creditors and debtors, laws of buying and selling and their like, similar in scope to the laws with which Israel was charged (Genesis 34:13).

But the more basic issue is whether or not Orthodox Jewry, believing in the divine origin of the Torah and in the eternity of its message, can tolerate the idea that the Bible when studied in the context of the ancient Near East seems to strongly attest to the fact that it bears the cultural imprints of the times in which it was given. These imprints are evident not only in its history and historiography but also in its temple architecture, its cultic practices, its sacred psalms and liturgy, its modes of divine communication, and even in its divinely given law. Thus the major challenge that such an approach to the Bible presents is the need to define the uniqueness of Torah in more subtle yet possibly more profound ways. The Bible when studied in the context of the ancient Near East also seems strongly to suggest that the "Jews" of ancient Israel were part of a cosmopolitan cultural complex with which their Torah interacted. The challenge of acknowledging such interaction comes at a time in which large segments of Orthodox Jewry advocate total separation from Western civilization whose culture is as morally bankrupt as the Torah's depiction of much of the ancient world; at a time in which large segments of Orthodox Jewry are rejecting science and the humanistic ideals of Western thought; at a time in which large segments of Orthodox Jewry are encouraging their young to withdraw from intercourse with the modern world around them. This is not to minimize the tensions that do exist between Orthodox Judaism and the modern world, which are, in many ways, similar to tensions that existed between biblical Israel and the other ancient Near Eastern civilizations. But despite these tensions, the Bible when studied in the context of the ancient Near East suggests that Torah rejects only those cultural aspects of civilization that are hostile to its worldview and indeed encourages *yapyuto shel yepet be ʾohelay shem.*

From the above discussion, it is clear that the study of the Bible in light of our knowledge of the ancient Near East has a much broader impact than merely on the meaning of the biblical text alone. The issues raised affect all of those who are committed to the ideals of Orthodox

Judaism and are concerned with its future. They are especially significant in addressing the role of the study of Tanach within Orthodox Jewish education.

Although all Orthodox Jewish educators would acknowledge the importance of teaching Tanach in Jewish schools, the goals of such study are often nebulously conceived, ill-defined, and poorly articulated. This is especially true of secondary- and college-level education where the need to transmit factual knowledge of the biblical tradition is no longer the primary consideration. At this juncture, emphasis is usually placed upon the acquisition of textual skills to enable the student to study Tanach independently as a lifelong *mitzvah* from which he is to gain both instruction and inspiration. The student improves his ability to read and understand the classical medieval exegetes who, in the main, confront the text personally in an attempt to determine the "plain sense of the text" and the message of Scripture. But educators must ask whether the Orthodox Jew today may still be trained to confront personally the biblical text and to wrestle with its meaning.

Today, in the modern period, when the intellectual climate is no longer dominated by religious dogmas, and humanism is the primary virtue, is it too dangerous to allow an Orthodox Jew to rely on his own intellectual resources in understanding the biblical text even when halachic issues are not involved? Do the times require a uniformity of thought that allows only authoritative understandings of the biblical text that are sanctioned by tradition? Must the Tanach be read today with reverent inattention so that internal inconsistencies and divergent tendencies remain unnoticed and unappreciated? If so, it is obvious that there is no place in the Orthodox Jewish curriculum for the study of the Bible within the context of the ancient Near East, for such study informs the student of the possibility of new insights and new appreciations of the text.

But even if one were to respond in the negative to the above questions, such study must be handled with great sensitivity, for there is potential danger in this approach. When viewing Torah against the backdrop of ancient Near Eastern culture, there is always the danger that the more impatient student may not make the effort to appreciate the subtle differences which allow one to view the unique worldview and message of Torah. In its stead, he may be left with a diminished belief in the uniqueness of Torah and a lessened sense of *yirat shamayim*. But again this is an ever-present danger in the teaching of Torah. Is this any different from introducing a difficult midrash in class whose literal sense seems incomprehensible to the student and which, if not properly presented, may leave the student with a lessened appreciation of Torah and rabbinic thought? Thus, great sensitivity must always be present in the teaching of Torah for the teacher's responsibility in properly communicating the truths of Torah is indeed awesome.

4

Rabbinic Midrash as Evidence for Textual Variants in the Hebrew Bible: History and Practice[1]

Yeshayahu Maori

This chapter sketches one aspect of the study of the Bible, namely the scholarly attempt to clarify the textual traditions of the Bible, as seen from one particular angle: the relevance of rabbinic literature. We will first examine the manner in which that literature serves as a source of data for textual inquiry. Part II is an appendix dealing with the halakhic conclusions to be drawn in cases of conflict between the received text and rabbinic literature.

---

[1]This article is a translation, edited and expanded, of the Hebrew article published in *Iyyunei Mikra u-Parshanut*, vol. 3, *Sefer Zikkaron le-Mosheh Goshen-Gottstein* (*Studies in Bible and Exegesis*, vol.3, *Moshe Goshen-Gottstein—In Memoriam*, ed. M. Bar-Asher, et al. [Ramat Gan, 1993]), pp. 267–286. See also Y. Maori, "The Text of the Hebrew Bible in Rabbinic Writings in the Light of the Qumran Evidence," in *The Dead Sea Scrolls: Forty Years of Research*, ed. D. Dimant and U. Rappaport (Leiden: Brill, 1992). I would like to thank Hayyim Angel for translating my article into English, and Prof. Moshe Bernstein for his helpful comments.

RABBINIC SOURCES AND THE BIBLICAL TEXT

Most current scholarship accepts the idea that rabbinic literature, despite the late date of its extant copies, contributes to the textual criticism of the Bible, and not only to its exegesis. It was largely the research of Victor Aptowitzer in *Das Schriftwort in der rabbinischen Literatur*[2] which broke the ground for modern investigation of this area.[3] The value of rabbinic literature for textual criticism is reduced somewhat by the fact that rabbinic texts postdate the period when the biblical text was already fixed, in addition to the complications connected to rabbinic citation of biblical phrases in Midrash. Nevertheless, given the paucity of relevant material, rabbinic literature is significant for the textual criticism of the Hebrew Bible.

As is well-known, deviations from the Masoretic Text (MT) are reflected in rabbinic literature in two forms: 1. The Midrash *quotes* a verse which differs from the MT. 2. The Midrash seems to be *based* on a variant text (henceforth: hermeneutical variant).[4] To take an obvious, if minor, example, the *derashah* (exegetical comment) on the 480 synagogues in Jerusalem (*Megillah* 3:1, 73d and elsewhere) which is based on the *gematria* of ML'TY (Isaiah 1:21),[5] indicates that the author of the *derashah* had the reading MLTY (without an *aleph*), since ML'TY=481.

Scholars assign, with good reason, greater importance to the hermeneutical variant than to the variant citation. With a quotation variant, it is always possible that the variant results from a copyist's error. But when the evidence is manifest in the Midrash itself, in the word play

---

[2]Victor Aptowitzer, *Das Schriftwort in der rabbinischen Literatur* (Vienna 1906–1915; reprint, New York, 1970). My references follow the pagination of the reprint.

[3]On the history of research and some of the problems involved in evaluating this rabbinic material, see also Aptowitzer's introduction.

[4]Accordingly, in the Hebrew University Bible Project (HUBP) edition of Isaiah, *The Book of Isaiah*, ed. M. H. Goshen-Gottstein, vols. 1–3 (Jerusalem: HUBP, 1975, 1981, 1993), we distinguished between simple quotation variants and hermeneutical variants, which are marked as *herm*. If the quotation, too, differs from MT, it is designated *var-herm*.

[5]Cf. the parallel midrashic sources referred to in the HUBP edition of Isaiah, ad loc.

or content, we are more likely to be confronting the biblical text available to the composer of the Midrash. For it is difficult to assume that the sage would have based his *derashah* on a misquotation or a faulty text. Therefore our discussion will be concerned primarily with hermeneutical variants.[6]

The *Geonim*, *Rishonim*, and *Aharonim* already addressed most of the issues pertinent to this study, and a brief survey of their opinions will clarify the topic. Aptowitzer's monumental work also began with an examination of the history of scholarship on the topic and other meth-

---

[6]Cf. *The Book of Isaiah, Sample Edition with Introduction*, ed. M. H. Goshen-Gottstein (Jerusalem: Magnes Press, 1965) sect. 66, p. 36. See also D. Rosenthal, "The Sages' Methodical Approach to Textual Variants within the Hebrew Bible," in *Isaac Leo Seeligman Memorial Volume*, ed. A. Rof and Y. Zakovitch (Jerusalem: E. Rubinstein, 1983), Hebrew section, pp. 395–417 in his discussion of Rabbi Hai Gaon's responsum; there he comments that "only in later periods did the rabbis (*Responsa of Rashba Attributed to Ramban*, 232) distinguish between quotation and hermeneutical variants" (p. 402, n. 42). This formulation is misleading. Rashba differentiated between "that which appears in the Talmud pertaining to legal matters" and other types of *derashah*. Meiri, when summarizing Rashba's position (*Kiryat Sefer*, ed. M. Hirschler [Jerusalem, 1956], sect. 1, pt. 3, p. 58, col. 1), distinguishes between those cases "in the Talmud pertaining to the law, where some legal matter arose from it," and those that "pertain to Midrash."

In other words, Rashba distinguishes between those *derashot* from which there is derived a *halakhah*, where one should rely on the rabbinic text against the MT, and all other *derashot*, including (most importantly) aggadic *derashot*, even where they reflect a hermeneutical variant. This is stated explicitly in Radbaz's recapitulation of Rashba's opinion (Responsa of Radbaz, 4, question 1020 [594], Warsaw 1882, p. 116d): "For every *male'* and *haser* that affects a law, like *BSWKWT—BSKT, KRNWT—KRNT*, we rely on the Talmud. . . . When no law is affected, then we retain the masoretic reading." For Rashba, and doubtless also for earlier rabbis, only hermeneutical variants created a quandary; quotation variants were dismissed as erroneous. Compare this to Rabbi Hai's response regarding the transposition of *Yehoyada ben Benayahu* to *Benayahu ben Yehoyada* (see below, note 27): "We cannot say that the biblical text of our Gemara was incorrect; rather, they are making a *derashah* on the verse." Moreover, it is certainly no coincidence that the three examples of textual discrepancies between the Talmud and our text that are cited by Tosafot (see below, note 28) appear to deal with hermeneutical variants.

odological issues. Although the list of rabbis enumerated in his introduction is truly impressive, his evaluation of the positions of certain rabbis
and his methodological discussion require further consideration. We
must also bear in mind the new material and methods that have been
discovered and devised in the more than eighty years since Aptowitzer's
study.

The import of the textual variants in rabbinic literature has always
been a sensitive issue, especially since this area of research attracted
scholars familiar with rabbinic literature, usually religious Jews. For them,
the mere existence of textual variants was problematic. Although they
could dismiss other textual witnesses such as the Septuagint, Samaritan
Pentateuch, and other Hebrew manuscripts as unreliable, they could not
do the same when dealing with textual witnesses in rabbinic literature.

How perturbing such matters can be to a traditional mentality can be
seen from the reaction of M. M. ha-Efrati to an article by D. B. Ratner.
Ratner rejected the assertion of Y. Reifman that the text of Habakkuk
2:16 found in a Midrash read WH'RM (as opposed to MT WH'RL).[7]
On this issue, ha-Efrati writes:

> Indeed, such matters would be worthy of publication, were it not that they
> would cause a rapid erosion of the tradition prevalent among Jews. One should
> avoid publication of material which undermines the tradition, for it brings
> no benefit to the larger community. Rabbi Y. Reifman has been a close friend
> of mine for over twenty years, and his words are dear to me; nevertheless,
> where there is concern for a possible breach within the community, there
> should be no tolerance whatsoever.[8]

To be sure, the religious outlooks of some rabbis often influenced their
explication of rabbinic texts that ostensibly contained textual variants.
Noteworthy are the comments of Rabbi Menaḥem de Lonzano[9] to *Sanhedrin* 4a: "Here it is clear that one of the three occurrences of *KRNT* in

---

[7]*Esther Rabbah* 3:1 (6c): "The entire household of that wicked man were judged
while *naked*, as it is written (Habakkuk 2:16) 'drink,' this is Nebuchadnezzar,
'also you,' this is Belshazzar, *ve-he'arel*, this is Vashti."

[8]*Ha-Tzofeh la-Maggid*, vol. 14 no. 44 (1870), p. 351 (ha-Efrati's response
follows Ratner's article).

[9]*Or Torah* (see below, note 45) to Leviticus 4, p. 13b. The two references
are from Lonzano's comments there.

this passage (Leviticus 4:25, 30, 34) is spelled *KRNWT*," unlike the MT. Lonzano continues: "It therefore seems right to me to interpret this talmudic passage in a manner consistent with the MT. If, upon close scrutiny, this interpretation seems somewhat forced, let the reader understand that it is preferable to offer a slightly forced interpretation than to explain in a straightforward way but to face a greater calamity." Through the modern period many scholars have reacted similarly when their studies touched on the issue of biblical textual variants. This is true not only because the biblical text has been preserved better than other texts, but because of the deep religious sensitivity of the scholars.[10] The remarks of M. Ish-Shalom[11] reflect the great pressure that the traditional individual faces in dealing with biblical textual variants:

> When I stated in *Me'ir Ayin* that "in the biblical text it is written, etc.," a prominent rabbi who is well versed in aggada criticized me. He cited the passage (*Avot* 1:11), "Sages, be careful with your words." His reasoning— one should not adopt positions which support those who pervert Scripture. But should we blind ourselves because there are those who pervert the text? I am familiar with the statement, "because he hid [his face], he merited the radiant countenance" (*Berakhot* 7a); but the same Sages also wrote "Why do you give heretics a support for their position?" And He answered: "Write! Though whoever seeks to distort will surely distort" (*Genesis Rabbah* 8:8). This teaches that only one who wants to err will do so, whereas one who does not wish to err on this matter will not.[12]

To the best of our knowledge, Rabbi Hai Gaon was the first to address the apparent divergence of biblical verses cited in the Talmud from

---

[10]They did not, however, state their views explicitly. Perhaps they did not even sense that, in their discussions of this issue, they were deviating from the scholarly approaches they would employ in dealing with nonbiblical sources.

[11]In his preface to his edition of *Seder Eliyahu Rabbah* (Vienna, 1902), p. 133.

[12]It is well known that not all editors of Midrash were careful to list the textual variants, even when the edition claimed to be critical as, for example, Adin Steinsaltz's introduction to *Midrash ha-Gadol on Leviticus* (Jerusalem, 1976), p. 13. In this manner, they perpetuated the pattern established by their predecessors. Obviously, this fact influenced HUBP's choice of editions of Midrashim used for the list of variants.

MT.[13] He was asked[14] about "talmudic citations of biblical verses not found in the Bible," and three examples are adduced.[15] The first (from *Berakhot* 48a, see below) appears to misquote Proverbs 4:8, replacing that verse with one found in Ben Sira. The second (*Berakhot* 61a=*Eruvin* 18b) appears to quote a verse not found in the MT. In the third example (*Megillah* 4a), the Talmud challenges Rabbi Yehoshua ben Levi's view— that Lod, Ono, and Gey' ha-Ḥarashim were walled cities at the time of Joshua son of Nun—from 1 Chronicles 8:12, which indicates that Elpaal built those cities. The Talmud then responds (in our printed texts):

---

[13]We know that Rabbi Yehudai Gaon had already been questioned on the issue of inconsistency between the text found in the Talmud (*Sotah* 10a) and the MT, but he did not respond to the question (cited in Aptowitzer, pp. 21–22; cf. R. Margaliot, *Ha-Mikra ve-ha-Masorah* [Jerusalem, 1954], pp. 10–11).

[14]*Teshuvot Ge'onim Kadmonim*, D. Cassel edition (Berlin, 1848), responsum 78. This responsum is cited in its entirety by B. M. Lewin in *Otzar ha-Ge'onim* on *Berakhot*, responsa on 48a (pp. 113–114) based on the Berlin ms. On the case in *Megillah* 4a, see *Otzar ha-Ge'onim* on *Megillah*, responsa, pp. 6–7. S. Abramson, in his *Ba-Merkazim u-ba-Tefutzot bi-Tekufat ha-Ge'onim* (Jerusalem, 1955), pp. 131–132, reprinted this responsum based on the fragment of the Cambridge manuscript, which we have used. According to this version, it was sent to Rabbi Elḥanan b. Shemarya, a leader of the Babylonian community of Fostat (and not to Rabbi Nissim) from Rabbi Sherira and Rabbi Hai.

The responsa attributed to both Rabbi Sherira and Rabbi Hai clearly reflect the views of Rabbi Hai (or else his name would not be associated with them). Regarding the responsa attributed to Rabbi Sherira, it must be pointed out that in Rabbi Sherira's later years, when his son Rabbi Hai worked under him, many people posed their questions to Rabbi Hai. Out of respect for Rabbi Sherira, however, they mentioned Rabbi Sherira's name. Cf. Abramson, p. 126; T. Groner, '*Alei Sefer*, 8 (*Tammuz* 1980), p. 21, n. 66; cf. also T. Groner, *The Legal Methodology of Hai Gaon* (Chico, 1985), pp. 118–119. Another responsum consistent with this one is that attributed to Rabbi Hai, see below. Cf. also the responsum on the variant that reverses *Yehoyada ben Benayahu* with *Benayahu ben Yehoyada*, below in note 27. The questioner there too is Rabbi Elḥanan, and the responsum is attributed to Rabbi Sherira and Rabbi Hai "the head" (of the judicial court). This responsum was sent when Rabbi Sherira was old (990 c.e.), and it is therefore probable that Rabbi Hai authored it.

[15]So in the responsum cited by Abramson, although *Teshuvot Ge'onim Kadmonim* contain only two examples (that from *Berakhot* 61a is missing).

According to your own view, Asa built the cities, for it is written (2 Chronicles 14:5) "And Asa built the fortified cities which are in Yehuda!"[16] R. Eleazar answers, these cities were walled from the time of Joshua son of Nun. They were destroyed in the episode of the concubine at Givah, and Elpaal rebuilt them. The walls fell again, and Asa repaired them. This explanation fits the text well, as it is written (2 Chronicles 14:6) "And he said to Yehuda, Let us build these cities"—we see from this verse that these were cities beforehand.

Rabbi Hai was then asked: "It is also written in *Megillah*, 'This explanation fits the text well, as it is written *and Asa fortified ("vayhazzek Asa),'* but in all texts we read *and Asa built ("vayyiven Asa)."* According to the questioner, the Talmud's inference, that Asa was not the first to build the cities, is based entirely on the word *vayhazzek*, which is absent from MT.[17] Rabbi Hai prefaces his detailed discussion as follows[18]:

Understand that the Sages never erred about a text, for consider how much effort they exerted to avoid confusing the attribution of the teaching of one Sage with that of another, and each Sage took great care to quote his teacher verbatim; this is certainly true regarding Scripture. Therefore, you must examine each case in question to determine the reason for the variant: 1) If it is a scribal error, or 2) the students who transmitted the quotation were not well versed, or 3) it is not a direct quotation of an actual verse.

According to the Gaon, it is inconceivable that a Sage erred in his own citation of a verse. Dismissing the possibility that the Sage had a variant text before him,[19] he proposes three alternatives.

---

[16]Note that the text differs from MT. We are concerned below only with the variant noted by the questioner: *vayyiven/vayhazzek*.

[17]Indeed, ten manuscripts (of the thirteen manuscripts and printed editions enumerated in *Makhon ha-Talmud*) read *vayhazzek Asa*. Ten manuscripts continue: "This explanation fits into the text, for it is written *vayhazzek Asa*." In six manuscripts, it continues: "And it is not written *vayyiven*." See Rashi and *Dikdukei Soferim* ad loc. I would like to thank Rabbi Y. Hutner, head of *Makhon ha-Talmud ha-Yisraeli ha-Shalem* of Yad haRav Herzog in Jerusalem, and Rabbi A. Rothman, a staff member there, who generously gave me access to materials on textual variants in the Talmud for this study.

[18]Rabbi Hai's response to the question from *Berakhot* 61a is also absent from the MS cited by Abramson.

[19]See my quotation of Rabbi Hai below in note 27.

The first (scribal error) applies only when we are not dealing with a hermeneutical variant, as defined above. Such cases are not pertinent to our analysis.[20] The second (deficient transmission) is particularly fascinating. According to the Gaon, the citation from 2 Chronicles is the result of error. The mistake cannot be scribal, since the discussion in the Talmud presupposes the variant; it is the "composer" of the passage who erred. This "composer" cannot be an *Amora*, to whom such an error cannot be imputed, but rather unreliable pupils, who compounded misquotation by inventing a *derashah* on the nonexistent word *vayḥazzek*.[21] Presumably it was the unlikeliness of this explanation that deterred later rabbis from resorting to it when discussing similar cases.

The third proposal (indirect quotation of the verse) is particularly significant to our investigation. With respect to the three instances in our responsum, it is possible that Rabbi Hai intended this claim to resolve *Berakhot* 48a. If so, then Rabbi Hai is suggesting that although his version refers to Proverbs 4:8, "[some] Sage[s] cited the verse from Ben Sira."[22]

Conceivably[23] Rabbi Hai here makes use of an idea found in a different responsum.[24] There he was asked about the passage in *Bava Kamma*

---

[20]Actually, this possibility does not even affect the Gaon's response to the questions he was asked (unless he employs this argument to explain *Berakhot* 61a, which, as we have seen, is missing from the extant text).

[21]According to Rabbi Hai, there is no need for the *dayka nami* (this interpretation fits well into the verse), since according to the version in the printed editions, the text is in fact difficult. (Cf. also the versions of Rabbi Ḥananel and the Arukh, cited by Lewin in *Otzar ha-Ge'onim* on *Megillah* 4a, p. 6, n. 3.)

[22]Cf. Ben Sira, 11:1 in Segal edition: "The wisdom of a poor man will lift his head, *u-bein nedivim t[o]shivenu*." According to this reading (which is also that of the questioner), the talmudic passage continues as follows: "Do not read, *BNGYDYM*, but rather *BYN NGYDYM*." According to Rabbi Hai's reading, the Talmud follows the citation from Proverbs by saying *bein negidim*, which is essentially the interpretation of the verse in Proverbs.

[23]Cf. Rosenthal, p. 402, n. 39. If this is truly the proper interpretation of these issues, perhaps there is room to reason that Rabbi Hai intended to explain the quotation in *Berakhot* 61a and *Eruvin* 18b, "and Elkana walked after his wife" (a verse which does not exist in the MT) as the explication of the verse, based on the *derashah* that one's wife is called also "one's house" (cf. Aptowitzer, *Das Schriftwort*, pp. 68–69).

[24]*Teshuvot ha-Ge'onim Sha'arei Teshuvah*, ed. Leiter (1946), p. 12; and in a similar manner: *Teshuvot ha-Ge'onim Musafia* (Lyck, 1864), section 27.

92b, where the Talmud states that the source for an aphorism (which, in English, means: "A decayed palm tree usually grows next to barren foliage"[25]) is "the writings" (*Ketuvim*), although the verse is not found in the Hagiographa (*Ketuvim*). The Gaon responds that this verse is found in Ben Sira, and immediately adds: "However, our Sages often convey the sense of biblical verses in language other than that of Scripture." The allusion to "the writings" is in fact an interpretation of Proverbs 13:20, "He that walks with wise men shall be wise, but a companion of fools shall suffer harm." In other words, some apparent cases of hermeneutical variants are merely deliberate paraphrases of the biblical text. As we shall see below, some scholars generalized this argument, and adduced further evidence that the talmudic Sages frequently engaged in paraphrase in order to counter the inference that our Sages had variant texts.[26]

When Rabbi Hai states that the Sages were never mistaken about the text he is not necessarily ruling out the possibility that their text differed from the MT. He might instead be claiming confidently that no error would affect their citation of a verse or generate a *derashah* on the basis of a faulty verse. The assurance with which Rabbi Hai states his views implies, however, that he held the stronger position.[27]

---

[25]This translation is Rashi's interpretation of the maxim.

[26]Rabbi Hai himself adduced support for this phenomenon from *Bava Kamma* 81b. See below note 50.

[27]Rosenthal (pp. 402–403), who understood his words thus, asserts that Rabbi Hai's position influenced the approach of later eastern scribes, but we have no concrete evidence for this claim. A similar approach is found in a different responsum of Rabbi Hai. The Gaon was asked about the citation of 1 Chronicles 27:34 in *Berakhot* 3b–4a (and *Sanhedrin* 16a): "And after Aḥitofel was Benayahu ben Yehoyada" (it would appear that the *derashah* is based on this reading), while the MT reads "Yehoyada ben Benayahu." The Gaon responded that one should emend the biblical text in the Talmud in accordance with the MT, and he himself does this (cf. *Otzar ha-Ge'onim* on *Berakhot* 3b–4a, res., pp. 3–6; to *Sanhedrin* 16a, Toibish ed. [Jerusalem, 1967], pp. 137–138). Regarding the possibility raised by the questioners that "there are corruptions in our verses," the Gaon responds: "[it is impossible] that there are corruptions in the text, for all of Israel read these verses in the same manner."

On attribution of responsa to Rabbi Sherira and Rabbi Hai, see above note 14. It is noteworthy that the reading of the questioners, *Benayahu ben Yehoyada*, is found in most printed editions and in the manuscripts of Makhon ha-Talmud on these two talmudic passages; and Rashi, too, had that reading.

Tosafot exerted a decisive effect on the *Rishonim* and *Aharonim* by noting three instances where the Talmud diverges from our versions of the *masorah*.[28] Since then, it has become a commonplace of rabbinic literature that our Sages occasionally had textual variants.[29] *Rishonim* and *Aharonim* have added to the list in Tosafot,[30] both from the Talmud and from elsewhere in rabbinic literature.[31] Whether one should emend our texts based on the *derashot*, or let the MT (or the text of the majority of manuscripts) stand, became an issue of serious concern.[32]

---

[28]*Shabbat* 55b, s.v. *M'BYRM ketiv*, and *Nidda* 33a, s.v. *ve-hanissa ketiv*.

[29]Some of these rabbis are listed (although for a slightly different purpose) by L. Bardowicz, *Studien zur Geschichte der Orthographie des Althebräischen* (Frankfurt am Main 1894), pp. 50–55. To that list one should add, for example: Rabbi Menahem ha-Meiri (*Kiryat Sefer* [see note 6 above], 57, col. 2–58, col. 1); Ran (novellae to *Sanhedrin* 4b, *KRNT KRNT KRNWT*); Rabbi Moshe Halava (S. Asaf, *Mekorot u-Mehkarim be-Toledot Yisrael* [Jerusalem, 1946], p. 184); Rabbi Shimon b. Tzemah Duran—Rashbatz (*Tashbatz*, vol. 3, res. 160, Lemberg edition, 1881, p. 27d); Rabbi Y. Mintz (*Responsa of Mahari Mintz and Maharam Padua*, res. 8, Cracow edition, 1872, p. 14a–b).

[30]Specifically, Rabbi Akiva Eiger in his *Gillayon ha-Shas*, *Shabbat* 55b and Rabbi Yeshaya Pik Berlin in his *Haflaa she-ba-Arakhin*, *m'h*, and in various glosses printed in the margins of printed Talmuds (see also his note in *Haflaa she-ba-Arakhin*, '*gn*) list many examples.

[31]Several *Aharonim* included textual variants from the Zohar. See, for example, *Responsa of Radbaz*, vol. 3, res. 1172 (101) (Warsaw, 1882), p. 28a (also in his comments at the end of the responsum cited in note 6 above). S. Y. Norzi in his *Minhat Shai* referred often to the Zohar instances when dealing with this issue. He was influenced by Rabbi Meir Azariah mi-Pano and by Rabbi Menahem de Lonzano. See below, end of note 50.

[32]Ramah, in his *Masoret Seyag la-Torah* (Florence, 1750; reprint, Tel Aviv, 1969) did emend the text in certain places based on *derashot*, comments on Genesis 25:6 (entry on *pilegesh*, p. 55a): "'And to the children of Abraham's concubines—In all accurate editions to which we have access, it [*HPYLGShYM*] is spelled with two *yods*; moreover, they [i.e., the masoretes] noted that this spelling of the word is unique in the Torah [in having both *yods*]. However, the *derasha* identifies Hagar with Ketura from the fact that it is written *HPYLGShM*, without a *yod* before the final *mem*. Hence we learn that the proper spelling is without that *yod*."

Consider Rabbi Menahem de Lonzano's reaction (*Or Torah* on the verse, p. 6b): "Ramah also noticed that in all accurate editions available to us, there

Despite the consensus regarding the general principle, it must be emphasized that the number of variants about which the rabbis concur is modest,[33] and most of them are distinctions of *male' ve-ḥaser*.[34] Since the Talmud itself concedes that "we are not experts" with regard to *male' ve-ḥaser*,[35] it was easy for later rabbis to acknowledge this category. This principle is particularly pertinent to *derashot* arising from these variants, such as YShKVN KTYV, HPYLGShM KTYV, and others like them— *derashot* where the textual divergence is hard to deny.[36] Yet, there are those who posit the existence of more substantial textual variants.

---

are two *yods*, and the Masoretic note indicates that this is the only place in the Torah where it is spelled in this manner. Despite all this, he still follows the reading of the *derashah* which says that there is no [second] *yod*. And he therefore acted and wrote it in his book without the *yod*, according to what we were told." Rabbi Abraham Bakrat draws the surprising conclusion that Ramah relied on precise manuscripts over the Midrash (*Sefer Zikkaron*, ad. loc., ed. M. Philip [Petaḥ Tikvah, 5738], 135).

Rashba (see above, note 6) established the principle that "the variants found in the Talmud which affect laws ... certainly should be altered" (regarding this reading of Rashba, see J. S. Penkower, "Textus 9 [1981], pp. 40–41, n. 3. It is cited also in *Orḥot Ḥayyim* [ms.], noted by S. Z. Havlin, *Alei Sefer* 12 [1986], p. 22, n. 102), and many rabbis accepted his position (see, for example, Meiri in note 6 above, p. 59 col. 2 [and cf. *Bet ha-Beḥirah*, *Kiddushin* 30a, A. Sofer ed. (Jerusalem, 1963), p. 178]; Rashbatz in note 29 above; Radbaz in notes 6 and 31).

In the final analysis, however, the rabbis determined that one should not emend the MT (i.e., that found in the majority of mss.), even where it is clear from the content of the *derashah* that our Sages had a different reading, and even in those cases from which laws are derived. See my discussion of the halakhic status of variant texts.

[33] And if we set aside those collected by Rabbi Akiva Eiger and Rabbi Yeshaya Pik Berlin, the number is negligible.

[34] *Yad Malakhi*, pt. 1, letter *ḥet*, para. 283 (Berlin, 1856, p. 63): "Certainly *male' ve-ḥaser* cases such as M'BYRM ... WHNS' ... HPYLGShM ... KLT Moshe, and others in this category. ... We see that it is acceptable to admit a divergence between the Talmud, Midrash, or Zohar and the MT. ... But when there are differences of verses or words, it seems unlikely that such an error crept into all of our texts or that there is a variant reading."

[35] *Kiddushin* 30a.

[36] As to those who disputed even this type of case, see below.

Take one of the three instances cited by Tosafot (*Shabbat* 55b): "We found in the Jerusalem Talmud (*Sotah* 1:8, 17b) that Samson 'judged Israel for forty years' [although another verse gives his term as twenty years]. This teaches that the Philistines feared him twenty years after his death as they had during his lifetime. In all of our texts, however, it is written 'twenty years.'"[37] This discussion clearly recognizes significant discrepancies between the text analyzed by the Talmud and that of the MT.[38]

It is crucial to note that the same rabbis generally seek to minimize the actual number of variants, even *male' ve-ḥaser*.[39] They resort to various explanations—often forced[40]—even when they could have appealed easily to their own principle, namely, that the Talmud's reading is different from the MT. Here, too, Tosafot set the standard.[41] Only in recent gen-

---

[37]Cf. Judges 15:20, 16:31. We will return to this case later. Rabbi Yeshaya Pik Berlin, in *Haflaa she-ba-Ararkhin*, m'h cites the variant, *Yehoyada ben Benayahu*—*Benayahu ben Yehoyada* (above, note 27) as an example where the reading of the Talmud is inconsistent with the MT. This is hardly a "minor" difference.

[38]The idea of textual variants in our context is mentioned by Rashba cited earlier. Compare this to the formulation of Radbaz (cited in note 6): "However, there arose discrepancies between the Talmud and the rabbis of the Masora in many places, such as PYLGShYM—PYLGShM, KLWT—KLT, and many others. Likewise, there are textual conflicts on legal matters, both in capital law and monetary." Cf. also the *Responsa of R. Yitzhak bar Sheshet* (Rivash), 284.

Rabbi Yeshaya Pik Berlin, in his *Haflaa she-ba-Arakhin*, m'h cites several examples from the Talmud (e.g., *Megillah* 15b), where the question is based on a verse, and the respondent (generally Rabbi Naḥman b. Yitzḥak) states that there is no question, since the word is written *ḥaser*. Rabbi Berlin comments: "It is conceivable that in all of these instances, the questioner had before him the reading which he cites, and R. Naḥman b. Yitzḥak (or the *setam Talmud*) responds that the correct reading is such and such (i.e., *ḥaser*), and not as the questioner cites it."

According to this, many arguments in the Talmud itself are based on disputes over the proper reading of Scripture. Regarding this issue, cf. the "conservative" words of S. Lieberman, *Hellenism in Jewish Palestine* (New York, 1950, p. 47, n. 1).

[39]Cf. *Tosafot Sanhedrin* 4b, s.v. *LTTPT LTTPT LTWTPWT* (cf. also *Zevaḥim* 37b; *Menaḥot* 34b), and *Tosafot Menaḥot* 39a, s.v. *Lo Yifhot*.

[40]Cf., for example, *Tosafot Arakhin* 18b, s.v. *u-peduyav mibben ḥodesh va-mala*.

[41]From the fact that Tosafot, unlike Rabbi Hai, acknowledged that the Talmud sometimes conflicts with our texts, Rosenthal (p. 401) wanted to conclude

erations have scholars changed direction, vastly increasing the total number of variants.[42] More important, they have identified many variants, affecting the meaning of the text, which would not have been discovered, for example, by merely contrasting the various Masoretic manuscripts.[43]

Tosafot's view, that rabbinic texts of the Bible are not always identical with the MT, was not universally accepted. Rabbi Menaḥem Azaria mi-Pano[44] and Rabbi Menaḥem de Lonzano are noteworthy among late medieval rabbis.[45] Among later rabbis, we may include Shemuel

---

that "it would appear that there is a fundamental difference between oriental and occidental rabbinic traditions." However, from what we have seen above, it is difficult to support the assertion that the western rabbis have a uniform position.

[42]See Aptowitzer's bibliographical notes. His book is the most outstanding example of this phenomenon.

[43]Cf. M. Cohen, "Some Basic Features of the Consonantal Text in Medieval Manuscripts of the Hebrew Bible," in *Iyyunei Mikra u-Parshanut* (*Studies in Bible and Exegesis—Arie Toeg in Memoriam*), ed. M. Goshen-Gottstein and U. Simon (Ramat-Gan: Bar-Ilan University 1980), p. 126 and n. 11.

[44]See his essays: *Shivrei Luḥot* (with *Yemin ha-Shem Romema*), (Safed, 1864; reprint, Israel, 1985), pp. 5b–7b (for similar language, changed order, and abridgment, see also *Yonat Elem* [Lvov, 1959], chapter 99); *Me'ah Kesita* (Munkatch, 1892), 72 (p. 38, cols. 2–3); *Em Kol Ḥai*, pt. 2, 35, in *Sefer Eser Maamarot*, reprint (Jerusalem, 1983), p. 42a–b. We have cited him, despite the limited scope of his words, because of his influence upon S. Y. Norzi's *Minḥat Shai*. Cf. J. S. Penkower, *Jacob Ben Ḥayyim and the Rise of the Biblia Rabbinica*, (Ph.D. Thesis, Hebrew University 1982), pp. 43–44, 318–319.

[45]His view is expressed several times in his essay, *Or Torah*, the central section in his book, *Shtei Yadot* (reprint, Jerusalem, 1970), pp. 3b–26b. Generally speaking, he rarely admits the existence of biblical variants in rabbinic literature. The characteristics of his approach are as follows: (1) He suggests forced interpretations to the rabbinic texts in order to reconcile them with the MT. (Cf., e.g., his remarks quoted above near note 9; S. Y. Norzi, in several places in *Minḥat Shai*, and Rabbi Shelomo Ganzfried in his glosses to *Keset ha-Sofer* [also called *Lishkat ha-Sofer*].) (2) He adopts the principle of the *Raaya Mehemna* (see note 50 below), stating that "one should not rely on Midrashim based on *male' ve-ḥaser* when they differ from the MT" (p. 6b, on "It is written *HPYLGShM*"). Although Lonzano limits the scope of the principle taken from *Raaya Mehemna* regarding *male' ve-ḥaser* (cf. p. 20a on the small yod in *Pineḥas*—Numbers 25:11), he eliminates, in effect, virtually all cases of hermeneutical variants.

Waldberg,[46] Simḥa Reuven ben-Ḥayil Edelman,[47] and, finally, the formidable Ḥayyim Heller.[48] These rabbis assert that all[49] those *derashot* that—according to Tosafot and their followers—contain a textual variant, could be adequately explained on the basis of the received text if only we understood the principles of *derash* ("the methods of the Talmud") operative in rabbinic literature. In other words, every *derashah* that appears to exhibit a contextual variant from the MT may be harmonized with the MT by showing that our Sages employed the "methods of the Talmud" to abridge, add to, and intermix verses, to switch consonants (and vowels), and even to cite (and base *derashot* on) paraphrased verses, in the light of their (simple or midrashic) intent.[50]

---

[46]In *Darkhei ha-Shinuyim* (Lemberg, 1870; reprint, Jerusalem, 1970). This work deals only with *derashot* based on letter variants; notwithstanding, we may still learn from his general outlook (not to mention that most *derashot* with apparent discrepancies from the MT are based on letter variants). Waldberg does admit that a few examples cited by Rabbi Akiva Eiger attest to a variant Talmudic reading. Cf. p. 25a of his book.

[47]In *Mesillot Kol Benei Ḥalof*, the first section of his book, *Mesillot* (Vilna, 1875), pp. 1–57; *Taar ha-Sofer* (a critical study of S. Rosenfeld's *Mishpaḥat Soferim* [Vilna, 1883]), in *Ha-Kerem*, ed. A. Atlas (Warsaw, 1888), pp. 225–256; cf. also his article, *Et Lifrotz ve-et Livnot*, in *Ha-Karmel*, section *Ha-Sharon*, vol. 4 (1864), no. 13, *et seq.*

[48]His comments are scattered throughout his works, especially in the glosses to his Peshitta edition (in Hebrew characters) to Genesis (Berlin, 1927) and Exodus (Berlin, 1929), and in the appendix to his study on The Septuagint References in Mandellian's Concordance, in the *Hekhal ha-Kodesh Concordance* (New York, 1943), which is devoted to our topic (pp. 54–67).

[49]It is possible that some of the scholars in this list admit a few variants (cf. my comments on Lonzano and Waldberg above); nevertheless, the forced answers which they present in order to avoid saying that the reading in the Talmud is inconsistent with the MT (and, *ipso facto*, the scant number of variants to which they concede) justify their inclusion in this group.

[50]On two occasions, the Talmud itself attests to citation based on intent. The first is discussed by Rabbi Hai (already discussed in notes 24, 26). There, the Talmud states that the quotation cited (*Baba Kamma* 81b = *Berakhot* 30a) is not from an actual verse ("*alav ha-katuv omer mihyot tov al tikre ra*"); rather, it conveys the meaning of a different verse, namely, Proverbs 3:27. The second instance, in *Berakhot* 55b, states that "all dreams [are fulfilled] according to their interpretations." The Talmud understands this to be the lesson derived from Genesis 41:13, where it says, "and it came to pass, that as he had interpreted for

Most of these methods were already noted, in connection with textual variants, by the Tosafists themselves, and were elaborated by the later rabbis, both *Rishonim* and *Aharonim*, who followed the Tosafists.[51]

---

us, so it was." (R. Z. H. Chajes, in his introduction to the Talmud, end of chapter 30 [*Kol Sifrei Maharatz Chajes*, vol. 1 (Jerusalem, 1958), p. 341b], attempted to include a third example, from *Baba Metzia* 110b, but that case does not appear to be a proof.)

Based on these two examples, many scholars have asserted that it is impossible to base a textual variant on a Midrash, since the "variant" might have been invented by the *darshan* in order to explicate either the meaning or to paraphrase the verse. The truth, however, is that these two examples are clearly labeled; moreover, these examples reflect a popular expression, and we therefore have no right to derive general principles of *derash* from them. It is quite another matter when a cited verse is accompanied by an explanation suited to its context (e.g., *Bava Kamma* 119a cites from Job 27:17, "*Yakhin [rasha] ve-tzaddik yilbash*").

Additionally, Aptowitzer (p. 27) correctly pointed out that we must also consider the art of the *darshan*, which might lead him to alter the text, in order, for example, to highlight a contrast. However, the example that he provides, from *Sanhedrin* 93b, referring to 1 Samuel 14:47 ("Of Saul the verse reads . . . *yarshia*, whereas of David, it is written . . . *yatzliah*." Cf. 1 Samuel 18:14, which reads, "and David was successful [*maskil*] in all his ways), is problematic since it is absent from all mss. in Makhon ha-Talmud and appears only in the Venice 1520 edition.

In this context, Lonzano, Norzi (e.g., *Minhat Shai* on Numbers 7:1), and others have quoted the *Raaya Mehemna* (on *Pinehas*, p. 254a) to explain the *derashah* "it is written KLT" (see below, note 53), which is inconsistent with the MT. The *Raaya Mehemna* writes that our Sages detracted from, added to, and altered (words and letters) in their *derashot*, and were unconcerned with the actual reading of the text. From this statement, many rabbis concluded that our Sages (i.e., the *Raaya Mehemna*) taught us that one may not infer anything regarding the actual biblical text from rabbinic literature.

[51]Cf., for example, Rabbi Yeshuah Halevi's *Halikhot Olam*, *shaar* 2 (Warsaw, 1883; reprint, Jerusalem, 1960), p. 15a, and his commentators Rabbi Yosef Karo (*Kelalei ha-Gemara*) and Rabbi Shelomo Algazi (*Yavin Shemuah*). *MinhatShai* contains many references (cf., for example, his comments to 1 Chronicles 5:24, where he also lists other references found throughout his work), as does *Ben Yohai*, by Moshe Kunitz of Uban, (Vienna, 1715), *shaar* 7. (Kunitz there responds to Rabbi Yaakov Emden's claim [in his book *Mitpahat Sefarim*] about the late authorship of the Zohar, based on the fact that the Zohar often cites verses inaccurately. Kunitz attempts to prove that these "deviations" are found in the Talmud also, and, based on his vast erudition in the Talmud, he tries to explain

Aptowitzer classified and analyzed some of these principles.[52] Because Heller and those sharing his view staked out such an extreme position, they did not get a full, serious hearing; nevertheless, they provide a counterpoint to those who think (in our opinion, correctly) that many *derashot* in rabbinic literature reflect textual variants.

It cannot be denied that the Sages, in formulating *derashot*, occasionally take great liberties, even when they do not resort to *al tikre* and similar formulas. Conceivably one can explain apparent textual variants using the principles of *derash*. In order to avoid recognizing textual variants, Heller and those sharing his view occasionally broadened these principles of *derash* to the point where the *derashot* of our Sages became little more than "free play" with Scripture. Even *derashot* prefaced by the word *ketiv* (it is written),[53] indicating that the *derashah* is based on orthography, Heller describes as examples of free play, which have no implications for determining the text. To quote Heller:

> All of these [*derashot*] and others, introduced by the word *ketiv*, differ from the previous two methods of *derashah* [i.e., a routine *derasha* and those with *al tikre*—Y.M.], only in their external form. The term *ketiv* does not indicate divergence from the text, but rather means, 'make a *derashah* (as if it were so written).'... However, many of our great rabbis did not understand this and therefore encountered difficulties to the point where they decided that the lection of the Talmud was different from our own.[54]

And while discussing Genesis 25:6, where the rabbis seemed to infer[55] from the defective spelling of the word HPYLGShM (without a *yod* after the *shin*), that only one *pilegesh* (concubine) is referred to, Heller writes:

> The truth is that this is not so, since our Sages never had a variant text here; rather, this is merely a method of *derash*—in order to furnish the aggada, that

---

the "deviations" in the Zohar as a typical method of the Talmud. Cf. also Y. Tishbi, *Mishnat ha-Zohar*, vol. 1 [Jerusalem: Bialik Press, 1949], p. 68.)

[52]pp. 21–28.

[53]See Genesis 25:6, *Genesis Rabbah* 61:4 (Theodor-Albeck edition, p. 661). Also *Numbers* 7:1, *Numbers Rabbah* 12:8 (Vilna 48b). There are many such examples.

[54]*The Septuagint*, (above n. 48) 60.

[55]Cf., e.g., Ramah's remarks cited in note 32 above.

Abraham had only one concubine (Hagar and Keturah being identical), with scriptural basis. . . . When they said "it is written," they meant this only as an external sign for a *derashah*, like cases of *al tikre* and routine *derashot* where they did not stress their exegetical device.

Where our versions of the Midrash explicitly state that a word is written *ḥaser* (defective)[56] or the like, the Heller position maintains that this is a scribal interpolation.[57]

Because there are so many facets to *derash* methodology, a scholar might ascribe a certain *derashah* to a textual variant, while another might validly argue against that conclusion. Hence, this issue naturally makes for polar opposition, even when the existence of rabbinic variants is accepted in principle. The following is one of many such examples.

The wise son, in the famous "four children" passage of the Passover *Haggadah*, quotes Deuteronomy 6:20, "What mean the testimonies, and the statutes, and the judgements, which the Lord our God has commanded you?" The wicked son's question is based on Exodus 12:26, "What is this service to you?" Why, ask the commentators, is the wicked child stigmatized for saying "to you" (*lakhem*), thus excluding himself from the group; does not the wise child too detach himself from the group by saying "you" (*etkhem*)? The usual answer is that the wise child's reference to God expresses his sense of solidarity with the group.[58]

Well-known variations on this passage are found in *Mekhilta of R. Yishmael*, *Masekhta de-Pisḥa* 18 (p. 73), and in *J. T. Pesaḥim* 10:4 (7d). In many manuscripts of Mekhilta, the Jerusalem Talmud, and various

---

[56]Cf., e.g., Rashi's reading of Genesis 25:6.

[57]It is interesting to note that S. Z. Schick, in *Torah Shelemah* (Satmar, 1909), troubled by the fact that Tosafot (*Shabbat* 55b) "openly" aver that the Talmud is inconsistent with our books, suggests that "either an errant student or a student of Balaam wrote these words in the margin, and the printers, either by mistake or out of ignorance, incorporated them in Tosafot" (p. 126a).

[58]I. H. Weiss, in his edition of the *Mekhilta*, offers a different explanation: "The wise child acknowledges his obligations, and asks only regarding the nature of these commandments. 'What are the testimonies,' in effect, means 'what is their meaning. . . .' However, the child who asks about the service, 'what are these to you,' asks in essence 'what purpose is there in this service,' thereby scorning those who are doing the service." Clearly, this interpretation is sermonic and devoid of any linguistic basis.

texts of the *Haggadah*, the wise child says "us" (*otanu*), and not "you" (*etkhem*), and this version is reflected in LXX and the Vulgate on Deuteronomy 6:20. For Abrahams,[59] this *derashah* was perhaps the most interesting of the many variants in the Mekhilta. Goldschmidt, by contrast, in his edition of the Passover *Haggadah*, suggests that "the reading, 'which the Lord our God has commanded us' (*otanu*), in the wise child's question, was deliberately inserted in place of the original reading (*etkhem*), to eliminate the problem posed by the lack of difference between the wise child's question and that of the wicked child."[60]

Medieval rabbis also disagree about the rabbinic text of Isaiah 43:14: "Thus says the Lord . . . for your sake I have sent (*shillaḥti*) to Babylonia." *Mekhilta* of Rabbi Yishmael, *Masekhta de-Pisḥa* 14 (pp. 51–52), expounds: "Where Israel is exiled, the Divine Presence, so to speak, is exiled too. . . . They were exiled to Bavel, the Divine Presence accompanied them, as it is written, 'For your sake I was sent (*shullaḥti*) to Bavel.'"[61] Ibn Ezra on this verse writes: "The phrase means: 'I [God] came hastily, as if I were sent.'" Radak (ad loc.) is perplexed by this explanation, implying that Ibn Ezra had the reading *shullaḥti*. Radak's received tradition was *shillaḥti* (vocalized with a *ḥirik*, in *pi'el* conjugation), which he found in all reliable manuscripts he had examined. Yet he acknowledges that the rabbinic *derashah* reflects the vocalization *shullaḥti*. The same is true of Abarbanel.[62]

---

[59]I. Abrahams, "Rabbinic Aids to Exegesis," in *Essays on Some Biblical Questions of the Day*, ed. H. B. Swete (London, 1909), pp. 174–175. Compare to H. L. Ginsberg, "The Dead Sea Manuscript Finds: New Light on Eretz Yisrael in the Greco-Roman Period," in *Israel, Its Role and Civilization*, ed. M. Davies (1956), pp. 56–57.

[60]In this case, one should not rule out the possibility that the rabbis were not quoting the biblical text verbatim. See the comments of R. M. M. Kasher in *Haggadah Shelemah* (New York, 1961), p. 121; and cf. D. Z. Hoffmann's remarks cited there from *Bet Vaad la-Hakhamim* 1:3 (5662); 17.

[61]In two manucripts (designated *aleph* and *kaf*) this passage is quoted with the defective consonantal reading of the MT. In several rabbinic parallels, however, not only is the *derashah* based on *shullaḥti* (*pu'al* form); it is also spelled *plene* (see HUBP, on this verse).

[62]Cf. Rabbi Shemuel Yafe Ashkenazi's commentary, *Yefeh Mareh* (a commentary and novellae on *aggadot* in the JT), on *Taanit* 1:1 (Berlin, 1625–26 [reprint, Ramat-Gan, 1984], vol. 1, p. 110a): "It appears that they had a tradition which read *shullaḥti*, even though it is not so in our versions." Cf. the interesting comment of Rabbi Abraham Bakrat (*Sefer Zikkaron* to Genesis 40:11, p. 176).

In contrast, Rabbi Yosef Kimhi, Radak's father,[63] writes of the reading, *shullahti* (in *pual* conjugation): "This reading never existed, for the word is vocalized with a *hirik*. Rather, our rabbis made a *derashah* in this manner." So too Rabbi Shelomo Yedidyah Norzi in his *Minhat Shai* (ad loc): "I am convinced that all the Midrashim had the text *shillahti*, as it is written in our books. . . . They read *shullahti* in the manner of *derash*, similar to the style of *al tikre*."

Because the list of Midrash-based textual variants (of the hermeneutical variety), compiled by the Hebrew University Bible Project (HUBP),[64] is rather liberal, the HUBP list of rabbinically based textual variants requires scrutiny. Our ability to obtain secure results depends upon several factors. How often is the hermeneutical variant attested in midrashic literature?[65] What may be learned from the midrashic parallels? Must we distort the simple sense of the Midrash in order to harmonize it with the MT? Then we must consider the accepted sources for textual criticism: is the variant attested in the ancient versions or in Hebrew manuscripts? What are the characteristics of the variant? These and other questions must be weighed into this discussion.

I hope to explore the usefulness of comparing variants with ancient versions and Hebrew manuscripts in a future study. Here, I shall limit myself to the evaluation of midrashic parallels. Professor M. Goshen[66] remarked that the HUBP, by definition, did not adduce evidence in favor of the MT, that is, the list includes variants from rabbinic literature, but not those midrashic passages that agree with the MT. When we speak of a hermeneutical variant, we ordinarily mean one found in all midrashic parallels. Where parallel rabbinic texts differ among themselves, this data may affect our judgment as to whether a particular Midrash attests to variants, or whether it merely reflects the operation of legitimate

---

[63]*Sepher ha-Galuj*, ed. H. J. Mathews (Berlin, 1887), p. 20. He is cited by Heller, *The Septuagint*, pp. 22–23 (see note 48 above).

[64]On the apparatus for annotating rabbinic variations, see Goshen (n. 6 above), sections 64ff., p. 35.

[65]For example, it is quite common to find Midrashim based on the interchangeability of the letters *heh* and *het*. This is not the case for substituting the letters *tet* and *tav* (cf., for example, *Numbers Rabbah* 5:6, Vilna 16d), where the *derashah* on Isaiah 48:9 interprets the word *AHTM* as though it were written with a *tav* instead of the *tet*.

[66]See n. 6 above, sec. 65, p. 35.

methods of *derash*. Let us consider an example already referred to in passing.

Earlier we mentioned that *Tosafot Shabbat* 55b quoted *Sotah* 1:8 (17b) as an instance where "our Talmud is inconsistent with our texts." The *derashah* in the Jerusalem Talmud (Venice edition) reads: "One verse states 'and he [Samson] judged Israel forty years,' and another verse reads 'and he judged Israel twenty years.' Rabbi Aḥa says, this teaches that the Philistines feared Samson twenty years after his death as they had during the twenty years of his life." Clearly, the two verses in their biblical text read "forty years" and "twenty years," respectively. In the MT, however, both Judges 15:20 and Judges 16:31 read "twenty years."

Despite Tosafot, several scholars tried to reconcile the Jerusalem Talmud with the MT; they proposed that the extra twenty years are derived from the repetition in Judges 16:31. Some adduced support from the midrashic "parallel" in Numbers *Rabbah* 14:9 (Vilna, 61b), on the verse (Numbers 7:71) "and for a sacrifice of peace offerings, two oxen," brought by the *nasi* of Dan:

> Another explanation: These correspond to the two references where it is written that he judged Israel for twenty years, namely, 'and he judged Israel in the days of the Philistines twenty years,' 'and he judged Israel twenty years.' This teaches you that he judged Israel for twenty years of his life, and that for twenty years after his death, the Philistines remained in fear of Samson and sat quietly.

The parallel in *Numbers Rabbah*, however, does not explain the language of the Jerusalem Talmud in Tosafot's version of it, which also appears in our own versions. Even substituting "twenty" for "forty" in the Jerusalem Talmud is not a satisfactory remedy.[67] The *Numbers Rabbah* text, agreeing with MT, is an independent source, neither cognate to our source in the Jerusalem Talmud, nor a later formulation of it.

Though comparisons of midrashic parallels are critical for analyses of midrashic sources, they are frequently misapplied. If one midrashic parallel agrees with the MT, many scholars are satisfied that the other parallels may also be harmonized with the MT.[68] In such instances, how-

---

[67]Cf. Aptowitzer, *Das Schriftwort*, p. 380.
[68]Cf. Heller, *The Septuagint*, pp. 62–65.

ever, each source must be examined independently. Often a parallel reflects the emendation of a later editor (sometimes even the copyist) who, having found the *derashah* problematic, attempted to "correct" it, as in the following example.

Isaiah 1:21: "It was full of (*mele'ati*) judgement; righteousness lodged in it, but now murderers." Edelman[69] examined the *derashah* in *Lamentations Rabbah* 2:4 (Vilna 21a): "There were 480 synagogues in Jerusalem, equal to *ML'TY*, which is spelled *MLTY*." Ostensibly, this reflects not the MT *ML'TY* (which equals 481), but rather the reading *MLTY* (without an *aleph*, equalling 480). Based on one parallel in *Yalkut Shimoni* (2:390), which actually reads "481," and another in *Lamentations Rabbah, Proem* 12 (Vilna 3c), which reads "in addition to the Temple, the numerical value of *mele'ati* is this" (i.e., 481),[70] Edelman concluded that the original version of the Midrash (in *Lamentations Rabbah* 2:4) spoke of 480 synagogues besides the Temple, for a combined total of 481, the numerical value of *ML'TY*—according to the MT.

Everything we know about the methods of redaction by editors and copyists, however, indicates that the process worked in the opposite direction. The original Midrash discussed 480 synagogues, and was based on the reading *MLTY*. A subsequent version of the biblical text, *ML'TY*, yielded a new number; the editor (or copyist) then emended the Midrash in order to reconcile it with the MT.[71]

In textual criticism, as in any investigation, there exist certain established disciplinary guidelines. In most cases, however, the evidence is ambiguous, so that in the end, "good judgment determines"[72] the verdict, as is the case in the following example. Isaiah 58:7 reads, "Is it not to share (*PRS*) your bread with the hungry." In a discussion of applicants for charity (*Bava Batra* 9a): "Rabbi Huna says: Applicants for food are investigated, but not applicants for clothes. . . . If you prefer a basis in Scripture, 'Is it not to share your bread with the hungry,' *PRWS BShY"N KTYV* [so that it could be read *parosh*-examine]; investigate and then give to him. Later it is written, 'When you see the naked, that

---

[69]*Ha-Mesillot*, p. 23.

[70]Parallels to this *derashah* are listed in the HUBP.

[71]Cf. the note in HUBP.

[72]This language is used by Ibn Ezra, in his introduction to the commentary on the Torah, sec. 3.

you cover him,' that is to say, immediately." According to Rashi, *s.v. parwsh*, the *derashah* is based on the reading *PR(W)Sh*, meaning investigation and clarification: before giving to a hungry person, investigate first. See also the gloss of Rabbi Isaiah Pik Berlin on the margins of the page and in *Haflaa she-ba-Arakhin, m'h*, asserting that the Talmud's version differs from the MT, where the word is spelled with a *samekh* rather than a *sin*.

Ramah (*Yad Ramah*, ad loc.) is reluctant to accept this interpretation, since "we see that this word is spelled with a *samekh* in all accurate texts." According to Ramah, Rabbi Huna derived the *derashah* from the semantics of the word *paros* (instead of the more usual *naton*). *Paros* implies that we dole out a slice (*perusah*) of bread pending verification that he has no other food; only after this investigation do we give him a larger gift.

Saul Lieberman[73] noticed that the words, *BShY"N KTYV* are missing from the manuscripts, and therefore concludes that "the most reasonable interpretation appears to be found in *Yad Ramah* ad loc. . . . . . Indeed, the *derashah* is based on the reading of *paros* with a *samekh*. The unusual spelling of *paros* with a *samekh* teaches that initially, one should give the poor person only a slice (*perusah*) of bread."

He adds, "nevertheless, there is still room for doubt, since the talmudic manuscripts . . . spell the word with a *shin*." To this we may add two points: (1) The talmudic manuscripts cite the word with a *shin* twice, once in the name of Rabbi Huna cited above and once in the name of Rabbi Yehuda in the continuation; (2) In four manuscripts, immediately following the citation, the Talmud explains, "it is written *parosh*" [with a *shin*]. Thus we have less reason than Lieberman to be doubtful that the original was spelled with a *shin*. The replacement of *sin* with *samekh* is well attested in rabbinic literature. The fact that the manuscripts retain the *shin* is adequate evidence that the Sages of the Talmud had the reading of *paros* with a *shin*; we therefore prefer Rashi's explication.

My last example is one that I find particularly troubling. The obscure verse (Isaiah 5:17), "Then shall the lambs feed as in their pasture" (*ve-ra'u khevasim ke-dovram—KDVRM*) is expounded in *Lamentations Rabbah* 1:33 (on *Lamentations* 1:6; Vilna 15b) as follows: "'Her princes were like gazelles' (*hayu sareha ke-ayyalim*)—Rabbi Yehuda says, when they are young, they are likened to lambs, as it says 'then shall the lambs

---

[73]In *He'arot le-Maamaro shel Y. Kutscher mi-Be'ayot ha-Milonut*, in *Meḥkarim be-Torat Eretz Yisrael*, ed. D. Rosenthal (Jerusalem, 1991), p. 507.

feed as in their pasture (*KDVRM*),' and when they are old, they are likened to gazelles, as it is written, 'her princes were like gazelles.'"

The second half of this Midrash is comprehensible—"gazelle" (*ayyal*) is also a term for power. How, though, did the word *rakkim* ("soft," meaning young) become entwined with the lambs (*kevasim*)? I suggested to the editor of the HUBP Isaiah edition that this *derashah* may be based on the reading *KDRKM* (instead of *KDVRM*), which could then be divided midrashically into *KD RKYM*, when they are soft and young.[74]

II

HALAKHIC STATUS OF VARIANT TEXTS[75]

As mentioned above, Ramah, in his *Masoret Seyag la-Torah* emended the text in certain places based on *derashot*. He writes on Genesis 25:6:

> "And to the children of Abraham's concubines"—In all accurate editions to which we have access, it (*HPYLGShYM*) is spelled with two *yods*; moreover, they [i.e., the transmitters of the MT] noted that this spelling of the word is unique in the Torah (in having both *yods*). However, the *derashah* identifies Hagar with Keturah from the fact that it is written *HPYLGShM*, without a *yod* before the final *mem*. Hence we learn that the correct spelling is without that *yod*.

Consider Rabbi Menaḥem de Lonzano's reaction (*Or Torah* on the verse, p. 6b): "Ramah also noticed that in all careful editions, there are two *yods*, and the Masoretic note indicates that this is the only place in the Torah where it is spelled in this manner. Despite all this, he still follows the reading of the *derashah* according to which there is no [sec-

---

[74]See M. Goshen-Gottstein, ed., *The Book of Isaiah, Sample Edition with Introduction* (Jerusalem: Magnes Press, 1965) on this verse.

[75]In writing this section, I am especially grateful to my friend Professor S. Z. Leiman for sharing with me his ideas and knowledge. The fourth reason listed below was suggested by Leiman, and is the one that he feels to be the most important. Note 80 below is based primarily on his work.

ond] *yod*. And he thus decided and wrote it in his book without the *yod*, according to what we were told."

Rashba established the principle that "the variants found in the Talmud which affect law . . . certainly should be altered," and many rabbis accepted his position.[76] In the final analysis, however, the rabbis determined that one should not emend the MT (i.e., the majority of manuscripts), even where it is clear from the content of the *derashah* that our Sages had a different reading, and even in those cases from which laws are derived.

Why did Rashba's unambiguous position virtually disappear from the halakhic horizon? Various explanations are worthy of consideration; perhaps all have an element of truth in them.

1. Rabbi S.Y. Norzi's position in his *Minhat Shai* may have been a factor. He himself was influenced by Rabbi Meir Azariah mi-Pano and Rabbi Menahem de Lonzano, and especially by the *Raaya Mehemna* section of the Zohar, all of whom state that rabbinic textual witnesses are not sufficiently authoritative to override the MT/the majority of manuscripts.[77] *Minhat Shai* comments on Leviticus 4:34: "Wherever the Gemara or Midrash is inconsistent with the MT regarding *male' ve-haser*,[78] we follow the MT. This is obvious regarding aggadic *derashot* such as (Genesis 25:6) *PYLGShM*, (Numbers 7:1) *KLT*, (Deuteronomy 1:13) *V'SMM*; but even in this case, where there are legal ramifications which affect the dispute between the Houses of Hillel and Shammai . . . "[79] Following the above statements of Norzi, as well as comments found elsewhere in his writings, Rabbi Shelomo Ganzfried (in his book, *Keset ha-Sofer*) established the principle that in all instances where the reading of the Talmud is inconsistent with the MT, we follow the MT.[80] Like Norzi, he also does not distinguish between halakhic and aggadic Midrashim.

---

[76]See, for example, Meiri in note 6 above, p. 59, col. 2 (and cf. *Bet ha-Behirah*, *Kiddushin* 30a); Radbaz in notes 6, 31.

[77]In contrast to these rabbis (see notes 44, 45, and the end of 50), Norzi's critical sense for language denied him the luxury of concealing the fact that on many occasions it was indeed imaginable that our Sages had a variant reading.

[78]For the emphasis on *male' ve-haser*, cf. Lonzano's comments (note 45).

[79]See *Sanhedrin* 4a, *Zevahim* 37b. A complete analysis of Norzi's approach to textual variants in rabbinic literature requires a separate study.

[80]Cf., for example, his remarks in the preface to vol. 2, 28. The profound

2. Minḥat Shai and his followers may have deviated from Rashba's position because they had access to the relevant responsum of Rashba in an ambiguous and confusing form. The collection of Rashba's responsa with which we are dealing was first published in Venice, circa 1519, and attributed to Ramban. Responsum 232, which pertains to our discussion, states, "Whatever comes up in the Talmud relating to a law . . . we certainly emend *ha-mi`ut* (lit. the minority)." The context, amplified by Meiri and Radbaz who cite it, indicates that the word *ha-mi`ut* does not belong in this sentence—it crept in from later references to the word in that responsum.[81] Nevertheless, one might (mistakenly) understand Rashba to have ruled that we emend the MT based on talmudic variants affecting *halakhah*, only when the majority of our texts are consistent with the Midrash. In reality, according to Rashba, if there is a variant reading in the *Gemara* or Midrash which has halakhic ramifications, one should emend the MT based on the *derashah* in all cases. Indeed, the Minḥat Shai, immediately after stating (on Leviticus 4:34) that the MT should be retained even when it differs from the text presupposed by the halakhic midrash, cites the responsum of Ramban (i.e., Rashba) as if his own position were consistent with that of Rashba!

Moreover, Rashba's responsum was also known to many rabbis in abridged form (this time, attributed correctly to Rashba, not Ramban). Rabbi Abraham Ḥasan haSofer cites the abridged version in his *Iggeret*,[82] and Rabbi Yosef Karo also quotes it in the *Bet Yosef* (*Tur, Yoreh De'ah*,

---

influence of Rabbi Shelomo Ganzfried on later rabbis needs no documentation. Moreover, Ganzfried's *Keset ha-Sofer* was prefaced by an enthusiastic letter of approbation by Rabbi Moshe Sofer (*Ḥatam Sofer*), the leading halakhic authority of the nineteenth century. In that letter, Ḥatam Sofer wrote *inter alia*: "Upon the publication of this book, no scribe shall be licensed as a professional scribe unless he is expert in this book and can cite it from memory." It should be noted, however, that the first edition of *Keset ha-Sofer* (Budapest, 1835)—i.e., the edition to which Ḥatam Sofer gave his letter of approbation—does not discuss, much less decide, the issue of discrepancies between biblical citations in the Talmud and the MT. Ganzfried incorporated these discussions in later editions of *Keset ha-Sofer*, published after Ḥatam Sofer's death.

[81]See Penkower cited above (n. 32).

[82]"The letter of R. Abraham Ḥasan of Salonica," ed. M. Benayahu *Sefunot* 11 (1978): 213. The letter was written c. 1523 (Benayahu, ibid., p. 190).

275).[83] We might compare also *Minḥat Shai* on Numbers 7:1 (s.v. *kallot Mosheh*), who distinguishes between "Ramban's responsum 232" and "Rashba's responsum cited in the *Bet Yosef* commentary on *Tur, Yoreh De'ah* 275."[84] In the shorter version, Rashba's distinction between halakhic and aggadic variants is missing.

3. We must also consider the influence of Ya'akov ben Ḥayyim. In his introduction to *Mikra'ot Gedolot*, Venice 1525, he discusses the fact that "in several places, we find that the Talmud is inconsistent with the MT." He establishes the principle (based on an analysis of Rashi and especially Tosafot) that "we follow the MT,"[85] thus completely ignoring Rashba's responsum.[86] Although Ya'akov ben Hayyim is not regarded as a great sage or halakhic decisor, his works circulated widely.[87]

4. The practical laws of writing *Sifrei Torah* were always the special province of professional scribes. These, especially the elite, had their own professional tradition (as did other religiously oriented professions), transmitted over the generations. At times, even the rulings of great halakhic decisors could not alter the actual practice (and tradition) of these scribes.[88]

5. It is possible that Tosafot's comments about divergence between the MT and rabbinic versions of those verses (*Shabbat* 55b, quoted above, and *Niddah* 33a) played a role. Tosafot makes no distinction between halakhic and aggadic differences, inviting the inference that Tosafot

---

[83]The abridgment was not invented by the author of Bet Yosef (cf. Penkower [n. 44], pp. 308–309, n. 113a).

[84]Rabbi Abraham Ḥasan also distinguishes between the two responsa. Cf. his letter to Rabbi Yosef Taitachak on p. 227.

[85]See Yaakov ben Ḥayyim's introduction, C. D. Ginsburg edition (reprint, New York, 1968), pp. 57ff.

[86]It does not concern us whether Yaakov ben Ḥayyim deliberately ignored the responsum (as Penkower appears to believe, ibid., p. 29).

[87]As Penkower writes, especially pp. 40ff. It is difficult to ascertain the influence of Rabbi Y. Mintz's responsum (see note 19), where he writes, following Tosafot, "regarding the texts, we accept the Masoretic reading and write as they have received it, and we do not incorporate the reading of our Talmud (Bavli) or the Jerusalem Talmud," without distinguishing between halakhic and aggadic Midrashim. His responsa were first published in Venice 1553.

[88]Cf. Y. Ta-Shema, "Halakhic Characteristics of Rabbinic Literature in Ashkenaz in the 13th and 14th Centuries," *Alei Sefer* 4 (1977): 20–41.

would retain MT even in matters of *halakhah*. (The example in *Niddah* 33a deals with a halakhic issue.)[89]

Despite all of these factors, Rashba's position did not vanish completely, and did play a role in later halakhic discussions. For example, the rabbis of Venice in the eighteenth century were asked about a Torah scroll which did not have the "lame" (i.e., broken) *vav* in the word *shalom* (Numbers 25:12) as prescribed by the Talmud. In rabbinic responsa on this issue, Rashba's position was considered at great length.[90] The talmudic discussion (*Kiddushin* 66a) reads:

> From where do we learn that the Temple service performed by a blemished priest is invalid? R. Yehuda says in the name of Shemuel, Scripture says "Therefore tell him that I now give him My covenant of peace (*shalom*)"— when he is whole [*shalem*] and not when he is deficient. But it is written SHLWM!? R. Naḥman said that the *vav* in *shalom* is lame [and therefore can midrashically be read *shalem*].

Ostensibly, this *derashah* affects *halakhah*, as the source of the law that a blemished priest is unfit for Temple service. Therefore, in their responsa on this issue, as well as on related questions,[91] the rabbis discussed Rashba's responsum. Insofar as they understood Rashba's position as stated by Radbaz (i.e., that where there are legal ramifications we should follow the Talmud even when most of our texts read otherwise),[92] they did not hesitate to accept this principle. To be sure, they challenged the specific aspects of the case, suggesting, for instance, that perhaps the

---

[89]My friend, Rabbi M. Rauchberger, who brought this case to my attention, considers this is the *only* factor explaining the failure of scribes to follow Rashba's decision.

[90]Cf., for example, Yitzḥak Hakohen Rapaport, *Batei Kehuna*, vol. 3 (*Bet Din*) (Salonica, 1754; reprint, Jerusalem, 1970), 20 (the responsum of the Venetian rabbis), 21; Ḥayyim Mosheh Amarillo, *Devar Mosheh*, vol. 3 (Salonica, 1750), 8; Yisrael Yaakov Algazi, *Ne'ot Yaakov* (Izmir, 1767), 1; Refael Shelomoh Laniado, *Bet Dino Shel Shelomoh* (Constantinople, 1772), 10.

[91]For example, *Responsa of R. Akiva Eiger*, 75.

[92]See especially *Ne'ot Yaakov* and *Bet Dino shel Shelomo*, ibid., and cf. *Responsa of R. Akiva Eiger*, ibid. As stated, other rabbis were uncertain about Rashba's intent.

derashah in question reflects only the opinion of Rabbi Yehuda in the name of Shemuel. Shemuel's father, on the other hand (whose position is accepted as the *halakhah* on this issue), dispenses with the need for this *derashah*. If that is the case, there is no legal ramification based on this *derashah*.[93]

Rashba's position was discussed not only in connection with technical problems of orthography, but even for more serious variants. Rabbi Yisrael Algazi, in his *Emet le-Yaakov*,[94] Constantinople 1764 (Levorno, 1774—photo offset, Jerusalem, 1976), in the chapter on "problems which invalidate Torah scrolls and those which do not," reaches the same halakhic conclusion as did Rashba (as presented by Radbaz[95]):

> Whenever *male' ve-haser* affects halakha in the Talmud, such as *KRNWT KRNT* and *SWKT SKT* . . . one should emend the text if it is inconsistent with the talmudic reading. In *derashot* based on *male' ve-haser*, with no legal ramifications, however, one should not invalidate any Torah scroll, either based on a *derashah* or based on the *masorah*; rather, we follow the reading of most Torah scrolls.

These comments, however, were offered as theory, not as a decision in response to an actual case. As such, this position is not different from what we have stated until now, and does not call for an actual emendation of our Torah scrolls.[96] Even in specific cases, such as: "A Torah scroll which spells the word *WHMShTW* (Leviticus 5:24) without the *yod* between the *tav* and the *vav*, one must fix the scroll, since there is a law (in *Perek ha-Zahav*) derived from it. . . . "[97] There is no practical ramification, since the *derashah* is in fact consistent with the MT.

No opinion adopts Rashba's position, that one should emend the MT from *haser* to *male'* in any of the three instances of *KRNT* in Leviticus

---

[93] Among the other questions that were raised: does the absence of a lame *vav* invalidate a Torah scroll? How is the question affected by rabbinic disagreement over the exact form of the broken *vav*?

[94] And from there, elaborated by Rabbi Hayyim Yosef David Azulay (Hida) in *LeDavid Emet*, 11:3 (Jerusalem, 1986), p. 41.

[95] The aforementioned reprint, p. 47a.

[96] At least the case of *KRNT KRNWT* is inconsistent with the reading in the Talmud (cf. *Minhat Shai* to Leviticus 4:34).

[97] *Emet le-Yaakov* 5, p. 47b.

4:25, 30, 34, or to write *WHNS'* instead of *WHNWS'* in Leviticus 15:10.[98]
Over time, traditions became rooted to the point where nobody was
willing to declare all Torah scrolls invalid; therefore, even after Rashba's
precise position became clarified, it had become impossible to reverse
the trend.[99]

---

[98]Cf. *Niddah* 33a and *Tosafot* s.v. *Ketiv WHNS'*. Ḥatam Sofer cites this example in his responsa, *Oraḥ Ḥayyim* 52, "We accept the law of the Talmud, but we spell the word with a *vav* in our Torah scrolls" (cf. also *Likkutei Teshuvot Ḥatam Sofer, Yoreh De'ah* [London, 1965], sec. 35).

[99]Despite this, Rashba's responsum could have practical application. According to Rabbi Y. Algazi and Ḥida, it is possible that textual variants (of *male' ve-ḥaser*) invalidate the Torah scroll only when the *male' ve-ḥaser* have some legal ramification, but not for a plain *male' ve-ḥaser* distinction (see Rama on *Oraḥ Ḥayyim* 143:4). Cf. also Rabbi Yaakov Katz, *Shav Yaakov*, vol. 1, 56 (Frankfurt am Main, 1742), p. 97c. (For a different opinion: Rabbi Yeḥezkel Landau, *Noda bi-Yehudah, Mahadura Tinyana, Oraḥ Ḥayyim* 12.)

5

On the Morality of
the Patriarchs in Jewish
Polemic and Exegesis[1]

David Berger

THE POLEMICAL WORLD OF THE MIDDLE AGES

On three separate occasions, Nahmanides denounces Abraham for sinful or questionable behavior.[2] The first of these passages asserts that "our father Abraham inadvertently committed a great sin" by urging Sarah to identify herself as his sister, and goes on to maintain that the very decision to go to Egypt was sinful. Later, Nahmanides expresses perplexity at Abraham's rationalization that Sarah was truly his half-sister; this appears to be an unpersuasive excuse for omitting the crucial information that she was also his wife, and although Nahmanides proceeds to suggest an explanation, his sense of moral disapproval remains the dominant feature of the discussion. Finally, he regards the treatment of Hagar by both Sarah and

---

[1] This article was originally published in 1987; for full publication data, see copyright page. It is a pleasure to thank my friend Professor Sid Z. Leiman for his careful reading of the manuscript. I am particularly grateful to him for the references to *Menahot* and pseudo-Jerome in n. 13, *Sefer Hasidim* and the *midrashim* in n. 14, and Ehrlich's commentary in n. 22.

[2] Commentary to Genesis 12:10, 20:12, and 16:6.

131

Abraham as a sin for which Jews are suffering to this day at the hands of the descendants of Ishmael. The bold, almost indignant tone of these passages is both striking and significant—but it is not typical.

Most medieval Jews were understandably sensitive about ascriptions of sin to the patriarchs, and the situation was rendered even more delicate by the fact that the issue of patriarchal morality often arose in a highly charged context in which Jews were placed on the defensive in the face of a Christian attack. Two thirteenth-century Ashkenazic polemics reflect a somewhat surprising Christian willingness to criticize Jacob as a means of attacking his descendants. Since the patriarch was a Christian as well as a Jewish hero, such attacks on his morality were problematical: Jacob may be the father of carnal Israel, but he is the prototype of spiritual Israel as well. While criticisms of this sort are consequently absent from major Christian works, it is perfectly evident that no Jew would have invented them. On the medieval street, then, Christians did not shrink from such attacks on Jews and their forebears. Jacob, they said, was a thief and a trickster; the implication concerning his descendants hardly needed to be spelled out.

In *Sefer Yosef ha-Mekanne* we are informed that Joseph Official met a certain Dominican friar on the road to Paris who told him, "Your father Jacob was a thief; there has been no consumer of usury to equal him, for he purchased the birthright, which was worth a thousand coins, for a single plate [of lentils] worth half a coin."[3] The technical impropriety of the reference to usury merely underscores the pointed application of this critique to medieval Jews. The next passage reports a Christian argument that Jacob was a deceiver who cheated Laban by exceeding the terms of their agreement concerning the sheep to which Jacob was entitled, and this criticism is followed by the assertion that Simeon and Levi engaged in unethical behavior when they deviously persuaded the Shechemites to accept circumcision and then proceeded to kill them.[4]

With respect to Jacob, the Jewish response was conditioned by two separate considerations acting in concert. First, religious motivations quite independent of the polemical context prevented the perception of Jacob as a sinner; second, the Christian attack itself called for refuta-

---

[3] *Sefer Yosef ha-Mekanne*, ed. Judah Rosenthal (Jerusalem, 1970), pp. 40–41.
[4] Rosenthal, *Sefer Yosef HaMekanne*, pp. 41–42.

tion rather than concession. Hence, Joseph[5] responded with a remarkable suggestion found also in Rashbam's commentary that Jacob paid in full for the birthright; the bread and lentils are to be understood as a meal sealing the transaction or customarily following its consummation. As Judah Rosenthal pointed out in his edition of *Yosef ha-Mekanne*, Rabbi Joseph Bekhor Shor reacted with exasperation to the apparent implausibility of this interpretation, which was almost surely motivated by both moral sensitivity and polemical need. As for Laban, the answer to the Christian critique was that Jacob was the real victim of deception, and his treatment of his father-in-law was marked by extraordinary scrupulousness.[6]

Joseph Official goes on to an uncompromising defense of Simeon and Levi which is particularly interesting because this was the one instance in which a concession to the Christian accusation was tactically possible. Jacob, after all, had denounced their behavior, and even if his initial concern dealt with the danger that could result from an adverse Canaanite reaction rather than with the moral issue (Genesis 34:30), his vigorous rebuke of his sons at the end of his life (Genesis 49:5–7) could certainly have supported the assertion that he considered their action morally reprehensible as well as pragmatically unwise. Nevertheless, there is no hint of condemnation in *Yosef ha-Mekanne*; if Christians denounced Simeon and Levi, then surely Jews were obligated to defend them, especially since a sense of moral superiority was crucial to the medieval Jewish psyche in general and to the polemicist in particular.[7] Thus, Joseph tells us that the Shechemites regretted their circumcision and were in any event planning to oppress Jacob's family and take over its property; consequently, their execution was eminently justified.[8]

---

[5] Despite the manuscript, this must refer to Joseph Official and not Joseph Bekhor Shor; cf. the editor's note, and see just below.

[6] Rosenthal, *Sefer Yosef ha-Mekanne*, loc. cit.

[7] On this point, see my brief discussion in *The Jewish–Christian Debate in the High Middle Ages: A Critical Edition of the* Nizzahon Vetus *with an Introduction, Translation and Commentary* (Northvale, NJ 1996), pp. 25–27. I hope to elaborate in a forthcoming study on the problem of exile in medieval polemic.

[8] Rosenthal, *Sefer Yosef ha-Mekanne*, p. 42. The persistence of Jewish sensitivity to this story in modern times can perhaps best be illustrated by a contem-

There is a certain irony in the fact that the Christian question in *Yosef ha-Mekanne* which immediately follows this series of objections to patriarchal behavior begins, "After all, everyone agrees that Jacob was a thoroughly righteous man; why then was he afraid of descending to hell?"[9] Although this is a return to the Christian stance that we ought to expect, there is in fact one more incident in Jacob's life that Christian polemicists apparently utilized in their debate with Jews, and this is, of course, his deception of his own father.

The anonymous *Nizzahon Vetus* presents the following argument:

> "I am Esau your firstborn" [Genesis 27:19]. One can say that Jacob did not lie. In fact, this can be said without distorting the simple meaning of the verse, but by explaining it as follows: I am Esau your firstborn, for Esau sold him the birthright in a manner as clear as day. It is, indeed, clear that Jacob was careful not to state an outright lie from the fact that when Isaac asked him, "Are you my son Esau?" he responded, "I am" [Genesis 27:24], and not, "I am Esau."
>
> They go on to say that because Jacob obtained the blessings through trickery, they were fulfilled for the Gentiles and not the Jews. The answer is that even the prophet Amos [*sic*] prayed for Jacob, for he is in possession of the truth, as it is written, "You will grant truth to Jacob and mercy to Abraham, which you have sworn unto our fathers" [Micah 7:20]. That is, had not the truth been with Jacob, then you would not have sworn to our fathers.[10]

The pattern holds. Once again Christians attack the patriarch's morality; this time the consequences for his descendants are spelled out with explicit clarity, and once again Jewish ingenuity is mobilized for an unflinching, unqualified defense.[11]

---

porary example of Jewish black humor. Simeon and Levi—so the explanation goes—were just as concerned as Jacob about adverse public opinion, and this is precisely why they arranged to have the Shechemites undergo the judaizing ceremony of circumcision. Once it would be perceived that it was a Jew who had been killed, no one would be concerned. Cf. *Kli Yakar* to Genesis 35:25.

[9] Rosenthal, *Sefer Yosef ha-Mekanne*, p. 42.

[10] Berger, *The Jewish–Christian Debate*, p. 56.

[11] For Rashi's rather different defense of Jacob's veracity as well as the persuasiveness of the version in the *Nizzahon Vetus* for later Jews, see my commentary in *The Jewish–Christian Debate*, pp. 246–247. It is worth noting that the

Nevertheless, the pattern does not always hold. Polemicists will do what is necessary to win whatever point appears crucial in a particular context, and on one occasion at least we find two Jewish writers displaying very little zeal in defending the questionable action of a biblical hero. Their motivation is hardly mysterious: Jesus had cited this action approvingly.

Jacob ben Reuben and the *Nizzahon Vetus* both comment on the story in Matthew 12 in which Jesus defends the plucking of corn by his hungry disciples on the Sabbath with reference to David's eating of the shewbread when he was hungry. In his late-twelfth-century *Milhamot ha-Shem*,[12] Jacob responds as follows:

> How could he cite evidence from David's eating of the shewbread when he was fleeing and in a great hurry? If David behaved unlawfully by violating the commandment on that one occasion when he was forced by the compulsion of hunger and never repeated this behavior again, how could your Messiah utilize this argument to permit the gathering of corn without qualification?

More briefly, the author of the *Nizzahon Vetus* remarks, "If David behaved improperly, this does not give them the right to pluck those ears of corn on the Sabbath."[13] Although Jacob provided mitigation for David's behavior and the *Nizzahon Vetus*'s comments might be under-

---

Nizzahon Vetus also reports a Christian argument that Moses' delay in coming down from Mount Sinai (Exodus 32:1) renders him "a sinner and a liar" (p. 67). Mordechai Breuer has suggested (*Sefer Nizzahon Yashon* [Jerusalem, 1978], p. 21, n. 57) that this argument *may* have originated among Christian heretics. On the other hand, since it ends with the question "Why did he delay?" it may have been leading to a Christian answer that Moses, who was not really a sinner, was testing the Jews and found them wanting. The ancient rabbis, of course, were generally not faced with the polemical concerns of the Middle Ages, and on rare occasions the Talmud ascribes sin to the patriarchs even where the biblical evidence does not require such a conclusion; see, for example, the accusations against Abraham in *Nedarim* 32a.

[12] Edited by Judah Rosenthal (Jerusalem, 1963), p. 148.

[13] Page 182. It is important to note that the Talmud (*Menahot* 95b–96a) had suggested a legal justification for what David had done. Note too the anomalous report in pseudo-Jerome cited by L. Ginzberg, *Legends of the Jews*, vol. 6 (Philadelphia, 1928), p. 243.

stood as a counterfactual concession for the sake of argument ("even if I were to agree that David behaved improperly"), the impression of sin is not only allowed to stand but is actually introduced by the Jewish writers. Even more striking, Jacob continued his argument by saying that once Jesus was permitting every act of King David, "why did he not permit sexual relations with married women since David had such relations with the wife of Uriah?" Now, the Talmud had made the most vigorous efforts to deny that Bathsheba was still married to Uriah and, indeed, that David had sinned at all, and the insertion of this question—which was not essential to the argument and is in fact missing from the parallel passage in the *Nizzahon Vetus*—is a telling illustration of the impact of the search for effective polemical rhetoric.[14]

Thus far we have seen Jewish defenses of biblical heroes for reasons both religious and polemical, and criticisms of their behavior which arose from a sensitive, straightforward reading of the text as well as from polemical concerns. It remains to be noted that the particular ideology of a Jewish commentator, if pursued with sufficient passion, could itself overcome the profound inhibitions against denouncing the morality of the patriarchs. I know of but one example of this phenomenon, but it is quite remarkable.

In his study of Jewish social thought in sixteenth- and seventeenth-century Poland, Haim Hillel Ben Sasson frequently pointed to the animus against the wealthy displayed by the prominent preacher and exegete Rabbi Ephraim Lunshitz. Among many examples of this animus, Ben Sasson draws our attention to Lunshitz's remarks about the rabbinic comment that when Jacob remained alone prior to wrestling with the angel, his purpose was to collect small vessels that he had left behind. Before Lunshitz, Jews had universally understood this as an exemplification of an admirable trait. Not so the author of the *Kli Yakar*: "A majority of commentators agree that this angel is Sammael the officer of

---

[14]It is, of course, difficult to say what Jacob's view of David's relationship with Bathsheba was in dispassionate, non-polemical moments. For Abravanel's rejection of the rabbinic exculpation of David (*Shabbat* 56a), see his commentary to 2 Samuel 11–12. See also the very interesting remarks in *Sefer Hasidim*, ed. J. Wistinetzki (Frankfurt am Main, 1924), sec. 46 (p. 43)-R. Margulies' edition (Jerusalem, 1957), sec. 174 (p. 181). Cf. also the less striking references in *Midrash Shmuel*, ed. S. Buber (Krakau, 1893), pp. 122–23, and *Seder Eliyyahu Rabbah*, ed. M. Ish-Shalom (Friedmann) (Vienna, 1902), p. 7.

Esau . . . whose desire is solely to blind *(lesamme)* the eyes . . . of the intelligence." Now, as long as Jacob refrained from the slightest sin, Sammael could not approach him, but once Jacob was guilty of even a small measure of sin, his immunity was lost. And for a rich man like Jacob to remain behind in a dangerous place for a few vessels is indeed the beginning of sin. Jacob had begun to blind himself, "for who is as blind as the lovers of money about whom it is written, 'The eyes of a man are never satiated' (Proverbs 27:20)? . . . Who is such a fool that he would endanger himself for such a small item? Rather, it is a mocking heart which turned him away from the straight path to succumb to such love of money, which causes forgetfulness of God."[15]

What makes this passage all the more noteworthy is that the talmudic source contains an explicitly favorable evaluation: the righteous care so much for their property because they never rob others (*Hullin* 91a). Moreover, if Lunshitz was uneasy with this talmudic evaluation, nothing was forcing him to mention the passage in the first place; the point is nowhere in the biblical text, and the *Kli Yakar* is in any event a discursive, selective commentary, which could easily have skipped the verse entirely. Clearly, he made the point because it served as an outlet for one of his driving passions. Patriarchal immunity from criticism, even in a traditional society, evidently had its limits.

BIBLICAL CRITICISM AND JEWISH EXEGESIS IN MODERN TIMES

As the Middle Ages gave way to the modern period, the content and context of this issue were radically and fundamentally altered. Inhibitions against criticizing biblical morality began to crumble, and both Enlightenment ideologues and nineteenth-century scholars gleefully pounced upon biblical passages that appeared morally problematical. In the first instance, the target was the Bible as a whole and, ultimately, Christianity itself; in the second, it was usually the Hebrew Bible in particular, whose allegedly primitive ethics served as a preparation and a foil for the superior morality

---

[15]*Kli Yakar* to Genesis 32:35. See Ben Sasson's *Hagut ve-Hanhagah* (Jerusalem, 1959), pp. 118–119.

of the Gospels. In effect, an argument originally directed against Christianity was refocused to attack Judaism alone.[16]

Modern biblical scholarship, then, transformed the essential terms of this discussion, and the transformation was so profound that it ultimately inspired a reaction strikingly different from the standard medieval response. The crucial point is that the attack was no longer on the morality of the biblical personalities. To many Bible critics, the very existence of the patriarchs was in question, and the historicity of specific accounts of their behavior was surely deemed unreliable in the extreme. The attack now was on the morality of the biblical author or authors—an attack that was almost impossible in the premodern period, when the author was ultimately presumed to be God Himself.[17]

Consequently, it now became possible—perhaps even polemically desirable—for traditionally inclined Jews (whether or not they were strict fundamentalists) to take a different approach by driving a wedge between hero and author. There were indeed occasional imperfections in the moral behavior of the patriarchs, but these are condemned by the Torah and required punishment and expiation. Whatever the exegetical merits of this approach, and they are, as we shall see, considerable, it would have been extraordinarily difficult both tactically and psychologically had the attack of the critics still been directed at the patriarchs themselves.

There is, however, a deeper issue here. The assertion that the Bible disapproves of certain behavior was not based on explicit verses of condemnation; rather, it depended on a sensitive reading of long stretches of narrative in which patterns of retribution and expiation emerged. On the simplest level, this approach demonstrated that the morality of the Torah is not inferior to that of Bible critics. On a deeper level, it undercut the effort of some critics to utilize the moral "deficiencies" of certain passages to establish divergent levels of moral sensitivity in the Penta-

---

[16]Cf. the similar medieval phenomenon in which arguments by Christian heretics against the Hebrew Bible were reworked by Orthodox Christians in their polemic with Jews. See my *Jewish–Christian Debate*, p. 6.

[17]For an exception, note Luther's remarks on Esther in his *Table Talk*: "I am so hostile to this book that I wish it did not exist, for it judaizes too much, and has too much heathen naughtiness." Cited approvingly by L. B. Paton in his discussion of "the moral teaching of the book" in *The International Critical Commentary: The Book of Esther* (1908; reprint, Edinburgh, 1951), p. 96.

teuch as a whole and in Genesis in particular. But on the profoundest level—at least for some proponents of this approach—it went to the heart of the essential claims of the higher criticism by arguing in a new way for the unity of Genesis. Many of the newly discovered patterns cut through the documents of the critics and emerged only from a unitary perception of the entire book; since the patterns seemed genuine, the only reasonable conclusion was that the unity of Genesis was no less real than its literary subtleties. These observations were not confined to narratives bearing on the morality of the patriarchs, but it is there that some of the most striking examples were to be found.

In the first half of this century, a number of Jewish writers—Martin Buber, Benno Jacob, Umberto Cassutto—began to note such patterns. Before going further, we are immediately confronted by a challenging, almost intractable methodological problem. I have suggested that this revisionist reading of the Bible is rooted in part in traditionalist sentiments, that it presented a new way of responding to people critical of sacred Jewish texts. At the same time, I consider the essential insights justified by an objective examination of the evidence (although my own motives are surely as "suspect" as those of the figures under discussion). Decades ago, Jacob Katz argued that one may not readily assign ulterior motives to someone whose position appears valid in light of the sources that he cites,[18] and more recently Joseph Dan has criticized a work about Gershom Scholem for attributing his view of Kabbalah to factors other than his accurate reading of the kabbalistic texts themselves.[19] Fundamentally, these methodological caveats are very much in order, and in certain instances they are decisive. At the same time, undeniable intuitions tell us that even people who are essentially correct can be partially motivated by concerns that go beyond the cited evidence, and there ought to be some way to determine when this is likely to be so. In our case, a figure like Cassutto was clearly concerned not only with the unity of Genesis but with the standing and reputation of the biblical text. Moreover, despite the fact that he was not a fundamentalist and that he

---

[18]Jacob Katz "Mahloket HaSemikhah Bein Rabbi Yaaqov Beirav Veha-Ralbah," *Zion* 15, secs. 3–4 (1951): 41.

[19]*Kiryat Sefer* 54 (1979/80): 358–362. Dan does note (p. 361) that even in Scholem's case, extratextual considerations can play some role.

was no doubt sincere in his protestation that his essential conclusions flowed solely from an objective examination of the text, the consistency of his conservative tendencies in issue after issue where the evidence could often point either way surely reveals a personality that was inclined to seek traditional solutions.[20]

In contemporary biblical scholarship, such an inclination frequently labels one a neo-fundamentalist whose conclusions are rejected almost a priori. This is a manifest error with the most serious consequences. Even people with much stronger traditionalist tendencies than Cassutto can be motivated by those tendencies to seek evidence that turns out to be real. Kepler's laws are no less valid because he sought them as a result of his religious convictions. In this instance, a change in the attack on biblical morality liberated and then impelled people with traditionalist inclinations to see things in the text that had gone virtually unnoticed before. At first, these figures were necessarily non-fundamentalists; genuine Jewish fundamentalists would not easily shed their inhibitions about criticizing the patriarchs. With the passage of time, however, even some uncompromisingly Orthodox Jews could adopt this approach,[21] while others—probably a majority—would retain unabated the religious inhibitions of the past;[22] fundamentalism is far from a monolithic phenomenon.

---

[20]While maintaining that Cassutto's work in essentially anti-traditional, Yehezkel Kaufmann nevertheless pointed to several examples of this conservatism; see "Me'Adam ad Noah," in *Mi-Kivshonah shel ha-Yetzirah ha-Mikra'it* (Tel Aviv, 1966), p. 217.

[21]Yissakhar Jacobson, *Binah ba-Mikra* (Tel Aviv,1960), pp 33–36; Nehama Leibowitz, *Iyyunim be-Sefer Bereshit* (Jerusalem, 1966), pp. 185–188 (English trans., *Studies in Bereshit [Genesis]* [Jerusalem, 1976], pp. 264–269); Leah Frankel, *Perakim ba-Mikra* (Jerusalem, 1981), pp. 102–104, 143–144.

[22]Professor Lawrence Kaplan has called my attention to Rabbi A. Kotler's "How To Teach Torah," *Light* 10, 12, 13, 15, 19 (1970/71), republished as a pamphlet by Beth Medrash Govoha of Lakewood. A Hebrew version appears in Rabbi Kotler's *Osef Hiddushei Torah* (Jerusalem, 1983), pp. 402–411. "If there were any fault," writes the author, "—however slight (Hebrew: *dak min ha-dak*)— in any of the *Ovos* [patriarchs], the very essence of the Jewish people would have been different" (English pamphlet, p. 6-Hebrew p. 404). Rabbi Kotler makes it clear that his work is a reaction to modern heresy (*kefirah*), which perceives the patriarchal narratives as ordinary stories. On the other hand, Professor Kaplan notes that the popular *Pentateuch and Haftorahs* edited by Rabbi J. H. Hertz (1936) extols Scripture precisely because it "impartially relates both

THE BIBLE'S JUDGMENT OF PATRIARCHAL BEHAVIOR: THE CASE OF JACOB'S DECEPTION

Let us turn now to a central example of an approach that we have thus far discussed only in the abstract. At Rebecca's behest, Jacob deceived Isaac by pretending to be Esau and thereby obtained a blessing intended for his brother. We have already seen a medieval Jewish defense of Jacob's behavior, and in the entire corpus of premodern Jewish exegesis there is hardly a whisper of criticism.[23] In the twentieth century, however, a number of scholars have noted a series of indications that make it exceedingly difficult to deny that the Torah implicitly but vigorously condemns Jacob's action.

First, the deception was motivated by a misreading of Isaac's intentions. The blind patriarch bestowed three blessings on his children: the first to Jacob masquerading as Esau, the second to Esau, and the third to Jacob. It was only in the third blessing, when he knew for the first time that he was addressing Jacob, that he bestowed "the blessing of Abraham to you and your seed with you so that you may inherit the land in which you dwell which God gave to Abraham" (Genesis 28:4). Although other

---

the failings and the virtues of its heroes" (commentary to Genesis 20:12, citing one of the passages from Nahmanides with which we began). Similarly, Arnold B. Ehrlich asserts that Scripture does not conceal the faults of the patriarchs; see *Mikra Ki-Feshuto*, vol. 1 (New York, 1898; reprint, New York, 1969), pp. 33, 73 (to Genesis 12:14, 16 and 25:27); his German *Randglossen zur Hebräischen Bibel* (Leipzig, 1908; reprint, Hildesheim, 1968) omits the first and more important passage. Ehrlich, a brilliant maverick who was neither a traditionalist nor a conventional critic, was in many respects *sui generis* and resists inclusion in any neat classificatory scheme. Finally, Rabbi Shalom Carmy has called my attention to the willingness of representatives of the nineteenth-century Musar movement to acknowledge minor imperfections in the patriarchs as part of the movement's special approach to the analysis of human failings.

[23]David Sykes, in his *Patterns in Genesis* (Ph.D. diss., Bernard Revel Graduate School, Yeshiva University, 1984), notes *Zohar, va-Yeshev*, 185b, which indicates that Jacob was punished for this act because even though something is done properly, God judges the pious for even a hairbreadth's deviation from the ideal. He also points to the Yemenite manuscript cited in *Torah Shelemah*, vol. 6, p. 1432, no. 181 (where the editor also notes the *Zohar* passage), which indicates that Jacob was deceived by his sons with a goat (Genesis 37:31) just as he had deceived his own father with a goat (Genesis 27:16). See also below, note 25.

interpretations of this sequence are possible, the most straightforward reading is that Rebecca and Jacob had gravely underestimated their husband and father. Isaac had indeed intended to bless Esau with temporal supremacy, but the blessing of Abraham—the inheritance of the holy land and the crucial mission of the patriarchs—had been reserved for Jacob from the outset. The deception was pragmatically as well as morally dubious.[24]

Jacob is then subjected to a series of misfortunes and ironies whose relationship to the initial deception cannot be accidental. He must work for his "brother" Laban (Genesis 29:15) instead of having his brothers work for him (Genesis 27:37); he is deceived by the substitution of one sibling for another in the darkness and is pointedly informed that "in our place" the younger is not placed before the older (Genesis 29:26); his sons deceive him with Joseph's garment and the blood of a goat (Genesis 37:31) just as he had deceived Isaac with Esau's garments and the skin of a goat (Genesis 27:15–16); his relationship with Esau is precisely the opposite of the one that was supposed to have been achieved—Esau is the master (Genesis 32:5, 6, 19; 33:8, 13, 14, 15) to whom his servant Jacob (32:5, 19; 33:5, 14) must bow (33:3, and contrast 27:29). Moreover, Jacob's debilitating fear of his brother results from the very act that was supposed to have established his supremacy.[25]

There is, then, ample evidence that Jacob had to undergo a series of punishments to atone for his act of deception. It is almost curious, how-

---

[24] *Binah ba-Mikra*, loc. cit. Cf. also Malbim on Genesis 27:1 and Leibowitz, *Iyyunim*, pp. 193–195.

[25] For premodern references to such arguments, see note 23; *Midrash Tanhuma*, ed. S. Buber (Vilna, 1885), *Va-Yetzei* 11, p. 152, and the parallel passage in *Aggadat Bereshit*, ed. S. Buber (Krakau, 1902), ch. (48) [49], p. 99, where Leah tells Jacob that he has no right to complain about being deceived since he too is a deceiver (although the midrash does not explicitly endorse her criticism); Eliezer Ashkenazi (sixteenth century) *Maasei ha-Shem*, vol. 1 (Jerusalem, 1972), p. 115b, who comments on Laban's remark about the younger and older but apparently considers it evidence of Laban's nastiness rather than Jacob's culpability. Note too *Genesis Rabbah* 67:4, which speaks of later Jews crying out in anguish because of Esau's agonized exclamation in Genesis 27:34, and the somewhat more ambiguous midrash of unknown provenance cited by Rashi on Psalms 80:6, in which Jews shed tears as a result of Esau's tears; see Leibowitz, *Iyyunim*, p. 190. Such isolated observations over a period of more than a mil-

ever, that no one has noted an additional—and climactic—element in this series, which can fundamentally transform our understanding of a crucial aspect of the Joseph narrative. One reason why the point may have been missed is that there are no key words calling it to our attention, and the presence of such words not only alerts the reader but serves as a methodological guide preventing undisciplined speculation. At the same time, we cannot permit ourselves to ignore grand thematic patterns, and in this instance I think that such a pattern has been overlooked.

Leah Frankel, utilizing the "key word" approach, has noted that the root meaning "to deceive" (resh-mem-yod) appears in Genesis three times. The first two instances, in which Isaac tells Esau that his brother deceitfully took his blessing (Genesis 27:35) and Jacob asks Laban why he deceived him (Genesis 29:25), are clearly related to our theme.[26] Perhaps, she suggests, the third instance, in which Simeon and Levi speak deceitfully to Shechem (Genesis 34:13), is intended to indicate that Jacob was "to taste deceit carried out by sons. He would have to stand in the place where his father stood when his son Jacob deceived him" [her emphasis].[27] While this approach is not impossible, it seems unlikely;

----

lennium and a half do not, I think, undermine or even significantly affect the thesis of this paper. For twentieth-century references, often containing additional arguments, see Martin Buber, Die Schrift und ihre Verdeutschung (Berlin, 1936), pp. 224–226; Benno Jacob, Das Erste Buch der Tora: Genesis (Berlin, 1934), p. 591 (abridged English translation, New York, 1974), pp. 197–198; Umberto Cassutto, La Questione della Genesi (Florence, 1934), esp. p. 227; idem, Torat ha-Teʻudot (Jerusalem, 1959), pp. 55–56-The Documentary Hypothesis (Jerusalem, 1961), pp. 63–64; idem, "Yaakov," Entziklopediyyah Mikra'it (EBH), vol. 3, cc. 716–722; Jacobson, Leibowitz, and Frankel (see note 21); Nahum M. Sarna, Understanding Genesis (New York, 1966), pp. 183–184; Jacob Milgrom in Conservative Judaism 20 (1966): 73–79; J. P. Fokkelman, Narrative Art in Genesis (Assen and Amsterdam, 1975), pp. 128– 130, 200, 223, 227; Sykes, op. cit. (note 23). With the exception of Fokkelman, all these figures, whether they are fundamentalists or not, more or less fit the traditionalist typology that I have proposed. Needless to say, the evident validity of many of these exegetical suggestions must (or at least should) eventually affect biblical scholars of all varieties.

[26]Cf. Tanhuma and Aggadat Bereshit in the previous note.

[27]Perakim ba-Mikra, p. 104.

although Jacob suffers indirect consequences from Simeon and Levi's trickery, he is in no sense its object, and the resemblance to his own deception is exceedingly remote.

But there is another act of filial deception in Genesis whose similarity to Jacob's seems unmistakable. Jacob concealed his identity from his father by pretending to be someone else. Similarly, his own misery and anguish reach their climax when his son Joseph conceals his identity and pretends to be something other than what he truly is. The fact that the direct victims of Joseph's deception were the brothers may be the main reason why this observation has been missed, but it is perfectly clear that Jacob is as much a victim as his sons. This point alone should make us reevaluate the key element of the Joseph cycle as the culmination of the process of expiation suffered by the patriarch, and the essential argument does not depend on anything more. But there *is* more. Joseph deceives his father while providing him with food just as Jacob deceived his own father while bringing him the "savory food" which he liked (Genesis 27:7, 14, 17, 25). It is not just that the brothers are Jacob's messengers and will report Joseph's deceptive words to their father (although this is quite sufficient); in the final confrontation between Joseph and Judah, the latter is explicitly a surrogate for Jacob, acting to protect Benjamin *in loco parentis* (Genesis 44:32).[28] Moreover, there is only one other place in Genesis where one person speaks to another with as many protestations of servility as Judah addresses to his "master" in that climactic confrontation; that place, of course, is the description of Jacob's servile behavior toward Esau upon his return from the house of Laban (Genesis 32:4–6, 18–21; 33:1–15).[29] In short, Joseph has not merely concealed

---

[28]It may be worth asking (with considerable diffidence) whether Judah's status as a surrogate for Jacob may help us resolve an old, intractable crux. In Joseph's second dream, the sun, moon, and eleven stars, presumably symbolizing his father, mother, and brothers, bow down to him (Genesis 37:9–10). But his mother was already dead at the time of the dream; less seriously, Jacob does not bow to Joseph until Genesis 47:30, by which time our intuition tells us (I think) that the dreams ought to have already been fulfilled. *Perhaps* two of the brothers who bow to Joseph represent both themselves and a parent; Judah is the surrogate for Jacob, and Benjamin, who is pointedly described as his mother's only surviving child (Genesis 44:20), is the representative of Rachel. Joseph's parents bow down to him through their offspring.

[29]For whatever this is worth, Jacob addresses Esau as "my master" seven times in these verses (32:6, 19; 33:8, 13, 14 [twice], 15 [32:5 is not addressed to Esau])

his identity from his father; by threatening Jacob's family from a position of mastery, he has actually taken on the role of Esau.[30] The parallel to Jacob's deception is genuinely striking.[31]

LITERARY PATTERNS AND
THE DOCUMENTARY HYPOTHESIS

During the last decade, J. P. Fokkelman,[32] Robert Alter,[33] and Michael Fishbane[34] have searched the narratives of Genesis for patterns out of purely literary motivations, sometimes with the implicit assumption that

---

and Judah addresses Joseph as "my master" seven times in his final speech (44:18 [twice], 19, 20, 22, 24, 33). Since seven is clearly a significant number and since Jacob is explicitly said to have bowed to Esau seven times (Genesis 33:3 ["complete subjection," says Fokkelman, in *Narrative Art in Genesis*, p. 223]), it is at least possible that this is more than coincidence.

[30]Note too that Jacob was most concerned with Esau's threat to Rachel and her child (Genesis 33:2), and it was Rachel's child Benjamin who was singled out for persecution by the Egyptian viceroy. Finally, Professor David Shatz has called my attention to the use of the rare verb *stm*, "to hate," with regard to both Esau's hatred of Jacob (Genesis 27:41) and the brothers fear that Joseph would hate them (Genesis 50:15).

[31]The fact that Joseph's actions were no doubt motivated by other factors involving his brothers does not, of course, refute the perception that we are witnessing the final step in a divine plan to purge Jacob of his sin. It is, in fact, possible that an even later incident in Genesis is related to Jacob's deception of Isaac. The successful expiation of that sin may be symbolized by Jacob's ability, despite his failing eyesight, to discern the difference in the destinies of his older and younger grandsons (Genesis 48:10–20). Cf. Benno Jacob, *Das Erste Buch*, p. 884 (called to my attention by David Sykes), and Cassutto, *La Questione della Genesi*, p. 232. (It need hardly be said that this new approach does not end with a denunciation of biblical heroes. After a process of retribution and moral development, the ethical standing of the patriarch is beyond reproach.) Finally, it must be stressed that other moral questions like the scriptural evaluation of the treatment of Hagar and the behavior of the young Joseph are also susceptible to this mode of analysis.

[32]See n. 25.

[33]*The Art of Biblical Narrative* (New York, 1981).

[34]*Text and Texture* (New York, 1979).

the conventional documentary hypothesis remains virtually unchanged no matter how many interlocking themes are discerned. In a reaction to one of Alter's early articles on this subject, I wrote that "I think he underestimates the impact of such literary analysis on the documentary hypothesis. You can allow the 'redactor' just so much freedom of action before he turns into an author using various traditions as 'raw material.' Such an approach must ultimately shake the foundations of the regnant critical theory, not merely tinker with its periphery."[35] More recently, the point has been made with vigor and documentation in David Sykes's dissertation, *Patterns in Genesis.*[36] To Alter's credit, he does confront the question in his later book, and although his conclusions are by no means traditional, they are not wholly consonant with those of critical orthodoxy.[37]

It is becoming clearer from year to year that Genesis is replete with linguistic and thematic patterns of subtlety and power which run through the warp and woof of the entire work. Despite the overwhelming force generated by a critical theory that has held sway for generations, scholars will not be able to hide forever behind the assertion that they are studying the art of a redactor as that word is usually understood. The issue will have to be joined.

---

[35]*Commentary* 61:3 (March, 1976): 16. It may be worth asking whether Shakespeare has ever been described as the redactor of the various Hamlet documents because he worked with earlier, related stories.

[36]35. See n. 23. My affirmation of the validity of this general approach does not, of course, imply an endorsement of every pattern or set of patterns that has been suggested, and it is self-evident that some proposals will be more persuasive than others. This mode of interpretation will always be vulnerable to the charge of arbitrary and subjective eisegesis. Nevertheless, such is the fate of almost all literary analysis, and a combination of methodological guidelines and a healthy dose of common sense can minimize, though never eliminate, undisciplined speculation. In any case, I am thoroughly persuaded that the recent literature contains more than enough convincing examples to sustain the essential point.

[37]P. 20, and especially chap. 7 (pp. 131–154). In the present climate, it requires some courage to express such views, and Alter has already been accused of involvement in *(horribile dictu)* "the new fundamentalism" (and he has already denied it); see *Commentary* 77:2 (February 1984): 14. Cf. also Fokkelman's very brief comment on the issue in *Narrative Art*, p. 4.

6

Introducing Rabbi Breuer

Shalom Carmy

It is impossible to encounter academic Bible scholarship pertaining to the Torah (the Five Books of Moses) without becoming aware of the hypothesis that the Torah is composed of at least four distinct documents. These sources, it is professed, took shape over a period of several centuries. As the authors represent differing outlooks and traditions about Israel's history and laws, their presentations abound in contradictions. The editorial process that combined them, arriving at our familiar text, is a mixture of conservative juxtaposition, preserving redundancies and contradictions, and a shrewd rewriting and interweaving of the original sources to eliminate difficulties. The Higher Criticism aims to reverse the process of redaction, to unearth, to the extent that this is possible, the traditions and sources out of which, in their view, the Torah developed, and to speculate about the historical situations that gave birth to the documents.

My purpose here is to set the stage for Rabbi Breuer's paper. With that goal in mind, let us quickly recall two salient ingredients of the Orthodox reaction. First, the sense of revulsion at the patent heresy entailed by the enterprise of Higher Criticism. If the Torah was given to Moses, it cannot have been compiled piecemeal for hundreds of years after his death; this difficulty becomes especially grave, as Rabbi Breuer notes, in view of the accepted teaching (enshrined in the seventh of Maimonides' thirteen dogmas) that the prophecy of Moses is qualitatively superior to that of other prophets of God. And how, moreover, can we revere the Torah as the word of God if it is replete with alleged inconsistencies?

The second feature of the Orthodox response was to emphasize that the traditional commentators were hardly naïve about the scholarly discoveries. They were well acquainted with the most significant inconsistencies and, far from being unsettled by them, had in their possession effective strategies of reconciliation. The critical analysis of Genesis, for example, was much concerned with the different names of God: by assigning all mentions of the Tetragrammaton to the source called J, a criterion emerged for distinguishing the passages ascribed to J from those attributed to E and P. But, countered the defenders of tradition, there is an ancient semantic distinction between the Tetragrammaton and the alternate divine cognomen *Elohim*: the former, if we may simplify the matter, denotes God's quality of mercy; the latter, the attribute of judgment. The Rabbis applied this distinction to the opening chapters of Genesis, teaching that God had intended to create the world according to the principle of strict judgment (chapter 1), conjoining it with the Tetragrammaton (meaning the quality of mercy) in chapter 2, only because a world of strict law is not viable. If the Rabbis were sensitive to inconcinnity in the narrative portions of the Torah, they were even more keenly aware of inconsistencies in the legal sections, as any student of Talmud and halakhic Midrash can attest. The methods available to the Rabbis from time immemorial can be expanded and extended to passages that were not exhaustively discussed by our predecessors, and Orthodox exegetes have continued to do so, not without success.

For almost forty years Rabbi Breuer has passionately argued for a more sophisticated, more systematic, and, above all, less defensive encounter with the challenge of the Documentary Hypothesis. But you will not grasp the nature of his seminal contribution to our understanding of Tanakh if you think of it as a mere refinement in the standard modes of harmonization. Rabbi Breuer explicitly advocates a novel frame of reference for the entire debate, and implicitly formulates a new criterion for the cogency of proposed resolutions to the difficulties we seek to comprehend.

Rabbi Breuer's method proceeds from one fundamental insight. The Torah must speak in "the language of men." But the wisdom that God would bestow upon us cannot be disclosed in a straightforward manner. The Torah therefore resorts to a technique of multivocal communication. Each strand in the text, standing on its own, reveals one aspect of the truth, and each aspect of the truth appears to contradict the other accounts. An insensitive reader, noticing the tension between the versions, imagines himself assaulted by a cacophony of conflicting voices. The perceptive student, however, experiences the magnificent counterpoint in all its power.[1] To use Rabbi Breuer's example: Genesis 1 (the so-called P account) describes one aspect of the biblical understanding of creation; Genesis 2 (the so-called J version) presents a complementary way of apprehending God's creation of the world and of man. Each text, isolated from the other, would offer a partial, hence misleading, doctrine of creation. In their juxtaposition, the two texts point the reader toward an understanding of the whole.[2]

This new approach does not obviate the need for the traditional strategies of harmonization, nor does it negate their success. It does, however, transform our idea of what it is that the traditional solutions are out to accomplish. Let me explain by commenting on one detail in one of Rabbi Breuer's studies. The laws of Jewish servitude (*eved ivri*) are expounded in three separate portions of the Torah: Exodus 21: 2–6; Leviticus 25: 39–55; Deuteronomy 15: 12–18. Leviticus diverges from the other two sources, in certain detail. Leviticus teaches that the Hebrew slave goes free in the Jubilee year, which is not mentioned elsewhere. Moreover, the legislation of Exodus and Deuteronomy includes the eventuality that the slave refuses to go free when his term of servitude is up, prescribing that his master bore his ear through with an awl, and subjugate him in perpetuity (*le-olam*); Leviticus does not recognize an enslavement that would override the Jubilee. The Rabbis (*Kiddushin* 21b) explain that the word *le-olam*, in this connection, means "for an extended term," not forever. *Le-olam* in Exodus and Deuteronomy does not conflict with Leviticus's Jubilee-based universal manumission. Thus the three texts can be amalgamated to form a consistent halakhic code on Jewish servitude.

---

[1]The analogy between the study of Torah and symphonic or contrapuntal music is taken from the introduction to Rabbi Yehiel Mikhal Epstein's *Arukh ha-Shulhan, Hoshen Mishpat*, where it is applied to the differing opinions found in the halakhic literature.

[2]Note that Rabbi Breuer's investigations are not limited to so-called doublets, in which internally consistent passages are juxtaposed. He devotes a great deal of attention to instances where the hypothesized sources are interwoven in the same chapter.

What is the plain meaning (*peshat*) of *le-olam*? Champions of the internal consistency of the Written Torah and the authoritative interpretations of the Oral Torah maintain that the word *le-olam* means what the Rabbis say it means. If this explanation cannot be justified on independent philological grounds, one must rely on rabbinic tradition as an authoritative record of biblical Hebrew. The alternative position, held, in this instance, by Rashbam and adopted by Rabbi Breuer, concedes that the plain meaning of *le-olam* implies unqualified perpetuity. The rabbinic explication of *le-olam*, according to this view, is *derash* rather than *peshat*. It cannot be treated as the plain meaning of the verses, as they appear in Exodus and Deuteronomy. But what does it mean to assert that the normative interpretation of a text is strained?

Rabbi Breuer[3] observes that each one of the three legal sections illuminates a different aspect of the Torah's teaching on Jewish servitude. To focus on what is pertinent to our example: the major theme of Leviticus, chapter 25 is that the children of Israel can never become genuine slaves, "they are My slaves, whom I took out of the land of Egypt" (Leviticus 25:55). In Deuteronomy, by contrast, the master is reminded "You were a slave in the land of Egypt and God redeemed you" (25:15). In Leviticus freedom is the inalienable right of the slave; it is the slave who left Egypt—whose servitude cannot extend beyond the limit of the Jubilee year. In Deuteronomy, it is the master who reenacts God's act of redemption, and who is therefore obligated to free his slave after his term of service. From the perspective of Deuteronomy and Exodus, stressing the master's responsibilities, the slave can forfeit the manumission extended to him by declining to go free. In that case his bondage is renewed *le-olam*, in the literal sense, forever. Leviticus, however, is concerned, not with the limits of the master's responsibility, but with the unconditional doctrine of freedom that knows no difference between master and

---

[3]See his *Pirkei Mo'adot*, vol. 1 (Jerusalem: Horev 1986), pp. 16–22, for a detailed discussion of the three passages. For the sake of brevity, I have left out Rabbi Breuer's comments on the distinctions between the Exodus and Deuteronomy versions. The persuasiveness of Rabbi Breuer's approach gains force from the accumulation of details, and thus may not be evident from our isolated discussion of the *le-olam* problem.

slave: there is no room to consider the possibility that the slave will re-linquish his right and choose to extend his servitude.

In the light of Rabbi Breuer's analysis, we may return to the question of *le-olam*. If we were to isolate the sections in Exodus and Deuteronomy, oblivious to the aspect revealed by the Leviticus passage, we would indeed interpret *le-olam* according to its plain meaning, and if this is all the Torah had to say on the topic, we would conclude that the Hebrew slave who declined his freedom is subject to interminable servitude. Conversely, were the Torah's teaching exhausted by the Leviticus pas-sage, we would be oblivious to the aspects embodied in the other texts. Had the Torah integrated the various texts, presenting a unified legal code (in the manner of Maimonides or the *Tur Shulhan Arukh*), the word *le-olam* would not have been used, because the plain meaning of the word (according to Rashbam and Rabbi Breuer) would not have conveyed clearly the ruling of the *halakhah*. But the Torah is not a straightforward legal code, and therefore the passages expounding the different aspects of the Torah's teaching are not amalgamated, but juxtaposed. The syn-thesis, interrelating the various aspects and determining their halakhic scope, is the proper domain of the Oral Law. The work of fusion some-times requires that the sources, which at the level of *peshat* are exam-ined independently of one another, undergo reinterpretation (*derash*) as part of the synthesis. The word *le-olam* carries its plain, unforced mean-ing in the isolated context, when the Torah speaks in one voice, as it were; when the Torah's theme becomes polyphonic, *le-olam* must be interpreted in conformity with the whole, even if the word is consequently burdened with an obscure and awkward sense.

Thus, for Rabbi Breuer, the harmonization of conflicting texts con-tinues to take place, but the frame of reference for which the solutions are proposed is the Torah as a complex system of texts, not the immedi-ate local context. Let me put it another way. In the past, the purpose of reconciliation techniques was to resolve an inconsistency or contradic-tion in the text. Those of us who are inspired by Rabbi Breuer's efforts may be satisfied with the time-honored answer, but not until we have investigated why the text contains a problem in the first place.[4]

---

[4]The prefatory character of these remarks leads me to dramatize the innova-tive thrust of Breuer's breakthrough. Of course his contribution is not completely

II

As we have already noted, a major theological objection to the Documentary Hypothesis has to do with the special role of Moses in transcribing the Torah. Rabbi Breuer is unwavering in his insistence upon this dogma as traditionally understood. If anything, he is convinced that the doctrine has been neglected by recent Orthodoxy, and blames much unnecessary resistance to the phenomena discovered by modern scholarship on the failure fully to take into account the unique theological-literary status of the Pentateuch. Precisely because the Torah's divine origin transcends all categories of literature, contends Breuer, it accommodates conflicts and apparent contradictions that would, in the case of any other composition, drive us to hypothesize authorship by diverse hands.

This is Rabbi Breuer's position as it is repeatedly stated in the present volume and in his other writings. At our conference, however, the topic posed to him was not confined to his own beliefs: it extended to the general question of compatibility between modern biblical scholarship and piety. Here Rabbi Breuer was forced to acknowledge the existence of scholars whose standard of religious practice is conscientious, despite beliefs that are incompatible with traditional doctrine. In an effort to understand the meaning of piety for such scholars, Rabbi Breuer entertains alternatives to the principles to which he is firmly committed. In

---

without precedent among classical medieval and modern sources. Rabbi Breuer himself has frequently alluded to the kabbalistic doctrine of *sefirot*, which considers the divine attributes as discrete qualities, as it were, reflecting the diverse aspects of the divine experienced by man, even while affirming their essential unity. In the opening chapter of the present volume I alluded to a convergence between Breuer's theory of aspects and the methods of Lithuanian *lomdut*. From an exegetical point of view one should also acknowledge the important work of Rabbi David Zvi Hoffmann. In discussing the relationship between Leviticus and Deuteronomy, for example, Rabbi Hoffmann seeks to demonstrate that each, at the level of *peshat*, addresses its own primary audience: Leviticus, the generation of the desert; Deuteronomy, the generation about to enter the land of Israel. One advantage of this sensitivity to the distinction between primary and secondary audiences (to which Breuer adverts at the end of his paper) is that it goes beyond resolving the difficulty to explain the reason we have the problem to begin with, thus anticipating my last remark in the text.

the opening section of his discussion he suggests that observant schol-ars who nonetheless deny *Torah min ha-shamayim* may justify their posi-tion by transferring to the Jewish people the authority to command that traditional religion invests in God. This position, in effect, is orthopraxy, as it severs normative behavior from normative belief.

Next, (in section II of his paper) Breuer formulates a "flexible" version of *Torah min ha-shamayim*. This view subscribes to a normative theologi-cal belief in the divine origin of the Torah, but dispenses with the unique role of Moses, thus allowing one to follow the critical approach respecting the Torah's provenance. Rabbi Breuer immediately rejects this option as well (section III of his presentation), on grounds of theological truth. He does not deny that an individual adopting this view may be studying the Bible in order to serve God, with the kind of subjective fervor that we associate with fear of heaven (*yirat shamayim*), and with an awareness of its divine origin. I have taken the trouble to rehash this part of Rabbi Breuer's discussion because many readers, unaccustomed to intellectually honest theological deliberation that attempts, empathetically, to present objectionable, even heretical, opinions, in the most tolerable light, are liable to become confused and irritable, carelessly attributing to an author the very ideas that he has so vigorously repelled.

III

Misunderstanding is the fate of the pioneer. Rabbi Breuer has persevered against the indifference of the academy and initial lack of comprehen-sion within the Torah community. But the lonely, courageous trailblazer is often at the mercy of his own exuberance, as yet unchecked by the intelligence of fellow seekers. Rabbi Breuer's work, including that found in this book, has occasionally succumbed to the temptation of one-sided formulas. If we are to build on his insights, it is important to moderate some of his excesses.

1. Rabbi Breuer believes that awareness of the phenomena highlighted by the methods and schools of Biblical Criticism should have led to a' new flowering of creative Orthodox study. His own program is a belated attempt to make the most of the opportunity. It is probably true that

the new approaches, stemming from the original work of Rabbi David Hoffmann and Rabbi Breuer, would not have become popular were it not for the challenge posed by the critics. Yet it can be argued that Rabbi Breuer, in his zeal to restore to Orthodox study its self-sufficiency, has permitted the academy to set our agenda. Although Rabbi Breuer and his school have consistently generated their exegesis from the biblical text and from the classical Jewish sources, it is tempting to assess any proposed interpretation in terms of its success in supplanting the theories of the critics.[5]

The tree is known by its fruit. As proponents of Rabbi Breuer's orientation advance in their work, steadily expanding the range of their study and leaving their detractors in the dust, this last criticism loses much of its sting. Yet Rabbi Breuer's exaggerated respect for critical presuppositions and speculations, to which he ascribes—within the limits of his theological method, of course—a solidity that is far from self-evident, may undercut the very autonomy he is striving to secure. It is quite possible to recognize the polyphonic character of the Torah, the presence of different voices in different passages (or even in the same passage), without acquiescing in many of the specific claims that Rabbi Breuer repeats without reservation. Nothing, except for the assertions of those who have concluded, on other grounds, that J precedes P, would lead me to think that Genesis 2 articulates an earlier level of religious consciousness than Genesis 1; Breuer, however, incorporates this assumption without questioning it. Many well-informed, intellectually honest individuals, contemplating the hypothesis that the J and E texts were produced by writers living in Judah and Ephraim, respectively, feel no impulse to believe it; Rabbi Breuer cites it as received truth. Most secular Israeli scholars, following Yehezkel Kaufmann, reject Wellhausen's

---

[5]Outside his programmatic essays, Rabbi Breuer rarely, if ever, cites Bible criticism as an essential background for his work. He is content to let the biblical text, augmented by its rabbinic explication, drive his discussion. *Pirkei Mo'adot* is subtitled (on the binding of both volumes, though not on the title pages!) "A Commentary to the Torah and the Festivals Deriving from (*mi-tokh*) the Biblical Text and the Words of the Sages"; while the reference to the Sages may be limited to chapters devoted to rabbinic texts, it can serve to characterize the work as a whole.

hypothesis according to which P is later than D; Breuer adopts it, though he apparently does not go along with the German professor's view that P comes after the exile to Babylonia.

Rabbi Breuer's sweeping concessions to a purportedly monolithic Bible criticism may have a purpose, from a rhetorical point of view. By ruling out, on a priori grounds, any combat with the Bible critics on their own home court, so to speak, we are spared a great deal of wasted effort. If it is neither necessary nor possible to refute the views of the critics issue by issue, our energy can be channeled into the cultivation of Rabbi Breuer's systematic solution.[6] But Breuer's theory of aspects does not depend on the credibility, in detail, of any particular corpus of modern biblical scholarship. As we endeavor to comprehend the various aspects of the multivocal Torah, we can surely afford to be more selective in our appropriation of the data served up by the critics. Intellectual honesty requires no less.[7]

----

[6]In section IV of his essay in this volume, Rabbi Breuer compares the conflict between faith and biblical scholarship to the old war between religion and scientific cosmology. He suggests that intelligent people are no longer bothered by this problem because they recognize that the scientific belief in the great age of the world rests on the premise that creation *ex nihilo* in six days cannot be allowed in scientific investigation. Most intelligent religious people known to me simply do not take the six days of Genesis as a literal statement about cosmology. Either under the pressure of scientific evidence, or as an outgrowth of theological reflection, they have come to the conclusion that the Torah is not, *in this particular case*, judging the scientific issue. Here, too, Rabbi Breuer seems to prefer an approach that short circuits the conflict once and for all, leaving one free to attend to more important matters. Here, too, it seems to me that the advantages of a sweeping solution cannot exempt us completely from considering problems individually, as they come up. Contemporary philosophy of science has become dubious of armchair attempts to delineate in advance the contours of scientific theory, and the same skepticism extends to a priorism in theological inquiry.

[7]The previous analysis parallels the first and third criticisms of Breuer in Moshe J. Bernstein, "The Orthodox Jewish Scholar and Jewish Scholarship: Duties and Dilemmas," *The Torah U-Madda Journal* 3 (1991–1992): 23–24. As the discerning reader will not fail to note, the differences in the way the discussion unfolds are as significant as the similarities.

2. According to Rabbi Breuer the literary complexity of the Torah can be explained in only two ways: either multiple voices of one Author, namely God, who transcends the one-dimensionality of human communication; or multiple authors, as taught by the critics. An individual human author, as authorship is normally construed, could not have brought it off.

It is not at all clear to me why this should be the case. Great writers are eminently capable of employing multiple styles: the stylistic variations among Kierkegaard's "pseudonyms," for example, are so thoroughgoing that they show up on computer analysis. It is even more obvious that masterly authors can authentically represent polyphonic perspectives.[8] When conflicting or contradictory motifs appear in a work of literary art or philosophy, we may dismiss it as a blemish in the work, but in studying a great author, we are wise to give him, or her, the benefit of the doubt, and to judge the obscurity essential to the communication of enigmatic subject matter. Only when we detect, in the production of a great author, convincing internal, or external, signs of carelessness or sloppy thinking, do we conclude, with a shrug of the shoulders, that even Homer nods. If we are to compare God's relation to the Torah with a human author's relation to his composition, we will, of course, compare God to a great author rather than a mediocre one. And since we believe that God's work is perfect, we will always treat any inconcinnity in the Torah as integral to the perfection of the whole. Thus we arrive at Rabbi Breuer's fundamental insight, that the complexity of the Torah's form corresponds to the profundity of its message. But we do so without Breuer's either/or, which makes a fragmented, intellectually shallow interpretation of the Torah the only possible alternative to the traditional belief in the giving of the Torah to Moses.

Our divergence from Rabbi Breuer's dichotomy between the Pentateuch and all other literature has implications for our study of the non-Pentateuchal books of the Bible, *Nevi'im u-Ketuvim*. Throughout the Bible we encounter texts whose inner complexity, or whose contrast with other texts, richly rewards the kind of analysis provided by Rabbi

---

[8]Within biblical literature, this is undeniably and trivially true of Job and Kohelet.

Breuer's theory of aspects. If *Humash* is *sui generis*, in the sense that Breuer's fundamental insight cannot be applied elsewhere, it is difficult to explain why his method applies equally well to *Nakh*. If, however, the coincidence of complexity and profundity distinguishes great literature in general, then all parts of the Bible display this character to an intense degree.[9]

3. The approach taken by Rabbi Breuer in the present essay is concerned exclusively with the literary analysis of the Torah. It is impossible for one man to do everything—certainly not at the same time. As I have argued earlier in this volume, the prosecution of a completely self-sufficient system of Orthodox biblical studies is not feasible, and unrealistic demands can only result in paralysis. Yet we cannot act as if the only problems raised by modern biblical studies are literary. And it is particularly important to realize that literary problems cannot be sequestered from historical questions.

IV

The idea of the multivocal Torah and the resolve to advance beyond reconciling the inconcinnities of texts to discover why the difficulties are there to begin with—these principles are an enduring legacy of Rabbi Breuer's work in this area. His courageous and uncompromising dedication to creating a *derekh ha-limmud* in *Tanakh* embodies the Rav's ideal of the *homo religiosus* who "calmly but persistently seeks his own path to full cognition of the world, [who] claims freedom of methodology; [who] has faith in his ability to perform the miracle of comprehending the world."[10] The questions and criticisms I have just raised demonstrate how much more work is required of us if we are to cultivate the fields he has

---

[9]In this section IV of his essay in this volume Rabbi Breur bemoans the consequences of what he percieves as the tendency of contemporary Ortodox Jews to reduce the Torah to the level of other biblical books . My own experience suggests the opposite: the natural prompting of piety leads most people to ascribe to all biblical books the highest possible level of divine involvement (See, for example, Malbim's preface to his commentary on Jeremiah.)

[10]See the dedication to this book (p. xvii).

plowed. As his own production continues unabated,[11] and the activities of his students and sympathizers pick up steam, it is a duty and a privilege to show gratitude for his initiative and inspiration.

---

[11]The bibliography in Rabbi Breuer's two volume Festschrift also lists his remarkable achievements in the study of the MT and the cantillation tradition (*taamei ha-mikra*). This work has implications for Breuer's approach to the issues belonging to the "lower criticism" of the biblical text, which are not discussed in the present volume. As an admirer of Rabbi Breuer I am pleased to note that, by the time the Festschrift appeared in print, his bibliography had already outstripped the one there compiled.

7

The Study of Bible and the Primacy of the Fear of Heaven: Compatibility or Contradiction?

Mordechai Breuer

The topic assigned to me implies a possible contradiction between the study of Bible and *yirat shamayim* (fear of heaven). The God-fearing student of the Bible must confront this presumed contradiction and seek to resolve it. Failing to do so, his wisdom will take precedence over his piety; even worse: as the result of psychological conflict, the scholar in him will undermine his piety and as one who is God-fearing he will reject his scholarship.

To address the alleged contradiction we must first define the concepts involved, the study of Bible, on the one hand, and *yirat shamayim* on the other hand. Then we shall see whether a real conflict exists and if it has a resolution. "Study of Bible," in our context, does not refer to the type of Bible study familiar to the Jewish people from the day the Torah was given. It is inconceivable that such Bible study could detract from one's *yirat shamayim*. To the contrary: not only is Torah study valuable because it leads to moral and religious action, but a strong grounding in all the areas of Jewish study, Bible, Mishnah, Jewish Law and Midrash, is essential to sustain the fear of God. The kind of study under scrutiny is that which has appeared in recent centuries, beginning with Jean Astruc, maintaining that the Torah is composed of distinct documents, each written in its own style, whose contents are in conflict. This paper will deal exclusively with the implications of this method of studying the Torah, by which I mean the Five Books of Moses (the *Humash*).

This hypothesis led to a new method of studying the Bible, known as "critical study of the Bible." This science, developed mainly by gentile scholars, achieved impressive results. The critics persuasively described the nature of the documents that, in their opinion, make up the Torah. Holding that the authorship of these documents by one person, as natural authorship is understood, is impossible, whether in Moses' generation or in any other, they inferred that several authors, differing among themselves in world outlook and literary style, wrote the Torah.

As we shall see below, when we look at the critical analysis of Genesis chapters 1 and 2, the author, called J, is distinguished by a sensitive, poetic soul. Another, dubbed P, was a man of law and order, of scientific mind-set, whose writing, exact and concise, lacks feeling and poetic flourish. The critics also characterized the other primary writers of the Torah, naming them E and D. These authors inhabit different spiritual worlds and different times and places. J came first, living in Judah at the height of the monarchy. Shortly afterward came E, who resided in Ephraim. Subsequent to and close to in spirit to E came D, who lived at the time of the prophet Jeremiah. P, the final writer, who had the most profound influence on the Jewish religion, lived either during the period preceding the destruction of the first temple or during the subsequent exile. Hundreds of years separate the first and last authors of the Bible. Yet these writers did not create their texts alone; they summarized and refined ancient traditions that reached them either through oral transmission or as written documents.

The transformation and development that made these sources into the Torah is often apparent between the lines. The editors exercised exquisite craftsmanship on centuries of tradition. The final stage of the Torah's composition is due to the redactor, R, who made an integrated text of these documents, which until then were distinct literary creations. When the redactor transcribed earlier documents without addition or subtraction, the strata are easily identified. When, however, he combined material from two or three documents, additions and deletions were necessary to avoid contradiction or repetition. Often the editor's patchwork does not disguise the gap between the original documents and the redactor's version.

The power of these inferences, based on solid argument and internally consistent premises, will not be denied by intellectually honest persons. One cannot deny the evidence before one's eyes. As committed believers, we cannot ignore what human reason points to with confidence; we cannot pretend that falsehood is truth. Therefore we cannot regard God's Torah as the unified composition of *one human author* in *one generation*. Willy-nilly, the Torah contains several documents, which, viewed as *natural products of human culture*, must have been written by different people over the course of many generations before their final redaction. It is the implications for *yirat shamayim* of the study of the Torah based on this method that we must investigate. But this requires that we define what is meant by *yirat shamayim*.

The accepted meaning of *yirat shamayim* is fear of sin. One who fears God is diligent in obeying His commandments, as meticulous in fulfilling the "lighter as the more grave," rigorously adhering to all that the halakhic literature determines as law. He wholeheartedly believes this law to be God's word, that God is concerned with the "four cubits of *halakhah*," that defiance of God's will is inconceivable. This is what Jews mean by *yirat shamayim*. This definition engenders no conflict between the study of Bible and *yirat shamayim*, provided that the person who accepts the tenets of Bible Criticism truly fears God and scrupulously executes the obligations of Jewish law, dreading sin and joyful in the performance of the *mitzvot*. We might draw an analogy from Rav Kook's comments regarding the debate over the date of the composition of the Mishnah:

> The sanctity of the basic measures of the Torah is the same, whether these units were transmitted to Moses at Sinai or decrees of a court of law, because it is the nation's acceptance that is significant, and it is due to their commitment that we fulfill in purity even matters that are only decrees of later generations, such as the decrees of R. Gershom. Likewise there should be no difference in our wholehearted loyalty to the oral law, whether it was completed earlier or later. (*Iggerot HaRe'iyah* I 194)

These comments about the Oral Law might be applied to the written Torah. We can imagine an individual who holds that it makes no difference to our attitude toward the sanctity of the written Torah whether Moses wrote the Torah or whether an editor at the time of Ezra compiled the text. The essential point, in the view of such an individual, is the commitment of the nation to accept as binding the words of the Torah in its present form. What obligates us is our tradition; our ancestors and sages declare that God commands us to follow the teachings of the Sages even when there is no clear source for this in the written Torah. And just as the Jewish people have always fulfilled the Sages' teachings, the individual we are considering is prepared to accept the demands of the Torah even though, for him, its authority is based on the Sages' affirmation.

From the perspective of this individual, there is no possible conflict between critical study and *yirat shamayim*: at worst, he will continue to observe the entire Torah faithfully based on the authority of the Sages. The Torah's power to obligate us is undiminished; it derives from God, who commanded us to abide by the Sages' decrees. This is enough to provide *yirat shamayim*. Just as the God-fearer would never mock the law of the *Shulhan Arukh*, the Jewish Code of Law, even when it encodes later decrees, just as, for example, he eschews leavened bread that had been owned by a Jew during the Passover as carefully as he avoids bread on Passover itself, just as he joyfully celebrates the second festival day of the Diaspora as he fulfilled the obligations on the previous day—so he will treat with sanctity the Torah whose origin, in his opinion, derives from a post-Mosaic redactor.

The previous discussion is not merely hypothetical. Quite a few scholars, and their students, identify with the findings of biblical scholarship, yet faithfully and reverently observe the full scope of *halakhah*, meaning that they adopt halakhic minutiae as determined by recognized rabbinic authority, even as they harbor no doubt about the late authorship of the Torah. This is because they see the acceptance by the Jewish people as the essential factor and they are committed to obeying the word of God, the *halakhah*, as transmitted by tradition.

If this position is true, then the contradiction implied by the title is nonexistent. But I do not accept it. The problem is not that of faithful observance, but rather of belief. And for this reason I cannot claim that the difficulties regarding critical study of Bible can be removed in this way.

II

The Liberal Solution

Belief is certainly no less important for Judaism than the network of laws and commandments. The framework of faith specifically includes belief in *Torah min ha-shamayim,* "the divinity of the Torah." At first glance it seems that this belief is compromised, if not totally destroyed, by the critical study of Bible. It is *this* contradiction between the scientific study of Bible and the belief in a heavenly Torah that must be addressed. For this purpose we must define the character of this belief. The observant scholars we are discussing might try to solve the problem by giving the divinity of Torah a relatively flexible, liberal, rationalistic interpretation. Divinity would then mean that the Torah derives from prophetic inspiration rather than human intellect. The author was not transcribing his own thoughts but acting as a "man of God," who saw divine images and heard God's speech. This Torah, we declare, is divine because a person who experienced the divine inscribed the heavenly directives.

This view does not, indeed cannot, assert that Moses alone wrote the Torah, as a human author composes a book. For even a prophet writing under divine inspiration retains his personality and style. The style of his prophecy manifests the depths of his soul; he hears God's word, but absorbs according to the nature of his soul. Nothing is revealed to him by God that his nature is incapable of comprehending. Moreover, when a prophet formulates what he heard and saw in his prophetic experience, he speaks in his own language, limited by his personality. Therefore Hosea could not have heard what was spoken to Isaiah, and Zephaniah would not utter the words of Jeremiah; it is inconceivable that Ezekiel's prophecy would have been transmitted to Amos or that Micah would speak Zephaniah's words. By this logic Moses could not have composed all the documents included in the Torah since, as suggested above, their content and style indicate different authors at different times. If Moses is the author of the Torah, as we normally think of an author, it is all the more difficult to believe that he would contradict himself so frequently, as the documents appear to do. To view Moses himself as the editor of the Torah borders on absurdity: having composed conflicting accounts, he then, on this scheme, labored strenuously to disguise the discrepancies. Biblical scholarship has argued convincingly, according to the view we are discussing, that no individual person, neither Moses nor any other prophet, could have composed the Torah. Yet, according to that approach, this in no way affects Jewish faith.

That is because the view we are discussing accepts *Torah min ha-shamayim* as a belief that the Torah was transmitted through prophecy, not that Moses was *the* unique prophet who received the Torah from heaven. If Moses is to be viewed as the "author" of the Torah, in the conventional sense of the term, he should have written "And God spoke to me saying," like other prophets who wrote their own prophecies. The view we are now discussing would argue that only one passage in the Oral Law explicitly asserts that "Moses wrote his book" (*Bava Batra* 14b), and that it is nowhere stated that one who denies Moses' composition of the Torah loses his share in the next world as is the case with one who denies the divinity of the Torah (*Sanhedrin* 90a). Many of the greatest scholars in the medieval and early modern periods deviated, on occasion, from a rabbinic dictum, when it flew in the face of the text's simple meaning.[1] Using their example as precedent, one might take the liberty of disregarding the view expressed in *Bava Batra*, insofar as a reading of the biblical text does not support the view that Moses wrote the Torah in the manner of a conventional human composition.[2]

---

[1] See, for example, Rashbam's introduction to the Torah; Ibn Ezra's introduction to the Torah; Abravanel's introduction to the Prophets; Or haHayyim's introduction to the Torah *inter alia*.

[2] This principle can also be applied to historical assertions that conflict with the text's plain meaning. Of the talmudic discussion (*Rosh Hashanah* 3b) that assumes "Cyrus is Darius is Artaxerxes," Rabbi Zerahia Ba'al ha-Maor observes that the biblical text plainly regards Cyrus, Darius, and Artaxerxes as three different people. This approach has also been applied to the talmudic passage immediately following the statement "Moses wrote his book." The Talmud in *Bava Batra* goes on to say that "Joshua wrote his book," and Abravanel (in his general introduction to early prophets) infers, from several verses in Joshua, that Joshua could not have authored his book. Similarly the author of *Shaagat Aryeh* posits, in opposition to the implication of another part of the talmudic statement in *Bava Batra*, that Ezra the scribe did not write the book of Chronicles himself but compiled documents of previous authors: he edited the book but did not write it. (See my article "The Documentary Theory of the *Shaagat Aryeh*," *Megadim* 2 [Fall 5747 (1986)]: 9–22.) Using such reasoning, the scholars we

The position we are discussing concedes that the Torah comprises several documents, written by different prophets in various eras. The documents are *min ha-shamayim*, because they are the words of the living God. There is an infinite gap between God, the source of the Torah, whose heavenly abode transcends space and time, and man, the recipient of prophecy, created from earth, who lives within the confines of space and time. The human intellect is limited; man cannot grasp or utter contradictory ideas. God is not bound by this constraint. Hence the one God reveals Himself in the world by exhibiting manifold traits and contradictory actions—like an old man seated at rest and a young man at war—with the attribute of justice and the attribute of mercy.[3] The unity of God is disclosed through the encompassing of opposing aspects and actions. The one God who embraces justice and mercy can communicate seemingly contradictory prophecies, corresponding to these aspects of divinity.

The prophecies given to individual prophets at different times thus reveal paradoxical elements. One prophet, oriented to justice and whose generation is particularly suited to hear the providential perspective of justice, received and transcribed the prophecy of judgment. Another, oriented to mercy and whose generation is particularly suited to hear of a world guided by mercy, will receive and transcribe the prophecy characterized by kindness. The diversity of these two prophecies reflects different authorship; yet both emanate from one source and from one shepherd. The view we are examining treats the composition of the Torah like the handing down of prophecy just described. The editor of the Torah had before him the various sources. But the Torah is not limited, as would be the prophecy of the individual prophet, to the perspectives of law (*din*) or mercy (*rahamim*); rather the Torah expresses the quality of harmony (*tiferet*), combining law and mercy. By God's instruction, the editor

---

are discussing might propose that Moses only wrote the part of "his book" that the Torah explicitly attributes to him (Deuteronomy 31:9). The rest of the Torah, however, could derive from other men of God, living at other times. These documents, redacted by a prophet who added and subtracted according to God's will, form one book, one *torah*, in which there is not one letter belonging to the human intellect, being wholly *Torah min ha-shamayim*, from the first word to the last.

[3]See Maimonides *Hilkhot Yesodei ha-Torah* 1:9.

inscribed the Torah, and this quality of *tiferet* governs the Torah as a whole. We shall have more to say about this further in this discussion. Now, however, we are still occupied with the liberal approach.

Except for its significant omission of the specific role of *Moses*, an issue to which we will return, the ideas already outlined avoid any conflict between the modern study of Bible and *yirat shamayim*. The scholars identify the documents that comprise the Torah and try to explain the centuries of development behind them, prior to the coming of the prophet who consolidated the sources. The religious student, for his part, recognizes the hand of God in combining the various aspects of His revelation.

So far we have described the discoveries of *Biblical Criticism*, not the beliefs of *biblical critics*. Our adoption of the discoveries of biblical scholarship does not, by any means, imply assent to the beliefs of the scholars. We must know that an iron curtain separates, not faith and scholarship, but many men of scholarship and men of faith. While the scholars view the Torah as a grand literary creation, composed by human beings, we believe that the Torah is from heaven. This is not a debate between faith and science but rather a confrontation of faith and heresy. Science can only investigate what reason apprehends. The human intellect cannot comprehend God and is therefore unable to certify prophecy. Scholarly study of the Torah postulates the biblical text as the product of human agency, and as the product of human activity the Torah must reflect multiple sources. But this presupposition of the scientific approach, which enables the human mind to proceed, is not subject to confirmation or refutation. Scholars cannot prove that the Torah is a human product, because that is the assumption that underlies the entire enterprise. At the same time it would be impossible to demonstrate that the Torah is divine, based on the assumptions of scholarship, because that belief contradicts the axioms with which the proof must be consistent; in any event, it would be an attempt to demonstrate something beyond the capacity of human reason. Whether the Torah is a human or divine creation cannot be decided by scientific reason, which has no authority over the domain that transcends reason. Where the intellect falls short faith responds confidently. Faith knows with certainty "the foundation of wisdom, to know that there is a first cause" (Rambam *Hilkhot Yesodei ha-Torah* 1:1) and it is a basic religious truth that God reveals Himself to man. An honest scholar acknowledges that this judgment is beyond his competence as a man of science.

In fact, scholars frequently reiterate their conviction that the Torah is a merely human composition, in no way different from other literary creations. But this claim already abandons the realm of science and enters that of faith. With this pronouncement they become spokesmen for a "faith," and its content is heretical. We who believe wholeheartedly in the divinity of the Torah must oppose them. But the debate about that which lies beyond science cannot be judged from within science. Only a heavenly voice acknowledged by all can resolve this conflict authoritatively.

Before addressing the role of Moses, let us summarize our conclusions so far. The position we are now describing is prepared to accept without reservation the views of scholarship so long as the scholars have not ventured beyond the limits of scientific method, which include the demarcation of the various documents in the Torah, the development that preceded them, and the editorial process that followed. Only when scholars deviate from the scientific framework and introduce heretical beliefs about the Torah's human composition must we reject their assertions and hold fast to our tradition. This traditional belief suffuses our personal lives. The Torah we study day and night is not a Torah propounded by human authors, but a divine Torah received by prophets who inscribed a vision revealed to them by God.

III

The Traditional Alternative

Everything we have articulated up to this point is compatible with the liberal definition of *Torah min ha-shamayim*, which ignores the specific role of Moses in transmitting the Torah. In reality, however, this definition of *Torah min ha-shamayim* does not prevail in Jewish thought. From antiquity, our Sages have never considered equating the Five Books of Moses with other prophecy. They regarded the equation, not as proper faith, but as utter heresy. The status of Moses is inherently different from that of all other prophets. The latter saw God in a vision, through a glass darkly; they heard His voice as a riddle that required clarification and interpretation. When they subsequently transmitted God's message to the people, when they wrote it down, they could not convey literally what they had seen and heard. Instead each adopted his own style and language. Moses was different. The loyal servant in God's house, to whom God spoke as one converses with a companion; he perceived God through a clear glass, as it were, and heard His message expressed precisely. Therefore Moses wrote the words of the Torah as God spoke them, without injecting his own. Thus the Torah of Moses was literally *min ha-shamayim*; the Lawgiver summoned His prophet to the heavens themselves. "Like an author dictating a book to his scribe," God dictated the Torah to His prophet from beginning to end.

Just as the content and style of the Torah are independent of Moses' personality, so too they transcend his particular time. The book of Jeremiah, for example, could only have been written during or after the life of Jeremiah, since it includes his spoken words, which could not have preceded him. Because the Torah, however, is not the words of a prophet but those of God who transcends time, the sages could speak of the Torah preexisting the world, "black fire upon white fire." By dating the Torah before the creation of time, the sages figuratively depicted the Torah's immediate relationship to God Himself, He who is an all-consuming fire. A thousand generations before the world's creation, when God and His name were still one, and no prophet existed to share in its composition, the Torah already existed. Thus God's direct creation of the Torah is like that of heaven and earth, on the first day of the world, when even the angels did not exist.

This midrash alludes to a specific analogy between the process of creation and the order of writing. Creation proceeds from the absolute free will of the divine, not subject to the law of natural development of the cosmos. The same applies to God's writing of the Torah, which derives from God's free will, not subject to the rules of literary development. God spoke, "And it was so" defines both creation of the world and creation of the Torah. The sages taught that the Torah preexists the world, like the architect's blueprint that precedes the building. The Torah is the blueprint because it incorporates the divine attributes employed in the creation as well.[4]

---

[4]The two blessings before the *Shema* reinforce this association of Torah and creation. The first praises God as "creator of light and darkness," while the second thanks Him for teaching us the Torah's commandments and laws. These blessings parallel the two halves of Psalm 19, which first recount God's glory and then extol the Torah. The same duality is found in the Sabbath prayers:

This definition of belief in the unique divinity of *Torat Mosheh* is the only one recognized by the Jewish people, adopted by all sages. Whoever views the Torah as an ordinary prophetic work denies its unique status. In the previous section we examined the *possibility* of interpreting the meaning of *Torah min ha-shamayim* liberally, insofar as this option is attractive to some scholars. It is impossible, however, to maintain this possibility as an account of the way this doctrine was understood throughout the generations of Jewish belief. Traditional belief means God's revelation of the Torah through Moses. Only Moses, the worthy scribe to whom God committed the task of writing every section, verse, and letter of the Torah from His very "lips." Other prophets did not attain this level: "No prophet arose in Israel like Moses, whom God recognized face to face" (Deuteronomy 34:11).

Let us revert to the statement in *Bava Batra* about the authors of the biblical books. As we saw, the Talmud ascribes the Torah and the book of Joshua to Moses and Joshua respectively. As we also saw, there were *Rishonim*, like Abravanel, who held that Joshua did not author his book. Analogous arguments of at least equal strength could have been deployed against Mosaic authorship, and although the commentators were duly aware of them, no one would have dared to propose such a conclusion. The reason for this difference is clear from the previous discussion. Whether the book of Joshua was written by Joshua or, as Abravanel thought, by Samuel, does not affect principles of faith; it is merely an historical query about prophetic authorship. Since Abravanel held that the simple meaning of the biblical text conclusively shows that *Joshua* was not written by the man Joshua, he did not adopt the rabbinic view. The role of Moses in writing the Torah, by contrast, engages fundamental issues of faith; *Torah min ha-shamayim* depends on Moses writing it. Had Abravanel concluded that Moses did not write the Torah he would ipso facto have dissented from the doctrine that the Torah is from heaven. Such a heretical notion could never have entered his mind.

---

the evening prayer celebates the Sabbath of creation; the morning prayer refers to the Sabbath of the Torah-giving. The blessing after *Shema*, Psalm 19, and the afternoon Sabbath prayer culminate with the world's redemption. The purpose of the creation and the subject of the entire Torah is nothing less than God's redemption of history.

Abravanel's distinction between the Torah and the book of Joshua is not a random imposition of dogma, but goes together with our entire conception of the Torah. Why shouldn't the arguments for post-Joshua authorship apply to the Torah as well? Many verses in the Torah are indeed incompatible with Moses' particular historical and personal situatedness. Hence Moses, *viewed as a flesh and blood author*, could not have written such a Torah. But this point is totally unremarkable: our Sages did not teach that Moses wrote the Torah in the same way that other prophets wrote their books. Since Moses inscribed the words of God, no conventional argument about authorship can undermine his role. God is beyond space and time, His writing is not subject to natural limitation; hence conventional scientific debate cannot determine the nature of the Authorship.

IV

The Point of Divergence

Let us review the salient positions of Biblical Criticism, as applied to the Torah. First, there is the thesis that the Torah contains discrete documents integrated by an editor whose work is evident throughout the Torah. We too must acknowledge these arguments because we too assert that God's Torah, in its plain sense, speaks "the language of human beings." When read by the rules that govern human speech, the Torah is consonant with the scholarly evaluation of the text.

In addition, the scholars assert that the Torah is a human composition, similar to other literary works. This view, as we have noted, presupposes itself. A human author is limited by his specific time and place, unable to grasp the conflicting aspects in one idea, unable to employ strategies of authorial multiplicity, unable to dispense with generations of development. If the Torah is a human document, the conclusion is inescapable that it was composed piecemeal in the manner that the critics imagine. Thus, the religious believer can reject the assumption about the source of the text without denying the literary analysis the scholars have proposed.

This is the position that we have staked out. God, who is beyond the limitations of time and space, prepared the Torah, declaring in one utterance what man can comprehend only as a combination of differing sources. Before the world was created, God redacted one document characterized by justice and one characterized by mercy, and synthesized them with the quality of harmony. After a thousand generations this Torah, "black fire on white fire," descended to earth. Moses, the faithful shepherd, was summoned to the upper realm, and brought it down to the terrestrial sphere.

Earlier we mentioned the relationship between the creation of the world and the Torah. This parallel is also relevant to the relationship between faith and science. Faith informs us that the world came into being in six days; science claims convincingly that the world was slowly formed over millions of years. Yet here it is commonly recognized that the conflict is imaginary. The scientific evidence assumes that the world coalesced spontaneously. But this very supposition, if it is not self-evident, is unprovable. For this reason men of faith can set this assumption aside and declare that God's free act created the world and that this untrammeled freedom is perfectly consistent with His creation of the world in six days through divine utterance. It is because of a division of domains of this sort that intelligent people today are rarely troubled by conflict between faith and the natural sciences.

Inexplicably, the truce between faith and science has not penetrated the discipline of biblical scholarship. Instead the emphasis is put on the contradiction between faith and science. Unable to withstand the contradiction, most men of faith consciously avoid biblical scholarship in order to safeguard their traditional belief. Few faithful Jews are prepared to risk their souls in order to resolve the tension. The truth is, however, that this conflict is illusory, the product of unsophisticated thinking. It arises because both men of faith and scientists have strayed from their disciplines and entered foreign areas. The scholars believe they have indisputably proven that Moses did not write the Torah, oblivious to the fact that this entire argument depends on their heretical assumptions. The believers, on the other hand, wearing the mantle of the "scientist," attack the scientific arguments of their interlocutors, instead of opposing their heretical presuppositions.

How did this situation come about? Why do so many believing Jews see a conflict in the area of Bible study? Possibly the historical context of the discussion is responsible, as much of early Biblical Criticism was nurtured in an ambience of antipathy to Judaism. But it seems that a

more significant reason for this situation is confusion about the meaning of *Torah min ha-shamayim*. It is likely that many believing Jews have
difficulty with *Torah min ha-shamayim* in its traditional connotation.
Consciously or unconsciously they equate *Torah min ha-shamayim* with
the divine origin of the other prophetic works, written by the prophet
himself, in his own language, based on his transcendental experience.
They naively think that their belief in the divinity of the Torah is intact
and that the Mishnah's stricture against one who denies the Torah's
divine origin does not refer to them. They also know well that the Sages
throughout history wholeheartedly affirmed that Moses wrote the entire
Torah, and that this belief is so fundamental to Judaism that one who
rejects it undermines the entire Torah. Yet they fail to recognize that
the traditional position regarding Mosaic composition of the Torah is a
corollary of the *primary belief* that God created the Torah. As a result of
this misstep, they are content to treat the Torah as Moses' composition,
like other prophetic books. But we have claimed that the scholars are
right: Moses, as a human individual, could not have composed the Torah,
and this is precisely what the *unique* status of Moses is all about. Unfortunately, these believers hold tightly to Jewish faith as they understand
it, combining belief in Mosaic authorship with a failure to recognize the
unique role of Moses. Consequently, they must wage war against science,
attempting to refute scientifically all that scholars and scholarship have
proven. The battle is lost from the start. The naïve believer is at a distinct disadvantage because the fight is neither between faith and heresy
nor between faith and science, but rather between faith and ignorance,
speaking in the name of a mistaken conception of faith. Science gets the
better of ignorance, undermining their imagined faith.

Even among people who do not tend to obliterate the distinction
between Torah and the Prophets, another factor is at work. They reject
the position proposed in this chapter because they view it as impossible
that the one God who created the Torah could possibly produce apparently inconsistent documents. In effect they are applying what is true of
secular literature to the holy. A secular author who contradicts himself
testifies to thoughtlessness and a lack of intellectual and spiritual integrity. The Torah, they argue, must be unified and uniform without contradictions and internal "flaws," like God Himself.

This position is correct in its definition of *Torah min ha-shamayim* but
seriously mistaken about the content of *Torah min ha-shamayim*. It displays a kinship with the pagan attitude that moves from an awareness of

the manifold nature of Divine actions to the assertion of divine multiplicity. God declared at Mount Sinai: "I am the Lord your God. I-in Egypt, I-at the Sea, I-at Sinai, I am past and I am future, I am for this world and I am for the next." For Jewish faith God's unity in the world is made manifest when He reveals His many aspects in what appear to be conflicting actions. This conception of God underlies the unity of the Torah. It is the pagan mentality that infers from contradictory aspects of God's activity, reflected in the multiple literary aspects of the Torah, the existence of multiple deities, and, correspondingly, multiple authors of the Torah. This wrongheaded approach leads one to think that conflicting documents in the Torah are irreconcilable with a unified Torah from God. Hence the strained denial that the discrepancies exist, and the compulsion to adduce scientific refutations of dubious cogency. Hence the attempt to persuade themselves and us that all biblical scholars, including the great minds among them, are deluded and deluding, motivated by wickedness, folly, or hatred of Jews.

The principle emerging from all of this is that there is no real tension between faith and science so long as the conception of faith is free of distortion. One who adopts the inferior (liberal) concept of *Torah min ha-shamayim* as no different from the other prophetic books is in danger of concluding that the Torah was not written by Moses at all. He is distinguished from the outright heretic only by his belief in the divinity of the Torah, as he understands it. The heretical scholars deem the Torah's writers and editors mere mortals, while the believer who adopts the liberal concept of *Torah min ha-shamayim* maintains that the Torah, like other prophetic works, was written and edited by men of God based on revelation.

In contrast to this, the superior (traditional) concept of *Torah min ha-shamayim* implies necessarily that only Moses could be its author. He accepts the results of the critical method, insofar as God's Torah was written in the language of human beings. The scholarly arguments, which rely on linguistic principles of human communication, are significant for him too, and require neither refutation nor opposition. But he rejects every word of what the scholars maintain with respect to the writing and editing of the Torah, because he is committed to God's authorship, and regards as heresy the view that the Torah is man-made.

Let us contrast the three views we have discussed. The secular scholarly position views the Torah as a collection of documents, written by J, E, P, and D, edited by R. The liberal religious view accepts this hypothesis, but ascribes the documents to authentic prophets of God. The traditional belief, which we advocate, holds that the Torah is directly authored by God. Since we acknowledge the phenomena uncovered by the scholars, this means that God provided J, E, P, D, and R the editorial layers. Our belief differs inherently from the first two, because those approaches see the Torah as the work of man. If, however, we consider, not the question of authorship but the nature of Torah study, the essential distinction is between the first view and the latter two. According to the first perspective the Torah presents a merely human understanding; according to both of the "religious" views the Torah manifests the supreme divine intellect. The scholar who adopts the first position studies Torah with the measure of detachment appropriate to other literary study. The believer, by contrast, learns Torah with holy trepidation and reverence, in the awareness that he is studying the word of God. This reverence is possible even if one believes that the Torah was formulated by prophets who heard God's word rather than by God Himself; either way it is the divine word. In fact, Jews cultivate this sense of awe toward all the biblical books: no one would think of distinguishing between the Torah, on the one hand, and the book of Isaiah for example, on the other hand. The Jew studies both with the same degree of assiduity, respect, and dignity due to the word of God.

V

Example: Genesis, Chapters 1 and 2

We have alluded to the many contradictions between passages in the Torah. For earlier generations these contradictions attracted exegetical attention, as each exegete strove to resolve the difficulties. The Documentary Hypothesis altered the situation. The contradictions now serve as markers for the various documents: questions of exegetical conflict now become questions about the accounts of different authors. The scholar aims to diagnose the personal and historical factors responsible for the conflicting versions of the documents.

Let us take one example: the well-known discrepancy between the first two chapters of the Torah. According to the scholarly consensus, P wrote the first chapter. P looked at the world like a natural scientist.

Therefore the order of creation follows the natural development of species: vegetation and animate beings precede man. The fundamental purpose of nature, in this account, is to preserve the created species. Hence one would not imagine man being created alone. God created him male and female; for only thus is his existence perpetuated. No doubt, the scholar concludes, this account bespeaks a late date, for it presupposes a highly developed consciousness of natural law.

The second chapter expresses a totally different perspective. J, its author, is a sensitive poetic soul who saw the world through the eyes of a poet. His world cannot be portrayed as alienated, governed by the mechanical forces of nature; its only goal, survival. Self-preservation in the biological sense is not enough; a spiritual end must be imported, a meaning beyond brute existence, one that radiates nobility, beauty, and love. Only man endows the world with meaning and only through him can a purpose be conceived. For this reason God formed him first. Vegetation and animal life are recounted afterwards: their significance is tied to their human meaning. Man, in this account, had to precede woman. Only thus could man experience the pain of being alone. When woman is subsequently created he rejoices over her like a groom over a bride. With the gifts of joy and love, the creation process is complete. This description, the critic might claim, befits the nation's early stages: a world full of song and imagination, consciousness of the mechanical nature still undeveloped.

The critic links the portrayals in the two documents to the distinct personal and historical backgrounds of their authors. The editor's achievement was to accept both portrayals and combine them into one book, thus embracing the truth that both express. Indeed the Torah articulates complementary aspects of the created world. In the wild forests, for example, vegetation sprouts without man's help; in settled regions grass grows only after man tills the earth. From one perspective God created male and female together to perpetuate the species. From another, He created the two sexes separately so that woman's creation would mark the entry of happiness, joy, and love into a lonely world. The critic does not believe that these respective interpretations were intended by the authors of the two documents. Each document presents the monochromatic outlook of its author. Only the editor, by distilling the partial truth in each version, uncovered the broad perspective which permitted him to embrace several true texts within one Torah. When traditional rabbinic commentaries reconcile the conflicting views, they are explaining the *peshat* of the redactor's final product.

When we, who believe in the divinity of the Torah, adopt the critical division of sources, we do not assign the contradictory portrayals of creation in the Torah to different human authors and redactors. Instead, we refer the distinctions to the different qualities of God. In chapter 1, God is identified with the quality of justice implied in the name *Elohim*, and creates a world governed by law. In chapter 2, the quality of mercy, associated with the Tetragrammaton, engenders a world of mercy. The internal differences between these worlds include discrepancies in the order of creation (vegetation, living things, and man), and in the way man and woman were created. The believer knows that God contains all variation within Himself as surely as His rainbow contains the spectrum of colors. He encompasses justice and mercy; He can therefore juxtapose conflicting accounts reflecting these conflicting qualities. The critics claim that J preceded P chronologically, in line with their presuppositions. We would say instead that, within human culture, the spiritual conception of the world precedes perception in terms of natural order. The Creator, who is beyond time and space, not subject to the laws of historical development, presents these two conflicting perspectives simultaneously.

God formed the world neither according to pure justice or pure mercy, but rather justice tempered by mercy and mercy limited by justice. The two qualities were not expressed in their pure form, but were synthesized. This offers a partial expression of the qualities of justice and mercy, but a complete realization of a creation manifesting both of these qualities. Man, who is unable to comprehend polar opposites, perceives contradiction. The divine narrative, however, integrates both versions and their philosophical perspectives. This integration takes place by means of the "redaction," which reflects the attribute of *tiferet*, "harmony." Neither source is to be read literally, as presenting one-dimensional aspects of justice or mercy. They should be understood, rather, in the light of the received text where the Almighty interwove these two aspects.

Unlike the secular scholar, for whom each document represents no more than the subjective perspective of a human author, the religious individual knows that each document expresses a partial truth, a divine truth, an articulation of His holy attributes. Each creation story, taken in itself, reveals how a world created exclusively according to one of these characteristics would have appeared. The textual components of the

Torah, like the Torah as a whole, are true. Israel was commanded to love truth and peace (i.e., the reconciliation of opposites) which derive from the God of Israel whose seal is truth and whose name is peace. Thus the study of Bible by the religious individual fortifies the bond between the Holy One, Israel, and the Holy Torah.

VI

Torah Lishmah and Intellectual Integrity

We have seen that the believer and the scientist differ most, not in their recognition of phenomena, but in their evaluation of the phenomena. This is eminently true of their respective attitudes toward the study of Torah. The scientist relates to the Torah as he does to all literary works. Having examined its content, and applied to it the critical method, he will accept it or reject it. The Torah, for him, does not speak in the name of a higher authority, compelling his submission. This is especially the case when it comes to the Torah's legal portions. The scholar will find some laws pleasing and progressive, others unseemly and inane. This attitude implies a lack of reverence even for *mitzvot* he chooses to fulfill. He adopts these laws not because of the Torah's normative demands but as the outcome of subjective attraction. Hence he never fulfills God's will but his own.

The believer, by contrast, does not subject the laws to his critical review: he declares, from the outset, *naaseh ve-nishma*, "we will follow and then understand"—whether he finds them attractive or not. He does not merely *study* Torah but *learns* from it. When he opens the Torah he enters the house of God, he brings himself before God for guidance.

Acceptance of the Torah's supreme authority does not, to be sure, relieve the believer from religious struggle. No individual can deny the truth in his heart, and God does not expect His children to suppress their inner sense of ethics and justice in the face of what is written in the Torah. Therefore the religious individual is allowed, and in fact is obligated, to wage the Torah's battle *within* the world of Torah itself. You ought not encourage falsity in your heart by negating your own truth as falsehood. God chastised Job's friends for their false justification of God. The tormented struggle between the heart's truth and what is written in the Torah is often a most difficult one. Yet the believer will never consider the secular student's judgment that some laws are acceptable and others are not. When he finds himself unreceptive to the Torah's truth he will put its words "on his heart," faithfully awaiting the hour when his closed heart will open and embrace the Torah's words. There is no way to know when this miraculous event will occur. Yet one may assume from the outset that it will never be demanded of him to abandon the truth of the heart. Eventually it will become clear that there never was a real contradiction between that truth and the Torah's. It was only his insufficient readiness for the Torah's truth that engendered the apparent conflict. His certainty in the triumph of truth supports him during the struggle of the conflict.

VII

The "Intention" of the Author

Our theological conception of *Torah min ha-shamayim*, distinguishing between the Torah given to Moses and the words of the prophet sent by God, has practical halakhic ramifications: no man or prophet has the authority to abrogate anything God has written in his Torah. Moreover this conception of *Torah min ha-shamayim* affects the study and interpretation of the Torah. This point requires an elaboration of our position on literary interpretation in general.

It used to be taken for granted that literary criticism meant understanding the author's intention. To ignore the author's meaning was to impose the critic's own meaning on the text. According to this approach the ideal commentator is the author himself. But the author is often an unreliable guide to his own work: the intentions informing the work may have been forgotten or unconscious, their imprint apparent though he fails to recognize it. Thus the critic, who can read between the lines and determine the author's conscious and subconscious intentions, becomes the superior authority. The critic can locate internal contradictions that the author missed, since these are due to conflicting attitudes the author has not acknowledged. Nowadays literary criticism is not preoccupied with the author's intention. Once the literary work has left his hands it occupies its own place, defining a world of its own. It is our possession to interpret as we understand it.

Taken without qualification, this approach would make literary study an exercise in anarchy, without rules or standards. One could comment as freely as he pleases, so long as the interpretation maintained some connection to the text. It would be impossible to discriminate between correct and incorrect interpretations; the only criterion would be plausibility to the reader. Any literary work could thus be approached with all the interpretive methods used to analyze the Torah: *peshat*, *derash*, *remez* and *sod*, *atbash* and *gematriya*. This is illegitimate. I would maintain that a literary critic's primary responsibility is to the author's conscious or unconscious intention, explicit or implicit in the work. The critic has every right to broach various ideas that emerge from the text, whether directly or indirectly. He may assert that these are implications of the work, although the author never intended them, and that the author's failure to say what the critic is saying is due to the limitations of his time and environment. Such an interpretation would artfully and effectively explicate the literary work without claiming to provide an accurate account of the writer's intention.

What I have proposed regarding a secular literary work surely applies to sacred scripture as well. The student of Bible must first understand what the writer intended to convey. The obligation to study Torah requires more than this. It includes the text's implications for future generations, especially its relevance for the reader's situation. Although the writer did not intend this specific meaning of the text it exists nonetheless. The Torah is "deeper than the sea," its possible ramifications are unlimited, and those who search will always uncover new features. Every idea found in the Torah engenders others, whether directly or indirectly. The full range of interpretations, derivations, and derivations of derivations pertaining to the Torah is pregnant with truth.

But this general principle regarding authorial intention does not apply to the Torah in the same manner that it pertains to other biblical books. The student of the prophets (and the same would go for the Torah acccording to the liberal understanding of *Torah min ha-shamayim* that we reject) can readily distinguish between the author's intention and the implicit intentions of the text. The prophet is rooted in a specific time and place. Hence his interpretation of his own prophecy is affected by his context and capabilities. Later readers may adduce new ideas from his prophecy, which were hidden from the prophet because their time had not yet come. This cannot be the case with respect to the Torah.

The Author's intention is not limited by the time of the writing since the Author—God—transcends time and His writing preceded creation. Nonetheless, we may suggest that when God transmitted the Torah, He directed it to a specific generation, that of the Exodus and the desert, that would receive it, and to later generations that would study the text.

This last point is pertinent to the scientific study of the Bible. When the biblical critics match a particular passage to the time period that suits its style of writing and content they have identified the generation that the passage addresses at the primary literary and historical level. Genesis, chapter 1, for example, may directly address those whose understanding of the world is suited to that version; that group would constitute the primary audience. There is, of course, a secondary audience, to whom the Torah is also transmitted. Although, when speaking of God as the Author, a distinction between the writer's intention and that which is written is inconceivable, one must distinguish between two different authorial intentions, one to the primary audience and one to other readers, the secondary audience.

The first level of intention in the Torah corresponds to the author's intention in the other books. This includes what is normally understood by the primary recipient generation. The second level of intention in the Torah parallels the implicit levels of the text in other prophetic works. What comprises the deeper meaning of other biblical texts is part of the Author's intended meaning in the divine Torah. Both levels become available to later students, though the primary audience may penetrate only the first level.

Thus the significant distinctions between the various definitions of *Torah min ha-shamayim*, which are central to our theological judgment about the compatibility of source division and Jewish piety, bear implications for the practice of Torah study as well. If one believes that the Torah was written by man, albeit with prophetic inspiration, his sense of the relationship between his understanding and the author's intention must be tenuous. The matter is entirely different for one who believes he studies *God's* Torah. This individual will attempt to seek undiscovered nuances in the Torah's meaning that will excite his heart and satiate his soul. Yet he will be confident that these novel interpretations are included in the Torah's design. He will bless God who has taught him Torah, who commanded him to immerse himself in the study of Torah, and who has made His words pleasant, generously endowing him with wisdom to understand the content of His creation.

8

Response to Rabbi Breuer

Shnayer Z. Leiman

1. Orthodoxy owes a genuine debt of gratitude to Rabbi Breuer for agreeing to address a very sensitive issue, namely the documentary hypothesis. He walks bravely where angels fear to tread. It is particularly refreshing to see an Orthodox rabbi who recognizes that the documentary hypothesis is alive and well, not dead and buried. Some well-meaning Orthodox defenders of the faith delight in repeating the canard that through the heroic efforts of Rabbis David Hoffmann and Hayyim Heller, the death knell was sounded for the documentary hypothesis decades ago—and it need no longer be taken seriously. Nothing could be further from the truth. The fact is that the critical study of the Bible, largely but hardly exclusively a Protestant enterprise, has long since penetrated the academic world. Wherever Bible is taught critically, that is, at Harvard, Yale, Oxford, and the Hebrew University, it is accompanied by the documentary hypothesis even as the twentieth century draws to its close. The first step toward the solution of a problem is the recognition that the problem exists. Those who cavalierly deny that the problem exists unwittingly enable others to fall prey to the very problem they wish to negate.

2. At the outset, it seems to me that the topic assigned to Rabbi Breuer, "The Study of the Bible and the Primacy of the Fear of Heaven: Compatibility or Contradiction?" needs to be carefully circumscribed.

181

Unquestionably, risks abound with regard to the critical study of the Bible. Not everyone needs to be introduced to comparative Semitics, textual criticism, problems in biblical history and chronology, and the documentary hypothesis. Regarding the Hebrew Bible, what is studied, how it is studied, when it is studied, who studies it, and who teaches it will depend on a variety of factors that need to be addressed even as one attempts to resolve the larger issue raised by the topic under discussion. Distinctions need to be made, perhaps, between private study and public discourse; between elementary school, high school, and college level students; between schools with different educational goals; and between adults with no background in Jewish study and the mature rabbinic scholar who has "filled his belly" with *Shas* and *Poskim*.

3. Addressing the implied tension (in the title of his presentation) between Bible study and fear of heaven, Rabbi Breuer states at the outset: "The kind of study under scrutiny is that which has appeared in recent centuries, beginning with Jean Astruc, maintaining that the Torah is composed of distinct documents, each written in its own style, whose contents are in conflict." Thus, Breuer identifies modern Bible study primarily with the documentary hypothesis. Indeed, the focus of the entire paper is confined to the issue of how the documentary hypothesis can be squared with the concept of *Torah min ha-Shamayim*. The implication is that having resolved the tension between the documentary hypothesis (or, as it is often referred to, higher Bible criticism) and *Torah min ha-shamayim*, the Torah-true Jew can now engage in the unimpeded study of the Hebrew Bible and modern Bible scholarship. But modern Bible scholarship consists of much more than higher Bible criticism alone. It also treats textual (or: lower Bible) criticism, biblical history, biblical archaeology, modern literary theory, and more. Each of these disciplines comes with its own set of problems for traditional Jewish teaching. Thus, for example, textual criticism will sometimes claim that a reading of the Masoretic text of the Torah is inferior to readings preserved in the Septuagint and the Dead Sea scrolls. Or, archaeology will claim that the camel was not domesticated in the patriarchal period, hence the references to domesticated camels in Genesis are anachronistic. Again, modern Bible scholarship does not recognize much of *Torah she-be'al peh*. Whatever *Mi-mohorat ha-Shabbat* (Leviticus 23:15) may mean, modern Bible scholarship is certain that it does not mean "the day after the first

day of Passover." Thus, even if Breuer has resolved the knotty problem of the documentary hypothesis, much of modern Bible study remains problematic for an Orthodox Jew.

4. A basic assumption of Rabbi Breuer's paper is the unimpeachability of the documentary hypothesis. His formulation on p. 161 is striking: "The power of these inferences, based on solid argument and internally consistent premises, will not be denied by intellectually honest persons. One cannot deny the evidence before one's eyes. . . . Willy nilly, the Torah contains several documents, which, viewed as natural products of human culture, must have been written by different people over the course of many generations before their final redaction." While I agree fully that the documentary hypothesis still lives, and even dominates discussion in some quarters, it remains a hypothesis. Indeed, in the eyes of some modern Bible scholars it is a beleaguered hypothesis. This is not the place to discuss the Scandinavian school, the proponents of *Überlieferungsgeschichte* and *Traditionsgeschichte*, and the documentary hypothesis. Suffice it to say that while by and large the documentary hypothesis still remains the centerpiece of higher Bible criticism, it is now accompanied, at least in some academic circles, by a healthy dose of skepticism, certainly regarding the absolute date of the documents, their relationship to each other, and the ascription of particular pentateuchal passages to J, E, or P. The following passages from J. Alberto Soggin's *Introduction to the Old Testament* are typical:

> Until recently, and even in previous editions of this *Introduction*, a series of texts which were supposed to be ancient were usually attributed either to source J or source E of the Pentateuch. These attributions were almost never justified by objective criteria, but simply because a parallel passage has been attributed to the other source. So it is not surprising that these attributions have meanwhile proved so problematical that they can no longer be supported in any case. . . .
>
> Attempts have been made in the past to attribute to the sources J and E of the Pentateuch the earliest legal texts contained in the Pentateuch. . . . Here, too, it is not possible to attribute the texts to these sources, since we have no objective basis for this procedure.[1]

---

[1] J. Albert. Soggin, *Introduction to the Old Testament* (Louisville: Westminster, 1989), pp. 78, 83.

Even if the vast majority of modern Bible scholars concurred on the plausibility of the documentary hypothesis, there is always room for honest dissent. The documentary hypothesis, in its most refined form, peaked during the lifetimes of Rabbi David Hoffmann and Professor Umberto Cassuto. Yet they took issue with it, even as they were *modeh al ha-emet* and intellectually honest to a fault. Since then, no new textual evidence of any significance has been discovered that "proves" the documentary hypothesis. Nor does there appear to be any imminent danger that a copy of J, E, or P will be discovered.

5. Rabbi Breuer's paper can be divided conveniently into two parts. The first (sections I–II) deals primarily with the documentary hypothesis and the notion of *Torah min ha-shamayim*; the second (sections III–VII) deals primarily with the documentary hypothesis and the notion of *Torah mi-Sinai*. In the first part of his discussion, Breuer suggests that the Torah is divinely inspired in exactly the same way as prophetic literature. It is irrelevant who the authors were or when they lived; what is crucial is that the authors were prophets who recorded the Divine Word. The documentary hypothesis creates no problem for the Orthodox Jew who believes this, for—according to Breuer—all the documents were authored by prophets. Since the Jewish community accepted the Torah as its constitution, it is binding for all time even if it is non-Mosaic in origin.

The second part is far more traditional in that it recognizes the Mosaic authorship/editorship of the Torah. Nevertheless, Breuer assures us that we have nothing to fear about the documentary hypothesis. After all, it is based entirely on the assumption that the biblical documents were authored by humans and therefore subject to the literary conventions that govern such documents. But Orthodoxy posits that the Torah is divinely authored, hence not subject to the literary conventions that govern documents authored by humans. What appears to the naked eye as literary strata in the Torah is in fact a divine code, speaking to different generations of Jews in different voices, and containing a multitude of meanings that often move beyond the plain sense of a specific portion of the text. With regard to the Torah, the whole is greater than the sum of its parts.

Breuer's position in the first part is sufficiently problematic that it really requires no discussion. It flies in the face of talmudic teaching (*Megillah*

2b; *j. Megillah* 1:5), Maimonidean teaching (*Commentary on the Mishnah, Sanhedrin* 10:1; *Code*, Introduction), and contemporary rabbinic discussion (e.g., R. Moshe Feinstein, *Iggerot Mosheh, Yoreh De'ah*, III, responsa 114 and 115), all of which state unequivocally that all the laws of the Torah are Mosaic in origin. No prophet could add to, or detract from, the Mosaic laws.[2] Well aware of the problematic nature of his suggestion in the first part of his discussion, Breuer largely rejects it in the second. Largely, but not entirely; after all, the first part is retained. The sense one gets is that the first part remains a safety net for those who will find the second part too difficult to swallow. It is this second part of Breuer's presentation that commands attention. At least in its present formulation, I find it problematic for a variety of reasons, some of which I turn to now.

6. Rabbi Breuer adopts an Hegelian thesis, antithesis, and synthesis approach to the Torah in order to account for its conflicting sources. The redactor (Moses) preserved one document (thesis), and its counterpart (antithesis), and even spliced them together (synthesis), the purpose of which was to teach the reader doctrinal or natural/scientific truths. Now these divine truths often become evident only after Breuer (or a master exegete of similar expertise) discovers them. One wonders why the Divine Economy could not have come up with a more frugal way of promulgating Torah teaching. Surely, a concise and lucid listing of essential Torah teachings, say, in a Maimonidean-type catechism or code, would have brought the message home to many more readers and with much less expenditure of intellectual energy.

7. In effect, Rabbi Breuer demonstrates convincingly that some doublets in the Torah complement one another. But to move from those few doublets to an overarching principle that resolves all doublets and inconsistencies requires a genuine leap of faith. One wonders how Breuer would reconcile the conflicting reports at Genesis 26:34 and 36:2; and at 28:9 and 36:3.

8. Rabbi Breuer argues that the documentary hypothesis is irrelevant (theologically) because modern Bible scholars treat the Bible as a secular document, applying to it the same literary conventions they would

---

[2]In general, see Rabbi Zevi Hirsch Chajes, *Torat haNeviim*, in *Kol Kitvei Maharatz Chajes*, vol. I (Jerusalem: Divrei Hakahmim, 1958).

apply to any ancient Near Eastern document. Orthodox Jews, Breuer
adds, can simply respond: for us, the Torah is the living word of God,
hence ordinary literary conventions cannot be applied to it. Now a proposed solution to a problem is persuasive only to the extent that it can
either be verified or falsified. What would persuade a rational observer
that Breuer's proposed solution is either true or false? The answer, of
course, is nothing. Since Breuer's claim is that we do not know how
divine writing works, it follows that we cannot know with certainty
whether or not human literary conventions apply to divine documents.
At best, Breuer's solution to the problem raises an interesting possibility that can neither be verified nor falsified. Since, by definition,
Breuer's solution to the problem can neither be verified nor falsified,
his solution remains problematic and unconvincing. On such a slen-
der reed, the Jew who confronts the modern study of Bible will lean
precariously, if at all.

9. The notion that the Torah in its present form is a divinely authored
document, hence not subject to ordinary literary convention, is not without problems. The rabbis taught long ago *Dibbera Torah ki-leshon benei
adam*. Moreover, there is a considerable gap (of over one thousand years)
between the Mosaic recording of the Torah and our oldest extant copies of the Torah text. Even if we were to concede that divinely authored
texts are not subject to human literary convention, this would apply only
to the text at the very moment it left the hand of God. Neither Breuer,
nor anyone else, can state with absolute confidence that no additions,
deletions, or changes of any kind were introduced into the Torah text
during the one thousand and more years that separate Moses from our
oldest copies of the text. As any public reader of the Torah can testify,
errors have crept into the best of Torah scrolls. Every so often, a Torah
scroll needs to be returned to the ark, due to an error discovered while
being read from in public. Apparently, divinely authored documents,
once transmitted to humans, are subject to the vicissitudes of human
textual transmission. This is certainly true with regard to the history and
development of the Masoretic text of the Hebrew Bible. This raises the
issue of just how much tampering with the divine text has taken place.
Given the occasional substantive differences among the Hebrew texts
of the Samaritan, Dead Sea scroll, and Masoretic versions of the Torah,
each claiming to have preserved the *ipsissima verba* of the word of God,
one wonders how much weight to give to an argument that claims un-

abashedly and confidently that the Torah text, as we have it, is a divinely authored document not subject to ordinary literary convention.

10. In sum, Rabbi Breuer's provocative essay confronts an important issue, one that in the Orthodox community has suffered mostly from neglect. We are indebted to him for his courage and wisdom, and trust that his essay will stimulate others to address the issue *le-hagdil Torah u-le-haadirah*. Its central thesis, however, that the modern study of the Bible is not problematic for the *yere shamayim*, is less than convincing at least in its present form. Breuer's solution, based as it is on a priori assumptions, preaches only to the converted. Only those with a prior faith commitment to the antiquity, unity, and immutability of the Torah text will find Breuer's solution persuasive.

Meanwhile, other strategies will need to be explored in order to respond to the challenges posed by modern Bible study in general, and in order to blunt the sharpness of the documentary hypothesis in particular. Some of the more promising strategies have been suggested by modern Bible scholarship itself. These include comparative and conceptual analysis of ancient Near Eastern and biblical law. Such analysis has shown that much that was thought to be contradictory in Torah law is, in fact, quite harmonious, each of the alleged contradictory laws treating a different aspect of law. Recent linguistic and philological advance suggests that even in biblical times colloquial and literary Hebrew coexisted. This paves the way for the possibility that different Hebrew terms with the same meaning reflect colloquial vis-à-vis literary usage, rather than two documents from different authors and centuries. Modern literary theory is suggesting new ways of reading and understanding texts that call into question some of the basic presumptions of the documentary hypothesis.

While we reject Rabbi Breuer's central thesis, we applaud his readiness to confront modernity, including the modern study of the Bible. There are undeniable risks in any such confrontation. Not to confront modernity, however, is more than risky for Orthodoxy, it is suicidal.[3]

---

[3] I am indebted to my colleagues Professors David Berger and Richard Steiner, who read and commented upon an earlier draft of this response. As they constantly remind me, I alone am responsible for the errors that remain.

9

Camino Real and Modern Talmud Study[1]

Shalom Carmy

You are studying the sections of *Bava Metzia* devoted to the four kinds of *shomer* (bailee). It is quite natural to begin with the *mishnah* (93a) that introduces, systematically, the four categories and the most fundamental laws pertaining to them. But you notice (for the first time?) that the placing of the *mishnah* is unexpected, at the end of a chapter dealing with the rights of employees. It would be more suitable, one would think, had this *mishnah* appeared in the third chapter (*ha-Mafkid*), which discusses responsibility for objects that are stolen or lost while in the possession of the *shomer*. Is this merely a case of the serendipity typical of talmudic discussion—"the words of Torah, poor in one place and rich in another" (J T *Rosh Hashanah* 3:5), or is it a phenomenon inviting, perhaps even requiring, closer scrutiny?[2]

---

[1]These remarks draw upon my correspondence with Rabbi Yitzchak Blau. On the question of integrating literary issues with standard *lomdut* I have profited from discussions with several students and friends, among them Jonathan Rabinowitz, Yosef Crystal, and especially Rabbi Yaakov Genack.

[2]For a far-reaching theory responding to these and other questions, see David Henshke, *Arbaa Shomerin Hem?*, in *Shenaton ha-Mishpat ha-Ivri* 16–17 (1991), 145–218.

Take another example in the same area. A borrower (*shoel*) is liable in almost all cases. One of the few exceptions is when the damage resulted from the use for which the animal was borrowed (*metah me-hamat melakhah*).[3] In studying this rule it occurs to you that the notion of *metah me-hamat melakhah* does not appear in the Mishnah, nor, for that matter, in any other Tannaitic source. Is the silence accidental? Does it imply that the rule did not exist in the Tannaitic period? Or shall we infer that cases of *metah me-hamat melakhah* were so infrequent that the possibility was rarely discussed?[4]

What are we to do with such questions? All things being equal, the student of Torah has good reason to want to know how the text he is learning attained its canonical form, and, if at all possible, he would like to reconstruct the original statements and debates of the *Tanna'im* and *Amora'im*. If academic methods promise assistance, why not employ them? What Rabbi Yehiel Weinberg said about philological and textual investigation of the talmudic text is just as true of the historical-literary inquiry he engaged in: "any influence and instruction from precise science should be accepted. For insofar as the subjects of talmudic-halakhic investigation are very old books, we find that, as with any philological investigation, the existence of an authoritative text is the first prerequisite."[5]

No room is provided for this interest, however, in the conventional *yeshivah* curriculum. The *yeshivah* scholar, following the *derekh ha-melekh*,

---

[3]According to Rambam, the previous sentence applies only when the animal was debilitated by the work; if the animal is dead, the borrower is exempt only if it died *during* the work. See *Hilkhot She'elah u-Pikkadon* 1:1,4 and commentators.

[4]Rabbi Yehezkel Abramsky, in *Hazon Yehezkel*, BM 8:8 (Jerusalem, 5712), pp. 133ff. discovers, in the failure of *Tosefta* to mention *meta me-hamat melakhah*, a possible basis for Rambam's limitation on the occurrence of *metah me-hamat melakhah* to the animal's death in harness. (See also his reference to *Mekhilta of Rashbi*, which does refer to *metah me-hamat melakhah*.)

[5]"On the Necessity for the Investigation of Halakhic Sources," in *Li-Prakim*, 2nd ed. (Jerusalem: Kirya Neemana, 1967), pp. 115–120. Passage cited from Shalom Carmy, "R. Yehiel Weinberg's Lecture on Academic Jewish Scholarship," *Tradition* 24:4 (Summer 1989): 15–23, 21. For a thorough study of the subject, see Moshe Bleich, "The Role of Manuscripts in Halakhic Decision-Making: Hazon Ish, his Predecessors and Contemporaries," *Tradition* 27:2 (Winter 1993): 22–55.

the royal road of learning, has little patience for such matters. His eye is fastened on the content of the *sugyot*, not their form or composition. Content, for most *benei Torah*, means conceptual analysis, as practiced in the archetypal Lithuanian *yeshivot* of the past century and at their successor institutions in Israel and the United States, as taught by great masters like Rabbi Hayyim Soloveichik of Brisk and Rabbi Shimon Shkop of Telz and their generations of disciples.[6] The goal of conceptual analysis is to discover the truth of *halakhah*, to formulate the principles inherent in the word of God. Literary and historical research, though its motivation may be the service of God, though the student attempts to infuse it with a religious passion, is about the background of Torah, and thus remains one step removed from the *camino real*.

Professors Sperber and Elman demonstrate, with great erudition, that historical and literary issues were not alien to the *Rishonim* and to many of the great *Aharonim*. They examine the range of methods made available by contemporary academic research, and show that the results of these investigations are not without interest, and, as Sperber argues, even have import for practical halakhic decision. But justifying certain aspects of the academic enterprise is not the same as providing a model for the interweaving of modern scholarship in the fabric of Talmud Torah. Both the *Bet Midrash* and the university Talmud department tend to regard traditional Talmud study, on the one hand, and literary-historical investigation of the rabbinic corpus, on the other hand, as hermetically sealed worlds. The *talmid hakham* dwells within the four cubits of traditional analysis; the professor, even when he shares the background and beliefs of the *talmid hakham*, sets aside the conceptual tools of the *yeshivah* when he takes up the implements of literary-historical analysis.

An important factor in this dichotomy is the condescension and superficiality that often characterize the academic attitude toward traditional learning. Academic scholars of Judaism regularly feign obliviousness to the primacy of conceptual content in the study of Torah. Not knowing better, sometimes despite knowing better, individuals aligned with the academic program frequently fail to see any significant distinction between Brisker analysis and high-class *darshanus*,crediting them-

---

[6]For historical, biographical, and methodological overviews, see Norman Solomon, *The Analytic School: Hayyim Soloveitchik and his Circle* (Atlanta: Scholars Press, 1993); Yitzhak Adler, *Iyyun be-Lomdut* (New York, 1989); and Rabbi Shlomo Zevin's classic *Ishim ve-Shittot* (Tel Aviv: A. Tsioni, 1958).

selves with the search for scientific truth, while patronizing the orientation they have abandoned as "inspirational Jewish studies."

Historians of philosophy, by contrast, generally recognize that investigation of the language and transmission of philosophical texts is ancillary to conceptual work and is of little value unless that work is pursued. Hence it is not surprising that the analytic approach, despite its failure to achieve predominance over the philological-historical in the university world of Jewish studies, has nonetheless penetrated the more conceptually sophisticated realm of legal studies. From this perspective Rabbi Yehiel Weinberg is merely stating the obvious when he writes:

> If the meaning of "scientific investigation" is the clarification of concepts, the extrapolation from cognate ideas of the fundamental concepts and their logical and methodical construction, then it is difficult to grasp precisely why a discourse on Talmudic ideas which presents them in the formal framework of formulated clarified concepts should not be worthy of the name "science."[7]

Surely the path of the *talmid hakham*, leading to the conceptual heart of the halakhic inquiry, is the *derekh ha-melekh* of our learning. Where does that leave the queries with which we began our discussion? So long as questions about the history of the sources and traditions are dismissed as extraneous to the *camino real*, we, who are committed to *lomdut*, can complacently pass them on to the professors, while we forge ahead with a wave of the hand and a merry cry of *weiter*, the compartmentalization of traditional Talmud Torah and modern scholarship intact. Let me remind you, however, that our opening questions, about the Mishnah's presentation of *shomer* and the history of a specific rule of *sho'el*, grew out of a conventional encounter with a text studied in a *yeshivah* setting; they were not conjured up by a graduate student looking for a topic. Are we really justified in ruling such questions out of order? Can literary and historical considerations be successfully and seamlessly integrated in the *derekh ha-melekh*?

Leaving aside the legitimacy and adequacy of the solutions offered by academic Talmud study, to which we shall return later, the major obstacle to the integration of modern scholarship and the *camino real* is the time and effort required to encompass a *sugya* from all angles. By the time the

---

[7]"R. Yehiel Weinberg's Lecture . . ." 19.

literary-historical aspects are properly covered, one is too overburdened and weary to progress from these preliminary inquiries to the conceptual analysis itself. Under present and foreseeable pedagogical constraints, this would rule out the combination of formal literary analysis and *lomdut* for the vast majority of students and teachers.[8] Even the sophisticated few, I imagine, are unlikely to engage in such synthesis on a systematic, global scale, rather than on an eclectic basis.

The convenient conclusion is that the majority of Talmud students should not be acquainted with formal literary-historical considerations. But this would be misleading, for it does not take into account the fact that these questions often arise spontaneously in the course of learning. The examples I drew, almost at random, from my own recent experience,[9] are far from exceptional. How often does the *Gemara* seem to construe the Mishnah by, in effect, rewriting it? How many contradictions are resolved only by bringing to bear a factor patently absent from the language of the primary texts being interpreted? Students who raise such problems, only to discover that nobody knows, or cares, what's bothering them, are likely to conclude that the *Gemara* "isn't supposed to make sense," or, as a mother once told an elementary school teacher, when asked how her son was adjusting to *Gemara*: "He thinks the Mishnah's O.K., but the *Gemara* is always looking for trouble."[10]

No doubt there are students who are either insensitive or undeterred by textual inconcinnity. But others, not always the least intelligent or the least earnest, are frustrated by literary difficulties which, if not acknowledged, may inhibit the student's growth as a *lamdan* or under-

---

[8]The claim that secondary issues should be curtailed lest they detract from the primary goal, that *tafel* is ever to be thrown overboard for the sake of *ikkar*, can be taken to an intolerable extreme, and risks becoming a self-fulfilling prophecy. If reading Aramaic interferes with formulating analytic *hakirot*, shall we consign the original text to cold scholarship and steer the majority of students to ArtScroll, as is commonly done in other areas of Torah? It need hardly be pointed out that relinquishing the Aramaic text of the Talmud would be a far more disastrous blow to the quality and future of Talmud Torah than omitting to appropriate newfangled methods of scholarship.

[9]At the time of the conference, Yeshiva was learning *Ha-Sho'el*.

[10]It is fitting that I heard this cautionary anecdote from my father and first teacher, Mr. David Carmy *zt"l*, who firmly believed that the *Gemara was* supposed to make sense.

mine his motivation. And even those who play the intellectual game of *lomdut* with panache, whose development appears to be unconstrained, may be hindered by the inarticulate awareness that the etiquette of learning places certain legitimate questions about the formation of the text outside the limits of discussion.

Fortunately, involvement in literary problems is not an all-or-nothing proposition. Earlier I suggested that even those well versed in literary-historical methods are likely to resort to them sporadically, as the need arises, rather than consistently. The same kind of compromise may satisfy less advanced students as well. There may be situations in which sensitivity to literary features of the text is encouraged, both *lishmah*, because reflecting on them is a legitimate part of learning, and because they are, in any event, apt to attract spontaneous attention; in other circumstances the literary history should be discussed only at the student's initiative. Lastly, as is many a time the case in mature learning, it is often appropriate to recognize, and bracket, the problem, deferring any attempt to resolve it, so that the student is able to turn back to the content, untroubled by the vague peripheral uneasiness that occurs when an unacknowledged difficulty is swept under the rug, as it were.[11]

So far I have insisted that an awareness of the phenomena discussed by literary-historical theorists occurs as a natural by-product of the traditional learning process, with the implication that the status of these phenomena is no different, in principle, from that of geographic information pertinent to learning. My purpose, in keeping with the title of this volume, was to sketch very briefly the possible integration of modern Talmud scholarship in the study of Torah. I did not challenge the theological legitimacy and intellectual coherence of the dominant academic theories, as these questions are more than adequately treated in the two long chapters by Professors Sperber and Elman.

It would, however, be misleading if we failed to observe that many *talmidei hakhamim* repudiate the entire synthesis of academic Talmud scholarship and traditional Torah study, not because of the practical

---

[11]The situation described here is analogous to what happens when philosophical or *taamei ha-mitzvot* issues intrude upon the study of Talmud and *halakhah*. The question may be valuable in itself; it may be so troublesome that the student simply cannot go on without addressing it. Often, however, once the matter is properly formulated, the student realizes that he, or she, can, for the moment, set the difficulty to one side and continue learning.

obstacles raised above, and not only as a reaction to the scholars' lack of comprehension and sympathy for the *derekh ha-melekh* of learning. They reject coexistence with the literary-historical methodology because they object to the specific theories and interpretations prevalent among its practitioners.

To begin with, many *talmidei hakhamim* believe that the fundamental arguments adopted by the scholars are eminently unconvincing, and their systematic judgments highly speculative. If this is so, then to spend time and energy on the whole exercise is wasteful at best, frivolous at worst. An even graver fault, from the viewpoint of Orthodoxy, is the tendency to explain away difficulties by assuming that the *Amora'im* regularly alter the original intent of Tannaitic statements and that the later editorial stages may deform both. What precedents might support this strategy, and what arguments might justify it, is part of the task reserved for Professors Sperber and Elman. Prima facie, however, it should be obvious that espousing this approach risks undermining the respect due to *Torah she-be'al peh* and the authentic bearers of its traditions. To take such objections seriously means that we would have to jettison large portions of these theories about the history of the sources and traditions. This would not, however, invalidate all insights based on the literary phenomena. In other words, my discussion of the desirability and feasibility of broadening the *camino real* to include ideas based on literary-historical factors is not dependent on any particular theory about those factors.

In setting the stage for my colleagues' presentations, I have concentrated on the literary-historical method, insofar as it is the area with the greatest implications for the everyday study of Torah. The tenor of my comments may leave both academic scholars and *talmidei hakhamim* dissatisfied—the former, because they are reluctant to accept the superiority of the traditional analytic approach, the *derekh ha-melekh*; the latter, because I would like to see whatever is valuable in the academic project incorporated, to the extent that this is practically possible, in our learning.[12]

As we have noted throughout, the primacy of the *derekh ha-melekh* in the study of Talmud is not merely a matter of intellectual preference. It

---

[12]Those with a foot in both camps may add their own criticism: that my proposals for a synthesis are not specific enough. To these I would reply that the development of a viable *derekh ha-limmud* requires a great deal of experimentation, and can only be achieved by trial and error, one stone on top of the other.

is intimately bound up with our sense of Torah study as a transcendent religious activity, confronting us with the word of God. Any admixture that threatens to divert us from the conceptual heart of the halakhic inquiry strikes at the heart of our religious vitality. Hence, the very notion that considerations insignificant in the current mode of study may be destined to take on a more consequential, albeit secondary, role can be profoundly unsettling to anyone who cares about Talmud Torah and *avodat ha-Shem*.

In this connection, it may be worth recalling that our own *derekh ha-melekh* was once regarded as something of a departure from the tried and true path. A century ago Rabbi Hayyim Brisker's method was derided as a radical innovation, as "chemical analysis." When Rabbi Henoch Agus decided to publish *Marheshet*, he feared that his approach was too old-fashioned to appeal to the up-and-coming Brisker faction. In the introduction to his book, he meditates on Rabbi Abba's prayer, when traveling, that his words of Torah be acceptable to his audience. Why, asks the author of *Marheshet*, did he utter this prayer on the road? Is the petition not equally appropriate at home? And he answers:

> He knew that his words were acceptable to the scholars of his town, and pleased his comrades and his audience. But that was good and fitting and pleasant in his town, where they were accustomed to his ways of learning and mode of analysis (*pilpul*). In another place, or in *Eretz Yisrael*, where they were accustomed to another mode and a greatly different style than in his own place, Rabbi Abba was worried that his words and thoughts would not find favor. Therefore he uttered this short prayer. . . .[13]

The prayer of the *Marheshet* was accepted; his book found favor, and is still studied lovingly wherever Litvisher Torah is cherished. As authors and readers of this volume we would do well to make his prayer our own.

This work is being done by various individuals, many of whom, I suspect, are unknown to one another, so that it is unclear whether these efforts have attained a critical mass. Some fine work has been done in journals, books, and dissertations devoted to *Mishpat Ivri*; other valuable essays have appeared in Torah journals like *Ha-Maayan*. The Herzog College (affiliated with Yeshivat Har-Etzion) has recently undertaken to publish *Netuim*, a journal of Mishnah study, edited by Rabbi Avraham Walfish and Rabbi Yehudah Shaviv.

[13]*Marheshet* I (Jerusalem, 1968), introduction. The book was first published in 1931.

10

On the Legitimacy, or Indeed, Necessity, of Scientific Disciplines for True "Learning" of the Talmud

Daniel Sperber

There is a well-known jibe attributed to the *yeshivah* world and directed against those involved in the academic study of Talmud. "We (*"Yeshivah-leit"*) wish to know what Abbaye and Rava said, but they (the academics) want to know what they wore." Now it is clear that anyone who devotes himself exclusively to the externals of talmudic literature, such as historical background, philology and linguistic characteristics of Babylonian Aramaic, and so forth, will be missing the main point of learning. But, on the other hand, those who believe they are involved in real learning, but lack certain systematic disciplines, often miss the point of the *sugya*, and may even err when attempting to derive from it the *psak halakhah*. In terms of the jibe with which we opened, at times it is indeed important to know *also* what Abbaye and Rava wore.

Let us demonstrate this with two examples. Who constitutes for us a greater paradigm, or role model, of classical talmudic learning than Rashi? In one of his responsa we read as follows:

Once I saw the master (Rashi) praying without a girdle. I was puzzled and
said: How is it that he is praying without his loins girdled? Surely they said in
Tractate *Berakhot* (24b), that one may not pray without a belt, and the reason is that one's heart should not behold one's privy parts. And he (Rashi)
replied: It seems to me that in those times the sages did not wear trousers,
but merely long cloaks that went down close to their ankles, and all their
clothes were closed front and back, left and right. Therefore they stated that
one may not pray without a girdle, for they had nothing to separate the heart
from the privy parts other than the girdle. (And indeed it seems likely that
they had no trousers, for in Tractate *Shabbat* . . . [120a] we have learned in
a Mishnah what one saves from a fire, and eighteen items of clothing that a
person may save on Shabbat are there enumerated . . . but trousers are not
mentioned.)[1] But we do wear trousers, and even without a belt there is a
clear separation between the heart and the privy parts, and therefore we may
pray without a belt.[2]

We see then that Rashi's views as to talmudic costume led him to rule
halakhically on a certain issue, or at any rate to justify an existing cus-
tom.[3] Actually his explanation is based on a conjecture, and borne out
only tentatively by oblique talmudic evidence.

---

[1]Elfenbein printed this section in brackets, perhaps indicating that it is not a
part of Rashi's statement, but a later gloss by a disciple. I here assume that this
is part of Rashi's statement. The whole responsum is found in *Or Zarua* I, sec.
128, 45a, and at the end is written: הכותב הוא הרב ר' שמע', ורבו היינו רבי שלמה זצ"ל,
that is to say Rashi (Rabbi Solomon b. Isaac). According to the editor (p. xxiii)
this is one of the late responsa. See further S. Albeck's note to his edition of
Sefer ha-Eshkol vol. 1 (Jerusalem, 1935), pp. 18–19, nn. 7–8, from which we learn
that this was already Rabbi Hai Gaon's view. Indeed this was already the view
of Rabbi Sa'adyah Gaon, as found in *Siddur* Rabbi Saadja Gaon, ed. Davidson,
Assaf, and Joel (Jerusalem, 1941), p. 29, and cited in *Shibbolei ha-Leket*, ed. M.
Buber sec. 17, p. 16. (My thanks to Dr. Moshe Sokolow, of New York, for point-
ing this out to me.) There were those who thought that even trousers are not
sufficient, and one always needs a belt (*Shibbulei ha-Leket* [in the name of *Sefer
ha-Terumah?*]). See further *Sefer ha-Raviah*, ed. Aptowitzer, vol. 1 (Jerusalem,
1964), p. 56, note 16. See also the responsum of Rashi, no. 263; Aptowitzer,
pp. 56–57, n. 17; Albeck, pp. 21–22, n. 15. This whole issue requires closer analysis and I hope to deal with it elsewhere.

[2]*Teshuvot Rashi*, ed. Elfenbein (New York, 1943), no. 262, pp. 305–306.

[3]See note 1. Cf. Ch. Tchernowitz's comment in *Ha-Goren* 10 (1928),
p. 85.

When we look into the issue somewhat more closely, we find that in point of fact it is somewhat more complex and problematic. For while indeed it is true that the Bavli does apparently not list trousers among its eighteen garments and reads ושני ספרקין, (which Rashi explains as פיישולש, probably meaning *faissole*, straps around the legs),[4] the Yerushalmi (ad loc., 16d 20) reads: שני סבריקין[5]ושני אבריקין, which latter word, אבריקין, probably corresponds with the Latin *braccae* (in Greek βρʹακαι, "trousers, pantaloons"),[6] an article of attire well-attested in Roman times. It is true that they were less commonly worn by Romans than by the Northern nations, such as the Celts—indeed the word is of Celtic origin[7]—or Asiatics, such as the Persians. However, in the second century C.E., the period of the Mishnah and Baraita, they appear to have been worn at Rome, too (though their use in that city was later forbidden by the emperor Honorius in 397 C.E.).[8]

Now the attestation of the word in the Yerushalmi, and indeed elsewhere in Palestinian rabbinic literature,[9] makes it clear that trousers were known of, and worn, in talmudic Palestine. Furthermore, מכנסיים, meaning trousers, are also found in the sources (e.g., *Mishnah Kelim* 27b, etc.). This strongly calls into doubt Rashi's supposition, and makes his reasoning suspect. That Rashi was ruling in accordance with the Bavli and not the Yerushalmi—with which he may not have been acquainted[10]—is a specious argument. For he based his ruling on an assumption as to real-

---

[4]See Darmesteter and Blondheim, *Les Gloses françaises . . .* (Paris, 1929), no. 456, p. 62.

[5]סבריקין=συβρίκον (σουβρίκον) "outer garment," *superaria*. See E. A. Sophocles, *Greek Lexicon of the Roman and Byzantine Period* (Cambridge, MA, & Leipzig, 1914; reprint, Hildesheim and New York, 1975), p. 1001a, s.v. συβρικός; S. Krauss, *Griechische und Lateinische Lehnwörter in Talmud, Midrasch und Targum* (Berlin, 1899; reprint. Hildesheim, 1964), p. 371a, s.v. סבריקין.

[6]Krauss, *Griechische und Lateinische Lehnwörter* 8a, s.v. אבריקין.

[7]It is related to Scottish *breeks* and English *breeches*.

[8]See *Codex Theodosianus* 14.10.3; Lampridius, Alexander Severus 40. See W. Smith, W. Wayte, and G. E. Marindin, *A Dictionary of Greek and Latin Antiquities* vol. 1 (London, 1890), pp. 314–315.

[9]*Yelamdenu* Genesis to Daniel 3:11, apud Aruch s.v. ברקין; see *Aruch Completum*, vol. 2, ed. A. Kohut, p. 201b.

[10]There has been a good deal written on this subject. See, e.g., A. Y. Bromberg, *Rashi ve-ha-Yerushalmi* (Jerusalem, 1945), and R. Zvi Hirsch Chayes' glosses to *Ta'anit* ad fin., and his *Imrei Binah*, sec. 5, and so forth.

life practices in talmudic times, and the assumption has been shown to be questionable. One may, of course, choose to separate the various elements in this responsum, accepting the *sevarah* (speculative reasoning), that "the heart may not see the privy parts," but rejecting the supposition that rabbis did not wear trousers and the proof for this from the Bavli. And in that case, the talmudic directives in *Berakhot* 24b would be addressed to people wearing loose cloaks, but not to people wearing trousers. Be this as it may, what remains significant is that Rashi (or his disciples) apparently regarded the issue of whether the *Tanna'im* wore trousers or not as meaningful to his argument, and hence consequential to his own style of prayer, and possibly to ours, too, for that matter. Thus, at times, a knowledge of everyday life in talmudic times can play a significant role in the understanding of a talmudic text, and even in the subsequent process of halakhic ruling.[11]

This will be even more evident in the next example which we shall bring, from the area of *Hilkhot Shabbat*. The *Shulhan Arukh, Orah Hayyim* 317:1, rules as follows:

> He who ties a permanent knot (*kesher shel kayyamah*) [on *Shabbat*], and one which is the work of an expert (*maaseh oman*), such as the cameleteers' knot or the sailors' knot, . . . and all such similar knots [is guilty]. But if the knot he ties is not that of an expert, though it is permanent, he is free of guilt.

Rabbi Yisrael Meir ha-Cohen of Radin, in his classic *Mishnah Berurah* and *Beur Halakhah* has lengthy descriptive analyses of the various views of the *Rishonim* as to what constitutes a "permanent knot" (*kesher shel kayyamah*), and the differing degrees of *isur* pertaining to these knots. One may summarize his findings as follows:

---

[11]In point of fact, Rashi's assumption does seem to be correct, namely that *Rabbis, Sages,* did not wear trousers, but merely cloaks. See, e.g., *Shabbat* 118a, on R. Yossi's *glimah*, תלמיד חכם, חלוק של in *Bava Batra* 57b, etc. Indeed, trousers were relatively unknown. See S. Krauss, *Kadmoniyyot ha-Talmud* 2/2 (Tel Aviv, 1945), p. 216; on girdles, see pp. 217–227; and on undergarments, pp. 200–215. For a full discussion of the girdle, "gartel," one should add the halakhic element of "hikon," "הכון"; see B. *Shabbat* 10a, *Shulhan Arukh, Orah Hayyim*, sec. 91:2, and a full discussion in J. Lewy's *Minhag Yisrael Torah*, vol. 1, (New York, 1990), pp. 141–143. For a similar issue, see *Mishnah Berurah Orah Hayyim* 2:1.

1. According to the Rif, Rambam, and Rabbi Josef Caro
   a) a permanent knot is one that is never untied (i.e., that in the first place was tied for an unlimited period of time and that can remain tied forever), and is also that of an expert. For tying such a knot on Shabbat one has to bring a sin offering.
   b) A permanent knot that is not that of an expert, or an expert knot that is not permanent—tying it is forbidden, but obligates no sin offering.
   c) A knot that is not that of an expert and is not permanent, one may tie in the first place (*le-hithilah*).
2. Rashi, Rosh, and other *Rishonim*, on the other hand, rule that the main consideration is not the *nature* of the knot and whether it is that of an expert or not, but:
   a) if it is permanent, that is, that it is intended to last permanently, it is forbidden, and one who ties it is obligated to bring a sin offering, even if it is not that of an expert.
   b) On the other hand, if it is intended to be a temporary knot, it is forbidden, but one does not bring a sin offering for tying it.
   c) And if it is the sort of knot that one unties on the same day, even if it is an expert knot, one may tie it in the first place, because such is not considered a forbidden knot.
3. Some opinions have it that any knot that will be untied within a week has the same halakhic status as a knot that will be untied in the same day.

Now the source of all these different views is to found in the first two (or three) *mishnayot* of the fifteenth chapter of Tractate *Shabbat* and their *sugyot* in *Shabbat* 111b–112a, and so forth. There we read as follows:

Mishnah 1. These are the knots for which they [that tie them on *Shabbat*] are culpable: cameleteers' knots, and sailors' knots. . . . R. Meir says: One is not accounted culpable if one ties a knot which can be untied with one hand.

Mishnah 2. There are some knots for which one is not accounted culpable [as one is] for a cameleteer's knot or a sailors' knot. [Thus] a woman may tie up the [corners of a] slit in her shift, or the strings of a hair-net or belt. . . . A bracelet may be tied to a belt but not to a rope; but R. Judah permits this. R. Judah laid down a general rule: no one is accounted culpable for any knot which is not permanent.

We see, then, that the Mishnah (1), when wishing to explain what is a permanent knot, gives the example of a sailor's knot (and a cameleteer's knot). The Gemara (111b) then further elaborates this point as follows: "What is a sailor's knot? If you say it is the knot they tie onto the *isterida*, that is not a permanent knot. No, it is the knot . . . of the *isterida* itself." This brief passage is the crux of the whole halakhic issue, for in it the *setama de-Gemara*[12] (the anonymous portion of the *sugya*) explains to us what constitutes a "permanent knot." And the understanding of this passage clearly depends upon the understanding of the word *isterida*, if that is the correct reading. I have discussed this word elsewhere in considerable detail.[13] There I demonstrated, convincingly, I believe, on the basis of Gaonic traditions, that the correct reading is actually *istedira*, and that this is the (otherwise unattested) Greek nautical term for a *parral* (*$\iota\sigma\tau o\delta\epsilon\iota\rho\eta$, "collar of a mast"). The parral is a rope twisted into a ring; its ends have been permanently married into one another thus forming a ring, or collar, that holds together the ship's yardarm to the mast. Through it is looped the halyard, with a slipknot, and this halyard is used to raise and lower the yardarm and sail into place on the mast. Without any doubt the parral has been permanently knotted (married), and it is equally clear that this has been done by an expert (mariner). Thus, even without going further into the rest of the *sugya*, we see that the correct lexicographic explanation of the technical term appears to corroborate the main normative halakhic opinion of the Rif, Rambam, and Rabbi Josef Caro, namely that a permanent knot is one that is knotted by an expert and is intended never to be untied. To arrive at this conclusion, which is surely significant for the understanding of the *sugya*, as well as for the establishment of the normative *pesak*, we had to determine the correct reading of the text (on the basis of manuscripts and early testimonia), interpret (and emend slightly) an obscure Gaonic gloss, rediscover (or reconstruct) a very rare Greek technical term belonging to

---

[12]We shall not go into the question of the possible dating of the *setama de-Gemara*, but merely note that it is probably late Amoraic. Halivni himself has changed his position on this issue several times as is evident from a comparison of the various introductions to the different volumes of his *Mekorot u-Masorot*. For details see note 30 below.

[13]See my *Nautica Talmudica* (Ramat-Gan and Leiden, 1986), pp. 40–44.

Roman nautical jargon, and corroborate our tentative findings with con-crete evidence from contemporary reliefs and mosaics.[14]

Every step in this process of research was directly aimed at the true comprehension of the talmudic *sugya* and the resultant halakhic appli-cations. In principle, the use of manuscript sources was no different from that of learning a gloss (*hagahah*) of the Bah or the Gra; and reference to Byzantine-Greek dialectic dictionaries was no different from use of the Aruch. Furthermore, only after extensive search and examination of Roman archaeological findings did we uncover that corroborative evi-dence without which the laconic (and slightly corrupt) Gaonic gloss could not be intelligently comprehended. And this gloss constitutes the major source for understanding the *sugya*. Thus a full understanding of the whole talmudic complex necessitates the use of, and, of course, compe-tence in, a number of so-called secular disciplines—linguistics, classical archaeology, and so forth. This is really a rather obvious point; but apparently it needs to be stressed and restressed in our day and age, when the gap between "learning" and "studying" is growing ever broader.[15]

There exists a school of scholarship that primarily is involved in unraveling the different strata of the talmudic *sugya* on the basis of sty-listic, linguistic, and logical criteria.[16] There is, I submit, nothing radi-cally new in this approach. Already the Geonim, such as Rav Sherira in his famous *Iggeret*, informed us that certain passages in the Talmud are Savoraic, that is, post-Aramaic.[17] And since the end of the Amoraic

---

[14]Sperber, *Nautica Talmudica*. A further corollary of the issue of the "per-manent knot" may be found in the responsa *Avnei Nezer Orah Hayim*, sec. 183, on the knots on phylacteries. See, on this, Lewy, *Minhag Yisrael Torah*, p. 72.

[15]I have elaborated on this issue in greater detail in my *Material Culture in Eretz-Yisrael during the Talmudic Period*, (Jerusalem 1993), (Hebrew), and hence I shall not pursue this point here any further.

[16]See, most recently, the excellent volume of S. Friedman, *BT Bava Mezi'a VI, Critical Editions with Comprehensive Commentary* (Jerusalem, 1970). For a methodological introduction to this approach see Friedman, *Mehkarim u-Mekorot* (New York, 1988), pp. 283–321.

[17]See, e.g., B. M. Lewin, *Rabbanan Savorai ve-Talmudam* (Jerusalem, 1937), pp. 26ff.; A. Aptowitzer, *Ha-Tzofeh le-Hokhmat Yisrael 4* (1875), pp. 17–19. The material has been summarized, with a full bibliography, by Friedman, *Mehkarim u-Mekorot*, pp. 284ff. On the *Savoraim* in general, see J. E. Ephrathi, *Tekufot ha-*

period is also "*sof horaah*,"[18] the end of a period of *pesak*,[19] it is surely essential (or at least valuable) to know which elements of the talmudic text postdate that point of "*sof horaah*." Hence, the search after Savoraic passages, and their characterization by language, style, and logical argumentation, is surely an integral part of *le-asukei shemateta aliba de-hilcheta*, understanding the talmudic text in order to derive from it the practical halakhah.

Indeed both the *Geonim* and the *Rishonim* were constantly aware of the stratification of the talmudic text. Thus, for example, the *Ritva* to *Bava Metzia* 3a writes: "All this formulation . . . is not an integral part of the Gemara, but the wording of Rav Yehudai Gaon, and the scribes inserted it into the Gemara proper, and there are many such cases in our tractate. . . . " And so also in his commentary to *Ketubot* 34b he writes: "And our great teacher [i.e., the Ramban] explained that that section is not the wording of the Gemara, but the interpretation of Rav Yehudai Gaon, of blessed memory, and one should not deduce from here with regards another text. . . . "[20]

Furthermore, attempts have been made to distinguish between the words of the *Amora'im* and the explanatory glosses in anonymous sections of the Gemara (*setama de-Gemara*),[21] and this has led to a whole flourishing area of talmudic research in recent times.[22] However, this distinction was already clearly made by the *Rishonim*, and most especially the *Baalei ha-Tosafot*.[23] Thus, for example, the Tosafot in *Shevuot* 25a

---

Savora'im ve-Sifrutah (Petah-Tikva, 1973), and my own entry in the *Encyclopaedia Judaica* (Jerusalem: Keter, 1971), 14:920–921, s.v. *Savoraim*, and in *Ha-Enzyclopedia ha-Ivrit* 25 (1975), 424.

[18] On *sof horaah*, see S. Albeck, *Sinai: Sefer Yovel*, ed. Y. L. ha-Cohen Maimon (Jerusalem, 1958), pp. 57–73, and Ch. Albeck, ibid., pp. 73–79.

[19] See M. Elon, *Ha-Mishpat ha-Ivri* (Jerusalem, 1973), p. 896, for an explanation of this concept. And further, the very important study of S. Z. Havlin, *Mehkarim be-Sifrut ha-Talmudit: Yom Iyyun le-Regel Melot Shemonim Shanah le-Shaul Lieberman* (Jerusalem, 1983), pp. 148–192, and more specifically pp. 160–162.

[20] See the plentiful material cited by Friedman, *Mehkarim u-Mekorot*, pp. 84ff.
[21] See note 12 above.

[22] See, e.g., the numerous writings of the late Avraham Weiss (and his disciples), and more recently of David Halivni Weiss, etc.

[23] See Friedman, *Mehkarim u-Mekorot*, pp. 287ff.

(s.v. Samuel) explain: "One may thus say that this is not a part of Samuel's *dicta*, but that the *shass* (*gemara*) explains thus according to his view, and there are many examples of this in the Talmud." And the Tosafot to *Yevamot* 8a (s.v. *ki*) even goes so far as to say: the Talmud *erred* in [understanding] the statement of Rava(!)[24] Apparently, the Tosafot found it legitimate to suggest that the later anonymous stratum of the *Gemara* contains misunderstandings of earlier Amoraic statements. For in their eyes these late anonymous glosses were less reliable and less canonic. Thus, the *Ritva* to *Bava Metzia* 40a writes: "And even though the above *sugya* explains thus . . . it is a *sugya de-talmuda be-alma* [i.e., this is not an authoritative passage], and does not constitute a contradiction (*kushia*) to Rav Hisda."

The great and saintly sage and scholar, Rabbi Yaakov Yehiel Weinberg (who followed in the footsteps of his mentor Rabbi David Zvi Hoffmann) was himself involved in this kind of methodological analysis.[25] He surely believed that while doing so he was fully engaged in "*limud Torah*." Let us cite a passage from one of his classic studies.[26] First he brings numerous examples of *Rishonim* who were obviously aware of the distinctions we have mentioned, and who solved difficult problems by positing that certain passages were, for example, "an explanation that was written in the margin and [subsequently] copied into the books."[27] He then continues as follows:

> From these examples, and many others like it, we see that the Rishonim recognized these additions through their sharp understanding, and this recognition sufficed them, and [hence] they did not attempt to solve contradictions with forced brilliance. However, our teachers, the greatest of the Aharonim, who established for us the [mainstream] path of understanding *sugyot* and whose books constitute *the* introduction to all who enter into the world of Talmudic learning, abstained from going along this path of unraveling the *sugya* into its component parts, presumably out of fear lest the authority of the holy Talmud be lessened and undermined, and in this way

---

[24]Friedman, *Mehkarim u-Mekorat*, p. 290.

[25]Y. Y. Weinberg, *Mehkarim ba-Talmud* (1937–1938; reprint [posthumously in his *Seridei Eish*, vol. 4], Jerusalem, 1969); see Friedman, *Mehkarim u-Mekorot*, p. 288.

[26]Apud *Seridei Eish*, pp. 119–120.

[27]Raviah, Weinberg, ibid., p. 119.

the basis upon which the halacha is founded will collapse. The truth is, however, that this method of study in no way touches upon the principles of our
received halachah. Such views are determinations of those Torah giants [i.e.,
Aharonim] and are holy to us, and God forbid we move away from their words
even in the smallest degree. Nonetheless, there is in this method of research
special importance for the clarification of *sugyot* and the understanding of
their issues. How many wonderously difficult problems, which can only be
solved in the most forced fashion or tiresomely sagacious argumentation,
simply vanish in the blink of an eye in the light of such examinations, and
passages, so obscure that scholars despaired of finding solutions for them,
suddenly became crystal clear of themselves.

He himself admits, then, that the latter-day giants of Torah scholarship
(with the exemption of a few lone examples, the Gra, the Neziv, etc.)
abandoned this line of research. He nonetheless strongly affirms its
legitimacy. He does, however, briefly mention in passing the possible dangers connected with this methodology, namely that the authority of
the talmudic text might be called into doubt, and the basis of practical
halakhah be undermined. He easily dismisses these considerations, probably for two (unstated) reasons.

1. He trusted that all involved in deep talmudic study had the greatest of respect for the basic integrity of the text, and any approach
   of the type described above would be borne out by traditions from
   the *Geonim* and *Rishonim*, by uncontrovertible linguistic and stylistic evidence, and by closely reasoned and wholly convincing
   deductive analysis.[28]
2. Perhaps it was his view that such discoveries do not affect practical *halakhah*, as already established by the classical *posekim*.[29]

However, had he been confronted with a situation where a whole new
basis for talmudic study was being promoted, one dealing almost exclusively with the separation of strata, and where the lion's share of explanations depended upon the supposition that members of the latter strata
had, at best, only a partial understanding of the statements of the predecessors from the earlier strata, he would have doubtless been filled with

[28]See Weinberg, ibid., p. 114.
[29]See note 31 below.

consternation, and, we suspect, would have been more cautious in his own practice of methodology, and certainly extremely critical of this whole "new school." Is it then merely a question of degree? Could he have set limits and parameters for the use of such a critical methodology? If it is essentially legitimate, how can it be limited in its application? Or is it perhaps a question of the basic attitude of the scholar to his source material and his degree of respect for the talmudic Sages and for the authority and perception of the early commentators? Or is it a question of the ability of the researcher, his control of the sources, and the stringency of his methodology?

For example, how would Rav Weinberger have viewed the works of Professor David Halivni (-Weiss), one of the most erudite, brilliant, and scholastically effective practitioners of this new school?[30] Of course, we cannot answer for him. But if we take the conclusions of Rabbi Irwin H. Haut as acceptable to the open-minded traditionalists, Halivni's work has much to be credited for, and is undoubtedly of value to traditional talmudic scholarship.[31] There are questions of emphasis and degree; Haut feels that Halivni's penchant for "literary solutions," as opposed to legal

---

[30]See mainly his series *Mekorot u-Masorot*, Moe'ed Jerusalem 1965, 1972, Nashim Tel Aviv 1965, etc.

[31]I. H. Haut, *The Talmud as Law or Literature* (New York, 1982). Certainly his questions are no less meaningful and provocative than those of Rabbi J. H. Dünner, chief-rabbi of Amsterdam (1874–1912), whose *"Anotations Criticae"* (*Hagahot*) to the Bavli Yerushalmi Tosefta and Midrashim have recently been reprinted by Mossad Harav Kook, under the title חידושי הריצ"ד, vols. 1–3 (Jerusalem, 1981–1983). And Halivni suggested answers that are usually more to the point. On Dünner, see the late Professor Benjamin De-Fries's biographical essay and appreciation at the beginning of volume 1 of the Mossad Harav Kook reprint (pp. 9–32). De-Fries raises the ideological question:

> However, R. David Zvi Hoffmann raised the issue of *psak*: would not [Dünner's] *Hagahot* in the present form be utilized, against his will, to undermine the whole structure of the *Shulhan Arukh*? . . . But one may answer that critical research comes only to delineate lines of growth and development of the halacha in a scientific fashion, but is not intended to refute the halacha and its conclusions in its dogmatic and mature form. . . . [The scientific approach] recognizes stages of development and the strange vicissitudes of evolution which at times bring about changes in interpretation and mutation of forms. But in practice we accept the *psak* as it is derived from the *sugya*, and as it evolved into its final form. . . . [p. 31]

And see De-Fries's continued analysis.

ones, is a little too weighted.[32] But he does not contest the legitimacy of his approach, or, for that matter, the competence of Halivni's praxis. Perhaps he feels that this "new approach" should be used as a kind of last resort, when all traditionalist legalistic deductive reasoning has proved unsatisfactory. But ultimately this too is a subjective criterion, and probably no two people would agree on how to judge the point.

One possible criticism of any methodology that posits the lack of, or partial, understanding of the later talmudic authorities of the *dicta* of their predecessors is that such a view diminishes our respect for those ancient giants. It also posits that we understand the matter better than did the later *Amora'im*. Can our latter-day understanding be superior to those of the early masters? They are angels compared to us mortals, and if they were mortals, then compared with them we are on the level of base animals (cf. *Shabbat* 112b). How dare we measure ourselves against them, even to the extent of correcting them?[33] To this we may respond in a number of ways. Either like Rashi in *Shevuot* 3b: "A mistaken student wrote this in the margin, and the copyists [subsequently] put it into the *Gemara*," that is, this is not really of genuine talmudic pedigree and authority[34]; or like Rashi to *Sanhedrin* 10b: "It is the way of the *tana* (the Amoraic memorizers of Tannaitic texts) to err as to the reading and miss out a word by lapse of memory; but he does not switch words. . . . " That is to say, textual errors were unconsciously introduced into the text already in Amoraic times by professional memorizers, who were not necessarily scholars. Indeed, they were likened to baskets laden with stacks of manuscripts. They could quote by heart, and knew not what they spake (see *Megillah* 28b, *Sotah* 22b).

Actually, the *Geonim* had already addressed themselves to the question of how blatant errors infiltrated the talmudic text. In a well-known

---

[32]Haut, pp. 70–71.

[33]For a similar such question in the later periods of halakhic development, see E. Schochetman's excellent article *Bar-Ilan* 18/19 (1985): 170–195, as to the problem of הוצאת לעז על הראשונים, casting doubts or aspersions on the earlier authorities.

[34]See Rabbi Yaakov Hayyim Sofer (the great-grandson of the "Kaf ha-Hayyim"), *Yehi Yosef* (Jerusalem, 1991), p. 132. Sometimes this is formulated thus: *Lav Mar bar Rav Ashi Hattim alei*, i.e., this passage does not bear the signature of the editor of the Talmud, Mar Bar Rav Ashi, or, in other words, this is not really a part of the Talmud.

Gaonic responsum in *Teshuvot Geonim Kadmonim* (sec. 78),[35] dealing with mistaken biblical readings in the Talmud, we read:

> . . . But you must examine carefully in every case when you feel uncertainty [as to the credibility of the text] what is its source (כיצד עיקרו), whether a scribal error, or the superficiality of a second-rate student (שטפא דתלמידי תרביצאי)[36] who was not well-versed . . . after the manner of many mistakes found among those superficial second-rate students, and certainly among those rural memorizers who were not familiar with the biblical text. And since they erred in the first place . . . [they compounded their error].[37]

Or perhaps we may respond that though we be midgets compared to those erstwhile giants, once we have succeeded in clambering onto their shoulders, we see further than they, and our horizon is broader than theirs. (This, as is well-known, is the usual justification for the standard ruling: הלכה כבתראי, the *halakhah* follows the view of the later authority.) Without pursuing this well-trodden area of discussion any further,[38] I believe we can state, without too much hesitation, that the criticisms we raised can be properly rebutted, leaving the methodology, where practiced with wisdom, respect, and restraint, methodologically legitimate.

We now turn to the question of the use of manuscripts and the discovery of alternative readings. Can we emend rabbinic texts on the basis of such testimonia, and what may be the long-term effect of such emendation upon normative *halakhah*? Well, the position of the Hazon Ish is fairly well known on this issue. In a letter[39] he wrote:

---

[35] Ed. Cassel (Berlin, 1848; photographic reprint, Tel Aviv, 1964), 23b.

[36] See, e.g., B. [M.] Levin, *Otzar ha-Geonim to Berakhot* (Haifa, 1928), *Ha-Perushim*, pp. 8–9: . . . *ve-sh'ar ama dela yad'ei perush kala ve-ishtif le-hu gemara ve-ta'u ve-osifa bah "parshiata de-kol shata. . . ."*

(From *Sefer ha-Ittim*, by Rabbi Judah b. Barzilai of Barcelona, ed. J. Schorr [Berlin, 1902], p. 244.) I shall not go into the question of what is the *Tarbiza* here. I hope to deal with this question elsewhere.

[37] The bracketed words are a free translation. Cf. *Teshuvot ha-Geonim Harkavy* (Berlin, 1887; photographic reprint, Jerusalem, 1966), sec. 229, p. 107; and *Menahot* 82b, *Aruch Completum*, vol. 8, ed. A. Kohut, p. 273, s. v. תרבץ, etc.

[38] See I. Ta-Shma's detailed study of this principle in *Shenaton ha-Mishpat ha-Ivri* 6/7, (1979–1980), pp. 405–423.

[39] *Kovez Iggerot*, ed. S. Greinemann, vol. 2 (Bnei Brak, 1990), no. 23, p. 37.

I received your [material]. I found in them nothing new. [As to] the photo-
graphs of the manuscripts, it is not my way to pay attention to them. For
we do not know who wrote them[40] and we may well assert that the scribe
wrote them according to his wont. And it is well known that one does not
rely too much on new discoveries,[41] but only on the works of the decisors

---

[40]This, of course, is not always the case. For example, the well-known manuscript of the Yerushalmi Ms. Leiden, Codex Scaliger 3, was copied by Rabbi
Yehiel ben Rabbi Yekutiel ben Rabbi Benjamin ha-Rofeh in the year 1280, the
author of the very popular medieval *musar* text *Maalot ha-Middot*, and a considerable *Talmid Hakham*. See Lieberman's introduction in the Kedem photographic edition, Jerusalem 1971, at the beginning of volume 1. And such is the
case with numerous manuscripts whose colophons survive. This then is a rather
questionable generalization.

[41]This is a very complex issue that requires an extensive study in its own right.
Here we shall merely point out that the majority position among the *posekim*
is that the principle of *halakhah ke-batrai*, we follow the latest opinion, does
not apply if the later authority was unaware of the opinions of earlier
authorities. And when this is the case we assume that had he known this earlier opinion, he would have judged accordingly. Hence, we follow the earlier
opinion, especially if it is that of a Rishon. See, for example, *Rema Hoshen
Mishpat*, sec. 25:2:

> But if at times there is a responsum of a Gaon which was not mentioned in the books, and we
> find them (later on) differing from him, we do not have to follow the later authorities,
> because it is possible that they did not know the view of the Gaon, and had they known they
> would have withdrawn their view (*Maharik*, sec. 96).

This, as mentioned above, is the majority view, see *Kenesset ha-Gedolah* to *Yoreh
De'ah* 37, *Beit Yosef* no. 50, 149. See further on this matter, Rabbi Yaakov Hayyim
Sofer, *Beit Yaakov* (Jerusalem, 1985), p. 19, n. 5, 52–53; and his *Tiferet Yitzhak*
(Jerusalem, 1981), pp. 46, 115, etc. Hence, discoveries of new early texts of
Geonim and *Rishonim* should certainly be taken into account. A case in point is
the Meiri, who was only recently fully discovered, and in whose writings we find
numerous *psakim* of relevance to our day. (See *Beit Yaakov*, p. 52, n. 17). See,
for example, Rabbi Ovadiah Josef, *Yabia Omer*, vol. 5, *Orah Hayim* 24:11, who
writes that "if the *Aharonim*, who ruled stringently [on a certain issue] had known
the words of the Meiri (to *Rosh ha-Shanah* 28b), who plainly holds the opposite
view, they would certainly have abandoned their own conclusions in favour
of his" (p. 103). And so too in vol. 4, *Orah Hayyim* 5:1, he writes, "and had
the aforementioned *Aharonim* seen the responsum of R. Abraham son of the
Ramban, they would surely not have differed from him" (p. 48). See further
Rabbi Ovadiah Joseph's "Opening Words" at the beginning of that volume.

In fact, I suspect that the Hazon Ish himself would agree with this view. This we may derive from the following: the Tur, *Hoshen Mishpat*, sec. 280, quotes the Ramah (Rabbi Meir Halevy Abulafia) in such a fashion that the Ramah's words contradict themselves. The *Beit Yosef* points this out but is left with the question outstanding (צריך עיון), while the *Darkei Moshe* (of the Rema, Rabbi Moshe Isserles) and the *Derishah* and the *Perishah* (of the Sma, Rabbi Joshua Falk Katz) struggle to solve the contradiction. The Hazon Ish (*Hoshen Mishpat* 15) rightly points out that "a copyist's error crept into the Tur, and the text should read thus . . . ", and he inserts a whole additional section that had fallen out of the text. He further points out "that the [full] reading is found in the printed edition, and because the Beit Yosef and the Rema did not have the Ramah's work they found difficulties with the Tur's text. But now that we have been graced with the writing of the Ramah, the copyist's error has been revealed to us." (The Yad Ramah was first published in Salonika 1790, *Bava Batra*, and Salonika 1798, *Sanhedrin*. Rabbi Joshua Falk Katz, the latest of the three afore-mentioned authorities, died in 1614.) See S. Y. Zevin, *Ishim ve-Shitot* (Tel Aviv, 1966), p. 327.

However, in the meanwhile my good friend and very learned colleague Rabbi Professor S. Z. Havlin points out to me that the issue is somewhat more com-plex than I made it out to be. First, he noted already implicitly in an article, published in *Ha-Maayan* 8:2 (5728/1968): 36, that this "discovery" of the Hazon Ish was first published by Rabbi Shimon Schkop in his *Shaarei Yosher*, vol. 2 (Warsaw, 5628/1928), *She'ar* 5, chap. 11. The Hazon Ish then discussed this same issue (without alluding to Rabbi Shimon Schkop) in his brother's journal, *Knesset Yisrael*, vol. 8, in an article under the name of איש וילנא, which was pub-lished in Vilna in 1912 (sec. 79, pp. 119–124) and thence to Hazon Ish, *Hoshen Mishpat* sec. 15. (In a note at the end of the *Knesset Yisrael* article he wrote as follows: Also in *Shaarei Yosher* . . . he discussed this issue at length, and con-cluded by saying that it is imperative [מצוה] to declare that the Rema's ruling is incorrect. However, according to what we have explained above, the ruling of the Rema is valid, and Mosheh [alluding to the Rema's personal name] is true and his Torah is true.) In a very complex discussion the Hazon Ish at-tempts to demonstrate that despite the error that crept into the text of the Rema, the resultant ruling nonetheless stands. He ends his discursive argumentation: והוראת הרמ"א אמיתית . . . , "and the ruling of the Rema is correct." It would there-fore appear that his aim was to demonstrate that the textual error does not, in fact, lead to an error in the operative *halakhah*.

For the whole issue of the effect of the discovery of new sources upon present-day *halakhah*, see Havlin (ibid., pp. 35–37), and most recently the excellent study by Rabbi Moshe Bleich, "The Role of Manuscripts in Halakhic Decision-Making: Hazon Ish, His Precursors and Contemporaries" (Tradition 27 [1993]: 22–55).

A further aspect of this issue may perhaps be seen in the frequently found argument that one does not have to follow a specific early authority because he did not yet know of the Zohar, which was only revealed after his time. See, for example, Lewy, *Minhag Yisrael Torah*, pp. 107, 132, etc. See also, similarly, other outstanding halakhic sources, such as the responsa of the Maharam (Rabbi Meir b. Barukh) of Rothenburg. See, for example Rabbi Josef Katz, *She'erit Yosef*, ed. Ziv (New York, 1984), sec. 62, p. 149, etc. The argument is, of course, that had they known the Zohar they would have ruled in accordance with it. And the same argument is applied to the rulings of the Ari ha-Kadosh (Rabbi Yitzhak Luria). Thus, for example, Rabbi Yitzhak Barda (*Responsa Yitzhak Yeranen*, vol. 3, sec. 13) writes "had the *Posekim* (decisors) known what the Ari knew, they would have reversed their opinions." So too, the Hida (Rabbi Hayyim Yosef David Azulai) writes (*Birkei Yosef, Orah Hayyim* 421:1, etc.), "We follow him (the Ari) often even when he rules contrary to Maran (Rabbi Yosef Caro). For the Rabbis knew (*kim le-hu Rabanan*) that if Maran had heard the words of the Ari, he would have changed his mind." (I own these reference to an as yet unpublished article by Professor Moshe Hallamish, that he most kindly gave me to read. He deals with this issue at length, and brings a wealth of evidence on the subject.)

Yet another aspect to this issue, and a very important one, is the relationship between the Hazon Ish's position and the principle of *halakhah ke-batrai*, the law is in accordance with the late authority. The rationale behind this principle is that, though we may be lesser intellects than our predecessors, of inferior knowledge and shallower understanding, we stand like midgets upon their shoulders, the shoulders of giants. And, hence, we have a broader horizon than they, see farther than they. (See note 38 above.) Thus, for example, the Radbaz (Rabbi David ben Zimrah) in his responsa, vol. 8 (B'nei Brak, no date), sec.141, writes:

> For if you do not say so, you have left no place for any of the latter-day authorities to make any innovation (*she-yitchadesh sham chiddush*) or add any point (*ve-lo shum dikduk*), not in reasoning nor learning (*lo sevara ve-lo gemara*), for we will say to him: If what you say is true, the earlier authorities would have said it. But this is not so. For no one's knowledge is complete, other than He to whom is perfection, may He be blessed. . . . For the latter-day authorities saw what the earliest ones did not see . . . and saw the writings of their predecessors and built upon them, and made their innovations, and it is for this reason we say the law is in accordance with the later authority. . . . [p. 108]

(This issue has recently been dealt with in depth in an as-yet-unpublished study by my colleague and former student, Dr. Meir Rafeld. My thanks to him for letting me peruse his paper with its wealth of information.) It would then seem, at least at a superficial level, that the Hazon Ish's view is not consonant with this widely accepted position in Jewish law, and constitutes a reversal from the normative trend in halakhic development. This question requires further careful examination. For yet a fuller understanding of the Hazon Ish's viewpoint

(*posekim*) that were handed down without interruption from generation to generation.[42]

And elsewhere he writes:[43]

You suggested an explanation of the *sugya* . . . emending the gemara on the basis of Ms. Munich [no. 95]. Surely [you cannot claim] that all the leading scholars throughout the generations from the time of the *Rishonim* till now did not get to the true meaning [of the passage], because a scribe erred and added something of his own in his gemara text and misled all the Sages. I will have nothing of it. . . . For the Rishonim were prepared to lay down their lives on behalf of the manuscripts that they had in their hands and divine providence protected them so that the Torah be not forgotten from Israel. And when they started to print the Talmud, the leading scholars of the day toiled endlessly to produce a correct and accurate text.[44] Albeit, at times,

---

on the development of the *halakhah*, see Hazon Ish, *Kodashim, Hilkhot Terefot* 5:8 (*Nashim, Hilkhot Ishut* 27:3) and *Orah Chayyim, Kuntres ha-Shiurim*, p. 115. And on this see most recently the discussion of Rabbi Zalman Menahem Koren in *Birurim be-Hilkhot ha-Raayah*, ed. M. Z. Neriah, A. Stern, and N. Gottel (Jerusalem, 1992), pp. 433–442. See the continuation of this article (pp. 442ff.) for an exposition of Rav Kook's view as to *Rema Hoshen Mishpat* 28, discussed above in this note. I have digressed somewhat at length in this issue, but this is because I believe it is an issue central to the understanding of the mechanism and development of *halakchah*.

[42] And see Hazon Ish to *Orah Chayyim*, p. 115, col. 2, sec. 6: " . . . and even though one does not rely on manuscripts representing a noncontinuous tradition . . . ", etc. For an interesting comparison, see *Minhagei Ziditchov*, ed. Josef Gottlieb (Jerusalem, 1971), *Hosafot Minhagim*, no. 102, p. 17:

One may not study from any book other than one which has a direct continuous tra-dition that it is from Elijah [the Prophet]: אסור ללמוד מאיזה ספר עד שהוא מקובל איש מפי איש מפי שהוא מפי אליהו.

For references, see editor's note, ibid.

[43] *Kovetz Iggerot*, vol. 1, no. 32, p. 59.

[44] Presumably he is talking about the first Venice edition, 1520 onward, which was printed by the Christian printer Daniel Bomberg. However, the text was prepared by scholars, such as Rabbi Hiyya, a Venetian Rabbi (mentioned in *She'elot u-Teshuvot Binyamin Zeev* sec. 71), Israel Cornelius Edelkind of Padua, some of whom did a very poor job, so that the text is replete with errors. See Rabbi R. Rabbinovicz, *Maamar al Hadpasat ha-Talmud*, ed. A. M. Habermann (Jerusalem, 1952), pp. 35–43, especially pp. 40–41.

one can benefit from a manuscript to weed out errors that have crept in over the ages. But an opinion that was licenced by all the Rabbis, without any doubt ever being raised, heaven forbid us destroying it.[45]

My good friend and very learned colleague Professor Shnayer Z. Leiman dealt with the Hazon Ish's views on this matter in an authoritative article in *Tradition*,[46] and I need not repeat his conclusions. However, I think it is fair to say that the position of the Hazon Ish is hardly a mainstream one. For throughout the generations the greatest Torah authorities made judicious use of variant readings and traditions, emended texts and rules accordingly. From the earliest *Geonim*, through the early *Rishonim*, such as Rashi and Rabbi Tam, to the later *Rishonim*, like the Maharshal, and the early *Aharonim*, such as the Bah and finally to the giants of more recent times, the Gaon of Vilna, the Neziv of Volozin, and so forth, all these, and very numerous others, made a constant use of this methodology. And returning to Ms. Munich, when Raphael Nathan Rabbinovicz published his monumental *Dikdukei Soferim* in the second half of the nineteenth century,[47] in which he systematically gave the alternative readings of the Munich manuscript,[48] he received the highest approbations from the great-

---

It should be further pointed out that in Bomberg's printing house, as well as the printing house in Cremona, apostate Jews were used as proofreaders, typesetters, etc., such as Vittorio Aliano in Cremona (Rabbinovicz, *Maamar*, p. 39, n. 8), Yaakov ben Hayyim ibn Adoniyahu in Venice, who prepared the Leiden manuscript of the Yerushalmi (n. 40 above) for the first Venice edition c. 1523, and who may have converted later on in life.

Perhaps the Hazon Ish did not know those facts about the early printing of the Talmud, or perhaps he was thinking of later editions, in which such great authorities as Rabbi Shlomo Luria (Maharshal), Rabbi Shalom Shachna, etc., were (directly or indirectly) involved. See Rabbinovicz, *Maamar*, pp. 61–62, on the first Lublin edition 1559, and n. 3 and pp. 85–91 on the third Lublin edition, etc. In any case, the Hazon Ish's generalization is somewhat idealized and probably bears little relationship to the historical facts.

[45] And of *Kovetz Iggerot*, vol. 3, no. 48, p. 69, and Hazon Ish to *Orah Hayyim* sec. 140, par. 3, p. 471.

[46] *Tradition* 19:4 (1981): 301–310.

[47] *Variae Lectiones in Mischnam et in Talmud Babylonicam quom ex aliis libris antiquissimis et scriptis et impressis tum e* Codice Monacensi *praestantissimo collectae, annotationibus instructae*, 1868–1897.

[48] See preceding note.

est authorities of his time: Rabbi Josef Saul Nathansohn, Rabbi Jakob Ettinger, Rabbi Itzhak Elhanan Spektor of Kovno, the Ktav Sofer, Rabbi Shlomo Kluger, and so forth. And the Gaddol of Minsk, Rabbi Yeruham Leib Perlman, wrote of it[49]: Come let us give thanks to the author of *Dikdukei Soferim*, who copied out [talmudic] readings from ancient manuscripts, and oft-times enlightened us with them. Indeed, his volumes were used by Rabbi Raphael Shapiro of Vienna, author of Torat Raphael, Rabbi Yeruham Perla, in his monumental commentary to Saadya Gaon's *Sefer ha-Mitzvot*, Rabbi Meir Simha ha-Cohen of Dvinsk, author of the *Or Sameah*, Rabbi Menachem Mendel Kasher, in his *Torah Shelemah*, and similar works. On further thought, the words of the Hazon Ish become even less readily understandable,[50] especially in view of the fact that he himself made numerous textual emendations when he felt it was necessary.[51] It certainly does not represent the main trend in traditional Torah scholarship. Perhaps it represents an attempt on his part to offset a tendency to overestimate the importance of new discoveries, manuscripts, *Rishonim*, and so forth, rather than part of a systematic philosophy of *halakhah*.

Paradoxically enough, one of his own very daring emendations in the Talmud is actually borne out by the Munich manuscript he so denigrated. Thus in *Berakhot* 35b we read: "The earlier generations used to bring the fruits in [to their houses] over roofs and through courtyards . . . in order not to have to separate their tithes." The Hazon Ish writes: "The word 'courtyards' is clearly an error, for the main way of entry is through the courtyards" (*Ma'asrot* sec. 5:15). He bolsters his emendation with suitable references—*Gittin* 81a, *Bava Metzia* 88a, *Menahot* 67b, and *Rambam Maasrot* 4.1—in all of which this word is missing. And so, in-

---

[49]*Yitron Or* to *Mishnah Sukkah* 1.1.

[50]See *Or Yaakov* by Rabbi Yaakov Hayyim Sofer, apud Yehi Reuven, by Rabbi Reuven David Nawi (Jerusalem, 1983), p. 119, n. 31; and see his *Berit Yaakov*, p. 229.

[51]See Leiman, p. 310, n. 21, for an example. See further *Kovetz Iggerot*, vol. 3, no. 19, p. 47, for what he wrote about the woeful textual state of the *Tosefta*, and also about inaccuracies in the modern editions of the Talmud (ed. Vilna?), and Hazon Ish, *Orah Hayyim* sec. 67, par. 12. See, on this, Rabbi Ovadiah Josef's comments in *Yabia Omer*, vol. 5, "Opening Words." The attitude of the Hazon Ish to textual emendation must be further examined and perhaps his guidelines to a consistent policy—if there be such—will be discovered.

deed, it is in the Munich manuscript, as cited by Rabbinovicz in his *Dikdukei Soferim* to *Berakhot* (p. 193). Furthermore, Rabbinovicz, in a long note (n. 4, ad loc.), discussed this matter, proving that since the talmudic statement in *Berakhot* "is that of Rabbi Yohanan, and he holds that a courtyard obligates tithes and everyone agrees that a courtyard obligates tithes [at least] by Rabbinic ruling," the word should indeed be deleted. He also notes that the Zelah [*Ziyyun la-Nefesh Hai* by Rabbi Yehezkel Landau, the author of the *Noda bi-Yehudah*] already pointed this out. (And see the continuation of his lengthy note, with additional comments of the Av Beit Din of Lvov). The Hazon Ish, then, could have gained additional verification of his emendation from the manuscript, and added argumentation from Rabbinovicz's comments.

Clearly, then, we should not place too much credence on the printed page, especially of late editions, and certainly one should not regard the printed edition as in any way canonic. And in order to underscore our warning not overly to rely on the printed versions of ancient texts and the dangers inherent in doing so, we shall bring just one example as a sort of cautionary tale.

Professor Saul Lieberman, in his *Ha-Yerushalmi ki-Fshuto*[52] discusses the passage in *Yerusahalmi Pesahim* 2.2, 29a, which according to the *editio princeps* reads as follows:

> *Hivkir chimtzo be-shelosh asar, le-achar ha-Pesach ma-hu?*
> *R. Yochanan 'asar. R. Shim'on ben Lakish amar: mutar.*
>
> He renounced ownership of his leaven on the thirteenth [of the month of Nissan]—what is [its status] after the Passover? R. Yohanan forbade it. R. Simon ben Lakish said: "It is permitted."

R. Baer Ratner, in his *Ahavat Tziyyon ve-Yerushalayim* (ad loc.),[53] cites six testimonia from *Rishonim* (Rashba, Ittur, Ramban, Rabbenu Yeruham, Ritva, and Recanati) that the reading is הפקיד, "he deposited," and that the Yerushalmi is discussing a deposit of *hametz* before Pesah, presumably in the hands of a gentile (see Ritva and Recanati). According to this the Yerushalmi is asking what is the status of this *hametz* after the

---

[52]Volume 1 (all that appeared) (Jerusalem, 1934), pp. 397–198.
[53]Pietrokov, 1908, pp. 28–29.

Pesah and Rabbi Yohanan and Rabbi Simon ben Lakish differ on this point. The reading in the Recanati is even more interesting, for it runs as follows:[54]

Hifkid chimzo be-yad goi

He deposited his leaven in the hands of a gentile, what is [its status] after the Passover?

Lieberman demonstrates conclusively that all these six testimonia have no validity whatsoever, "as is usually the case with him (i.e., Ratner).[55] For anyone with a taste (רח) of Torah will understand that this reading is impossible."[56] He goes on to prove this from the continuation of the Yerushalmi itself, and shows that every one of the passages in the *Rishonim* must be emended in accord with the true Yerushalmi text. Thus the passage in the Rashba is found in another parallel place, and there the reading is הפקיר. The Ramban has in the *editio princeps*: הפקיר. Rabbenu Yeruham was quoting from the Rosh, who in turn has: הפקיר. Internal evidence is brought to correct the reading in the Ritva and the Recanati. In the latter case, the context makes it completely clear what is the correct reading. Thus the whole passage reads:

הא למדת שהמפקיר על מנת לחזור ולזכות הוי הפקר אף על פי שחזר וזכה בו. וההוא
דפרק כל שעה: הפקיד (!) חמיצו ביד גוי, לאחר הפסח מהו? ר'... יוחנן אמר אסור
היינו דחייש לשמא לא יפקיר כלל. אבל אם הפקיר בודאי שרי כדפרישית.

Thus you have learned that he who renounced ownership, this is a true renunciation of ownership, even if afterwards he regains ownership. And that which [we have learned] in [the Yerushalmi] chapter Kol Shaah: הפקיד (!) his leaven in the hands of a gentile, what is [its status] after the Passover? R. Yohanan says it is forbidden—This is because he suspects that he might not really have renounced ownership. But if he *did*, it is certainly permitted, as we have explained.

Here, then, two errors made their way into the text: הפקיר turned into הפקיד, making nonsense of the strain of halakhic argumentation. And

---

[54]*Piskei Recanati*, sec. 157.
[55]*Ha-Yerushalmi ki-Fshuto*, p. 398.
[56]Ibid., p. 397.

בשלשה עשר must have been abbreviated in later editions to בי"ג, which was interpreted as standing for ביד גוי. Thus "the thirteenth [of *Nisan*]" turned into "in the hand of a gentile"![57] Obviously the *hametz* had to be deposited into the hands of a gentile, since had it been deposited with a Jew, in no way could it be construed as permissible after the Passover. Therefore, if it was deposited—הפקיד—it had to be in the hands of a non-Jew. So there is a sort of internal logic in this perverse corruption.

Now even though it is true "that anyone with a taste of Torah" should have understood that this reading is patently absurd, nonetheless the

---

[57]On corruption of abbreviated numbers, etc., see what I wrote in *Sinai* 62:5–6 (1968): 278–280, and Rabbi Reuven Margaliot, *Mehkarim be-Darkei ha-Talmud ve-Hidotav* (Jerusalm, 1967), pp. 21–30, 51–61. There may be another interesting example of such a corruption. The Yerushalmi in Sanhedrin 4.7, when discussing who is qualified to judge monetary laws, including bastards (*mamzerim*) brings a statement in the name of Rabbi Judah that: אין מדקדקים ביין נסך—one does not examine carefully *yayin nesekh*. The classical commentators were unable to make any sense of this statement, which of course, bears no relationship to its context. Rabbi Reuven Margaliot, in his *Mehkarim be-Darkei ha-Talmud ve-Hidotav*, pp. 31–331, after surveying earlier explanations and refuting them, made a bold attempt to explain the statement by suggesting that the letters יין נסך were the initial letters of six rules concerning judgment of monetary laws. But his suggestion, though brilliant, is forced.

Louis Ginzberg, in his notes to Abraham Geiger's *Kevutzat Maamarim* (ed. S. Poznansky [Warsaw, 1910], p. 404), makes a more convincing suggestion, namely that the text read originally: *ain medekdekim be yod gimmal*—one does not carefully examine [a] thirteen[-year-old], i.e., to check whether he has physical signs of maturity, but accepts him as an adult on the basis of his age. As such it would be parallel to what we have learned in *Berakhot* 47b:

קטן שהביא שתי שערות מזמנין עליו, ושלא הביא שתי
שערות אין מזמנין עליו, ואין מדקדקים בקטן

A child who has grown two [body] hairs (a sign of maturity) may be use for *zimmun*, and one that has not may not. And we do not carefully examine a child.

(See the *Gemara*'s discussion ad loc.) Ginzberg explains that a child who has reached the age of thirteen need not be examined for two hairs; we assume he has indeed reached physical maturity. Similarly, he argues in the case of monetary judgments. If he is thirteen, we may assume he has reached physical maturity, and as such is qualified for adult privileges and duties. The scribe misread י"ג, "thirteen," as י"נ, interpreting these as the initial letters of יין נסך, and hence our meaningless text.

garbled version of the Yerushalmi was used by Rabbi Hayyim Ha-Cohen Rappaport in one of his responsa[58] to emend the Yerushalmi, and this corrupt passage formed the basis of his practical ruling. Some time later, Rappaport's ruling was cited by Rabbi Moshe Nahum Yerushalimsky, in his *Minhat Moshe*,[59] who wrote: "Even though what he writes in his responsum is against the views of many *gedolim*, nevertheless, he does have a great pillar upon which to support himself, especially when great loss is involved (הפסד מרובה)."[60]

Let us give yet another example of the importance of a critical approach to the printed text, and, in addition, the importance of bibliographic knowledge, again taken from the field of *halakhah*. In *Shulhan Arukh, Orah Hayyim* 685:7 we read:

> There are those who say that *Parshat Zachor* (Deuteronomy 26:17–19) and *Parshat Parah Adumah* (Numbers, chapter 19) have to be read *mi-de-Oraita* [by a command of biblical authority]. Consequently, villagers, who do not have a *minyan* [quorum of ten], must come to a place where there is a *minyan* on those Sabbaths [when those portions are read] so as to hear these readings which are *de-Oraita* [in a *minyan*].

The author of the *Shulhan Arukh*, Rabbi Josef Caro, expresses the same opinion, that *Parshat Parah* is also *mi-de-Oraita*, in a different halakhic context in *Orah Hayyim* 146:2, where he writes: "and all the aforesaid has no relevance to *Parshat Zakhor* and *Parshat Parah*, which have to be read in [a quorum of] ten *mi-de-Oraita*." However, Rabbi Yehezkel da Silva (1659–1698), in his *Peri Hadash* (to *Orah Hayyim* 146:2) asks in surprise: "But that *Parshat Parah* [is *mi-de-Oraita*], whence do we know this?" Similarly, the Shelah, Rabbi Isaiah Halevy Horowitz (c. 1565–c. 1630) argues that *Parshat Parah* is not *de-Oraita*. And so too the Bah, Rabbi Joel Sirkes (1561–1640) (see *Orah Hayyim* 685).

Rabbi Josef Caro, however, in his *Beit Yosef* to *Tur Orah Hayyim* 685, cited his source for the opinion that *Parah* is also *mi-de-Oraita*, namely: "The Tosafot in the beginning of chapter היה קורא (*Megillah*, chapter 2,

---

[58]*Mayyim Hayyim*, Zitomir 1857/8, sec. 11.

[59]Warsaw, 1882, in *Kuntrus Hukkat ha-Pesah*, sec. 4.

[60]See Margaliot, ibid., p. 56 (where the bibliographic details require some correction).

17b) wrote that these are chapters which have to be read *mi-de-Oraita*, such as *Parshat Zachor* and *Parshat Parah Adumah*." Furthermore, Rabbi Israel Isserlein, in his *Terumat ha-Deshen* (responsum no. 108), wrote that the brief Tosafot (*Tosafot Ketzarot*)[61] to *Berakhot* chapter two explains that *Parshat Zachor* and *Parshat Parah* must be read *min ha-Torah* (i.e., *mi-de-Oraita*). However, in the *Tosafot*, as we have them in our editions, both in *Berakhot* and in *Megillah* there is no mention made of *Parshat Parah*. In *Megillah* 17b, s.v. בל, the Tosafot read: *ve-kashe, she-harei keriat ha-Torah einah min ha-Torah ela' mi-de-Rabbanan, levad mi-Parshat Zakhor de-havei de-oraita*. Similarly in *Berakhot* 13a, s.v. הלשון, we read: *ve-yesh lomar de-mairi be-parshiyyot he-hayyavin likrot de-Oraita, kemo Parshat Zakhor*. We see then that only *Parshat Zakhor* is mentioned as being mandatory *mi-de-Oraita*. So too in *Haggahot Asheri* to *Berakhot* chapter six (seven) (cited in *Terumat ha-Deshan*, ibid., and thence in *Magen Avraham* to *Orah Hayyim* 685) we are told that *Parshat Zakhor* must be read in [a quorum of] ten *mi-de-Oraita*. Likewise, the *Tosafot Sens* (cited ibid.) knew of no reading of biblical authority other than *Parshat Zakhor*.

On the basis of the above evidence, the Gaon Rabbi Elijah of Vilna, (the Gra, 1720–1797), in his note to the *Shulhan Arukh* (685) wrote:

"and *Parshat Parah*" (citation from the *Shulhan Arukh*)—In our Tosafot there is no mention [of *Parah*], neither in *Berakhot* nor in *Megillah* 17b. Similarly, in *Asheri*, chapter 6, there is no mention of anything other than *Zakhor*. And [Rabbi Josef Caro] chanced upon a corrupt version [of the Tosafot texts].

The truth of the matter is, however, somewhat different. The Maharshal, Rabbi Solomon (ben Yehiel) Luria (Brest-Litovske, 1510–Lublin, 1574), in his critical marginalia to the Talmud, entitled *Hokhmat Shlomoh*, to *Berakhot* (Cracow, 1581)[62] wrote as follows:

---

[61]See E. E. Urbach, *Baalei ha-Tosafot* (Jerusalem, 1980), pp. 600–601 (and especially n. 9), that this term refers to our *Tosafot* to *Berakhot*—which are an abbreviation of the *Tosafot* of Rabbi Judah Sir Leon.

[62]On the nature of these emendations see the excellent study of I. Ron, *Rabbi Solomon Luria and the Textual Development of the Talmud* (Ph.D. diss., in Hebrew, Bar-Ilan University, 1989). The emendations were based primarily in *severa* (logical thought processes), rather than on manuscript evidence.

תוס' בד"ה בלשון הקודש וכו' - פרה אדומה נמחק ונ"ב: טעות הוא וכן בתוס' דמגילה.

Tosafot s.v. בלשון הקודש, etc. [The words] *Parah Adumah* [are] to be de
leted, and the following marginal note added: This is an error, and so too in
Tosafot to *Megillah.*

Now the Maharshal's emendations were all incorporated into the text
of the third Lublin edition of the Talmud, printed during the years 1617
and 1634 (see note 44), and, as a result from that edition onward in all
subsequent printings of the Talmud the words *Parshat Parah Adumah*
are, indeed, absent. Understandably, then, neither the Peri Hadash
(1659–1698) nor the Gra (1720–1797), who had access to the *emended*
talmudic text, could find any mention of *Parshat Parah* in either of the
Tosafot. However, in earlier editions of the Talmud, prior to those emendations based on the Hokhmat Shlomoh's corrections, the words *Parshat
Parah Adumah* do appear, as already noted by that remarkable scholar,
Rabbi Hayyim Yosef David Azulai, the Hidah. In his *Petah Einayyim* to
Berakhot ibid. (14b) he writes as follows:

> "And chapters which have to be read *mi-de-Oraita*, such as *Parshat Zakhor*
> ..." So [is the reading in] our versions, and it is on the basis of the emenda-
> tion of the Maharshal in [his] Hokhmat Shlomoh. But the old (i.e., origi-
> nal) reading is: *Parshat Zakhor* and *Parshat Parah*, and it was cited by the Beit
> Yosef and the Bah in *Orah Hayyim* 685.

Furthermore, such a reading is found in *Tosafot Rabbi Judah* (b. Isaac)
Sir Leon to *Berakhot*, ibid. (ed. Rabbi Nissan Sachs [Jerusalem, 1949],
p. 161, especially no 37, pp. 161–162). Incidentally, this version was
noted by the Hidah in his *Mahazik Berakhah* to *Orah Hayim* 146:1, as it
was, too, in *Tosafot Rabbenu Perez* to *Berakhot*, ibid., (ed. M. Herschler
[Jerusalem, 1984], p. 24); and also in *Tosafot Rosh*, ibid. (*apud Berakhah
Meshuleshet* [Warsaw, 1863; reprint. Jerusalem, 1968]). And this same
view is found in the Rashba to *Berakhot*, ad loc.,[63] and in the Ritva to
Megillah ibid. (ed. I. M. Stern [Jerusalem, 1976], col. 120; see editor's

---

[63]However, see Rashba to *Megillah* 17b, ed. Dimitrovsky (New York, 1965),
p. 72. n. 20, where he mentions only *Parshat Zakhor*. And see Lieberman's note
in square brackets.

note 44. Likewise, see *Tosafot-Rosh* to *Sotah* 33b (ed. J. Halevy Lipshitz [Jerusalem, 1968], p. 66; and see editor's note 15).[64]

Indeed a careful examination of our *Tosafot* in *Berakhot* will reveal traces of the original reading. For the *Tosafot* reads as follows: " . . . aside from the *chapters* which one has to read *mi-de-Oraita*, such as *Parshat Parah*." But why write "*chapters*" in the plural, if there is only one example of such a case? Clearly, then, the original reading had at least two examples of chapters that one must read *mi-de-Oraita*. (This point was already noted by Rabbi Nissan Sachs, in his note to *Tosafot* Rabbi Judah Sir Leon [p. 162].) Thus it was not the Beit Yosef who chanced upon a faulty version of the *Tosafot*, as the Gaon of Vilna thought. But, quite to the contrary, it was the Gaon who studied in an emended version of the Talmud and its supercommentaries, one which did not preserve the original readings.[65]

Of course, there is a view that printed books are more reliable than manuscripts. We may refer to the words of Rabbi Moshe Hagiz, who writes that " . . . we do not even have [reliable] scribes in our days, and the majority of the scribes are spoiled and their quill has been corrupted."[66] Consequently, he says, he does not quote from manuscripts, only from printed books (with the exception of the Zohar).[67] However,

---

[64]See also *Tosafot Evreux* to *Sotah*, ed. Lifshitz (Jerusalem, 1969), p. 94, where we read: ‏כגון פרשת זכור ופרשת עגלה ערופה ופרשת פרה?!‏

[65]Furthermore, most of the testimonia of the *Rishonim* that we have cited above were not available to him. Thus Tosafot Rabbi Judah Sir Leon first appeared in *Berakhah Meshuleshet* (Warsaw, 1863), and so, too, Tosafot Rosh to *Berakhot*. The Ritva to *Megillah* appeared in Mikhtam le-David (Livorno, 1782), only some five years before the Gaon died, and then in Sdilkow, 1833, etc. So too the full version of Tosafot Rosh to *Sotah* only appeared for the first time in print in 1968, in Lifshitz's edition. Only the Rashba to *Berakhot* should have been available to him, as it was first published in Venice in 1523, and after being long out of print it was republished in Amsterdam in 1715, and then again in Fürth, 1751, etc. It is, therefore, not clear to me how the Gaon apparently overlooked this source. Perhaps he merely disagreed, and only stated that the Tosafot texts were corrupt.

[66]*Mishpat Hakchamim* (Wansbach, 1733), "the twenty-seventh level," sec. 548.

[67]See I. Z. Kahana, *Mehkarim be-Sifrut ha-Teshuvot* (Jerusalem, 1973), p. 303, n. 175.

he is speaking of manuscripts written during his own day, after the advent of printing. But ancient manuscripts have a somewhat different status; for they were assiduously checked and corrected before they were allowed into a private house.[68]

That is not to say that we should always give credence to readings in manuscripts. At times, even when a group of manuscripts all agree as to a reading, it may still be incorrect, as Lieberman very brilliantly demonstrated in his review of L. Finkelstein's edition of *Sifre* to Deuteronomy.[69] An intelligent reading of the text, based on a sound knowledge of rabbinic reasoning and a broad acquaintance with the literature, is always a prime prerequisite for critical textual analysis in this area.

If real learning aims at getting to the true meaning of the talmudic passage, it must concern itself with the accuracy of the text and the meaning of the words. This is self-evident, and probably would go uncontested by the *yeshivah* world. But these requirements necessitate the competence in philological and lexicographic disciplines, rarely to be be found in the standard *yeshivah bochur*. Perhaps the advantages to be gained from such long and hard-earned knowledge is so marginal that the investment in them is not considered worthwhile. But is the process of their mastery to be viewed as *bitul Torah*? If it is intended to deepen one's understanding of Torah, surely it comes within the category of "*amala shel Torah*," the toil and labor of Torah!

In addition, I would suggest that an understanding of the historical and real-life contexts within which the *Tanna'im* and *Amora'im* made their statements is necessary for a full understanding of the text. This might well be contested by our theoretical polemic "*yeshivah bochur*." He might argue that the legal opinions of the Sages are meta-historical; they are not dependent upon historical periods and changes, but upon some kind of absolute legal logic and unchanging ethical values. Indeed this

---

[68]See *Ketubot* 19b; *Tur Yoreh De'ah*, sec. 179.

[69]*Kiryat Sefer* 14:3 (1938): 329–330. However, one must be very careful before emending, especially against manuscript evidence. See Lieberman; comments in *Kiryat Sefer* 15 (1939/40): 56–57. Normally, of course, one would not correct a whole group of independent readings. See *Tiferet Yitzhak*, p. 68, with copious references.

is the position of those of its dogmatist school.[70] (Some have even gone so far as to liken law to mathematics, whose laws are immutable and correct in any context. But this is an extreme position held by few.) When different principles come into play it is not because the rules have changed but because the situation or context has changed.[71] We shall not enter into this complex arena of philosophical argumentation. Suffice it to say that even the positivist-dogmatist would agree that in order to understand why a certain "absolute" legal principle (*sevarah*) is used in a specific text, one has fully to understand the context or situation in which it was formulated or to which it refers.[72] Again this seems obvious. But let us approach it somewhat differently.

When reading a contemporary responsum on a technological issue, such as the use of a refrigerator on *Shabbat*, or a dishwasher on *Yom-Tov*, if the author of the responsum has, as is usually the case, not given any technical data, such as the company that produced the machine and its model number, the principles upon which it functions, the date of when the question was raised, and so forth, we may find ourselves needing to reconstruct it. For such information is often crucial to the subsequent relevance of the responsum. One has to know whether the light switches on and off as the door opens and closes, what degree of heat is reached, whether thermostatic controls are involved, and so forth.[73] Or again, many a responsum dealing with the issue of smoking (on *Yom Tov*, e.g.) from before a certain date is based on the supposition that smoking is healthful![74] Whereas since the dangers involved in smoking have been

---

[70]See I. Englard, *Mishpatim* 7:6 (1976): 34–65. His seminal article was followed by a number of fascinating responses: M. Elon, 8:1 (1977): 99–137; B. Shiber, *Mishpatim* 8:1 (1977): 91–98, etc.

[71]See Albeck's position, as described by Englard, ibid., p. 60. See Albeck, *Iyyunei Mishpat* 3, p. 710; and cf. Shiber.

[72]For a quaint example of this see *Shulhan Arukh, Orah Hayyim*, sec. 275:1, and the *Be'ur Halakhah* ad loc., s.v. לאור הנר, where there is a lengthy and detailed description of oil lamps of his day, and the difference between them and those of earlier times.

[73]In contrast to the classical type of responsum, see the writings of Rabbi Levi Yitzhak Halperin, of the Institute for Sciences and Technology, such as, for example, *Maaliyyot be-Shabbat* (Jerusalem, 1983), pp. 15ff.

[74]E.g., *Pnei Yehoshua* to *Shabbat* 34b, to *Tosafot* s.v. מתירין.

scientifically determined and widely publicized, the tone of the responsum has radically changed.[75] Thus, a knowledge of the historical context of the responsum may be esssential to determine its validity and relevance for present day *pesak*.

The situation is not essentially different when dealing with ancient halakhic sources. A fuller understanding of all aspects of the text is not only legitimate but essential. Hence, we should approach any given talmudic passage with all new-found disciplines available to us. At the same time we must be humble enough to realize that ultimately our conclusions will never move out of the realm of conjecture. Nonetheless, we may have understood the *sugyah* a little more, a little deeper, and a little better. We may have solved some additional problems that irked the earlier authorities. And we will have advanced in our *limud Torah*.[76]

---

[75]See Rabbi Dr. M. Halperin's essay in *Emek Halachah—Assia* 1986, pp. 306–310.

[76]For a very thoughtful study of the differences between "learning" and "studying" Talmud, see Menahem Kahana, "*Mehkar ha-Talmud ba-Universita ve-ha-Limud ha-Mesorati ba-Yeshivah*," in *Be-Hevlei Masoret u-Temurah* (Rehovot, 1990), pp. 113–142.

11

Progressive *Derash* and Retrospective *Peshat:* Nonhalakhic Considerations in Talmud Torah[1]

Yaakov Elman

The bulk of Orthodox Jewry has looked upon academic Jewish studies with suspicion from its inception. Even before *Wissenschaft des Judentums* entered the Academy in the last quarter of the nineteenth century, the movement was viewed as part and parcel of the Enlightenment and of the Reform movement, and thus as attempting to supersede traditional learning in scope, method, and result, as well as advocating major changes in educational methods and curriculum.[2] On the whole, the attempts of

---

[1]My thanks to Professors Shalom Carmy and Shnayer Leiman, and Rabbi Irwin Haut, for their comments on an earlier version of this paper. I cannot forbear thanking Mr. Zvi Erenyi and Mr. Zalman Alpert and the staff of Gottesman Library for numerous favors in connection with this paper and others, and Rabbi Martin Katz for the loan of several works and general and generous access to his personal library. Please note that I have not updated the literature cited; the paper remains essentially as revised in the summer of 1991.

[2]M. Steinschneider's comment regarding giving Judaism "a decent burial" comes to mind; see S. W. Baron's interesting discussion of Steinschneider's

Rabbi Azriel Hildesheimer and others to find a place for academic scholarship within Orthodoxy failed. The task has not become easier in the
last half century, though the possibilities of doing so have increased tremendously.

In the following discussion I intend to examine some of these pos-
siblities; I will survey some increasingly common methods currently
employed in academic scholarship on *Torah she-bev'al peh* with an eye
to defining their usefulness within the context of traditional learning.

The fact that there is value to be found in some current trends does
not guarantee that this will continue in the future. Academic studies
and traditional scholarship are on divergent paths, and that fact is not
likely to change. It is doubtful that full certainty can ever be attained,
and this is particularly true for the humanities; this ceaseless search for
radical methodological innovation has been anathema to most traditional
Jews in the recent past. Nevertheless, I intend to concentrate on what
seem to be "assured results" (read: "not improbable conclusions"),[3] or
methods that seem likely to lead to such results in the future—in particular, methods that seek to uncover the structural elements and aesthetic considerations that are inherent in the texts of *Torah she-be'al* in

---

attitude to the religious side of Jewishness, which ranged from indifference to
hostility, "Moritz Steinschneider's Contributions to Jewish Historiography," in
Alexander Marx Jubilee Volume on the Occasion of His Seventieth Birthday, ed.
S. Lieberman (New York: Jewish Theological Seminary, 1950), English Section,
pp. 83–148, esp. pp. 85–100, and see Gershon Scholem, "The Science of
Judaism—Then and Now," in *The Messianic Idea in Judaism and Other Essays on
Jewish Spirituality* (New York: Schocken, 1972), pp. 305–313.

It may be argued that certain Orthodox institutions and individuals looked
upon such studies with favor, chiefly those who regarded Rabbi Azriel Hild-
esheimer as their exemplar of *talmid hakham cum* Jewish scholar. However, we
cannot ignore the fact that, for reasons sociological, individual, and religious,
Rabbi Hildesheimer's experiment faced opposition, some of it fierce, in
Orthodoxy as a whole, and even in Germany; see Mordechai Breuer, *Juedische
Orthodoxie im Deutschen Reich, 1871–1918: Sozialgeschichte einer religiosen
Minderheit* (Leo Baeck Institute) (Frankurt am Main: Juedische Verlag bei
Athenaum, 1986), pp. 164–166, 170–186; and David Ellenson, *Rabbi Esriel
Hildesheimer and the Creation of a Modern Orthodoxy* (Tuscaloosa: University of
Alabama Press, 1990), pp. 78–114, and esp. 143–156.

[3]See Nahmanides' comments quoted below, p. 237.

the form in which they eventually took. The following lengthy survey will thus be rather narrowly focused; that narrow focus will, I hope, make it more rather than less useful.

I

Examination of the compatibility of academic work on *Torah she-be'al peh* with traditional methodologies requires first a definition of the salient characteristic(s) of those "traditional methodologies" to which academic methods will be contrasted.

This becomes all the more urgent given the vast number of method-ologies developed over the centuries since the reduction of *Torah she-be'al peh* to written form, including some that, vigorous for centuries and employed by some of the great names of Jewish learning, now lie neglected and more than half forgotten. What common thread joins all of them?

Broadly speaking, if one statement may be said to exemplify all of traditional Jewish study it is *ki lo davar rek hu mikkem—im rek hu —mikem:* "for it is not an empty thing for you, [it is your very life, and if it appears devoid of meaning]—it is you [who have not worked out its significance]."[4] The methodological consequences of this prin-ciple of "omnisignificance" is the Bavli's statement that *kol heikha de-ika le-midrash darshinan:* "wherever we can interpret midrashically we do."[5]

The primary focus of this talmudic principle is clearly *Humash*. But its area of application is much broader, for the techniques that *Hazal* employ in their interpretation of *Humash*, and by extension, *Nakh*, came to be used, *mutatis mutandis*, for *any* hallowed text—tannaitic texts and amoraic texts in turn, *Rishonim* and *Aharonim*. In particular, the doc-

---

[4]*Yerushalmi Ketubot* 8:11 (32c), based on Deuteronomy 32:47.

[5]*Bekhorot* 6b; see *Pesahim* 24a–b; I have dealt with this principle more extensively in "'It Is No Empty Thing? Nahmanides and the Search for Omni-significance," *Torah Umadda Journal* 4 (1993), pp. 1–82.

This coinage has gained some currency through its use by James Kugel in his *The Idea of Biblical Poetry: Parallelism and Its History* (New Haven and London: Yale University Press, 1981), pp. 103–104.

trine that Torah texts of immediately divine origin are formulated with a wondrous exactitude and tolerate no superfluities became a template for the key that fits all properly constructed locks, all hallowed texts of *Torah she-be'al peh.*

Moreover, not all results are equally desirable: the significance which is sought excludes the merely aesthetic as well as the particularistic. As to the latter, that means that the text's significance must be, whenever at all possible, of more than local importance, that is, for a limited time or place, or of limited applicability.[6] As to the former, literary or aesthetic values are not allowed to obtrude into canonical texts—almost by definition. Clearly, a canonical text is—almost by definition—too important for aesthetics to play an important role in its formulation.

The thrust of learning is always to demonstrate the harmony of a particular text within as wide a halakhic context as possible, and to build a halakhic system out of the disparate—and sometimes inconsistent—elements of its sources. In this context, significance almost always involves a substantive halakhic or quasi-halakhic point, or in the case of aggadic texts, a moral or theological point. To achieve that purpose, all hallowed texts serve as renewable resources to be exploited in every way possible. Thus, the Mishnah can be interpreted in the same way as a biblical verse.

For example, *Mishnah Shabbat* 11:4 is interpreted *both* in Bavli and Yerushalmi—in Bavli, *Shabbat* 100b, and Yerushalmi, *Shabbat* 11:4 (13a)—as a *yittur lashon,* no different than a Pentateuchal superfluity. The Mishnah reads:

> If one throws [an object] four cubits in the sea, he is not liable. *If there is a pool of water and a public road traverses it, and one throws [an object] four cubits therein, he is liable.* And what depth constitutes a pool? Less than four handbreadths. *If there is a pool of water and a public road traverses it, and one throws [an object] four cubits therein, he is liable.*

---

[6]Again, there are always exceptions; Tosafot, in continuing the program of the Bavli, often creates distinctions in applicability in order to reconcile contradictory texts. This method, which reaches back to the earliest texts of *Torah she-be'al peh* and which was originally used to reconcile contradictory biblical verses, came naturally to be applied to texts of *Torah she-be'al peh.*

On this the *Gemara* records the following discussion:

> One of the Rabbis said to Rava: The duplication of "traversing" is fine—it informs us that "traversing with difficulty" is [still] considered "traversing"[7] while "use with difficulty" is not considered "use." But why the duplication of "pool?"

The *sugyah* concludes with three suggestions as to the cases covered by this duplication. One is that the Mishnah wishes to distinguish between summer and winter; the second, attributed to Abaye, distinguishes between pools that are less than four cubits across, where people will wade through it, and those that are four cubits across, when they prefer to go around it; finally, Rav Ashi modifies Abaye's suggestion, proposing that people are wont to step across pools less than four cubits rather than wade through them.[8] Naturally, each distinction must be provided with a reason for the necessity to state both possibilities, a *tzerikhuta*.

The application of scriptural exegetic techniques to the Mishnah is panrabbinic; it is found in both Bavli[9] and Yerushalmi. In this respect at least, the Yerushalmi is no more *peshat*-oriented than the Bavli.[10]

---

[7]The Yerushalmi (*Shabbat* 11:4 [13a]) attributes this explanation to the fifth-generation Amora Rabbi Hananiah, in the name of Rabbi Pinhas, a contemporary of Rava and Abaye.

[8]Note that there are three proposals for the *tzerikhuta*; this will assume greater importance in light of our discussion in the section of this chapter that deals with literary considerations.

[9]Modern scholarship is gradually coming to understand the change in the status of the Mishnah that gave rise to such modes of interpretation; see the summary sections of chapters 2–8 of Y. N. Epstein, *Mavo le-Nusah ha-Mishnah* (Jerusalem: Magnes, 1963–1964); and, most recently, Avinoam Cohen, "Bikoret Hilkhatit leᶜumat Bikoret Sifrutit be-Sugyot ha-Talmud (Perek be-Hithavvut ha-Shikhvatit shel ha-Bavli)," *Asufot* 3 (1989/90): 331–339, and the literature cited in nn. 1, 14, and 30; and see David Hanschke's important observations, "Abaye ve-Rava—Shtei Gishot le-Mishnat ha-Tannaim," *Tarbiz* 49 (5740): 187–193, where he attributes this approach to Rava.

[10]*Contra* the conventional academic view. See most recently David C. Kraemer, *The Mind of the Talmud: An Intellectual History* (New York: Oxford University Press, 1990), pp. 16–19, based in part on Zechariah Frankel, *Mevo ha-Yerushalmi* (Breslau: Schletter 1870; reprint, Jerusalem, 1967), pp. 152–153.

Because the Mishnah of the Bavli and Yerushalmi seem to have been transmitted independently, they serve as independent witnesses to the text, and so the redundancy cannot be attributed to scribal error (dittography).[11] It also has no obvious structural, literary explanation.[12]

There are of course limits to Amoraic and post-Amoraic *derash* of the Mishnah. As in Scripture, *kol* is considered a *ribbuy* (e.g., *ha-kol la-atoyei mai*);[13] reinterpretation is often employed (e.g., *peshita* implies that the plain sense of the Mishnah or *baraita* cannot be its intended meaning since that is too simple; it thus constitutes an introduction to a *derash*). But not all the *middot* appear; there is no mishnaic analogue to the scriptural *gezerah shavah*, for example. The essential point is that the text is taken to encompass more than a common-sense exegesis would allow.

This concern with accounting for every aspect of the text in terms of halakhically substantive interpretations was applied to Talmud as well, despite the demurrer of the Rid cited below. Thus one of the standard approaches to the Bavli in the *pilpul* of the late *Rishonim* and their suc-

---

[11]The Mishnah text of the Bavli and Yerushalmi may be considered independently transmitted versions of the original, of equal validity in many of the cases in which they differ. See Saul Lieberman, *Tosefet Rishonim* vol. IV (Jerusalem: Bamberger and Wahrmann, 1939), introduction; and David Rosenthal, *Mishnah Avodah Zarah: Mahadurah Bikortit u-Mavo* (Jerusalem: Hebrew University, 1980), introduction, pp. 3–21.

[12]Modern scholarship generally finds here a conflation of two sources, without wondering overmuch why the formulation in both is identical. See Hanokh Albeck, *Shishah Sidrei Mishnah*, vol. II (Tel Aviv: Devir, 1952), "Hashlamot," p. 415; and Avraham Goldberg, *Perush la-Mishnah: Masekhet Shabbat* (New York: Jewish Theological Seminary of America, 1976), pp. 224–225.

Note also that Hazal themselves are quite capable of providing source-critical explanations of such cruces (e.g., *Mishnah Berakhot* 7:3, see bBer 50a, though admittedly there the sources seem contradictory; however, see GRA ad loc.). Apparently in this case the sources were simply not available. The matter requires more investigation.

Finally, here neither Tosafot Yom Tov nor the GRA, who are exemplars of the recognition that the Mishnah may be interpreted in terms of *peshat* and *derash*, nor Tiferet Yisrael, who praises the *peshat* Mishnah-exegesis of Rabbi Menashe of Ilya (see section II of this discussion), remarks on this exegesis.

[13]See Y. I. Ephrati, *Tekufat ha-Sabboraim ve-Sifrutah be-Vavel uve-Eretz Yisrael* (Petah Tikva: Agudat Benei Asher, 1973), pp. 159–273.

cessors, developed in the *yeshivot* of the Rhineland of the fifteenth century, is the pair of *qushyot* called *farbrengers* and *oisbrengers*.[14] These are
applied when a two-part *baraita* is cited in a *sugyah* but only one part is
directly relevant to the issue at hand; it is standard practice for the Bavli
to quote the whole *baraita*.[15] If it is the *resha* that is superfluous, the
question is called a *farbrenger*, if the *sefa*, it is an *oisbrenger*.[16] The standard solution to these *qushyot* is to prove that both parts of the *baraita*
are necessary, for a difficulty could be raised if only the one were quoted;
the seemingly superfluous part thus comes to repair the breach before it
can be made.

Note that this exegetical principle was first formulated in the fifteenth
century; presumably these cases were not considered problematic before
then, and this particular phenomenon was considered as merely part of
the Bavli's style of citation. It was widely used for centuries, and is recommended by the Shelah, employed (without the terminology) by the
Maharam Schiff,[17] and appears in *Yad Malakhi*[18] and *Halikhot Olam*[19] and
elsewhere, *despite the fact that a simple redactional principle can account for
all these cases*. That is, it is standard practice for the Bavli to quote the
complete *baraita* in order to place the *baraita* "in the record," so to speak,
and this was recognized by many *Aharonim*; indeed, by some of the same
Aharonim who recommended the use of these *qushyot*.[20]

---

[14]See *Shenei Luhot ha-Brit, Masekhet Shevuot*, p. 30; Mordecai Breuer, "ʿAliyat
ha-Pilpul veha-Hillukim bi-yshivot Ashkenaz," in *Sefer Zikkaron le-Moreinu ha-
Rav Yehiel Yaakov Weinberg* (Jerusalem, 1969–1970), pp. 241–55; and H. Z.
Dimitrovsky, "ʿAl Derekh ha-Pilpul," in *Salo Baron Jubilee Volume* (New York:
Columbia University Press, 1975), pp. 111–191 [Hebrew section].

[15]To this, as to nearly every statement that can be made of the Bavli, there
are of course exceptions; on occasion even the parts of the *baraita* relevant to
the discussion are never quoted; see for example *Pesachim* 48a.

[16]See Dimitrovsky, "ʿAl Derekh," pp. 144–149; for the distinction just presented, see pp. 148–149, and see *Shelah, Torah she-be'al peh, Kelal Baraitot*, who
recommends it as a proper *kushya* (*inyan amiti*) so long as the contradiction that
is said to eventuate is not *be-derekh ha-pilpul ha-rahok*.

[17]See "Al Derekh," p. 145, n. 185. Maharam Schiff *ad Gittin* 52a, s.v. *ha-
reshut be-yado*, where it is clear the *baraita* concerned is cited in full (including
interpolated *laatuyeis!*) in order to present a collection of "*Hilkhot Apotrofin*."

[18]Alef, n. 87; see "Al Derekh," p. 144, n. 178.

[19]See "Al Derekh," p. 146, n. 192.

[20]"Al Derekh," p. 145.

The purpose of this technique and similar ones is thus to give a halakhic meaning to every formal textual characteristic. In time, this desire led to the replacement of the aesthetics of form with various conceptual symmetries. When this could not be done, the original structures were often ignored and fell into oblivion. Halakhic, moral, or theological edification became the criterion by which the success of a *hiddush* was measured; merely aesthetic considerations were irrelevant.

By the same token, scholastic edification required that aesthetic embellishments be integrated as vital pointers to *conceptual*—in this context, halakhic, moral, or theological—elements of the proposed interpretation.

This distinction may be found in other contexts as well; compare the attitude toward the use of parables by Maimonides and Maharal.

> Know that the prophetic parables are of two kinds. In some of these parables each word has a meaning, while in others the parable as a whole indicates the whole of the intended meaning. In such a parable very many words are to be found, not every one of which adds something to the intended meaning. They serve rather to embellish the parable and to render it more coherent or to conceal further the intended meaning; hence the speech proceeds in such a way as to accord with everything required by the parable's external meaning. Understand this well.[21]

Maimonides' view, that details may merely serve as embellishment, did not prevail, either in regard to parables or to any other hallowed text. Quite apart from the controversies surrounding the *Guide*, it would seem that this view ran counter to the deeper currents of Jewish textual interpretation, which demanded holistic textual exegesis which gives meaning to every element and simply abhors the idea that "not every [word] adds something to the intended meaning."

This is a far cry from what became the mainstream interpretation of *Aggadah*. Compare Jacob Elbaum's characterization of the Maharal's exegesis: "In fine, the strange episodes, the far-fetched statements, *the details and stylistic usage which appear as no more than ornamentation are all intended to convey deeper meanings. Nothing, not even the seemingly most trivial detail, is mentioned in vain.*"[22]

---

[21]Moses Maimonides, *The Guide of the Perplexed*, trans. Shlomo Pines (Chicago: University of Chicago, 1963), introduction to pt. 1, p. 12.

[22]See Jacob Elbaum, "Rabbi Judah Loew of Prague and his Attitude to the

The recognition that aesthetic or rhetorical considerations play a role in the construction of *sugyot* has been almost totally rejected. Rather, the principle of omnisignificance with its concomittant emphasis on halakhic and theological factors continued to gain in importance, and was applied as widely as possible.[23]

Naturally, the halakhic significance of texts of *Torah she-be'al peh* tends to make their study self-referentional. One consequence of this was that it could become increasingly abstract and irrelevant to *halakhah le-maaseh* and matters that relate to the external world; the model it works with is seldom subjected to independent verification. Because of its emphasis on the universal, it is impatient with the limitations of geographical and historical context, and blind to cultural context. All of Torah learning exists *sub specie aeternitatus*. All is subordinated to the production of *hiddushim* in substantive matters of *halakhah* or *musar*,[24] or to show that an inconnicinity in wording hints at such a *hiddush*, known from another source.

The proof of the pudding is in the eating, however, and much of our *pilpul* has ever been considered inapplicable to halakhic determination. Thus, the Shelah felt compelled to differentiate between *pilpula de-kushta*, "pilpul of truth," and *pilpula de-havla*, "pilpul of futility." The *Rishonim* were very well aware of the need to distinguish between a *shinuya dehiqa*, a forced solution, and the proper sort; the former carried little weight in halakhic determinations.[25] Halakhic decision making could not be allowed to divorce itself from textual, and hence this-worldly, consider-

---

Aggadah," in *Studies in Aggadah and Folk-Literature*, ed. Joseph Heinemann and Dov Noy (Jerusalem: The Magnes Press, 1971), pp. 28–47; the quote is from p. 39. The italics are mine.

[23]This analysis attempts to trace the direction of Jewish exegesis of sacred texts in broad strokes; it cannot account for every exegetical method ever developed. In some cases, as in the various forms of Brisker analysis, the mode of analysis applied the principle of omnisignificance to nontalmudic texts (e.g., *Mishneh Torah*) and so to some extent talmudic interpretation suffered by comparison.

[24]See Rashi on *Megillah* 14a, s.v. *nevuah she-hutzrekhah*, where he defines *hutzrekhah le-dorot* as a concern with these matters.

[25]See Hanokh Albeck's collection of sources on this matter in *Mavo la-Talmudim*, pp. 545–556.

ations. And so along with the increasingly abstract, purely theoretical *lomdut* or *pilpul* there always existed a practically oriented, and thus (to some extent) more *peshat*-oriented hermeneutic. Again, however, the need of the halakhic system to take account of changing conditions did not permit this latter to develop devoid of *derash*; the cutting edge of *halakhah* required the creation of new interpretations of old texts.[26]

In this unreconstructed world, where, as information theory teaches us, entropy and disorder increase in the realm of knowledge and its transmission no less than in the material world, the principle of omnisignificance serves as a bulwark against disorder; it is the Torah's analogue of the Law of Conservation of Matter and Energy. Omnisignificance smoothes the jagged edges of contradiction and redundancy, but those edges remain to goad us on to new and more inclusive systematization, to allow scope for the intellectually edifying to overcome the world's irrationalities, which at base mirror this world's basic hostility to truth— the intellectual equivalent of Heisenberg's Uncertainty Principle, so to speak. In this sense, the Torah too is in exile.[27] Omnisignificance is a foretaste of the world of *tikkun*.

Omnisignificance is the concrete embodiment of the doctrine of *Torah min ha-shammayim*; all recognized Torah compositions are treated as divinely inspired, with some of the same canons of interpretation applied

---

[26]Study of the extent to which the reciprocal relationship between these two streams in promoting this endeavor is a desideratum; my impression is that their relationship was never stable.

[27]Rabbi Zadok ha-Kohen of Lublin puts it this way:

[God alone] has this understanding, that contrary propositions may be true; [in this case,] the Torah [which prescribes sacrifice for atonement, see *Makkot* 2:6] is true while [the power of repentance], which is its contrary, is also true. This matter is not yet to be understood by the human intellect, and [thus] one must forgo his own reasoning as against a Sinaitic halakhah in practical matters, for in practice two contraries cannot be true, as is explained at the end of *Tikkunei Zohar Hadash* [p. 121a] regarding [God's fore-]knowledge and [man's] free will—knowledge is intellectual, [that is, theoretical,] while free will involves action. [The same point is made] at the end of the Ari's *Arbaᶜ Me'ot Shekel*, that is, that in thought [it is possible] for two contraries to be true, but not in practice. [*Dover Tzedeq*, p. 149b]

What is contradictory in this world will in the end be thoroughly resolved, or rather, understood as not contradictory at all.

to them as to Holy Writ itself. All of them fall under the stricture of *lo davar rek*.[28] Nevertheless, the abstract and ahistorical nature of such learning is not without its problems.

For one thing, there is the problem of language, which is ultimately limited on the human plane, no matter how ingenious and far-reaching our means of *derash* may be. In the case of *Torah she-be'al peh*, the amount of play[29] via inconsistency left in the system of the Bavli, say, is not sufficient to allow all points of view to be equally well-founded; not all *hiddushim* will be logically compelling. Thus, Nahmanides long ago noted that

> every student of our Talmud knows that there are no absolute proofs in the disputes of its commentators, nor unanswerable difficulties (*qushyot halutot*) on the whole, for in this science, unlike the calculations of areas or the data of astronomy, there are no clear demonstrations. Rather, we put all our efforts in every disputed case to cast doubt (*leharhiq*) on one of the opinions with considerations that tend [in the opposite direction] (*sevarot makhri'ot*), and to show that textual difficulties arise from it (*ve-nidhoq ᶜaleha ha-shemuᶜot*) and place the advantage with its opponent from the plain meaning of the [relevant] *halakhot* and proper meaning of the *sugyot* [involved], together with the agreement of an understanding intellect (*sekhel ha-navon*).[30] This is the purpose of our efforts and the intent of every God-fearing scholar in the science of Gemara.[31]

Why should this be so? I suggest that this is because most *hiddushim* worth pursuing are not inevitably and absolutely *reasonably* implicit in the texts that are cited in support of them. From the time of the *Geonim* on we have striven to go beyond the text, and the greater the departure of our own context from that of the text we employ, the less certainty we have regarding the result. Fairly soon we must deal with relative weights of competing arguments, and the only way to deal with such

---

[28]Needless to say, the comments of Rashi and the codification of the Rambam have been and continue to be subjected to just this kind of analysis. Indeed, every work that is an accepted object of study may be included in this category; see section II of this discussion.

[29]Note the Yerushalmi: if the Torah had been given absolutely determined (*hatukhah*), no creature could live (*lo hayatah le-regel ᶜamidah*) (*Sanhedrin* 4:2 [22a]).

[30]Reading *navon* rather than *nakhon*.

[31]From the Introduction of Nahmanides' *Sefer Milhamot*.

problems of interpretation, in the absence of a universally recognized authority, is consensus. But the distance between consensus and certainty is often sizable. To some extent, attention to *peshat* allows us to measure that distance and orient ourselves.

For the *Rishonim*, for example, the weight of sources, plainly understood, was of decisive importance in halakhic decision making. It was vital to distinguish between *shittot* that followed the plain meaning of relevant sources fairly closely and those that had to resort to *shinuya dehiqa* to reconcile those sources.[32]

Peshat thus remained an important consideration in *pesak halakhah*. But its importance lies primarily in the realm of deciding between alternate views; the formation of those views is not likely to owe much to *peshat*.

This is in sharp contrast to the role that *peshat* in the exegesis of *Torah she-bi-Khtav* played in such determinations. It may be appropriate at this point to cite the Rashbam's rationale for his interest in *peshat* despite the lack of interest Hazal showed for this particular facet of exegesis.

> Let those who love right judgement understand well that which our Rabbis taught us that "no verse departs from its plain meaning."[33] Even though the essentials of Torah come to teach us and let us know the haggadot, the halakhot, and the laws by means of hints of *peshat*, [that is,] linguistic superfluities and the Thirty-two Rules of R. Eliezer son of R. Yose the Galilean, and by the Thirteen Rules of R. Ishmael, the earlier authorities, because of their piety occupied themselves with the *derashot* which are the essence (*ʿiqqar*), and due to this were not accustomed to the profundities of the plain meaning of Scripture. [Furthermore,] this [occured] because the Sages said: "Don't allow your children to [spend] much [time][34] with *higayon*."[35] They also said: "He who occupies himself with Bible is of intermediate merit; he who occupies himself with Talmud—there is no greater merit."[36] Because of

---

[32]See n. 25 above.

[33]*Shabbat* 63a.

[34]Current editions of *Berakhot* read: "Keep your children from . . .".

[35]*Berakhot* 28b; on this see Mordecai Breuer's illuminating article, "Mineʿu Beneikhem min ha-Higayon," in *Mikhtam le-David: Sefer Zikaron ha-Rav David Ochs z"l*, ed. Y. D. Gilat and E. Stern (Ramat Gan: Bar-Ilan University, 1978), pp. 242–261; Rashbam, in accordance with the predominant view among Ashkenazi *Rishonim*, interprets this word as referring to the study of Bible, while the Sephardim take it as the study of philosophy.

[all] this they were not so accustomed [to deal] with the plain meaning of verses, as it states in Tractate Shabbat: "I was eighteen years old and had learned all the Talmud and I did not know that 'a verse does not depart from its plain meaning.'"[37]

. Rashbam felt that the importance of *peshat* had to be established as a valuable aspect of biblical exegesis. That battle was unnecessary in regard to *Torah she-be'al peh*, since lip service had been and continued to be paid to the primary importance of *peshat*. Nevertheless, *peshat* was rather narrowly defined, and the study of the Bavli—which in geonic times became *Torah she-be'al peh par excellence*—hardly concerned itself with aspects of the text other than the halakhic or moralistic. Very early in his learning career the student learned that these are irrelevant and of no interest to those to whom one looks for approval.[38]

Thus, while the awareness that pilpulist methods would not uncover the plain meaning of the talmudic text was common, the primary concern with halakhic and moral considerations in the study of the Bavli led to the almost complete neglect of other aspects of the text.

One distinction should be made in this connection, however. Purely halakhic literature—responsa and codes—by its nature is centered on *halakhah*, and other aspects of authoritative texts are truly irrelevant to its concerns. Here *derash* in its widest sense is the cutting edge of *halakhah*

---

[36]*Bava Metzia* 33a. Rashbam has condensed the *baraita*.

[37]Rashbam to Genesis 37:2, ed. Rosen, p. 49. The Talmudic quote is from *Shabbat* 63a.

[38]Before leaving the Rashbam's analysis I would venture one more observation. It seems to me that the Rashbam's—and, needless to say, that of Rashi's (see Mizrahi on Exodus 22:8)—matter-of-fact acknowledgment that much of *halakhah* is not based on *peshat* is intellectually and spiritually healthier than the attempt of some *Aharonim* (Malbim and Rabbi Yaakov Mecklenberg come to mind) to wrest *halakhah* from the toils of *derash* and treat every halakhic pronouncement as the product of a profound understanding of *peshat*, a *tour de force* that often does little to enhance our understanding of either *Torah shebi-Khtav* or *Torah she-bev'al peh*.

This point has been made by Yehudah Copperman, "Ha-Ra'uy ve-ha-Ratzuy ve-ha-Mehayyev bi-Peshuto shel Mikra," in his *Li-Peshuto shel Mikra: Kovetz Ma'amarim* (Jerusalem: Haskel, 5734), pp. 68–75, and his "Horaat ha-Torah be-Misgeret Bet ha-Sefer ha-'Al Yesodi, Helek II," in the same volume, pp. 53–67, esp. pp. 62–67.

as it faces new problems and conditions, and fashions new analogies to meet them. *Perush* and *tosafot*, which were originally equivalent and which originally emphasized the local *peshat*, as did Rashi in his commentary, gave way to the Tosafists' extended meta-*peshat*—the local *sugyah* as seen against the backdrop of all of Shas.[39] But even in the realm of *peshat*, *perush* gave way to *hiddush*, and *hiddush* requires at least a modicum of *derash*, a turning away from the concerns of the text at hand, and placing it into a context to some extent foreign to it. As we shall see, these contexts seldom allowed certain aspects of the text to emerge.

II

The realization that the Mishnah may be interpreted as both *peshat* and *derash* is not new; it goes back to the *Tosafot Yom Tov*[40] and the GRA,[41]

---

[39]See E. E. Urbach, *Baalei ha-Tosafot* (Jerusalem: Mosad Bialik, 1980), p. 21. Rabbi Kalman Kahana's distinction, adopted from Dr. Philip Bieberfeld, between *mashmaut*, the local *peshat*, *peshat* in terms of the verse or *parashah*, as opposed to *peshat*, or meta-*peshat* in our terms, the *peshat* in terms of the entire Torah, comes to mind. See K. Kahana, *Heker ve–Iyyun: Kovetz Ma'amarim* (Tel Aviv, 5720), pp. 91–94.

[40]The *locus classicus* is *Mishnah Nazir* 5:5, where the analogy to Biblical interpretation is explicit.

[41]See Binyamin Rivlin, *Gevi'i Gevi'a Kesef* (Warsaw, 5618), p. 23b. On the whole issue and its relationship to the ongoing development of Jewish study, see the interesting exchange in *Shematin*: Y. A., "Parshanut she-lo ka-Hazal," *Shematin* 8:31 (5731): 63–65; A. Neuman, "Parshanut she-lo ka-Halakhah," *Shematin*, n. 32, pp. 17–19; A. Kurman, "Parshanut she-lo ka-Halakhah ve-she-lo ka-Hazal," *Shematin* 9:32 (5732): 8–17, n. 33, pp. 36–41. See also Kalman Kahana, "*Darkei Perush ba-Mishnah*," *Heker ve-Iyyun*, pp. 132–152. A fairly large literature has grown up around the issue; see most recently Yaakov S. Spiegel, "Derekh Ketzarah bi-Lshon Tanna'im ve-al Peshat u-Derash ba-Mishnah," *Asufot: Sefer ha-Shanah le-Mada'ei ha-Yahadut*, vol. 4 (5750), pp. 9–19, and his bibliographical notes on pp. 20–21, nn. 36–42; my thanks to Professors S. Carmy and D. W. Halivni for drawing my attention to this article. My approach and that of Spiegel are somewhat different but convergent; see my "Rabbi Zadok HaKohen on the History of Halakhah," *Tradition* 21 (1985): 1–26, esp. p. 16. See too my "Rabbi Moses Samuel Glasner: The Oral Torah," *Tradition* 25 (1991): 63–68, esp. p. 68, and see Spiegel's remarks, "Derekh Ketzarah," p. 24.

and may even be traced back to the Rid,[42] and even to the Yeru-shalmi.[43]

Once this realization took hold, especially in the GRA's time and af-ter, the question became: Since the Bavli does not always provide us with *peshat* in the Mishnah, are we permitted to pursue the plain meaning of mishnaic texts and ignore the Talmud's exegesis? Essentially, the answer *Klal Yisrael*[44] gave was a qualified yes, with the proviso that the one pro-posing the nontraditional interpretation be of recognized stature. The GRA might do so, Rabbi Manasseh of Ilya might not.[45] But once the gate was opened, others pushed through.[46]

The wider implications of this undoubted fact do not seem to have been clearly enunciated until the late nineteenth century, primarily,

---

[42]See A. Y. Wertheimer and A. Lis, eds., *Piskei Ha-Rid le-Rabbenu Yeshayah di-Trani le-Massekhtot Berakhot ve-Shabbat* (Jerusalem, 1964), p. 229; Rid notes that "the Mishnah is to the Amoraim as the Torah is to the Tanna'im." How-ever, Rid there distinguishes between the Amoraim and the Tannaim in this regard. As we shall see, this distinction was obliterated in the course of time, and any accepted work was given the same status as Torah in this regard.

[43]See *Yerushalmi Pe'ah* 2:6 (17a), ed. Vilna 2:4, 13a: *havivin hen ha-devarim ha-nidrashim min ha-peh min ha-devarim ha-nidrashim min ha-ketav.*

[44]On the role of *Klal Yisrael* in this process, see immediately below.

[45]The *maskilim* later in the century found fairly ample precedent for their en-deavors; see S. Y. L. Rappoport, *Erekh Milin* (Warsaw, 5674), pp. xii–xiii, and the literature cited in n. 41. On Rabbi Menashe of Ilya see Isaac E. Barzilay, "The Life of Menashe of Ilya (1767–1831), *PAAJR* 50 (1983): 1–37, and especially his "Manasseh of Ilya (1767–1831) as Talmudist," *JQR* 74 (1984): 345–378. One in-teresting and instructive instance involves his interpretation of *Mishnah Shabbat* 20:4, which drew the fire of the *Sho'el u-Meishiv*, but turns out to have been that of Rabbenu Hananel and other *Rishonim*, then still in manuscript, unknown to Rabbi Joseph Saul Nathausen; see *Heker ve-Iyyun*, pp. 139–143.

My thanks to Professor Barzilay for giving me the benefit of his work on Rabbi Menashe.

[46]See my discussion regarding "the opening of gates" in this discussion. In truth, the proposition is hardly radical in the context of Jewish learning and ample precedent exists for new interpretations of old texts; on the matter of proposing "un-talmudic" interpretations of the Mishnah, see the literature cited in Irwin H. Haut, *The Talmud as Law or Literature: An Analysis of David W. Halivni's Medorot Umasorot* (New York: Bet Sha'ar Press, 1982), p. 49, nn. 14 and 15. His sources include Rabbi Hayyim Ibn Attar, Rabbi Naftali Berlin, Rabbi Yehezkel Landau, Rabbi Yaakov Emden, the Maharal, and the Reshash.

though not exclusively,[47] in hasidic works.[48] However, hasidic thought addressed the question from a different point of view, one whose relevance to the problem of *peshat* and *derash* is not immediately apparent. I must thus venture a short digression.

Given the belief in the continuing presence of Divine inspiration (*ruah ha-kodesh*) over the centuries,[49] a mainstay of hasidic thought for which ample precedent can be found in the works of the *Rishonim* and *Aharonim*, two questions arise. How are we to distinguish works written under its influence, on the one hand, and what practical difference does the presence of that inspiration have, on the other? I hasten to add that this use

---

[47]Not only among *hasidim*; this view is attributed to Rabbi Hayyim of Volozhin in a letter from Rabbi Shelomo Hakohen of Vilna to Rabbi Hayyim Berlin and published in *Hameir* 2 (5724); see D. Eliach, *Kol ha-Katuv la-Hayyim* (Jerusalem, 5748), p. 160, n. 9, and cited by Y. S. Spiegel, "Derekh Ketzarah," p. 26.

[48]As indicated above, however, the beginnings of this realization, as applied to specific texts, can be traced back much further. However, this insight does not seem to have been generalized and used to justify the regnant methodologies of Torah study until the nineteenth century, presumably in the wake of the challenge of Reform and biblical criticism, just as the Karaite challenge sparked an interest in *peshat* in Geonic and post-Geonic times.

From all the foregoing, however, it is clear that the enunciation of this point of view in the late nineteenth century represents the distillation of much earlier thought; a study of the process remains a desideratum.

[49]Note the citation of Psalm 51:13 in the *Selihot* services; the implication of our request not to be deprived of *ruah ha-kodesh* is that it is still available to us. See too Maimonides' *Guide of the Perplexed*, II:45, where the lowest grade of *Ruach ha-Kodesh*, *siyata di-Shemmaya*, would still seem available to us. This is quite apart from the question, which A. J. Heschel answered in the affirmative, as to whether Maimonides (and other *Rishonim*) believed that prophecy was still possible; see A. J. Heschel, "*Ha-he'emin ha-Rambam she-Zakhah li-Nevu'ah?*" in *Sefer ha-Yovel li-Kvod Levi Ginzberg*, A. Marx, et al., eds., (New York: American Academy for Jewish Research, 5706), pp. 159–188 [Hebrew section] and "Al Ruah ha-Kodesh bi-Ymei ha-Benayim (ad Zemano shel ha-Rambam)," in *Sefer ha-Yovel li-Kvod Alexander Marx li-Mlot lo Shiv'im Shanah*, ed. Saul Lieberman (New York: Jewish Theological Seminary, 1950), pp. 175–208. See also Reuven Margaliyot's introduction to his edition of *She'elot u-Teshuvot min ha-Shammayim* (Jerusalem: Mosad Harav Kook, 5717). Most recently, see Bezalel Naor, *Lights of Prophecy* (New York: Union of Orthodox Jewish Congregations, 1990), especially pp. 3–11 [English section].

of *ruach ha-kodesh* does not carry the theological freight of scriptural or prophetic inspiration. In our context *ruach ha-kodesh* refers to the exegetical strategies permitted in interpreting these texts; it does not extend the infallability of scriptural divine or prophetic inspiration to posttalmudic works.

Rabbi Zadok Hakohen of Lublin answers the first question, on how to distinguish works written under the influence of *ruach ha-kodesh* from more mundane texts as follows:

> What is clear to the intellect and is known as stemming from God,[50] may He be blessed, is as *Torah she-bi-khtav*, and all that is written in a book can be viewed (*hu me'ein*) as Torah *she-bi-khtav*, . . . even what is written in *Shulhan Arukh* and in the Posekim at this time. . . . [51]

What does Rabbi Zadok mean by "known as stemming from God"? He explains this in a comment one of his earlier works:

> In writing from God [what] He gave him to understand[52]—in the composition of *Shulhan Arukh* and its glosses[53] which were accepted in all of Israel[54] as a book of decisions in our generations in all areas of Torah law and a

---

[50]See *Resisei Laylah*, *maamar* 56, 165b, where Rabbi Zadok himself writes that as long as *Torah she-bi-Khtav* was not clearly perceived by the soul in total revelation (*ki lo nitatzemah adayin ba-nefesh be-gilluy gamur*) so that the root of the soul be totally [enlightened] by the light of *Torah she-be'al peh* which permeates the body. For until the Talmud was sealed there was no *Torah she-be'al peh* in it perfection (*shelemutah*) in its total revelation in this world. Another rendering of *shelemutah* is possible, though less likely: "in its totality." If this is what Rabbi Zadok intended, the last sentence would add another condition to the *heter* of reducing Oral Torah to writing: it must be *complete* in extent as well as being totally revealed in depth of understanding. He might then be referring to the Maharal's distinction between Oral and Written Torah in *Tiferet Yisrael*, ch. 68 (London ed.), p. 211.

[51]*Peri Zaddik* V, p. 16b.

[52]Based on 1 Chronicles 28:19. The use of this verse in this context itself has a history. Rabbi Zadok apparently drew it from *Urim ve-Tumim* on *Kitzur Tekafo Kohen*, nn. 123–124, but the Shelah had already used it; see *Torah she-be'al peh*, *Klal Mishnah*.

[53]I.e., the glosses of the Rema.

[54]See immediately below; Rabbi Israel Dov Ber of Zledniki requires even less.

person's conduct according to the Torah—certainly their words did not come by happenstance (*mikreh*); rather, God, may He be blessed, sent His spirit over them that their words should correspond to [matters] which they [themselves] had not intended, for God does not abandon His pious ones,[55] and in a matter such as this composition which was accepted by Klal Israel.[56]

Klal Yisrael thus can recognize the presence of *ruach ha-kodesh* in a work. This is hardly surprising in the context of hasidic thought, given the kabbalistic triad of God, Israel, and Torah.[57] Note that Rabbi Zadok does not speak of the role of the *sages of Israel*, as he so often does in

---

[55] A reference to Psalms 37:28.

[56] *Mahshevet Harutz*, pp. 6a–b. Rabbi Zadok finds this doctrine implicit in the Rabbi Jonathan Eibeschuetz's *Urim ve-Tumim* on *Kitzur Tekafo Kohen*, nn. 123–124, 48b (end); but the condition of acceptance by Kelal Israel is later; see below. Rabbi Yonatan writes:

> Once the Rav[, the author of] *Beit Yosef* and Rema disregarded [the doctrine of *kim leh* against the majority of decisors] there is no need to concern oneself with it; the scholars of the generation accepted upon themselves (*kiyyemu ve-kibbelu*) to keep and act according the formulation contained in the short version [of *Beit Yosef* contained in] the Shulhan Arukh and the glosses of the Rema. In my opinion, there is no doubt that this was all 'in writing from God [what] He gave them to understand.' [This is because] there is no doubt that they could not have intended [to advert to] all the *kushyot* that the Aharonim posed on them and the sharp and profound answers given, and likewise the many laws included in smooth and compact form (*be-metek ve-kotzer leshonam*). How could [this be, given] the great amount of work—the work of Heaven—which was laid upon them; who is the man who can produce a compilation on all the Torah, taken from all the words of the Rishonim and Aharonim without the work—the work of Heaven—being all but impossible (*yikhbad alehem*)? Rather, [we must assume] that the spirit of God stirred in them that their formulation should correspond to Halakhah without the conscious intention of the writer—[rather] it was God's desire that allowed them to succeed [in this endeavor].

[57] See *Zohar* 3:73a for the first two elements; the third first appears as part of the triad in the works of the Ramahal; see see Y. Tishby, "'Kudsha' Berikh Hu', Oraita ve-Yisrael Kula' Had Hu"—Mekor ha-Imrah be-Ferush 'Idra' Rabba" le-Ramhal," *Kiryat Sefer* 50 (5735): 480–492 and "Hashlamot le-Maamari al Mekor Imrah 'Kudsha' Berikh Hu,' Oraita ve-Yisrael Had Hu," in the same issue, pp. 668–674.

connection with the unfolding of *Torah she-be'al peh*; instead, *Klal Israel* takes on the function of such determinations.[58] Naturally, *hakhmei Yisrael* play a role, but in this matter the *klal* too must signal its agreement.

Rabbi Zadok thus offers an "operational definition" of *ruach ha-kodesh*.[59] What then of the consequences of such categorization? While the answer is implicit in the citation from Rabbi Zadok's comment that "their words should correspond to [matters] which they [themselves] had not in-tended,"[60] the point is made more precisely in a work published in Rabbi Zadok's own lifetime, but is attributed to the Besht by Rabbi Israel Dov Ber of Zledniki, a disciple of Rabbi Mordekhai of Tchernobil.

> Works composed[61] until the [time of] the Maharsha—including [those of] the Maharsha—were [composed] by Divine inspiration (*ru'ah ha-kodesh*), and

---

[58]Though he does not cite them, it is hard to avoid associating the pivotal role of *Klal Yisrael* in the granting of prophecy to the prophets (see *Yevamot* 64a; the *Shekhinah* does not rest on fewer than 22,000 of Israel) or Rashi to Leviticus 1:1 s.v. *le'mor*, based on *Sifra* ad loc., see Albo, *Sefer ha-Ikkarim* 3:12. Communication requires two pivots, even when it is not a two-way process, and the parameters of *ruach ha-kodesh* or *ruach ne-nevu'ah* will be determined by recipients as well as the giver. See below.

[59]This applies to *any* text which is accepted by *Kelal Yisrael*; in *Peri Tzaddik* II, p. 117b, he applies this principle to *piyyutim*.

[60]Taken from Rabbi Jonathan Eibeschuetz; see n. 56. The same point is made in the *responsum* of Rabbi Hayyim Halberstam (see n. 63); he also uses the text in *Bava Batra* 12a so beloved by Rabbi Zadok.

[61]As it stands, this statement leaves open the possibility that works *composed* but not *published*, or published and neglected, were nevertheless written under the influence of Divine inspiration. This is quite apart from the question of the status of Karaite and other ancient heretical works, of which neither Rabbi Israel may have been aware. However, Divine inspiration implies some dissemination of the work in question at some time; otherwise, why would the writer have been impelled to compose it in the first place?

In the case of the Maharsha (1555–1631), his fame in his own time and the publication of much of his work during his own life insured that his work would not be neglected. Some of his *hiddushim* were published as early as 1602, and no decade thereafter passed without another volume appearing.

Why the pre-Maharsha era constituted such an apparent "golden age" is not altogether clear. Undoubtedly the relative scarcity of surviving works of *Rishonim* and of printed works altogether had something to do with this. However, it seems

since they were by Divine inspiration, they are [considered as] Torah itself
(*hu Torah atzmah*). . . . [As for] works after the Maharsha, some have Divine
inspiration and some do not; nevertheless, once they are accepted by
[or: among] Jews (*etzel benei Yisrael*), even if they are not accepted by [or:
among] all (*etzel ha-klal*) but only a segment (*bi-frat*) which is called a community (*ha-nikra be-shem tzibbur*),[62] the power of Divine inspiration extends

---

most likely that the catastrophe of Tah Va-Tat and the ensuing Sabbatean heresy, which began some seventeen years after the Maharsha's passing, signaled a
change of an era for Rabbi Israel. In this regard it is noteworthy that Rabbi Yonah
Landsofer (1678–1712), writing in the very early eighteenth century, advised
his sons to study the Maharsha's works carefully, since "the spirit of God spoke
through him, for without Divine inspiration it would have been impossible to
compose such a book" (*Derekh Tovim* [Frankfurt, 1717; undated Brooklyn
reprint, Zhitomir, 1875], p. 13).

This also provides an estimate of the elapsed time necessary for such judgments to be rendered. Rabbi Landsofer wrote about a century after the first volume of the Maharsha's *hiddushim* appeared, and about eighty years after his death.
Note also that the reason he gives stems more from the charisma of the work
than of the man. Undoubtedly, charismatic individuals of whatever time are
said to possess divine inspiration in their own times; whether this extends immediately to their works is a moot point, though two such examples, the Ari
and the Besht, are known more from their disciples' works.

[62]Clearly Rabbi Israel refers here to works accepted by *hasidim* and rejected
by others. Note that his litmus test is less severe than Rabbi Zadok's; the work
must be accepted only by part of *Kelal Yisrael*.

It may not be out of place to consider the problem raised by the apostasy of
a large segment of Israel, as in the days of Elijah, for example (see 1 Kings 19:18),
or of a smaller segment, perhaps, as in the time of Shabbatei Zvi. As to the first,
it may be that this rule was not in effect when prophecy itself was available and
the edifice of *Torah she-be'al peh* had not yet been completed; the role of *Klal
Yisrael* is a result of the linkage of the souls of all Jews to the Mishnah (see *Resisei
Laylah*, p. 165a). The outcome of this reasoning is somewhat surprising: *the triad
of God, Torah, and Israel is historically determined!*

The case of Shabbatai Zvi is less problematic; it merely took some time for
the consensus of *Klal Yisrael* to develop. There is also a time lag involved. Until
the consensus of the community forms, the work's status is, as it were, in sus-
pension. Spiegel makes this point in regard to Maimonides' *Mishneh Torah*; see
"*Derekh Ketzarah*," p. 26, and note his reference to *Teshuvot ha-Rashba* 4:118.

Rabbi Israel provides for this by stipulating that the rule applies "as long as it
is not against the Will of the Creator."

Nevertheless, the questions of who constitutes *Klal Yisrael* or a *tzibbur* for

to that work as long as it is not against the Will of the Creator, may He be blessed.[63]

Rabbi Israel Dov Ber goes on to spell out the consequences of this very clearly. Works composed under the influence of Divine inspiration may be interpreted with all the methods of PaRDeS—*peshat, remez, derash,* and *sod*—just as the Torah itself.[64]

---

the purposes of determining what texts have this status, and the bounds of "the Will of the Creator" are undeniably troublesome.

[63]Rabbi Israel Dov Ber of Veledniki, *She'erit Yisrael* (Zhitomir, 1867; enlarged edition Koenigsberg, 1877; reprint, New York, 1985), 6c. See A. Wertheim, *Halakhot va-Halikhot ba-Hasidut* (Jerusalem: Mosad Harav Kook, 1989), p. 58, n. 98; and see Spiegel, "Derekh Ketzarah," pp. 25–26, where other sources for this idea are cited.

This idea has become increasingly popular over the last few centuries; aside from the references Spiegel cites, which deal primarily with the Mishnah, more general statements, or statements referring to works other than the Mishnah, can be found in Rabbi Moshe Sofer, *She'elot u-Teshuvot Hatam Sofer, Even ha-Ezer* II, no. 102, 49c–d, on the *siyata di-Shemmaya* which a *talmid hakham* receives, and Rabbi Hayyim Halberstam, *She'elot u-Teshuvot Divrei Hayyim, Yoreh De'ah* II, no. 105, 33d–34a, regarding the inspired nature of Rabbi Hayyim ibn Attar's *Or ha-Hayyim*; see also n. 61 above. My thanks to Rabbis Shalom Carmy and Menahem Silber for much stimulating conversation on this topic.

[64]While Rabbi Zadok does not state this directly, the same view may be derived from his comments. According to Rabbi Zadok (based on *Me Shilo'ah, Nedarim*), God created two books, the Torah and the world; the former is a commentary on the latter. It is clear however that each functions in a symbiotic relationship, with events in the world illuminating the Torah as well. *Hiddushim* in Torah can influence events in the world (*Tzidkat ha-Tzaddik, maamar* 90, p. 25b). (In essence this adds a fourth corner to the zoharic triad of God, Torah, and Israel.) Since actions in the world may be interpreted according to PaRDeS (*Tzidkat ha-Tzaddik*), *maamar* 177, p. 62a–b), it follows that so can those works which are considered "as Torah." Though this may seem a rather roundabout argument, it is implicit in the system of equivalences Rabbi Zadok has set up.

Nevertheless, given the number of times Rabbi Zadok mentions the idea that *hiddushim* in Torah can effect changes in this world, or the importance of *hiddush* in his system in general, it is a matter of amazement that he does not state this directly. While it is possible that he did so in his lost works, or that I have missed the reference, the very absence of this point in all extant discussions of *hiddush* tends to cast doubt on my interpretation.

Thus, *peshat* and *derash* exist in all mainstream Jewish texts, but they are not equal in perceived value; the drive for omnisignificance, on the one hand, and for *hiddush*, on the other, tips the balance in favor of *derash*. This is not to say that all periods are equal in this respect; as we might expect, periods of creative ferment alternate with periods of creative tension, which prepare the way for another cycle, for the next "paradigm change."[65] Moreover, the preference for *derash* is often disguised or over-

---

Moreover, his interpretations of rabbinic texts, even when they involve *sod*, are not dependent on the more usual methodologies of *sod* as on a systematic approach to his sources, which gives each a place in his complete system, usually by identifying concepts in Nigleh with their concomitants in Nistar. When a source for such identification is lacking, Rabbi Zadok carefully delineates the exact relationship, usually by means of the word *mistama*, which serves as a marker for lack of a direct linkage. Thus, the type of wordplay that Rabbi Israel Dov Ber has in mind, as is evidenced by *She'erit Yisrael*, is more in the mainstream of hasidic discourse than Rabbi Zadok's methods.

Despite this, I think that Rabbi Israel Dov Ber has enunciated a principle that is implicit in most of rabbinic learning.

[65]See Thomas Kuhn, *The Structure of Scientific Revolutions*[2], (Chicago: University of Chicago Press, 1970). Sociologically, the role of *Klal Yisrael* may be defined as one of setting the parameters within which *hiddushim* will be developed. The process may be exemplified by the Maharal's unsuccessful attempt, persistent though it may have been, to restructure the curriculum of rabbinic study in the *hadarim*, with an emphasis on a thorough mastery of basic texts (Tanakh, Mishnah) before proceeding to Gemara, and Gemara and Rashi before proceeding to Tosafot; see S. Asaf, *Mekorot le-Toledot ha-Hinnukh be-Yisrael*, vol. 1 (Tel Aviv: Devir, 1954), sec. 30, pp. 45–52; and see Aharon Fritz Kleinberger, *Mahshavto ha-Pedagogit shel ha-Maharal mi-Prag* (Jerusalem: Magnes, 1962), pp. 143–155; Otto Dov Kolko, "Ha-Reka ha-Histori shel Mishnato shel ha-Maharal mi-Prag," *Zion* (*Sefer ha-Yovel*) (1984/5): 277–320, esp. pp. 297–307. But since such cultural processes can carry human reason far from the intentions of the Torah's Creator, *Klal Yisrael*'s collective cultural consciousness requires a gyroscope to keep it on course; *ruach ha-kodesh* serves that function.

It may be argued that it is the *talmidei hakhamim* who, as primary preservers and innovators of Torah, control the process; but such a view ignores the mutuality inherent in their leadership role. It also minimizes the role that responsa play in determining—directly or indirectly—the direction of *Talmud Torah*. Moreover, the extent to which *Klal Yisrael* lives up to its ideals of the democraticization

laid with a strong concern for what is considered *peshat*. It is rather the value placed on innovation or omnisignificance that in the end determines whether what eventuates is *peshat* or *derash*. Other factors also come into play. Thus, the extent to which the Bavli (or any other document) actually coheres as a complete system will determine whether Tosafot's attempts to understand each and every passage as part of a large, overarching system are actually *peshat* or *derash*. In some cases this approach will yield *peshat*, in others *derash*. In the latter case, the Tosafists are *creating* a system rather than *describing* an already existent one. It is not the conscious intent that determines the outcome, but the extent to which the assumptions that govern the exegetical methodology actually mirror the concerns of the text. Needless to say, since many of these problems have not yet been fully solved, we are sometimes hard put to determine whether a particular interpretation falls under the heading of *peshat* or *derash*.

In general, however, *peshat* represents the past, the known; *derash* represents *hiddush* and the future, the cutting edge of learning. Thus the *Gemara* gives priority to *derash*—*kol heikha de-ika le-midrash darshinan*—wherever we can *darshn*,[66] we do; it is only when we cannot, when our ingenuity fails us, that we resort to *peshat*.

Thus, *peshat* and *derash* coexist but in tension, with the drive to *hiddush* overcoming intellectual inertia inherent in traditional or traditionalist cultures.

It must be stressed however that one need not accept a hasidic understanding of the role of Divine inspiration in human affairs to recognize

---

of rabbinic learning will determine not only the role of the laity (the *hamon am*), but the vitality of the Torah that the rabbinic class produces. *Talmidei hakhamim* are also members of *Klal Yisrael*, and do not, in the best circumstances, remain a caste unto themselves, hermetically sealed off from the rest of *Klal Yisrael*. In the long run, certainly in the posttalmudic era, controversies that are *le-shem shammayim* are mitigated, and yield melds and blends of tendencies rather than pure types, and even movements that are rejected by the body of Israel, such as Karaitism and Sabbateanism, contribute to the tradition, if only negatively, and, if some modern scholars are to be believed, even positively. On this latter point, see section VI of this discussion.

[66]As used by the *Amora'im* who enunciate this principle, Rav Ashi and Mar b. Rav Ashi, *darash* = *shannuyei* = to make distinctions; see *Pesahim* 24b and *Kiddushin* 4b.

that this description of the process of learning and *hiddush* actually corresponds to historic reality. Although we may reject *sod* as a legitimate interpretive strategy for Shas, as Rabbi Yisrael Dov Ber asserts it is,[67] various alternatives to *peshat*, loosely termed *derash*, remain to us.

Nevertheless, human beings differ in abilities and perceptions, and some are born literalists; the community of Torah must find a place for them. In the dynamic equalibrium of differing methodologies of Torah study, *pashtanim* serve as anchors, showing us how far we have gone in our embrace of the new. Often we have so lost sight of the old that it seems new to us.

The recognition that the *Amora'im* at times employ *derash* in their interpretation of the Mishnah naturally led later commentators to interpret these *mishnayot* in a fashion closer to the *peshat*. Of the many examples that might be cited,[68] Rabbi Menashe me-Ilya's interpretation of *Mishnah Bava Metzia* 1:1, which contradicts the *Gemara's* explicit *derash* of the superfluities in this mishnah, but was praised by *Tiferet Yisrael, ad loc.*, is noteworthy. In contrast to the *Gemara*, which understands the mishnah's redundancies as referring both to cases of lost objects and disputes over sales, Rabbi Menashe denies that the mishnah deals with the latter at all.[69] The redundancies are thus "merely" stylistic.

Since the Renaissance, when sensitivity to any challenge to *emunat Hakhamim* has increased tremendously, this right of interpretation has itself been challenged.[70] The question need not detain us since, as noted, ample precedent exists for the alternate point of view.

---

[67]He practiced it as well, as an inspection of the section entitled *"Likkutim"* will bear out.

[68]See literature cited in nn. 40–42. Although Tosafot Yom Tov's comments on *Mishnah Nazir* 5:5 have become a *locus classicus* for this principle, and have engendered much debate, I have chosen an example that is less open to criticism, even though it postdates the GRA. As to the latter, one example of many is his interpretation of *Mishnah Berakhot* 7:3; see *Shenot Eliyahu ad loc.*, s.v. *ehad asarah*.

[69]See papers referred to in n. 45 above.

[70]See Rabbi Meshullam Roth, "He'arot le-Sifrei ha-Tosafot Yom Tov," in *Li-Kvod Yom Tov: Maamarim u-Mehkarim*, ed. Y. L. Maimon (Jerusalem: Mosad Ha-Rav Kook, 5716), pp. 70–109, esp. 90–94. His comments vis à vis the GRA are clearly tendentious; see the second part of Kurman's article cited in n. 41 above.

III

Even if *peshat*-oriented exegesis remains of secondary importance, it has always had a place within our *derash*-oriented system. Generally speaking, as noted above, however, it is only when our ingenuity fails that we resort to *peshat*.

However, *peshat* is the essence of an academic study of *Torah she-be'al peh*; therein lies its glory and usefulness, and therein lie the problems it brings in its wake.

To arrive at the plain meaning of the texts, both traditional learning and academic study requires an accurate knowledge of their provenance in every sense of the word: their historical provenance, in all its senses—political, cultural, religious, socioeconomic, including matters of realia; their linguistic, geographic provenance; it requires concern for structural and literary elements, for form-critical and source-critical matters; it requires first and foremost establishing a text, and thus brings text-critical matters into its purview.

Little need be said of source-critical approaches, since the *Gemara* itself pioneered the method. Traditionally the statute of limitations on these methodologies has been considered expired since the close of the Bavli, and the revival of such investigation marks academic scholarship in the eyes of the world of the *yeshivot* and is thus viewed with suspicion. In principle, however, and in stark contrast with the impossibility of employing such methods in Humash,[71] the view of most rabbinic compositions as *compilations*, and the consequent desire to trace them back to their component parts (and in this respect Mishnah differs little from *Mishneh Torah*)[72] is clearly the regnant view of the *Amora'im*.

While source-critical concerns did not pass over the great divide of the close of the Bavli to the *Rishonim*, most of the methods enumerated above did. Some of them were of great concern to the *Rishonim*, chiefly those

---

[71]I do not say "Bible" in general. See Rabbi Aryeh Leib of Metz, *Gevurot Ari* (Jerusalem, 5721), p. 56a on *Yoma* 54a, s.v. *teyuvta*, where he notes that Ezra followed his sources in compiling the Books of Chronicles. See M. Breuer, "Torat ha-Te'udot shel Baal Shaagat Aryeh," *Megadim* 2 (5747): 9–22. Note also that M. Eisemann cites this source and others of similar nature in his introduction to the Artscroll *Divrei ha-Yamim*, (Brooklyn, NY: Mesorah Publications, 1987).

[72]See my "History of Halakhah," especially p. 19.

involving textual and lexicographic matters, including realia when relevant, but also historical and geographical matters at times, and even redactional questions were taken up in episodic fashion. In short, the *Rishonim* were alive to nearly all the elements that go into achieving a proper understanding of the text that is alive to all its nuances. The major differences between their methodologies and those of modern academics have to do with the relative importance of these questions and the differing amounts and sources of information regarding the world outside the texts. But beyond that I daresay that there is little in method for which precedents cannot fairly easily be found in the words of the *Rishonim*.

THE NEW SOURCE CRITICISM

Arguably the most important "discovery" of academic scholarship of the last generation, or at least the increasing awareness of academic talmudists, is the recognition of the importance of the *stama di-Gemara*.[73] The "*stam*," as it has come to be known, plays a decisive role in the presentation, arrangement, *and wording* of many of the constituent elements that comprise Shas. The stam serves in large measure to organize and orient the (earlier) sources contained in the Bavli. Increasingly, the focus of research has turned to an examination of the stam's viewpoint vis-à-vis those of its sources and an assessment of its substantive contribution to the Bavli.

RECONSTRUCTING THE *SUGYA*

This brings us to perhaps the first question an Orthodox would-be academic must ask himself: How does *emunat Hakhamim* bear on all this? It is clear that new methodologies are not ipso facto forbidden; the history

---

[73]A consensus has grown up that sees the *stam* as generally late and post-Amoraic, and that sees these anonymous portions of the Bavli as constituting a stratum of its own, whenever dated; see S. Y. Friedman, "Al Derekh Heker Ha-Sugya'," in *Mehkarim U-Mekorot: Ma'asaf Le-Mada`ei Ha-Yahadut*, vol. I, ed. H. Z. Dimitrovsky (New York, 1977–1978, pp. 283–321; D. W. Halivni, *Mekorot U-Mesorot* (New York: Jewish Theological Seminary, 1982), *Moed*, vol. I [*Shabbat*], introduction; and *Midrash, Mishnah, and Gemara: The Jewish Predilection for Justified Law* (Cambridge, MA: Harvard University Press, 1986), pp. 76–92.

of *darkei limmud* is a long and fascinating one, though little researched. In particular, the Orthodox would-be academic student of *Torah she-be'al peh* must ask himself whether *emunat Hakhamim* requires us to take the *sugya* as we find it.[74] For example, if the *sugya* involves a dialogue between two *Amora'im*, must we take it at face value? At first blush, the answer would seem to be yes. But in this, as in so many other matters, our instincts are more *frum* than the practice of the *Rishonim*. Perhaps *Gemara* is too important to be left to the theologians.

In any case, whether on the level of the *memra* or the *sugya*, Tosafot saw clearly that we do *not* possess the *ipsissima verba* of the *Amora'im*, but a redacted text. This proceeds directly from the observation that *memrot* are preserved in different versions in different *sugyot*. For example, the following *pesak* of Rabbi Papa is reported in *Bava Batra* 176a and *Kiddushin* 13b. In *Baba Batra* the formulation is as follows:

The Memra

> Rav Papa said: The *halakhah* is that a verbal loan may be recovered from the heirs [of the debtor] but may not be recovered from purchasers. It "may be recovered from the heirs"—*in order not to lock the door in the face of borrowers*; "but it may not be recovered from purchasers"—because there is no general knowledge of the transaction.[75]

In *Kiddushin* we find:

> Rav Papa said: The *halakhah* is that a verbal loan may be recovered from the heirs [of the debtor], but not from purchasers. It "may be recovered from

---

[74]The question of post-Amoraic additions to the text of the Talmud has long been answered in the positive; Rav Sherira already noted the Saboraic origin of the first *sugya* in *Kiddushin*, and the *Rishonim* comment as Geonic additions to the text; see *Iggeret Rav Sherira Gaon*, ed. B. M. Lewin (reprint, Jerusalem: Makor, 5732), p. 71; idem, *Rabbanan Sabora'ei ve-Talmudam* (Jerusalem, 5697) [originally in *Azkarah le-Nishmat ha-Rav A. Y. Kook* (Jerusalem, 5697), pt. 4, pp. 145–208]; Y. S. Spiegel, "Leshonot Perush ve-Hosafot Me'uharot ba-Talmud ha-Bavli," in *Mehkarim be-Safrut ha-Talmud, bi-Lshon Hazal u-ve-Farshanut ha-Mikra*, ed. M. A. Friedman, et al. (Tel Aviv: Tel Aviv University Press, 5743), pp. 92–112.

[75]Literally, "there is no voice." No witnesses or scribe can testify to the loan having been made.

the heirs"—*because the obligation is biblical*; "but it may not be recovered from purchasers"—becasue there is no general knowledge of the transaction.

Tosafot in *Bava Batra*[76] suggest that Rav Papa only made the initial statement; the following interpretation is that of "the *Gemara*." In the one case, the explanation selected can be accepted whether or not one holds that the obligation is biblical, while in the parallel in *Kiddushin*, the statement is only acceptable to the former.

It is noteworthy that Tosafot in *Kiddushin*[77] attempt to reconcile the two sources by suggesting (in Rabbenu Tam's name) that Rav Papa's initial dictum applied only to loans of biblical authority, such as damages, valuations (*arakhin*), and sacrificial vows.[78]

Shakla ve-Tarya

The same may be said of *shakla ve-tarya*; talmudic dialectic has been carefully arranged, in some cases, with an eye to literary effect. For example, there is an interesting comment found in collections of Tosafot that were not included into the standard editions of Shas.[79] In the course of a discussion (in *Bava Metzia* 14b) as to whether one who sells land that does not belong to him can collect its produce (*perot*) and the

---

[76]S.v. *goveh*.

[77]S.v. *amar R. Papa*.

[78]See Urbach, *Baalei ha-Tosafot*, pp. 630–633 and 651–654, regarding the identity of the compilers of the printed Tosafot to *Kiddushin* and *Baba Batra* 144b–176b; both were apparently compiled by disciples of the Ri.

A similar case, where the *setama di-gemara* adds explanatory material to earlier traditions, is noted in Tosafot *Bava Metzia* 112a, s.v. *umman* regarding the query made to Rabbi Sheshet there and its parallel in *Bava Kamma* 99a; see also *Tosafot Niddah* 34b, s.v. *ki*.

On the question of later accretions to earlier texts, see Rabbi Y. Y. Weinberg, *Mehkarim ba-Talmud* (Berlin, 5697–5698), pp. 174–179; reprinted in *Seridei Eish* (Jerusalem: Mosad Harav Kook, 1977), pp. 121–124.

[79]According to E. E. Urbach, *Baalei ha-Tosafot*, pp. 646–648, the printed Tosafot are Tosafot Touque, taken in part from Tosafot Sens. This is not to say that literary comments were either edited out or excluded from the printed Shas; after all, we have cited a number of redactional comments culled from our printed collections of Tosafot.

increase in its worth (*shevah*), a matter in dispute between Rav and Samuel, Rav Nahman proffers an interpretation of Samuel's position, which Rava disputes. He does so on the basis of the *sefa* of whose *baraita* whose *resha* is not only cited next but is determinative for the proper interpretation of the *baraita*. The Tosafists, alive to incongruity, ask why the *sefa* is dealt with before the *resha*. Our printed Tosafot suggest that this is because the *makshan*[80] wished to utilize a source—the *sefa*—that dealt directly with the question of *shevah* rather than the *resha* that dealt with *perot*, since the dispute was essentially about the former.

However, the incongruity remains. Since the desired deduction cannot be made from the *sefa* in any case, why not go immediately to the *resha*?[81] This question is taken up in two collections of *tosafot* that did not "make it" into Shas, *Tosafot Ha-Rosh*[82] and *Tosafot Rabbenu Peretz*.[83] It is worthwhile citing their solutions in the exact wording in which they are given: "*orheih de-Talmuda le-hakshot tehillah davar she-yakhol lidhot*

---

[80]Apparently Rava, but see below.

[81]There is an interesting dispute between Maharsha and Maharshal on the exact nature of this question. According to Maharsha, the question is why Rava, who eventually makes his point from the *resha*, should begin with the *sefa*. Maharsha's answer is simply that Rava did not yet derive his point from the *resha*. Maharshal separates the two *makshanim*; according to him—hotly disputed by Maharsha—the second *makshan*, that is, the *makshan* who employs the *resha*, was not aware of Rava's interpretation of the *resha* and could not understand why he first had recourse to the *resha*.

The exact nature of Maharsha's objection to this interpretation, which he terms *dahuq*, is unclear; either he considers the separation of Rava from the second *kushya* as forced, or he considers that the second *makshan* must have known of Rava's deduction. It is noteworthy that this latter technique of positing lack of awareness by one master of the statement of another is now considered one of the controversial aspects of modern scholarship, but it was not always so; see *Helkat Binyamin* on *Shabbat*, published in 1913 in Pietrkov (reprint, 1954 by Temple Sholom of Philadelphia) with the *haskmah* of Rabbi Hayyim Soloveichik.

It should be noted that the incongruity discussed here is stronger than that which gave rise to an *oisbrenger*.

[82]Moshe Hershler and Yehoshua Dov Grodzitzki, eds., *Tosafot Ha-Rosh al massekhet Baba Metzia* (Jerusalem, 5719), 48b, s.v. *ka-tani miha*.

[83]Hayyim Ben Zion Hershler, *Tosafot Rabbenu Peretz le-massekhet Bava Metzia* (Jerusalem, 5730), 37a, s.v. *mide-resha*.

be-kal" (*Tosafot Ha-Rosh*); *"orheih de-Talmuda hu le-havi tehillah re'ayah she-yesh lidhot"* (Tosafot Rabbenu Peretz).[84] It is the way of the Talmud first to ask a question which may easily be pushed aside, or to bring a proof which can be rejected. Note that while *Tosafot Ha-Rosh* emphasizes *lehaqshot*, *Tosafot Rabbenu Peretz* has *le-havi re'ayah*. It is noteworthy also that both refer to *talmudic* style, and not to Rava personally. It marks a recognition that Rava did not determine the shape of the *sugya* that includes his comments, but that his comments have been arranged and organized by the *Talmud*. It is also noteworthy that these comments are not included in the *Otzar Mefarshei Ha-Talmud*.[85]

The *Sugya*

The same observation applies to *sugyot*. There are some thirty-odd *sugyot* that contain detailed debates between Rabbi Yohanan and Resh Laqish. Several of them contain contradictory accounts of the positions held by the two disputants, but rather than present the parallel debates as alternatives (*ika de-amri, ika de-matni lah*), the *sugya*'s redactor(s) first present one version, and then, in response to a problem, the attributions are reversed,[86] or the dispute is redefined.[87]

Tosafot mentions several such cases, and[88] the point has been the subject of hot debate in modern scholarship, particularly between Abraham Weiss[89] and Samuel Atlas[90] in the last generation. Atlas took Tosafot's view; Weiss insisted that these *sugyot* merely reflect divergent traditions that were spliced together, and denied vehe-mently that they constitute so-called fictitious *sugyot*.

---

[84]This is of course the embodiment of the principle of *ein adam omed al divrei Torah ela im ken nikhshal ba-hem tehillah* (Gittin 43a), and see Rabbi Zadok, *Tzidkat ha-Tzaddik, maamar* 49, pp. 13b–14a; for the nonce see my "History of Halakhah," p. 15.

[85]Again, Maharsha and Maharshal dealt with quasi-substantive issues, not literary-redactional ones.

[86]This occurs in *Bava Batra* 154b.

[87]*Bekhorot* 4b; see Tosafot s.v. *ella iy itamar*.

[88]Tosafot *Bava Batra* 154b, s.v. *beram; Bekhorot* 4b, s.v. *'ela*.

[89]*Le-Heker ha-Talmud*, vol. 1 (New York: Feldheim, 5715), pp. 18–32; and his "Sugyot shel Keta'im," *Ha-Tzofeh le-Hokhmat Yisrael* 9:2 (1925): 97–116.

[90]"Le-Toledot ha-Sugya," *Hebrew Union College Annual* 24 (1952–1953): 1–21 [Hebrew section].

Weiss's vehemence may be traced to the singular importance he placed on these dialogues between Rabbi Yohanan and Resh Lakish. According to his reconstruction of the history of the *sugya as a literary form*— and a literary form is merely one way of reconstituting reality—the sugyatic form was devised in Eretz Israel in early Amoraic times, perhaps in Rabbi's *bet midrash*. These early, well-developed debates between Rabbi Yohanan and Resh Laqish thus assume a great importance in tracing this history.

In at least one case Weiss has a powerful argument. For each divergent and contradictory part of the *sugya* involved (*Bava Batra* 154a–b) we can find parallels in the Yerushalmi (*Bava Batra* 9:8 [17a]), thus suggesting that the *sugya's* contradictions reflect a problematic reality. The question of whether Rabbi Yohanan had actually changed his mind was evidently put to him directly, and his denial was essentially disregarded in both Talmuds, by being recorded alongside reports of his contradictory statements. But in a large sense Weiss begs the question. If the redactor of these *sugyot* had two divergent traditions about the views held by each of the disputants, and about the nature of the dispute to begin with, why not compile an *ika de-matni lah sugya* rather than making an about-face after presenting us with what seems to be a bona fide dialogue? The *sugya* is *arranged* so as to *force* us to arrive at Tosafot's conclusion—that we are to reject the initial formulation of the dispute and the initial debate. *Ein adam omed al divrei Torah ela im ken nikhshal ba-hem tehillah.*[91] It is almost as if the redactor wants to teach us that not every tradition is to be given full faith and credence.[92]

This element of artifice, of redactional art, points to one of the cornerstones of academic Talmud scholarship of the last twenty years: the discovery of the importance of the *stama di-Gemara* as the organizing voice of the Bavli. It is noteworthy that the *Rishonim* speak of *orheih de-Talmuda* or *Gemara*, thus giving the redactional part of Shas a cohesive character as against the variegated *memrot* and other sources contained therein. Again, the *Baalei Tosafot* were there first.

---

[91]*Gittin* 43a; see n. 84 above. On the existence of "educational *sugyot*" see L. Jacobs, "Further Evidence of Literary Device in the Babylonian Talmud," in *Studies in Talmudic Logic and Methodology*, (London: Valentine, 1961), pp. 60–69.

[92]David C. Kraemer has made much of this point in his *The Mind of the Talmud: An Intellectual History of the Bavli* (New York: Oxford University Press, 1990), see especially pp. 99–170.

The Redaction of the Bavli

Despite the recognition by some *Rishonim* in some cases of the important role of the *stam*, the notion of an anonymous, collective authorship was rejected, without apparently ever seriously being considered. The notion was foreign; it was clear that such an important work had to bear the imprimatur of an important sage or group of sages—"R. X *va-haverav*" or "R. Y. *u-vet dino*." Thus, though *Iggeret Rav Sherira Gaon*, the prime historical source for this period, makes no mention of Rav Ashi as the redactor of the Bavli, most *Rishonim* came to see him as such.

One proof for this was discerned in the opening *sugya* of *Hullin* which contains a discussion between Rav Ashi and Rav Aha b. Rava regarding the exact implications of the opening *ha-kol* of mHul 1:1 and the use of the participle *shohatin*. In the course of this discussion Rav Ashi has cause to explain the exact significance of a point he had made earlier. However, as Tosafot (2b s.v. *ana*) points out, that earlier point is not presented in the *sugya* as having been made by Rav Ashi, but rather by *sugyat ha-gemara* or *setama di-gemara* itself. From here, Tosafot conclude, is proof that Rav Ashi redacted (*sidder*) the *Gemara*.

However, because of the episodic nature of interest in such questions, Tosafot did not pursue such matters with the same intense interest as substantive issues were given. Again, redactional issues did not figure into the principle of omnisignificance, and so remained of secondary importance. Thus, the fact that there are *sugyot* that testify to a *stama di-Gemara later than Rav Ashi* was not noted, at least not here and not by Tosafot.[93] But the works of the *Rishonim* are replete with comments that testify to their recognition that parts of the Bavli date to Saboraic or Geonic times.[94]

---

[93]See for example the post-Rav Ashi debate in *Bezah* 40a; see also J. Kaplan, *The Redaction of the Babylonian Talmud* (New York: Bloch Publishing House, 1933), pp. 95–101; and D. W. Halivni, *Mekorot u-Mesorot: Be'urim ba-Talmud le-Seder Mo'ed* (New York: Jewish Theological Seminary, 5735), pp. 348–350.

[94]See Yaakov L. Spiegel, "Leshonot Perush ve-Hosafot Me'uharot ba-Talmud ha-Bavli," in *Te'udah: Kovetz Mehkarim shel Bet ha-Sefer le-Mada'ei ha-Yahadut al shem Hayyim Rosenberg 3, Mehkarim ba-Safrut ha-Talmud bi-Lshon Hazal u-ve-Farshanut ha-Mikra*, ed. M. A. Friedman, A. Tal, and G. Brin (Tel Aviv: Tel Aviv University, 5743), pp. 92–112, based on his unpublished dissertation, *Hosafot Me'uharot (Sabora'ot) ba-Talmud ha-Bavli* (Ph.D. diss., Tel Aviv University, 1976).

In all candor, however, it must be admitted that despite the attention paid to these questions from the beginnings of the *Wissenschaft des Judentums* movement, academic scholarship cannot claim to have progressed much beyond the *Rishonim* in these matters, at least in devising generally accepted answers to the most general questions of the date and process of redaction of the Bavli or other early rabbinic compilations.[95] Nevertheless, some claim to progress can be made, at least in the matter of the framing of general questions and devising methods to answer them.

It is generally accepted that the most methodologically meaningful division of the Bavli's text is between the *setama di-gemara* and its attributed sources, *mishnayot, baraitot,* and *memrot*. In my own work, I generally avoid the matter of absolute dates, and treat the *stam* phenomenologically[96]; at most I hope for a limited (i.e., limited to the text at hand) relative chronology. But, as I hope to have demonstrated, even that may yield results that are useful for the construction of an intellectual history and interesting from a theological standpoint.[97]

---

[95]Indeed, both in America and in Israel, there are some who consider the entire enterprise futile. Jacob Neusner rejects the possibility of source criticism for rabbinic compositions entirely and concentrates on whole "documents," as he terms them, and many Israeli scholars concentrate on lower, or textual, criticism with little if any attention paid to wider issues.

[96]The consensus noted above (see n. 73) of the role of the *stam* as a late redactional layer is important in this regard. A late date for the *stam* implies that it is evidence that redactional activity came at the end of the formation of the Bavli, as opposed to theories of punctuated or continuous redaction; see the summary in Rabbi Kalmin, *The Redaction of the Babylonian Talmud: Amoraic or Saboraic?* (Cincinnati: Hebrew Union College Press, 1989), pp. 1–11, and charts on pp. xvii–xviii.

The theory of punctuated redaction is far from dead, however; see most recently D. Rosenthal, "Arikhot Kedumot Hameshukka'ot ba-Talmud ha-Bavli," in *Mehkarei Talmud: Kovetz Mehkarim ba-Talmud u-vi-Tehumim Govelim,* ed. Y. Sussman and D. Rosenthal (Jerusalem, 5750), pp. 155–204; and the works of N. Aminoah, in which he has systematically focused on redactional problems in his series *Arikhat Masekhta/ot . . . ba-Talmud ha-Bavli*—in order of publication: *Kiddushin, Bezah, Rosh Hashanah, Taanit, Sukkah, Mo'ed Katan,* (Tel Aviv: Tel Aviv University Press, 1976/77–1988).

[97]See "Righteousness as Its Own Reward: An Inquiry into the Theologies of the Stam," *Proceedings of the American Academy for Jewish Research* 57 (1991): 35–67, and "'Is There Then Anger Before the Holy One?' Aspects of the The-

These post-Amoraic additions range from whole *sugyot*, as in the case
of the opening *sugya* of *Kiddushin*, which Rav Sherira Gaon in his famous epistle attributes to the *Sabbora'im*, to smaller pieces within *sugyot*,
which nearly every Rishon can be shown to have noted. This information is not particularly esoteric or hard to find. But because of the way
the principle of omnisignificance has been applied, it is unconsciously
downplayed, and most *yeshiva leit* are unaware of the extent of the phenomenon. Nevertheless, consideration of all these redactional aspects on
the part of the *Rishonim* remain a very minor matter within the matrix of
their approaches to Talmud study, for the reasons I have set forth. Academic methodologies, while anchored in the works of the *Rishonim*, clearly
diverge from them by making these methods the center of their interest.
And as the principle of omnisignificance more and more excluded any
elements but substantive ones, these matters slowly all but sank out
of consciousness in the work of the *Aharonim*, with very few exceptions.

I have already quoted the Rashbam's observation on the history of
biblical exegesis as he understood it. After the comments quoted, he then
adds the famous report of Rashi's feelings on the matter toward the end
of his life:

> Even Rabbenu Shlomo, my mother's father, Enlightener of the Eyes of the
> Exile, who interpreted the Torah, Prophets and Writings, paid attention to
> the plain sense of Miqra, and I Samuel son of Meir, his son-in-law, z.t.l.,
> debated with him and before him [on these matters] and he admitted to me
> that if he had time, he would have to produce other commentaries accord-
> ing to the *peshatot* which are newly discovered every day.[98]

Evidently he felt himself as part of a vital, burgeoning movement that
would uncover aspects of the biblical texts neglected for centuries. Here
we have not "the opening of new gates," in Rabbi Zadok's terms, but the
reopening of old ones. To some extent that feeling can be found among
those who are sensitive to literary and structural aspects of the texts of
Torah she-be'al peh in our own time.

---

ology of the Stam," AJS Twenty-first Annual Conference, Boston, December
19, 1989.
[98]*Perush ha-Torah le-Rashbam*, ed. Rosen, p. 49.

IV

LITERARY CONSIDERATIONS

Traditionally, as noted above, aesthetic considerations in textual exegesis come into play only when our ingenuity fails. This failure of interpretative power occurs most often, it seems to me, in the face of structural elements or literary features that do not lend themselves to halakhic innovation or moral edification; they remain in the realm of the aesthetic. Because of our drive for edification, we tend to ignore those elements in a text that cannot be used as grist for our mill. This was not always so; the *Gemara* is certainly aware of such elements in tannaitic texts,[99] and the *Rishonim* are aware of such elements in *sugyot* and—be it known—in Bible as well.

I would like to begin with an example of the latter. Most halakhic verses in *Humash* are in prose form; one of the few exceptions are the laws of the Jubilee and *shemittah* year of Leviticus 25, much of which is couched in loose poetic form, that is, the parallelism that typifies biblical poetry: one verse is tightly constructed in synonymous parallelism (*kefel inyan be-millim shonot*),[100] and legal distinctions between the two stichs of the verse can fairly easily be proposed.

One exception to this is 25:37, which is composed in good chiasmic style, with the first word of the first stich parallel to the last of the second, and the last of the first with the first of the last.

> *et kaspekha lo titten lo be-neshekh,*
> *u-ve-marbit lo titten okhlekha.*

> Your silver you shall not give for interest (*neshekh*);
> For increase (*marbit*) shall you not give your foodstuffs."

---

[99] As for example in the *eidi de-tanna* . . . exegesis of *mishnayot* and *baraitot*.

[100] This phrase recurs with monotonous regularity among the Sephardic *pashtanim*, Ibn Ezra, and Radak, and, when no moralistic comment lies at hand (*kol heikha de-ika le-midrash* . . .), by Abarbanel, but not with such regularity that we do not find even Radak making distinctions rather than achieving synonymity by force majeure.

Conceivably we might distinguish between the words *neshekh* and *marbit*, or perhaps silver and foodstuffs; the anonymous, presumably redactional, introduction to the first *sugya* of *Bava Metzia* 60b will have none of it, and goes to considerable lengths to prove that *neshekh* (the "bite" taken from the borrower) and *marbit* (the "increase" that the lendor gets) cannot be separated; when there is *neshekh* there is *marbit*, and when there is *marbit* there is *neshekh*.

This discussion serves to introduce a *memra* of Rava, which explains the redundancy of the conventional parallelistic structure of biblical poetry as being halakhically motivated. According to Rava, one who collects interest transgresses two prohibitions (*laavor alav bi-shenei lavin*).[101] Thus, in standard fashion, a matter of biblical style is given halakhic significance. Of interest here, however, is the comment of Tosafot.[102] Rava's halakhic interpretation accounts for the redundancy of parallelism (*"kefel inyan be-millim shonot,"* as Radak or Ibn Ezra might say), but why does the Torah use two synonyms for usury (*neshekh* and *tarbit*) where one would suffice: why not *neshekh-neshekh* or *tarbit-tarbit*? The answer proposed is purely aesthetic: because the variation in wording is *na'eh yoter*—more aesthetically pleasing. The same point is made by Rabbenu Tam in regard to the use of *keret/kiryah* in Proverbs 11:10–11; the biblical writer will not repeat the same word in successive verses if at all possible.[103]

---

[101]The whole issue of multiple *lavin* requires examination; for the time being my unpublished "The Exegesis of Redundant Passages in Rabbinic Literature: The Unfolding of an Exegetical Principle," presented at the Association for Jewish Studies Twenty-second Annual Conference, Boston, December 17, 1990, must suffice.

[102]Ad loc., s.v. *lamah hillekan*.

[103]This principle is cited again in Tosafot *Bava Metziah* 111a, s.v. *lamah hillekan*. Urbach, *Baalei ha-Tosafot*[4], pp. 646–648, notes that though these are basically Tosafot Touque, based on Tosafot Sens, the redactor added material of his own as well. Since the Rosh, too, drew on Tosafot Sens (see Urbach, p. 590; p. 594, n. 30 and text), that may have been his source, but since these comments are oddities, and not typical of Rabbi Shimshon of Sens, or the Ri for that matter, that is not overly likely. Urbach notes that Tosafot ha-Rosh to *Bava Metzia* are "longer and more detailed than our Tosafot, and many comments are cited there in the name of the Rivan, the Rashbam, Rabbenu Tam, Riva and the Ri which are not in our Tosafot" (p. 595). Among the compiler's other sources are his teacher the Maharam, as well as the commentaries of Rabad

Even halakhic texts may allow scope for the writer's aesthetic sense. This, too, is an application of the *heikha de-ika* principle; once the *Gemara* foreclosed the option of making substantive halakhic distinctions between the two cola, all that remained was a nonhalakhic explanation. Note also that the use of parallelism functions to add a count which the usurer has transgressed; the Tosafists address themselves to the question of why the Torah employed two synonyms for one halakhic concept. Though their approach constitutes a *pis aller* in the context of traditional exegesis, it is noteworthy for being stated so openly.[104]

The *Amora'im* (in their *eidi de-tanna* exegeses) and *Rishonim* (as Tosafot here)[105] clearly recognized that not every word in tannaitic or talmudic texts, respectively, is to be construed as halakhically meaning-

---

and Ramah. Others comments of this type may have been filtered out in the course of time. Maharsha and Maharam do not discuss this Tosafot, Maharam Schiff suggests an emendation, to which the Reshash objects on the basis of Tosafot *Bava Kamma* 65a, s.v. *likhtov*. However, aside from the question of authorship of the relevant Tosafist comments, Reshash counterposes two different types of repetitions, those which occur in parallel and those which occur in certain expressions, whose specialized use for *derashot* is clear.

It is significant that this suggestion was mostly ignored by the *Aharonim*; indeed, as perspicacious a commentator as Rabbi Aryeh Leib Zinz, in his *Maayanei he-Hokhmah* (Warsaw, 5634; p. 95b), after noting Tosafot's question, totally ignores the proferred solution (and the *sugya*'s assertion that *neshekh* and *tarbit* cannot be separated) and proposes one that is casuistically omnisignificant. While his solution is not without philological merit, his utter disregard—he does not trouble to refute it—for Tosafot's solution is striking.

As to Rabbenu Tam, see *Sefer Teshuvot Dunash ben Labrat im Hakhra'ot Rabbi YaaKov Tam*, ed. Z. Filipowski (London, 1855), pp. 13–14. He makes similar remarks on pp. 44–45, 54, 91–92; see Richard C. Steiner, "Meaninglessness, Meaningfulness, and Super-Meaningfulness in Scripture: An Analysis of the Controversy Surrounding Dan 2:12 in the Middle Ages," *Jewish Quarterly Review* 82 (1992): 442, n. 59. Unfortunately, none of these examples occurs in an halakhic context.

[104]It is noteworthy that Tosafot Ha-Rosh ad loc., ed. Hershler-Grodzitzki, p. 163b, s.v. *laavor alav*, adds an alternative possibility: *i nami le-shum derashah sheni shani kera be-dibbureih!* Tosafot Rabbenu Peretz does not discuss the matter at all.

[105]See also Rashi on *Sanhedrin* 60a, s.v. *hakha ketiv*.

ful. Some statements, queries, proferred solutions, phrases, and clauses
are included for their rhetorical, mnemonic, educative power, or "merely"
aesthestic appeal. In my opinion, it is in this province of Torah learning
that academic scholarship, with its concern for rhetoric, for the literary,
formulaic, structural aspects of *explication du texte*, can make its contribution.[106] In our search for interpretations ever more edifying and ele-
gant, we lose sight of some of the elegancies inherent in the texts we so
laboriously study.

STRUCTURAL CONSIDERATIONS WITHIN THE BAVLI

Aesthetic Aspects

My first example is a case in which the structure serves only as an aesthetic means of arranging a fairly large body of material. The structure is
essentially external to the meaning and the flow of the sugya. The first
sugya of *Pesahim* is arranged somewhat like those *sugyot* already discussed,
where a putative dispute turns out to be contrived. In this case, the *sugya*
concludes that a dispute between Rav Huna and Rav Yehudah is simply
a matter of terminology with no substantive implications at all. Ostensibly the question at dispute is the meaning of *or* in the expression *or le-
arbaah asar*; according to Rav Huna, the meaning is said to be *naghei*,
taken at first to mean "light" or "day," while Rav Yehudah interprets it
as *leylei*, "night." In the end, Rav Huna's *naghei* is taken as a euphemism
for "night," and the dispute—is no dispute.[107]

My primary concern here, however, is not with this aspect of the *sugya*,

---

[106]See my "The Order of Arguments in *Kalekh*-Baraitot in Relation to the
Conclusion," *JQR* 79 (1989): 295–304.

[107]For a somewhat similar case see the first *sugya* of *Gittin*. It has not escaped
the notice of scholars that initial *sugyot* seem disproportionately contrived and/
or linguistic in nature—recall Rav Sherira Gaon's characterization of the first
sugya of *Kiddushin* as Saboraic. Abraham Weiss classified nearly all such *sugyot*
as Saboraic; see his lecture, *Ha-Yetzirah shel ha-Sabora'im* (Jerusalem: Magnes,
5713).

but with the interesting, symmetrical arrangement of introductory terminology, a symmetry that is lacking in our printed editions, but which
may be detected in some manuscripts.[108]

The *sugya* takes up the question of whether *or* can refer to darkness
or night in good philological fashion,[109] with no fewer than fifteen proofs,
both biblical and rabbinic, though mostly the former, back and forth. In
our editions, the first thirteen are prefaced with *metivei*, and the last two
with *ta shema*. In the manuscripts of the Oriental tradition, the proofs
are divided into two groups, one of seven and one of eight. The first seven
are prefaced with *motivei*, and of the last eight, seven are introduced with
ta shema, with the exception of the middle—the fourth—argument,
which is marked with *motivei*. The symmetry goes beyond mere order,
however. Of the first group of seven, the first three and the last three
conclude that *or* means "day," while the middle—the fourth—proof
concludes the reverse. Of the group of eight, the first three conclude
that *or* is "night," as do the last three but one, while the middle of this
group of seven—the fourth again—concludes the reverse.

---

[108]We are uniquely blessed with manuscripts for Pesahim; indeed, E. S.
Rosenthal managed to divide them into two families. The following remarks
are based on his article, "Kamah Dugmot Boletot le-Yihudah shel Masoret Nusah
Ito," printed as an introduction to MS Valmadonna of *Pesahim*, *The Pesahim
Codex: Babylonian Talmud: the facsimile of the ca. 1447–1452 Provence [?] manu-
script* (London: Valmadonna Trust Library, 1984), pp. 7–59.

[109]Note that the opening *sugya* of *Kiddushin*, attributed to the Saboraim by
Rav Sherira Gaon, is also concerned with philological matters, in this case the
gender of the word *derekh*. According to Avraham Weiss, most opening *sugyot*
are of Saboraic origin; see n. 107.

[110]See diagram on the next page, taken from E. S. Rosenthal's analysis
(n. 101). But not quite; here too Izhbitz has its say. See Rabbi Yaakov Leiner
(son of Rabbi Mordecai Joseph), *Seder Haggadah shel Pesah im Sefer ha-Zemanim*
(Lublin, 1910), p. 8, cited in S. Y. Friedman, "Mivneh Sifruti be-Sugyot ha-
Bavli," *Divrei ha-Kongres ha-Olami ha-Shishi le-Madda'ei ha-Yahadut*, vol. 2
(Jerusalem: ha-Iggud ha-Olami le-Mada'ei ha-Yahadut, 1979), p. 402. There is
no mention of this in his father's *Mei Shiloah* (New York, 1984), "Likkutei
ha-Shas," p. 115a.

'מותיב מר זוטרא :...., מכלל דאור אורתא   12 '*מתיב* מר[10] זוטרא : (כריתות פ״א

הוא, "שמע[15]» מינה'!   מ״ג) ...שמע[11] מינה[11] אור אורתא הוא.

                                       שמע מינה'.

'תא שמע :...., שמע מינה: אור אורתא   13 'מתיבי[12] : (ברי' ב' זבחים נ״ו ב')...

הוא, שמע מן[ינה] !   אלמא אור אורתא הוא, שמע מינה'

'תא שמע]..., שמע מינה: א[ור אור]ת[א]   14 'תא שמע[13] : (ברי' ב' יומא פ״ז ב'[14])

הוא, שמע מינה'!   ...אלמא אור אורתא הוא, ש״מ[12] !

'תא שמע דתאנא דבי שמואל: לילי....   15 'ת״ש דתני דבי שמואל: לילי... אלמ'

שמע מינה: אור אורתא הוא –   אור אורתא הוא ! ?

<אלא[16]> בין רב הונא ובין רב יודא[16] דכולי עלמ' אור אורתא הוא, ולא פליגי' מר כי אתרי'
ומר כי אתרי'; באתרא דרב הונא קרו: נגהי, ובאתרי' דרב יהוד' קרו: לילי'!

מכל השינויים השונים[17], שיש בסוגייה זו בין שתי מסורות־הנוסח, הצגנו כאן רק את
החילוף שבין 'דיבורי־ההצעה' שלהן. שכן זה יש בו כדי לחשוף את יסודות
'הסידור' של סוגייה מורכבת זו.

מן נוסח 'הוולגאטה' ניכר, שאינו מקפיד על צורת המבנה של השמועה. מתוך חמשה
עשר פיסקי־ראיות' – ... אלמא אור יממא [או: אורתא] הוא' וכו' – פותחים שנים
עשרה, לפי רוב־רובן[18] של עדי נוסח זה, בדיבור־ההצעה : 'מתיבי'. לעומתן

---

10   בכ״י ש רב זוטרא.

11   כך ד״י + כ״א (= כ״י ע !) אבל כ״י מפקש (בלא לרשום כאן חילופים קלים) "אלמא". וכך גם
     בקטעי גניזה גא, גג !

12   בקטע גניזה גג נתחלפו המספרים 13–14. מס' 13 : ת״ש אור יום הכפורים וכו'. מס' 14 : ת״ש (!)
     דתניא : יכול יהא נאכל לאור לשלישי (!) כך גם להלן <הא> מדקאמ' : יכול יהא נאכל לאור
     לשלישי !) וכו'.   לכאורה נשמט מס' 13 : 'מיתיבי דתני' יכול יהא נאכל לאור לשלישי' וכו',
     ב*אביו* של קטע גג הושלמה בגליון וחזרה שלא במקומה – ובשביל זה אף הוצעה ת״ש [אך
     ר' להלן הסימן בהערה 18].

13   'מיתיבי' כ״י א ! הש' גג.

14   ב' נדה ח' ב'.

15   נוסף בגליון מימין, וכצ״ל !

16   חסר בנוסח 'לישנא אחרינא' (כ״י ע).

17   ר' הע' 5.

18   גם עדים מזרחיים אינם חורגים מן המסגרת. כגון קטע גניזה אוף : – עד כמה שיש לדון ממה
     שנישתמר הימנו (הוא מתחיל באמצע מס' 10). הוא מצע במס' 11, 13 מתיבי, ורק במס' 14–15
     תא שמע. בקטע גניזה נ״י יש התחלפות מעניינת :
     מס' 10 : <משאין עומד מלמד אור יכול סימן > מיתיבי אין משיאין וכו'.
     מס' 11 : 'ת״ש' [ומעל לתיבה זו נכתב (כנראה בידי הסופר עצמו ?) בין השורות 'מיתיבי'] : היה עומד
              ומקריב וכו'.
     מס' 12 : מתיב מר זוטרא וכו'.

נוסה הוולגאטה: לישנא אחרינא:

'קס"ד: דמאן דאמר "נגהי" – נגהי ממש,   'קא סלקא אדעתין: דמאן דאמ' "נוגהי" –
ומאן דאמר "לילי" – לילי ממש'.   צפרא, ומאן דאמ' "לילי"–אורתא'.

1 'מתיבי: (ברא' מד:ג) ...אלמא אור   'מותיבי:..., אלמא אור יממא הוא',...',
   יממא הוא...', נדחה.   נדחה.

2 'מתיבי: (שמואל ב כג:ד) ...אלמא   'מותיבי:..., אלמא אור יממא הוא...',
   אור יממא הוא...', נדחה.   נדחה.

3 'מתיבי: (ברא' א:ה) ...אלמא אור   'מותיבי:... — ⁸ — — — —⁸,',...',
   יממא הוא...', נדחה.   נדחה.

4 'מתיבי: (תלים קמח:ג) ...אלמא   'מותיבי:..., אלמא אור אורתא הוא...',
   אור אורתא הוא...', נדחה   נדחה.

5 'מתיבי: (איוב כד:יד) ...אלמא   'מותיבי:..., מכלל דאור איממא הוא...'
   אור יממא הוא...', נדחה.   נדחה.

6 'מתיבי: (איוב ג:ט) ...אלמא אור   'מותיבי:..., מכלל דאור איממא הוא...'
   יממא הוא...', נדחה.   נדחה.

7 'מתיבי: (תלים קלט:יא) ...אלמא   'מותיבי:..., מכלל דאור איממא הוא...',
   אור יממא הוא...', נדחה.   נדחה.

8 'מתיבי: (פס' פ"א מ"ג) ...אלמא   'תא שמע:..., מכלל דאור אורתא הוא,
   אור אורתא הוא, ש"מ'!   שמע מינה'!

9 'מתיבי⁶:(~תוס' פס' פ"ג י"ג)   'תא שמע:⁹..., מכלל דאור... אורתא
   ...אלמא אור אורתא הוא,...',   הוא,..., ...', נדחה.
   נדחה.

10 'מתיבי: (ברי' ב' ר"ה כ"ב ב')   'תא שמע:..., אלמא אור אורתא הוא,
   ...אלמא אור אורתא הוא, ש"מ'!   שמע מינה'!

11 'מתיבי: (ברי' ב' זבחים י"ט ב')   'תא שמע:..., שמע מינה: אור איממא
   — — — — נדחה⁷.   הוא,...', נדחה.

---

6 תא שמע ש ק"ה ובגליון משמאל: נ"א: מתיבי. [ור' להלן הע' 22—21].

7 מספר זה קצר ביותר: בנוסח הוולגאטה בכל העדים נקטע אפילו ניסוח ה'תשובה': "אלמא אור
   יממא הוא" (או כיו"ב) ואילו הדחייה חתוכה וקצרה! (הינו: 'אורה' ודאי יממא).

8 מס' 3 נתקטע הרבה בכ"י ע: 'מותיבי: ויקרא אלהים לאור יום, למאיר ובא קראו יום' הינו:
   מותיבי: ויקרא אלהים לאור יום ‹אלמא אור יממא הוא. הכי קאמ':› למאיר ובא קראו יום!

9 בכ"י עת כתובה ברייתא זו להלן נז, ב שלא במקומה ובקיטוע, סימן שתוספת היא זו מתוך
   התוספתא, כסיום לתלמוד שעל פ"ד מ"ז (במקום זה שעל מ"ה סופה: 'ביהוד' היו עושים מלאכה
   בערבי פסחים' וכו') אבל דווקא כלשונה של תוספתא פס' פ"ג י"ג (הוצ' ליברמן עמ' 155 ש' 58
   ואילך): "תנו רבנן: מאימתי ארבעה עשר אסור במלאכה? ר' אליעזר בן יעקב אומר: מאור ארבעה
   עשר. ר' יהודה אומ': משעת הנץ החמה. אמ' לו ר' אליעזר בן יעקב: היכן מציגו יום אחד שמקצתו
   מותר בעשיית מלאכה ומקצתו אסור' וכו'.

In this case the arrangement seems totally aesthetic, and as such was totally ignored by the commentators.[110] At times, however, such symmetrical literary arrangements seem to imply more than they are meant to, and cause the *Rishonim* no end of trouble.

Structural Considerations that Bear on Halakhic Interpretation

My next example is one in which recognition of the structure of the *sugya* has important consequences for the proper understanding of its flow of argumentation. The opening *sugya* of *Perek ha-Ishah Rabbah, Yevamot* 87b–88a, deals with the source of the principle that the testimony of one witness can in certain circumstances be accepted in matters of *issur ve-heter*. The case involves a woman whose husband has gone abroad and disappeared. A single witness comes to court and claims that the woman's husband is dead. The *Gemara* concludes that such testimony may be accepted; the question is why. The *sugya* makes several attempts to determine that source, all of which come to naught, at which point it concludes that since the case is that of a woman who may ultimately be faced with the catastrophe of losing both her first husband, presumed dead until now, her second husband, whom she will now have to leave, and to have her children by him declared *mamzerim* (not to mention losing her *ketubah*)—we treat her leniently. The conclusion of the *sugya* runs:

> Rav Zera said: Because of the severity with which you deal with her in the end, you deal leniently with her at the start.
> Let him not deal leniently or severely!
> The Rabbanan deal leniently with her because of her [state of] *iggun*.

As Avraham Weiss pointed out, the *sugya* does not in the end answer the question it posed at the start. The terms of the investigation involve the essential question of whether this rule (of accepting the testimony of one witness in such cases) is either of biblical or rabbinic[111] origin.[112]

---

[111]It is true that the question as it now stands is posed as *mi-de-oraita minalan*, but since the discussion involves tannaitic texts this reading is difficult to maintain.

[112]See A. Weiss, *Al ha-Yetzirah ha-Sifrutit shel ha-Amora'im* (New York: Horeb, 1961–1962), pp. 34–40; and S. Y. Friedman, "Perek ha-Ishah Rabbah ba-Bavli, be-Tzeruf Mavo Kelali al Derekh Heker ha-Sugya'," in H. Z. Dimitrovski, *Mehkarim u-Mekorot* I, (New York), pp. 275–441; his analysis of this *sugya* is on pp. 323–330. Friedman concludes that the word *mi-de-Oraita* is Geonic.

But in the end the answer seems to be that it is rabbinic (Rabbanan). And, indeed, the *Rishonim* disagree about the matter. Rabbi Aharon Halevi, cited in *Nimmukei Yosef* and *Tosafot Yeshanim*, holds it to be of biblical origin, for halakhic reasons, while Rashi, the Meiri, and Ri[113] take it (for different reasons) as rabbinic, as the text itself seems to indicate.

The *sugya* is highly organized, and its structure may be illustrated diagramatically.[114]

הסוגיא הראשונה: עד אחד נאמן (פז ע"ב – פח ע"א)

מדקתני . . . אלמא עד אחד מהימן[1]

ותנן נמי הוחזקו . . . אלמא עד אחד מהימן

ותנן נמי עד אחד אומר אכלת חלב . . . אלמא עד אחד מהימן

א. מדאורייתא מנא לן: דתניא או הודע . . . ש"מ עד אחד נאמן

— וממאי משום דמהימן, דלמא משום דקא שתיק . . . תדע דקתני סיפא . . .

ב. אלא סברא היא, מידי דהוה אחתיכה ספק של חלב ספק של שומן ואתא עד אחד . . . דמהימן

— מי דמי . . . הא . . . הא לא דמיא אלא לחתיכה דודאי חלב . . . דלא מהימן. מי דמי התם אפי' אתו בי מאה לא מהימני, הכא כיון דכי אתו ביתרי מהימני, חד נמי ליהימני', מידי דהוה אטבל דהוה אטבל הקדש וקונמות

   (1)   האי טבל היכי דמי . . .

   (2)   הקדש נמי . . .

   (3)   קונמות נמי . . .

ג. אלא[2] אמר ר' זירא מתוך חומר שהחמרת עליה בסופה הקלת עליה בתחלתה[3]

— ולא[4] ליחמיר ולא ליקיל

משום[5] עיגונא אקילו בה רבנן.

---

[113]See Tosafot 88a, s.v. *mitokh*, and 89b, s.v. *kevan*; he meets Ra'ah's objection re *akirat davar min ha-Torah* by suggesting that the Rabbis may do so in cases closely analogous to one in which the Torah permits the particular course

1. בד"ח: נאמן.

2. כ"ה בכי"ו, כי"מ, כי"ל, כי"א, כימ"ב, וכ"ה בנמקי יוסף ובחדושי הריטב"א. בד' ליתא
   תיבת "אלא".

3. כ"ה בכי"ו. כי"ל, כי"א, כימ"ב וכי"מ. בד"פ: בתחלה.

4. כ"ה בכי"ל, כי"א, כי"ו, כי"מ, וכימ"ב; בד"פ: לא.

5. בכי"מ כימ"ב וכי"ל: אלא משום, וראה מאירי, עמ' 320. וכ"ה "אלא משום" ברשב"א
   ובנמקי יוסף, ובפירוש ר' אברהם מן ההר בשם "אית [דגרסי]", ומסיים: "והכל אחד" (עמ'
   רי). והשוה כללי התלמוד לר' בצלאל אשכנזי, ספר לדוד צבי, סי' 59. אולם ר"י קולון כתב
   "בשום ספר' לא גרס אלא" (שו"ת מהרי"ק, שרש לב, הראשון, ועיי"ש לדעתו מה נפקא
   מינה בדבר).

Thus the *sugya* may be divided into three sub-*sugyot*, each dealing with
one possible solution to the problem posed: either the rule is biblical,
rabbinic, or the product of *sevarah*. Each of these possibilities is provided
with a three-step proof, but the proofs of the first two sub-*sugyot* are refuted, while the third is hardly subjected to much analysis or discussion.

The *sugya* in its current form has thus been arranged as an introduction to Rav Zera's comment, and some of its constituent elements can
be traced to other parts of Shas.[115]

The subordinate character of the analysis can be illustrated in another
way; not only is Rav Zera's *memra* accepted without much ado, but the
earlier arguments seem to have be selected only to be refuted. Why, we
may wonder, should proof I(1), which can be so easily refuted, be proposed altogether?[116] On the other hand, why have better proofs, available elsewhere in Shas, not been proposed?[117]

However, as Friedman points out, once the literary character of the
sugyah is recognized, the halakhic problems it engenders assume a different character. This *sugya* is thus a more elaborate example of the rule
cited above in the name of *Tosafot Rabbenu Peretz: orheih de-Talmuda
hu lehavi tehillah re'ayah she-yesh lidhot*, the Talmud's way is first to bring
a proof that can easily be refuted.

---

of action (*davar domeh*), or, to put in another way, *be-davar she-yesh ketzat taam
u-semakh lo hashiv oker davar min ha-Torah*, it is permitted.

[114]The diagram is based on one prepared by S. Y. Friedman, "Perek," p. 323.

[115]See the analyses cited in n. 107.

[116]See Weiss, pp. 38–39.

[117]Friedman, "Perek," p. 327; see *Sotah* 2a, 31b, and 47b.

It is noteworthy—and typical—that here, too, there is no halakhic deficit incurred by the fact that the *Rishonim* did not take the literary nature of the *sugya* into account, at least not explicitly. The debate on the halakhic basis of *ed ehad ne'eman be-issurim* was conducted on halakhic grounds, as well it should be.

That being the case, the *Rishonim* could hardly ignore the halakhic difficulties noted above, and others besides. In particular, the great divide of the absolute invalidity of one witness for matters concerning a woman's personal status (*davar shebi-ervah*) as contrasted with less severe prohibitions for which one witness may sometimes suffice. Thus, the arguments attempted from *tevel*, *hekdesh*, and *konamot* in the last half of the *sugya* seem totally irrelevant to the issue at hand. These cannot serve as a precedent for releasing a woman from her marital ties on the testimony of one witness. Why then does the *sugya* include them?

The Ramban faces this issue squarely, and suggests that these are "*she'elot be-alma*"—merely questions that raise a point of interest, rather than offering pertinent arguments, or as he writes, "*hahi sugya le-hagdil Torah u-le-haadirah*,"[118] "this *sugyah* [was constructed merely] to enlarge and magnify Torah," that is, to extend the discussion without regard to halakhic necessities in the here and now. And the Ramban proceeds to ignore this *sugya* in his halakhic discussion of the issue of the status of the testimony of one witness in matters of *issura* anent *Hullin* 10b.

On the other hand, Rashba in his *hiddushim* to Hulin strenuously objects (without mentioning the Ramban by name!) to this understanding of this *sugya*. "Did they then debate this issue for no reason, since [this debate has] no practical effect in halakhic decision-making? Even though I have seen the greatest among the commentators explain [this *sugya*] in this way, it is not clear in my eyes, since this is not the way of the Talmud."[119] And

---

[118]See *Hiddushei ha-Ramban al kol Masekhet Hullin*, ed. S. Z. Reichman (Bronx, NY, 1955), col. 30a. The phrase, which appears in approximately this form in Isaiah 42:21 appears in *Hullin* 66b, and entered rabbinic literature from there.

[119]See *Hiddushei Ha-Rashba le-Rabbenu Shelomo b'R Avraham Adret: Masekhet Yebamot*, ed. Shmuel Dickman (Jerusalem: Mosad Harav Kook, 1989), cols. 479–480: "*Atu bikhdi shakli ve-tari bah kevan de-la nafka lan minah midi, ve-af al pi she-ra'iti le-Gedolei ha-Mefarshim she-pershu ke-inyan zeh eino mehuvvar be-einai she-ein zeh shitat ha-Talmud.*" Later still he comments, "*ve-ein ha-taam ha-zeh maspik be-einai,*" "this reason is not sufficient in my eyes" (col. 480).

indeed, in his comments to this *sugya*, the Rashba struggles mightily to impart halakhic significance to each part of this difficult *sugya*.

The disagreement may be seen as one regarding the nature of Shas itself, as the Rashba himself notes, since he denies that presenting "*she'elot be-alma*" is the way of the Talmud. The Ramban however uses this exegetical principle elsewhere in his *hiddushim*, and clearly sees the essentially nonhalakhic nature of other ostensibly halakhic discussions.[120] And though the Ramban does not explicitly discuss the tripartite division of the *sugya*, he is keenly aware of distinction between proofs and mere discussion, not only in his discussion of the last part of the *sugyah*, but also in his analysis of the other part, and particularly the introduction.

Thus an awareness of the structure of this *sugya*, and others, adds to our appreciation and understanding of the text, even when it does not add to our halakhic knowledge. In this case, as in others, it serves to explain some of the difficulties a purely halakhic interpretation encounters; in this case, these difficulties essentially reduced this *sugya*, but for its conclusion, to a cipher that had little if any influence on the subsequent course of halakhic determination. As noted above, the *Rishonim* distinguished between weak and strong arguments; the aesthetic aspects of the text often explain the existence of the former.

The Preference for Threes

The discussion above has alerted us to the importance of the number three as a structural element in some *sugyot*. This preference for a division into threes,[121] where the first two attempts are unsuccessful, while the third is ac-

---

[120]See his comments on *Shevuot* 24b, or *Avodah Zarah* 52a (ed. Chavel, col. 208).

[121]Note that the *sugya* examined in section 1 (*Shabbat* 100b) presented three suggestions for the *tzerikhuta*. In that case it does not seem that Rav Ashi's proposal was considered superior to the others.

Jewish learning has long appreciated the significance of the number three. Rabbenu Tam went so far as to opine that *rov divrei Hakhamim meshullashin* (*Sefer ha-Yashar*, ed. Schlesinger, p. 71). But its use in determining the make-up structural elements of compositions, large and small, has in general been ignored. For a discussion of the significance of this division into threes, see S. Y. Friedman, "Al Derekh Heker ha-Sugya," pp. 316–319, and the literature cited there; see especially p. 318, n. 132, and p. 329 n. 24 and text; see also his "Mivneh Sifruti be-Sugyot ha-Bavli," pp. 387–402.

cepted, is recognized by the *Rishonim*, though fitfully. More important, this method of analysis never achieved popularity; omnisignificant, halakhic solutions were always preferred, even when they encountered difficulties.

This preference for division into threes as an organizing principle applies both on the macro and micro level, as our analysis of *Yevamot* 87b–88a demonstrated. This preference operates outside the sugyatic form, as well. For example, the Bavli contains thirty-four[122] collections of three halakhic deductions introduced by the phrase *shema minah telat*, but only four cases of *tartei shema'it minah*.[123] This is not because three deductions are more common than two. Indeed, there are instances in which two deductions are listed, but not marked by an introductory phrase.[124] Clearly, and not surprisingly, Babylonian rabbinic culture evinced a strong preference for division or collation by threes.

On occasion this preference overcomes halakhic considerations. Thus, two of the three deductions of Rav Huna b. Rav Joshua in *Pesahim* 98a are not independent statements, and thus the three can be reduced to two.[125] The opposite also occurs; *Bava Batra* 90b contains four deduc-

---

[122]Actually, there are twenty-seven cases and seven duplicates. The cases are: *Berakhot* 27a, *Shabbat* 40b, *Eruvin* 10a, 101b, *Pesahim* 4a (=*Mo'ed Katan* 20b), 5b, 78a (=*Kiddushin* 7b, *Zevahim* 12a [*Temurah* 26b, *Keritot* 27a]), 107a, *Bezah* 35b, *Mo'ed Katan* 16a, 18a, *Yevamot* 46b, *Ketuvot* 21b, 90b, *Nedarim* 7b, 8b, *Kiddushin* 46a, 52a, *Bava Metzia* 63a, *Bava Batra* 24a, 90b (=*Menahot* 77a, *Bekhorot* 5b), *Sanhedrin* 19a, *Avodah Zarah* 43a, *Zevahim* 78a, *Menahot* 42b, *Hullin* 106a, *Niddah* 30a.

[123]*Pesahim* 91a, *Bava Kamma* 66a, 94a, *Menahot* 99a.

[124]See *Pesahim* 77b.

However, *Yoma* 25a, where Abaye makes two deductions from a *baraita*, is not altogether certain, since it may be attributed to Abaye's stylistic preference; as it happens, there is no other case of Abaye's use of the phrase on his own (in contrast, three attestations of Rava's use of the phrase exist: *Pesahim* 5b, *Kiddushin* 46a, *Bava Batra* 24a). Likewise, though *Menahot* 42b is based on a query Abaye made of Rav Samuel b. Rav Judah, the deductions in the form we have them are anonymous, though they predate Rav Ashi. Again, though Abaye uses the phrase in *Eruvin* 10a, he does so in reminding Rabbi Joseph of his own earlier statement; finally, his son Rav Bibi's use of the phrase in *Eruvin* 101b tells us nothing about his father's preferences.

[125]See Tosafot s.v. *u-shema minah yesh dihui be-damim*, where Ri notes that *dihui me-ikaro hevei dihui* is coeval with *yesh dihui be-damim*. In the end he has to produce an unlikely *uqimta* to justify the inclusion of both deductions, one that

tions, but two are combined to reduce the number to three.[126] As David W. Halivni puts it, "[the phrase] *shema^c minah telat* became a formula (*melitzah*) that was used even when [applied to a case] in which there were not exactly three [deductions]. There is no need to emend the passage here; if there are not exactly three, there certainly are close to three [deductions]."[127]

THE COST OF OMNISIGNIFICANCE

We pay a price for omnisignificance; our millennia-long obsession with it has caused us to lose our appreciation of *peshat* and its parameters. We

---

does not fit the case in *Pesahim*; see also Tosafot *Kiddushin* 7b, s.v. *shema minah*, where the same collection appears, but anonymously, and with a different *ukimta* proposed. Rabbenu Hananel *ad Pesah'im* 98a (ed. Metzger, p. 210) explains the matter differently; he apparently does not hold that the rubric requires independent deductions.

Similar cases occur in *Ketuvot* 21b (see Tosafot s.v. *u-shema minah*) and *Bava Batra* 24a (see Tosafot s.v. *u-shema minah*).

D. W. Halivni discusses this phenomenon in his analysis of *Nedarim* 8b (*Meqorot u-Mesorot*, Nashim [Tel Aviv: Devir, 1968], pp. 271–272) where one deduction is artificially divided into two. However, Halivni asserts that *Nedarim* 8b is a unique occurence (but see his comment re *Berakhot* 27a and *Pesahim* 4a. It seems to me that he defines this artificiality too narrowly).

[126]Similarly, see *Niddah* 30a, and Tosafot ad loc., s.v. *shema minah telat*, where Tosafot raises the possibility of a fourth deduction, but Rabbenu Tam concludes that it is not cited because it is too obvious (*"peshita leh leha-Shas"*). In the light of the evidence presented here, we may classify Rabbenu Tam's solution as omnisignificantly inclined, the upshot being that this collection was put together after the decision was made regarding Abaye's *ye'al kegam* opinions. Rabbenu Tam's suggestion serves to tighten Shas' cohesion.

In contrast, see *Menahot* 42b, where two deductions seem to have been raised to three. Indeed, the first and third deductions are so close in meaning and phraseology as to have constituted a lower critical problem for the *Aharonim*; see *Tzo'n Kodashim* ad loc., and the first two constituted a problem for the late *Amora'im*, and Rav Ashi concluded that they were not at all independent deductions, but that the second gives the reason for the first (*"mah taam"*).

[127]Halivni, *Mekorot U-Mesorots*, p. 272. See Irwin H. Haut, *The Talmud As Law or Literature*, pp. 30–34, where he strenuously defends a halakhic interpre-

have become locksmiths with but one key, a master key for, say, all Yale locks, but one that cannot deal with those of other manufacturers. At best, this makes us blind to aspects of the text we are bound to study, and thus render them less meaningful. At worst, by reading out of context, we misread texts without realizing it. Now, misreading is a species of creative reinterpretation, but, I submit, the difference inheres in precisely this point: creative reinterpretation is conscious; misreading is unknowing and misguided.

This misreading most often occurs in *Tanakh* because commentators—especially *Aharonim*—ignore the nature of the text. Thus poetic or narrative texts are treated no differently from halakhic ones. This is not the place to go into the vexed problem of the meaning of parallelism in biblical poetry, a matter that has been the subject of increasing debate in the last few years,[128] but clearly the more we ignore form-critical aspects of the texts we deal with, the more we are likely to misread them, to take them out of context. Reading poetry as a legal brief, or a legal brief as pure narrative, will not aid our understanding of either. Admittedly, this is a greater problem in *Tanakh*, where the variety of forms and *genres* is far greater than we meet with in *Torah she-be'al peh*, but there are such cases there, too, especially in aggadic material.

The "Rabbah b. Bar Hanna stories" in *Bava Batra* 73af are a case in point. Of all the complex and esoteric explanations that have been offered for these outwardly seeming "tall tales," no mainstream traditional commentator, to my knowledge, has considered that these stories were

---

tation of *Pesahim* 4a. In the light of the data presented here, which neither Halivni nor Haut adduced, it would seem that the literary nature of this phrase cannot seriously be in doubt.

[128]A partial bibliography would include Rabbi Alter, *The Art of Biblical Poetry* (New York: Basic Books, 1985); E. R. Follis, *Directions in Biblical Poetry* (Sheffield, *Journal for the Study of Old Testament Supplementary Series* 40, 1987); A. Berlin, *The Dynamics of Biblical Parallelism* (Bloomington: Indiana University Press, 1985); J. L. Kugel, *The Idea of Biblical Poetry: Parallelism and Its History* (New Haven: Yale University Press, 1981); D. Pardee, *Ugaritic and Hebrew Poetic Parallelism: A Trial Cut (ᶜnt I and Proverbs 2)* (Leiden: E. J. Brill, 1988); T. Collins, *Line-forms in Hebrew Poetry* (Rome: Biblical Institute Press, 1978); S. A. Geller, *Parallelism in Early Biblical Poetry* (Chico, CA: Scholars Press, 1979); M. O'Connor, *Hebrew Verse Structure* (Winona Lake, WS: Eisenbrauns, 1980).

meant to be taken as read. The cultural gap betwen Amoraic Babylonia, and its canons of polite discourse, and those of sixteenth-century Central Europe or nineteenth-century Baghdad, has been taken as nil. And yet Shas is full of stories that require latter-day apologetical interpretations. Again, a *peshat*-oriented commentary, uncomfortable as we might find it, would give us an index of our distance from the cultural standards of our forebears.[129]

This is not to say that even a partial literary approach is without its problems. For such a recognition brings with it a new perception of the nature of the Bavli. It is one thing to recognize the existence of structures alongside halakhic considerations, or where there are no halakhic ramifications, as in our analysis of *Pesahim* 2a-3a; when we deal with *sugyot* that the *Rishonim* took as purely halakhic, and find that aesthetic considerations have affected the redaction of the text, our perception of the Bavli as a legal work must change. And, as I have stressed throughout this chapter, Jewish learning has always proceeded in the halakhic direction.

I offer no solution, nor is it my place to do so. If, as seems likely,[130] the aesthetic element in the formation of *sugyot* must be factored in to achieve a proper understanding of their true dynamic, we ignore it to our peril, as we have done, until very recently, in Bible. The difference is that biblical interpretation does not have the same quality of urgency for Orthodox Jews that halakhic discussion does.[131] By right, such considerations vis à vis Talmud ought to be more difficult to ignore, but given the momentum of current and past methodologies, I suspect that the points I have raised will not make much headway, except among those whose inborn literary sense makes such patterns compelling.

---

[129]For an excellent example of the opportunities that some aggadic passages provide for understanding that gulf and the socioreligious tensions that lie behind our talmudic texts, see Daniel Sperber, "On the Unfortunate Adventures of Rav Kahana: A Passage of Saboraic Polemic from Sasanian Persia," in Shaul Shaked, *Irano-Judaica: Studies Relating to Jewish Contacts with Persian Culture throughout the Ages* (Jerusalem: Ben-Zvi Institute, 1982), pp. 83–100. This area of scholarship has recently been enriched by a number of important books and studies, but they lie beyond the scope of this already overlong paper.

[130]The evidence of this has been steadily accumulating and does not seem likely to stop.

[131]See my review of *Sinai and Zion* in *Tradition* 24 (1989): 99–104, especially 99–100.

V

In a sense our discussion up to now has concerned what might be termed matters of taste—aesthetic considerations—or the importance of redactional and literary questions as opposed to halakhic ones, though I hope to have shown that these can be closely intertwined at times. Nevertheless, *pesak halakhah* has its own canons of proof and evidence, and there is no reason that aesthetically oriented methodologies should affect practical or even theoretical *halakhah*. I would be remiss if I did not at least devote a little space to one area of study that has ever and anon been considered dangerous to tradition.

INTELLECTUAL HISTORY

Because the Academy has for a century placed a supreme value on history as the means to a true understanding of texts and cultural phenomena, questions of redaction and/or authorship have achieved major importance. Textual understanding in this view is to be gained only by viewing the text under study in its *context*. For reasons that lie within the province of the sociology of knowledge, context has nearly always meant *historical* context. One consequence of this view is that academic study tends to emphasize differences—between texts and within texts— in the attempt to trace the *development* of the text and the ideas it contains. Thus it is most likely to clash with traditional learning in matters that flow from this emphasis, since traditional scholarship has an entirely different agenda, one which tends to minimize dissension[132] and multiply legal distinctions, one which sees Torah *sub specie aeternitatis*, and so all but denies the applicability of the intellectual history to Torah.

One index of the homogenization process is that individual *Tanna'im* and *Amora'im* often lose their individuality in our tendency to look at Shas as one piece. This applies not only to individual sages, but to texts as well. One of the most delicate areas in which few Orthodox scholars care to tread is that of historical development and cultural differentiation.[133] For a century and more, Western humanistic scholarship has

---

[132]See Rashi *Ketubot* 57a, s.v. *ha qa-mashma^c lan*.

[133]Rav Yitzhak Hutner draws an explicit connection between the fear of studying Yerushalmi without a sure guide and that of studying history; see his

emphasized the key role of history and historical development in understanding the nature of any social institution.[134] Since all Torah is, as noted above, *sub specie aeternitatis*, we tend to read traditional texts in light of the whole of tradition, and thus lose the flavor of each time and text. More precisely, since the triumph of the Bavli, we read all texts in the light of normative *Torah she-be'al peh*, the Bavli. Once again, aside from missing many of the nuances of texts outside the Bavli, and the contribution to the pluralism of Torah, we also lose another element of *peshat*. For example, even in the matter of a seemingly panrabbinic subject such as theodicy, a careful examination of Babylonian sources and those of Eretz Israel will indicate that there is indeed a difference between the approaches of the two Talmuds.[135]

Generally speaking, the *Tanna'im* link the the sufferings of the righteous to some spiritual shortcoming or to the presence of the wicked in this world, and are disinclined, at least as portrayed in the surviving material, to allow for exceptions to the rule of "measure for measure."[136] Amoraic sources in *Eretz Yisrael* do not go much beyond the tannaitic response, essentially limiting such occurrences to isolated instances.[137] The one notable exception is the matter of vicarious atonement and collective retribution, where *Genesis Rabbah* and other homiletical *midrashim*[138]—but apparently not the Yerushalmi—admit to a certain inequitable distribution of suffering.

Pahad Yitzhak: Iggerot u-Mikhtavim, n. 86. A partial translation is provided in my "History, Pure and Impure," *Jewish Action* 47:1 (5747): 17–20.

[134]See Robert A. Oded, Jr., *The Bible without Theology: The Theological Tradition and Alternatives to It* (San Francisco: Harper & Row, 1987), pp. 1–39, for an account of this obsession with history and historical development.

[135]See my "The Suffering of the Righteous in Palestinian and Babylonian Sources," *JQR* 80 (1991): 315–339.

[136]See for now the discussion in E. E. Urbach, *Hazal: Emunot ve-De'ot* (Jerusalem: Magnes, 1978), pp. 227–253, 428–454; and see A. Aderet, *Me-Hurban li-Tekumah: Derekh Yavneh be-Shikkum ha-Umah* (Jerusalem: Magnes, 1990), pp. 149–157, especially his observation on p. 152; see my "Righteousness As Its Own Reward," sect. 2, and compare Urbach, p. 237.

[137]An exception is the marked Palestinian concern to explain the fact that although death was brought into the world by sin, the righteous suffer that penalty as well as the wicked; see A. Marmorstein, *The Doctrine of Merits in Old Rabbinical Literature* (reprint, New York, 1968); pp. 67–70.

[138]See in particular the material on Genesis 18 collected in *Genesis Rabbah*

A number of scattered but significant *sugyot* in the Bavli, however, propound the view that suffering in its widest sense (including poverty, lack or loss of children, and the like) may be undeserved, and this for reasons having nothing to do with collective retribution or vicarious atonement. Suffering may be ascribed to the effects of unfocused divine anger,[139] the exigencies of historical necessity,[140] the hazards of everyday life,[141] astrological circumstance,[142] the sin of Adam and Eve,[143] and more.

How did this difference come about? The key figure in the introduction into rabbinic circles of this new approach to the age-old problem of theodicy seems to have been Rava. Rava's name[144] recurs over and over in *sugyot* that tend to limit the operation of Divine providence, on the one hand, and the applicability of a measure for measure understanding of providence. For example, it is he who holds to the principle of *ein*

49; see J. Theodor and Ch. Albeck, *Midrash Bereshit Rabbah*, 2nd ed. (Jerusalem, 1965), pp. 496ff.

[139]*Berakhot* 7a, *Avodah Zarah* 4a–b, *Sanhedrin* 105b; dealt with these *sugyot* in detail in "'Is There Then Anger Before the Holy One?' Aspects of the Theology of the *Stam*," AJS Twenty-First Annual Conference, December 19, 1989.

[140]*Taanit* 5b.

[141]*Kiddushin* 39b; see "Righteousness As Its Own Reward: An Inquiry into the Theologies of the Stam," *Proceedings of the American Academy for Jewish Research* 57 (1991), section 3.

[142]*Hagigah* 28a; see "Righteousness As Its Own Reward," sec. 6. I hope to deal with this further in "The Image and Function of Death in Babylonian Rabbinical Literature," D.v., scheduled for delivery at the 1991 AAR/SBL Annual Meeting, November 23–26, 1991.

[143]*Shabbat* 55b; see "Righteousness as Its Own Reward," sec. 2.

[144]Even in the manuscripts. The question of the reliability of attributions in rabbinic literature has been a matter of dispute for the past decade; see J. Neusner, *Judaism: The Evidence of the Mishnah* Chicago: University of Chicago Press, 1981. pp. 15–22; J. Neusner and A. J. Avery-Peck, "The Quest for the Historical Hillel," in *Formative Judaism: Religious, Historical and Literary Studies*, ed. J. Neusner (Chico, CA, 1982), pp. 49–51, 62–63. These strictures do not apply to our case, where an unusual, not to say controversial, opinion is consistently attributed to one Amora in a variety of settings, and the manuscript evidence is fairly consistent. See D. W. Halivni, "*Sefekei de-Gavrei*," *PAAJR* 46–47 (1979–1980), pp. 67–83 [Hebrew section].

somekhin al ha-nes, "one does not rely on a miracle," in his dispute with Abaye regarding the opening of the Temple doors (*Pesahim* 64b); it is he who modifies Rav Joseph's more expansive formulation of the role of Torah study in protecting the one occupied from misfortune. Rava points to the cases of Doeg and Ahitophel,[145] the classic rabbinic instances of scholars come to a bad end, and he proposes that

> Torah protects [one from misfortune] and rescues [one from the evil incli-
> nation] when one is occupied in its study; when one is not occupied with it,
> it protects but does not rescue.[146] Mitzvot protect one [from misfortune]
> whether he is actively occupied with them or not, but they certainly do not
> rescue him [from the evil intention].[147]

Bava Kamma 60a–b establishes the existence of an *ʿidan ritha,* a time of plague, famine, or other communal misfortune, during which the righ-

---

[145]Note that Rabbi Ammi is supposed to have noted that Ahitophel did not die before he had lost all his knowledge of Torah (*Bava Batra* 106b)!

[146]According to *Berakhot* 5a, "whoever engages in Torah study—sufferings are kept from him." This dictum, attributed to Resh Laqish, is reworked by his colleague Rabbi Yohanan as follows: "If one has the opportunity to study Torah and does not study it, the Holy One, blessed be He, brings disfiguring diseases on him to stir him up." It is significant that Rabbi Yohanan is quoted (*ibid.*) as asserting that even sufferings that interfere with Torah study and prayer may yet be considered "sufferings of love" (suffering that is not occasioned by sin but demonstrate God's concern for the sufferer's spiritual well-being; see E. E. Urbach, *Hazal,* p. 394) in contrast to the view of others (Rav Jacob b. Idi and Rav Aha b. Hanina) that chronic or disabling illness cannot be considered "sufferings of love." As Rav Huna is reported as having stated a generation later, "If the Holy One, blessed be He, is pleased with someone, He crushes him with sufferings."

Nevertheless, it is clear that mainstream rabbinic opinion (to the extent to which it can be determined from the Bavli) held that sufferings could be warded off by Torah study or other *mitzvot.* And, on the other hand, the Rabbis could not deny the evidence of their senses: even scholars of note fall victim to disease and suffering. This question falls outside the area of the present summary, which is primarily concerned with communal suffering in times of divine anger: plague, war, famine, and the like.

[147]*Sotah* 21a.

teous and wicked suffer alike.[148] The *sugya* contains advice, attributed to Rava,[149] to close one's windows in time of plague—not bad advice at all, but not quite in the same category as fasting, prayer, donating charity, and so forth. In *Mo'ed Katan* 28a, Rava concludes, based again on an argument from experience, in this case the lives of Rabbah and Rav Hisda, that "[length] of life, children, and sustenance do not depend on [one's] merit, but on *mazzal*."[150] In essence, then, merit has no part, or, perhaps, little part, in determining the basic circumstances of one's life.

---

[148]See my "When Permission is Given: Aspects of Divine Providence," *Tradition* 24:4 (Summer, 1989): 24–45. Rav Joseph's espousal of the view of the *Mekilta* does not contradict his insistence—as interpreted by the *stam*—in *Ketubot* 30a–b that, though the four modes of execution by a human court have ceased, God carries them out by other, natural means. bB. Q. 60a refers to communal catastrophe; bKet 30a–b to individual sin and punishment.

Whether this *baraita* is original to the Mekilta is doubtful, since it occurs in no other Palestinian source, and is one of a number of such teachings that the Bavli attributes to Rabbi Joseph; see E. Z. Melammed, *Halachic Midrashim of the Tannaim in the Babylonian Talmud* [Hebrew], 2nd ed. (Jerusalem, 1988), pp. 87–88; and my "Suffering of the Righteous," p. 339, n. 62, and associated text.

Finally, it is likely that the protection afforded by Torah study and the performance of *mitzvot*, in Rav Joseph's view (*Sotah* 21a), does not apply to cases of *idan ritha*.

[149]So in all manuscripts and witnesses but for *Aggadot Ha-Talmud*, which reads Rabbah; see *Dikdukei Soferim ad loc.*, n. *tet*.

[150]See Tosafot ad loc., *Rosh Hashanah* 18a (=*Yevamot* 105a) and Tosafot, *ad loc.*, s.v. *Rava va-Abaye*. The Talmud there explains Rabbah's short lifespan as stemming from his descent from the high priest Eli (see 1 Samuel 3:14). The *stam* there counterposes Rabbah and Abaye; the former, who engaged primarily (or exclusively) in Torah study, lived forty years, while Abaye, who devoted himself both to Torah study and good works (*gemilut hasadim*), lived sixty years. According to Tosafot in *Yevamot*, Rava holds, like Rabbah, that Torah study alone provides atonement, but this contradicts the information provided by *Sanhedrin* 98b, not to mention *Mo'ed Katan* 28a, in which Rava attributes Rabbah's short life span to his *mazzal* (though it might be argued that it was his bad luck to be born a descendant of Eli!). Tosafot in *Rosh Hashanah* takes this problem into account, and suggests that while Rabbah did engage in good works, Abaye did more in this regard.

Rava's view apparently struck root, and I have elsewhere traced its influence on a number of anonymous *sugyot* or anonymous interpolations in earlier *sugyot*.[151]

What historical or cultural factors predisposed Babylonian scholars to accept such a view when those in *Eretz Yisrael* did not must for the moment remain a matter of speculation, though the Babylonian ambience, with its ancient fatalism, cannot be ruled out as a factor.[152]

At any rate, once we cease viewing the Bavli as a unitary document that sustains only those opinions that later generations deemed normative, we will notice patterns that will add to our understanding not only of *Torah she-be'al peh*, but of our lives in God's world as well.

Again, because of the idea that Torah is *sub specie aeternitatis*, a certain chronological homogenization has taken place, with later *hiddushim* read back into texts that did not originally contain the idea.[153] In part,

---

As to the tradition itself, note that Rabbah and Rav Hisda are classified as "absolutely righteous" men because their prayers for rain were immediately effective (*Mo'ed Katan* 28a); according to *Taanit* 24a, however, Rabbah once called for rain unsuccessfully and lamented that he and his generation, though their study of the Mishnah was more extensive, were not as worthy as the second generation Rav Judah [b. Ezekiel], a statement otherwise attributed to Abaye in *Berakhot* 20a. It would seem that the variant Rava (see *Dikdukei Soferim* ad loc., pp. 144–145 n. *lamed*) is to be preferred. Then again, these may be conflicting traditions.

[151]See my "Righteousness as Its Own Reward."

[152]I hope to return to this matter at a later date; for now, see Thorkild Jacobsen's essay, "Ancient Mesopotamian Religion: The Central Concerns," reprinted in his collection, *Toward the Image of Tammuz and Other Essays on Mesopotamian History and Culture*, ed. William L. Moran (Cambridge, MA: Harvard University Press, 1970), pp. 39–47.

[153]Since by definition a traditional system will seek its validation in the past, the past, by remaining alive, is constantly subject to conscious and unconscious reinterpretation. Thus the *Amorai'm* will read back into the Mishnah concepts or terminology that must be dated as post-Mishnaic; see for example R. D. Z. Hoffmann, "Zur Einleitung in dem Midrasch Tannaim zum Deuteronomium," *Jahrbuch der Judisch-Literarische Gesellschaft*, 7, pp. 304–33, specifically, p. 312, n. 2, on post-Mishnaic terminology the Bavli provides for its analysis of *Mishnah Nedarim* 1:1. In this case, the distinction between *yadot* and *kinnuyim* is tannaitic, though in all probability the term *kinnuy* in this sense is not.

this is natural and unconscious, and given the need for integrating new ideas into the body of Torah thought, inevitable and necessary. All traditional systems do so.[154] But by ignoring the chronological aspect of the process we lose a certain self-awareness that is useful in keeping track of where this constant process of omni-interpretation is taking us. Here too the Academy is—by default—the custodian of *peshat* as a benchmark.

Again Izhbitz offers us a paradigm.

> As is known, whenever anyone understands any matter clearly, the light of that Gate [of knowledge] becomes open to the world and is open to all, for this is the principle that God established for all the generations, even though they continually decline in ability. For once these lights are made available to each generation by the sages of Israel by the great ones among the sages of Israel, they are not sealed up; they remain open forever, and become fixed laws for all Israel. Therefore, even though later generations are inferior [to earlier ones], they nevertheless maintain their awareness [of knowledge], as dwarves [on the shoulders of] giants . . . and they themselves continue the process of this opening of new Gates. Even though they themselves are greatly inferior [in comparison to their forebears, their insights] are more profound, for they have already passed through the Gates opened for the earlier generations.[155]

Once these insights have been gained, they become part of Torah, "and become fixed laws for all Israel," and, as integral parts of Torah, lend their weight to the interpretation of the whole. This is the process of the unfolding of *Torah she-be'al peh*, and it is one of the functions of academic scholarship to reverse the process and study its unfolding. This not only gives us a deeper understanding of how we have arrived at where we are, but allows us to examine the options not chosen by *Klal Yisrael*. Some may be worthy of resurrection in the light of later circumstances and challenges; in other cases, we will understand even more clearly why the particular viewpoint was ignored or consigned to oblivion. *Ein adam omed al divrei Torah ela im ken nikhshal ba-hem tehillah.*

There is also a moral point in all this, which should not be lost. Those who open the gates and thus open the way for a new understanding of all of previous learning should be given the credit for their discovery.

---

[154]For those who doubt that our system is progressive, see my "History of Halakhah."

[155]*Resisei Laylah, maamar* 13, p. 14b. See my "History," p. 6.

VI

As the central endeavor of Jewish intellectual activity, *Talmud Torah* requires special sensitivities, whether carried out within or without the walls of the *yeshivah*. My discussion of the role of academic methodologies cannot be complete without some mention of the interaction of an Orthodox academic with those whose *yirat Shamayim* is either suspect, lacking, or in some sense defective.

Undoubtedly, the Rambam's principle of accepting truth from wherever[156] it comes is relevant, but its application, never without difficulty, has become increasingly controversial in recent times. The consensus of *Klal Yisrael* seems to militate against cooperation of any sort with those outside the camp of the strictest understanding of *Torah min ha-Shammayim*.

This is so whether we speak of Jews whose understanding of *Torah min ha-Shammayim* puts them beyond the pale, so to speak, or non-Jews whose contribution to *Talmud Torah* might be expected, at first glance, to be nil, since we have Hazal's word that while *hokhmah* is to be found among them, Torah is not.[157] This is so despite such precedents as Aher and Rabbi Meir, or Doeg and Ahitophel, or even Menasseh, king of Judah, the halakhic consequences of whose dream conversation with Rav Ashi were eventually enshrined as *halakhah le-maaseh*.[158]

Again, current consensus discountenances such possibilities for us. Here, too, however, the role of such people within the realm of *Torah shebi-Khtav* can serve as a paradigm for the case of *Torah she-be'al peh*. The fact that the words of such *koferim* as the Pharoah of the Exodus could be included in the Torah, *become sanctified thereby, and interpreted in the same ways as any other part of Torah*, was of singular significance to Rabbi Zadok.[159]

In one place Rabbi Zadok derives this principle from Moses' encounter with God in Exodus 33.

---

[156]*Mishnah im Perush Rabbenu Moshe ben Maimon*, introduction to Avot, ed. Kafih, vol. 2 [Hebrew only ed.] (Jerusalem: Mosad Harav Kook, 5725), p. 247b.

[157]See *Eikhah Rabbah* 2:13, ed. Buber, p. 114.

[158]*Sanhedrin* 102b; Menasseh's *halakhah* is codified in *Shulhan Arukh, Orah Hayyim* 167:1.

[159]Though he does not mention the source in his discussion of this issue, we may add the debate between the Pharisees and a Galilean Sadducee regarding dating documents by (non-Jewish) regnal years in a similar vein; see *Yadayim* 4:8.

"I call in the Name of God"[160]—Hazal took this to refer to the Thirteen *Middot ha-Rahamim*;[161] and, as is known, these [correspond also] to the *middot* by which the Torah is interpreted, which [constitute] the foundation of *Torah she-be'al peh* and the wisdom of the sages of Israel. And then He revealed [to Moses] all that a veteran disciple would innovate, as Hazal have said.[162] Regarding this He said: "I will be gracious to those to whom I would,"[163] etc., *even though he may not be worthy* [italics mine—Y.E.]. For [Moses] saw that even junior disciples were destined to innovate great things which were hidden from the great ones of the prior generations.[164] Nevertheless, they left room for each one to complete [the building of Torah (*le-hitgadder*)] with his own portion of wisdom which [God] grants those who fear Him.[165] This applies even to one who is by nature [*be-toladah she-nigzar alav*] either wise or foolish, [and] even though the righteous and wicked are not mentioned [in this context], [which] depends on personal choice [free will, as opposed to ingrained nature], it is uncontrovertible that there are scholars who acted in as evil a manner as Doeg, Ahitophel and Aher[166]—whose Torah nevertheless was not rejected. For the bestowal of wisdom is not according to [one's] apparent deeds but according to the Supernal Will, without a revealed reason, and therefore He says regarding

---

[160]*Exodus* 33:19.

[161]*Midrash Hagadol* ad loc.; see also *Leket Tov*. As is common in *Peri Tzaddik* no source is given; Rashi *ad loc.* cites *Rosh Hashanah* 17b on Exodus 34:6, and it may be to this that Rabbi Zadok refers. If so, he has equated the two verses because of the occurrence of the verb *qara* in both. However, his use of another part of Exodus 33:19 below favors the first possibility.

[162]*Peah* 2:6 (17a); see also *Exodus Rabbah* 47:1, *Leviticus Rabbah* 22:1.

[163]*Exodus* 33:19.

[164]See n. 153 above and the article therein cited.

[165]See my "From the Pages of Tradition: Rabbi Moses Samuel Glasner: The Oral Torah," *Tradition* 25:3 (Spring, 1990).

[166]Compare *Takkanat ha-Shavin*, pp. 67b–68a:
Many words of Torah were given over to outside [forces] [and] need to be taken out from them, just as there are in the Written Torah many *parashiyot* from the Nations [containing] the words of Laban, Esau, and Pharaoh, and similarly, the section of Bilaam and Balak and so on; these are words of Torah that were given over to wherever they were, from [the time] of the sin of Adam, and which returned to their holiness at the time of Mattan Torah, when the entire Torah was taken out of its storage place, to be revealed to the souls of the Israelites in its entirety.

this: "I will be gracious [to whomever I will]," even though he is not worthy or merits such [insights].[167]

Elsewhere he derives this principle from the very fabric of Creation.

Everyone may attain an understanding of hokhmah and divrei Torah, even though he has no [ein lo] yirat Shamayim which precedes [Torah], [nor] the inner urge from Below ['itoreruta dile-tata] which arouses him to the study and attainment of understanding of Torah for the sake of the Honor of His Name, may He be blessed, [nor again] does he recognize that [the subject with which he occupies himself] is the Torah of God. Nevertheless [mi-kol makom] God, may He be blessed, is always prepared to grant Torah insights [divrei Torah] even without the inner urge from Below. [This is the meaning of] "the One Who renews in His goodness the Work of Creation every day always."[168] Just as the Work of Creation took place without an urge from

---

[167]Peri Tzaddik I, p. 43a [Kedushat Shabbat, maamar 7]. Presumably Rabbi Zadok had Sabbatean texts or the works of suspected Sabbateans in mind, according to Professor Shnayer Leiman (personal communication).

[168]The use of this line from the Shaharit Prayer is highly significant in this context, because elsewhere this is connected with those sages who can discern the special hiddush of each day, and thus control the Work of Creation by means of the Torah learning. See Tzidkat ha-Tzaddik, n. 216, p. 92a.

Every day there are hiddushei Torah, for Hashem renews Maaseh Bereshit every day, and Maaseh Bereshit [was accomplished] by means of the Torah, as is stated at the beginning of Genesis Rabbah—and thus, most likely [mistama] the hiddush too is by means of hiddushei Torah. For this reason the berakhah of Yotzer Ha-Me'orot, which [embodies] the recognition of the renewal of Maaseh Bereshit, is followed by a second berakhah which is a sort of birkat ha-Torah (Berakhot 11b)—for [the one who recites these berakhot] seeks to know the hiddushei Torah which reflect this renewal.

[And] as I heard, that Hashem made a book, that is the world, and a commentary on that book, that is the Torah, for the Torah so to speak, explains God's relationship to [His] creatures [qinyanei Hashem ba-nivra'im]. Happy is the one who merits apprehending this after Keriyat Shema, which constitutes the fixed Torah study for the day, for with the morning and evening recitation of the Shema one fulfills the requirement of Talmud Torah (Menahot 99b) . . . and by discussion of divrei Torah he apprehends the hiddushim of each day.

Thus Rabbi Shimon b. Yohai and his companions, whose profession was only Torah, would not halt [their Torah study] for prayer (Shabbat 11a), for they knew each day's hiddushei Torah of Maaseh Bereshit with which the universe is continually renewed. Since the Sages were aware that not everyone merits this knowledge, they provided a prayer to beseech Hashem to mercifully allow us to merit reception of each day's renewed shefa.

I hope to deal with this in detail elsewhere, D.v.

Below—since, after all, humanity had not yet been created, so too every day always He renews in His goodness alone without the prior effort [*hishtaddelut*] of the lower beings.[169]

The essential creation of *Torah she-be'al peh* is the work of the "true sages of Israel," inspired by God, but because of God's imponderable grace, others, not only of lesser intellectual caliber but also of lesser spiritual character, can contribute to the work. In more prosaic terms, the enterprise of *hiddush* has many divisions, requiring varied talents and capacities, employing different methodologies; each has a place in the polishing of the seventy facets of Torah.

Similarly, every one of Israel is unique in one respect [*meyuhad le-ezeh davar*] and one must not claim superiority over him [*le-hitnasse'ot*]; just as one is necessary for Torah so too the other, since a Torah [scroll] is invalid if it lacks but one letter. [Each is like] one limb [of the body of Israel], and with the loss of one limb the body is endangered [*nitraf*]; and so one may not act arrogantly over another. Even though one may be on a higher level than another, nevertheless each is as necessary for the body as another.[170]

---

[169]*Tzidkat ha-Tzaddik*, n. 226, p. 102a.
[170]*Tzidkat ha-Tzaddik*, *maamar* 231, pp. 108b–109a.

Contributors

David Berger is professor of history at Brooklyn College and the Graduate Center, City University of New York and a visiting professor at Yeshiva University. He is author of *The Jewish-Christian Debate in the High Middle Ages* among several scholarly studies.

Mordechai Breuer teaches at Jacob Herzog College at Alon Shevut. His major work of creative biblical interpretation is the two-volume *Pirkei Moadot*. He has also published books on the Masoretic text of the Bible and related subjects.

Shalom Carmy is consulting editor of *Tradition*. A veteran teacher of Bible and Jewish thought at Yeshiva University, he has published many essays on these subjects. He is editing the seventh volume of the Orthodox Forum publication series, treating Jewish perspectives on suffering.

Barry Eichler is professor of Assyriology at the University of Pennsylvania and has published in his field and its relation to Bible.

Yaakov Elman is professor of Jewish Studies at Yeshiva University. He is the author of *Authority and Tradition* and *The Living Prophets*. He is a prolific writer on talmudic literature, biblical interpretation, and hasidic thought.

Shnayer Leiman is professor of Judaic studies at Brooklyn College and a visiting professor at Yeshiva University. He is the author of *Canoniza-*

tion of Hebrew Scripture and has published widely on a variety of subjects in Jewish Studies.

Barry Levy is professor of Judaic studies at McGill University and has published major studies on the history of biblical interpretation and Jewish biblical study.

Yeshayahu Maori is professor of Bible at the University of Haifa. He is an authority on the Peshitta and on rabbinic textual traditions of the Bible.

Daniel Sperber is professor of rabbinics at Bar-Ilan University. A prolific author on rabbinic literature and realia, and the recipient of the Israel Prize for Rabbinic Scholarship, his most recent books are *Magic and Folklore in Rabbinic Literature* and volume V of *Minhagei Yisrael*.

Index

About the Editor

Shalom Carmy is consulting editor of *Tradition*. A student of the late Rabbi Joseph B. Soloveitchik and a veteran teacher of philosophy, Bible, and Jewish thought at Yeshiva University, he has published many essays on these subjects. He is currently editing the seventh volume of the Orthodox Forum publication series, treating Jewish perspectives on suffering.